Ace the Verbal on the SAT*

Loren Meierding

ScarecrowEducation
Lanham, Maryland • Toronto • Oxford
2005

Published in the United States of America
by ScarecrowEducation
An imprint of The Rowman & Littlefield Publishing Group, Inc.
4501 Forbes Boulevard, Suite 200, Lanham, Maryland 20706
www.scareroweducation.com

PO Box 317
Oxford
OX2 9RU, UK

British Library Cataloguing in Publication Information Available

Library of Congress Cataloging-in-Publication Data

Meierding, Loren Edward.
   Ace the Verbal on the SAT / Loren Meierding.
       p. cm.
   Includes bibliographical references and index.
   ISBN 1-57886-198-5 (pbk. : alk. paper)
   1. Scholastic Assessment Test—Study guides. 2. English
language—Examinations—Study guides. I. Title.
LB2353.57 .M45 2005
378.1'662—dc22   2004020820

** SAT is a registered trademark of the College Board, which was not involved in the production of and does not endorse this
product.*

Contents

My experience of studying vocabulary and succeeding in increasing my verbal reasoning score over one hundred points to near perfect gives me reason to believe that writing this book can help others to improve their scores on the SAT and to enable their improvement to occur more quickly.

I was blessed with a high aptitude for math, but my verbal ability was not as great. When applying to college, I took the SAT two times and scored 757 and 749 on the mathematics section and 634 and 679 on the verbal section. When I took the preliminary version of the test, I scored 77 on the mathematics section (equivalent to 770 on the SAT) and 67 on the verbal section (equivalent to 670). I had straight As and was accepted at Yale.

When I was a senior at Yale, I was considering going to graduate school and took the GRE.* On the night before the test, I got only an hour of sleep and was very tired as I took the test the following day. It did not, however, affect my performance on the mathematics section, where I was able to concentrate sufficiently to score an 800 (99th percentile of college seniors taking the test), but by the time I took the verbal in the afternoon, I could hardly keep my eyes open. I scored 610, which was about sixty points short of what I would have expected to achieve.

Three years later I applied to graduate schools to study philosophy and used my old scores on the GRE. Unfortunately, when I applied to the University of Texas, there was a problem with my grades. When my Yale numerical grades were converted to alphabet grades by the University of Texas's conversion scale, my average was slightly under the B average required to get into graduate school. For example, my 91 in European History, the second-highest of four hundred Yale freshmen, was translated as a B since the University of Texas required a 93 for an A grade. The chairman of the philosophy department told me that if I raised my verbal score, he could probably get me in.

Since I had a strong desire to attend the University of Texas—it had the kind of philosophy department I was interested in—I had a strong incentive to work hard to improve my vocabularly and hence my verbal score. The method I devised to conceptualize relationships between pairs of words for answering analogy questions probably enabled me to increase my score on the GRE by an extra fifty points. I also took sample tests in one of the self-help books published to help students take the GRE. When I took the GRE the second time, I scored 780 on the verbal and 780 on the mathematics section.

My interpretation of my 170-point improvement on the verbal section broke down as follows: sixty points were due to getting enough sleep and coming to the test alert; sixty points were due to increased vocabulary; and about fifty points were due to having developed a system for answering questions using analogies. I believe that if other people follow my suggestions, they can increase their scores, too. Knowing effective strategies for approaching both the sentence completion questions and the critical reading passages and questions can also lead to some improvements in scores. To improve one's score through increasing vocabulary, however, requires a great investment of time, which is minimized by using this book.

The purpose of this book is to help well-prepared students who expect to score well on the verbal section of the SAT attain near-perfect scores. The difference between a 670 and an 800 score is about ten questions. The difference between a 720 and a (best) 800 score is only about five questions. The well-prepared student who has a broad and

---

*GRE is a registered trademark of the Educational Testing Service, which was not involved in the production of and does not endorse this product.

confident knowledge of vocabulary, a well-developed set of verbal comprehension and reasoning skills, and a good knowledge of grammar should expect to score high on the verbal section of the SAT. But even a well-prepared student may wish to answer a few more questions correctly. The student who is able to answer the easy- and medium-difficulty questions and who wishes to obtain a very high score must improve performance on the more difficult questions.

Students are helped primarily by expanding their vocabulary and by acquiring effective techniques for finding the answers to the questions. In addition to helping the well-prepared students, this book will help average students do better as well. Likewise, it can help those who are not planning to take the SAT but want to expand their vocabularies. Thus, this book will help

1. students who can score high on the SAT but want to attain near-perfect scores,
2. students with average preparation who can significantly improve by learning vocabulary and how to approach the various kinds of questions and the essay,
3. students who want to attain quick improvement without having much time to invest,
4. teachers and parents wanting to help students prepare for the SAT, and
5. people who are not interested in taking the SAT but want to significantly and quickly improve their vocabulary by studying the vocabulary learning chapters.

It is not possible to learn over the short term (a few weeks or months) most of the skills needed to do well on the SAT. Some advice can be given about how to approach critical reading and sentence completion questions, and vocabulary can be expanded sufficiently in a short period of time. But strong, comprehensive knowledge of grammar as well as good reading comprehension and good verbal reasoning needed to score high are developed only over many years of reading.

From my experience, I believe that I can help students improve their scores by providing them with vocabulary organized by Indo-European roots, which will facilitate their learning the many important words likely to occur on an SAT. I can also help by pointing out the basic strategies they should use to answer the questions. Had I possessed the help provided in this book, I could have improved my score over one hundred points in a fraction of the time.

The book provides the vocabulary with definitions and the sources needed to expand vocabulary by three thousand words. It provides understanding of what to look for in reading the critical reading passages. It shows how to find the correct answer on sentence completion questions. It provides advice on how to prepare for the new writing section of the SAT. The book provides the information needed to make improvements over the short term. Since increasing vocabulary is needed for most well-prepared students to score very high, the majority of the book is devoted to vocabulary learning.

The high scorer on the SAT does not need to clutter his or her mind with too many pieces of advice. There are a number of books in the marketplace that provide help for taking the SAT. Most of them are aimed at average students. They tend to provide advice that helps students answer easy- and medium-difficulty questions. They also tend to provide many rules to follow that, while true, are not all easily remembered or followed while taking the SAT.

The published self-help books for the SAT tend to be about 550–800 pages long. Most of them try to provide advice enabling average and even poorly prepared test takers to solve all the basic math problems and verbal reasoning questions. The books focus primarily on solving easy problems and therefore waste the time of well-prepared students.

I believe my book is better for achieving a high score. It has good basic advice as well as specific explanations that clarify and enable test takers to have better thought processes. I believe it enables students to achieve a faster acquisition of vocabulary at the level needed to answer questions on the SAT, as well as better retention through knowing the associations with roots. I believe that just reading the first seven chapters and then browsing through the vocabulary lists in the final twenty chapters will enable almost anyone to improve their score on the verbal section.

I found the standard reference work on Indo-European roots—*Indogermanisches Etymologisches Worterbuch* (1959) by Julius Pokorny—to be quite helpful. Also useful were *The American Heritage Dictionary of Indo-European Roots* (second edition; edited by Calvert Watkins) and *The American Heritage Dictionary of the English Language* (fourth edition) for finding information about roots for various English words. For those interested in finding out more detail about Indo-European roots, I highly recommend the latter two dictionaries. Furthermore, I found much interesting information in *The Loom of Language* by Frederick Bodmer about the grammatical and vocabulary relationships of Germanic and Romance languages to Indo-European languages.

ABBREVIATIONS

Some abbreviations occur with frequency in the lists of words and their definitions: 'esp.' for 'especially,' 'rel.' for 'related (to),' 'pert.' for 'pertaining (to),' 'alt.' for 'alteration of,' 'priv.' for 'privative,' 'intens.' for 'intensifier,' 'imit.' for 'imitative,' 'dim.' for diminutive,' 'compar.' for comparative,' 'superl.' for 'superlative,' 'pp.' for 'past participle (Latin),' 'pfp.' for 'perfect participle (Latin), and 'freq.' for 'frequentive (Latin).' Parentheses are used for definitions of prefixes and prepositions or to indicate that the preceding Latin form is a participle of a Latin verb. Some prefixes act as privatives—that is, they indicate a lack of an attribute or just act as intensifiers strengthening the meaning of the root to which they are connected. Some defined words have the same form functioning as a noun, verb, or adjective. This is sometimes indicated by a '(n),' '(v),' or '(adj).'

PART 1

BASIC ASSISTANCE WITH THE VERBAL SAT

CHAPTER 1

Improving on the Verbal Section of the SAT

The purpose of this book is to help students prepare to take the new SAT given beginning in March 2005. This book is designed to give help to those who want to achieve high verbal scores. It is also designed to provide quick help where possible. This chapter addresses what can be done to improve scores on the verbal section of the new SAT. Chapter 2 addresses what can be done to improve scores on the writing section of the new SAT. Another book will address what can be done to improve scores on the quantitative section of the new SAT. This book is intended to help students—whether well prepared or not—learn vocabulary and improve verbal reasoning for significant improvement on the SAT.

There are two areas in which this book can help students. First, it will help students augment their vocabulary with several thousand important words, thereby greatly reducing the chance that they will find unknown words on the test. It will also help test takers to learn the thought processes they should follow to make correct decisions on answers and to do so more efficiently.

SKILLS NEEDED TO SCORE HIGH ON THE VERBAL SECTION OF THE NEW SAT

Students who achieve very high or near-perfect scores on the verbal section of the new SAT require five capabilities:

1. Ability to comprehend analytical nonfiction and narrative material
2. Logical ability to interpret, make inferences, and draw conclusions from analytical and narrative material
3. Ability to analyze sentence completion questions and interpret clues
4. Good knowledge of grammar and grammatical nuances of sentence completion questions
5. Knowing all the vocabulary found in critical reading passages, questions, and sentence completion questions and answers

IMPROVEMENTS ARE POSSIBLE

Most of the five skills and abilities needed to do very well on the SAT are not acquired, remedied, or improved over the short term. No doubt, a part of the logical and analytical abilities have an innate basis and are not teachable. Nevertheless, most of the abilities are acquired. Yet all of them are partially or fully acquired by learning. All of them take considerable time to develop. Comprehension of difficult material is only acquired from considerable reading of complex and difficult material. Knowledge of good grammar and usage is generally acquired only after considerable reading of well-written fiction and nonfiction and at least one good grammar course.

Obviously, most of the abilities needed to score very high on verbal reasoning cannot be acquired over a short term of a few months or less. But there are four things that can be done that will help improve scores for well-prepared students:

1. Expand vocabulary to significantly improve verbal reasoning—that is, unknown words prevent correct answers.
2. Learn good strategies for approaching critical reading passages and sentence completion questions.
3. Know how to analyze sentence completion questions.
4. Practice taking a real SAT and solving realistic critical reading and sentence completion questions.

I believe that using this book—even just reading the review material, strategies, and the italicized words of the vocabulary lists—can help the reader achieve an improvement on verbal test scores and writing sample. More extensive study should prove of even greater help. The book is designed to help students know how to approach the harder problems and achieve high scores most efficiently. It does not provide help sufficiently comprehensive to make up for major deficiencies.

EXPANDING VOCABULARY

The verbal section of the new SAT consists of two types of problems: sentence completion and critical reading. For both types some practice and study can help to improve scores. The activity that promises the greatest payoff is learning vocabulary. For both kinds of questions, vocabulary and good reasoning are the primary factors that determine success. Comprehension of reading depends on understanding the words and being able to evaluate arguments and make inferences. Understanding grammatical, conceptual, and logical relationships also depends on understanding the words, although many questions will use words that are not especially difficult. Both kinds of problems have questions of varying degree of difficulty. The main factor making them more difficult is use of words with greater-than-average difficulty and, in particular, use of words likely to occur in college-level reading.

It is probable that one-half or more of missed answers can be attributed to deficiencies of vocabulary. The direct remedy to eliminate such misses is to learn vocabulary. Of course, learning vocabulary takes some time. We can figure that there are two thousand or so words not usually known by the average adult speaker of English that often occur on the SAT or are likely to occur on an SAT. If these words can be learned quickly, it is all to the good. This book has been designed to enable students to learn these words sufficiently enough to answer questions correctly on the new SAT.

To improve scores, especially to achieve high scores, test takers must possess a large vocabulary that includes the kinds of words likely to be used in the more difficult sentence completion and critical reading questions. Hence, the most important means to improve scores on an SAT, and certainly to obtain very high scores, is to spend some time and effort on expanding vocabulary. Because this is true, the design of this book is oriented toward enabling students taking the SAT to improve their vocabulary as quickly and easily as possible. A large portion of the book is devoted to vocabulary lists and vocabulary building. The vocabulary is organized to maximize learning and retention. There is also help for using good strategies and making good inferences.

This book provides helps for learning key vocabulary words. Knowledge of the two thousand italicized words can make a big difference. Important word groups of synonymous words include about six hundred words. The majority of words are arranged by common roots to improve word association, memory retention, reduce boring repetition, and improve quickness of learning. Mastery of italicized words will enable the confident answering and finishing of all test questions. The large number of defined words should not overwhelm the student. (Most are a bonus since they are derived from common root words. Focus on the italicized words.) He or she should begin by reading the basic information concerning the Indo-European, Latin, Greek, and Germanic roots and by examining the bold and italicized words. Other information can be perused as time and interest permits.

ANALYZING SENTENCE COMPLETION QUESTIONS

Test takers need to know how to make good inferences and how to understand the nuances of grammar and vocabulary for correctly answering the more sophisticated sentence completion and critical reasoning questions. This book provides practical strategies for approaching sentence completion and critical reading questions. The aim of the book is to go more deeply into the thought processes needed to make correct choices of answers to the questions. We want to provide ability to analyze and not just offer maxims to follow. Over forty examples of sentence completion questions are examined and analyzed to show how to figure out which words would fit the blanks. It is important to pay attention to connective words to figure out possible answers.

GOOD STRATEGIES FOR APPROACHING VERBAL REASONING QUESTIONS

To do well, one should know the vocabulary used in sentence completion and critical reading, and learning vocabulary will help primarily on the more difficult verbal questions on the SAT. Many of the critical reading questions depend more on logical thinking than on a large vocabulary. Comprehension involves more than understanding words. Even if there are a few words that are not well understood, the test taker may be able to correctly answer most of the questions on a passage or make good guesses from understanding the context. By strategies we mean giving test takers knowledge of what they should be looking for while reading the passages.

For almost any activity, improvement will occur from practice and experience. Someone who has not taken the SAT or a similar test can do the following activities to improve scores:

Know in advance what the instructions are and how to fill in the answers. Time is not then wasted while taking the test. It is useful to take the SAT at least once, just to be familiar with the procedures, before taking it for the sake of providing results to colleges and universities. Some time will be saved on a second round.

Take a practice SAT to gain experience. Taking practice tests also teaches the instructions and how to fill in the answers. One can purchase the College Board's *The Official SAT Study Guide: For the New SAT* and take some of the eight practice tests found therein. Students can also access problems and information on taking the SAT by accessing the website www.collegeboard.com.

Taking the test at least once before taking it to count and taking some of the ten practice tests on the *The Official SAT Study Guide: For the New SAT* provide experience in taking the SAT. Moreover, taking one or more of the tests in *The Official SAT Study Guide: For the New SAT* has an added advantage over taking the real test. Correct answers are given. The book offers a method of determining one's score so that the taker can determine what kinds of problems and questions give the most trouble and what kind of questions deserve an investment of time and effort.

This book does not provide practice test examples for the different types of problems, because it is better to practice on problems that have really occurred on past SATs. Nevertheless, just reading this book and working on its vocabulary chapters will help significantly. It is highly recommended that students spend some time working some sample sentence completion questions as well as reading some critical reading passages with questions. Some practice with real questions from an SAT is useful. The student can determine his or her weaknesses. Time is saved by knowing the process of taking the test before actually taking it. More important, practice enables a student to learn the proper pace for taking the test, a pace that will enable all questions to be attempted without rushing needlessly. To score high, a test taker needs to have a good sense of pace.

To understand how to score high on the new SAT, test takers must consider the purpose of the test. As in the past, the new SAT is a test intended to measure aptitude for mathematical and verbal understanding and reasoning. The new SAT also evaluates writing skills. This book focuses on verbal and writing skills. The verbal reasoning exam indicates the level of mastery for an English vocabulary and the capacity to understand and reason about college-level reading material. The scores therefore give college-entrance officers a good idea concerning which applicants are best prepared for college. They can compare students from different high schools with different grading systems. The SAT helps entrance officers determine students' relative achievement and ability so that they can make objective judgments about which applicants should be accepted. The test is therefore important for selecting the students who should receive large scholarships.

HOW TO USE THIS BOOK

How the reader will decide to use this book must depend on his or her needs and objectives. This book is intended especially for helping good students to achieve very high scores and significantly improve their scores on the verbal section of the SAT in a relatively short period. Very high scores are needed to gain entrance to the most prestigious schools and to obtain good scholarships. But medium scores are needed to gain entrance to many colleges and universities. There are several classes of students planning to take the SAT who may wish to spend some effort to improve their scores:

1. Students who can do very well on the SAT without further preparation but who want to score very high to gain entrance and scholarships at top universities. A student with strong preparation for verbal and quantitative problems may feel the only need is to improve vocabulary. Students who expect to do very well on the SAT without further preparation should just spend time going through chapters 7 through 27.
2. Students who are moderately or well prepared to take the SAT who want to have a modest improvement in their scores but who can expend only a modest or minimal time and effort to improve their scores. Students in this category may want to spend some time studying the vocabulary chapters 7 to 27 and reading through the material in chapters 2 through 6 to learn how to better approach taking the various kinds of problems.
3. Students with moderate preparation but who are prepared to expend considerable effort to make significant improvement in their scores to gain entrance to better schools. Students in this category may want to spend more time studying vocabulary chapters and reading through the material in chapters 2 to 6, designed to teach how to approach taking the various kinds of problems and questions. They ought also to take practice tests in *The Official SAT Study Guide: For the New SAT* or *10 Real SATs*.
4. Students who are poorly prepared to take the SAT and desire and need considerable improvement to gain admission to their local school or some other school. Careful reading of this book and study of vocabulary should enable students to improve significantly on vocabulary and verbal questions. Nevertheless, those who have some basic deficiencies in reading comprehension should not expect to overcome the deficiencies without significant effort and study of books designed to provide help on easier questions. Students in this category should definitely take some practice tests to diagnose their areas of weakness, and they should devote significant time to overcoming those areas of weakness. Studying books designed to help on easy- and medium-difficulty questions may be needed.

VOCABULARY LEARNING

Some additional remarks on vocabulary learning and its importance follow. The organization of vocabulary is designed to facilitate its learning and retention. Anyone who masters the words in this book will have an excellent chance of recognizing all the words encountered on the SAT. The words studied in this book are especially valuable when used on the written-essay part of the test (and when used in one's life in general).

The SAT is a test in verbal and quantitative reasoning. Ability to reason is probably mostly learned but also partially a result of innate abilities. Insofar as it is innate, no book can help. Insofar as it is learned, it is learned largely through experience and practice over a long period. Poor ability to comprehend reading selections usually results from having neglected vocabulary development through inextensive reading. It also results from failing to read difficult materials. Since extensive reading of difficult material takes considerable time, poor comprehension is not easily remedied. A person who has great reasoning ability will not score high on the verbal reasoning part of the

SAT if he or she has a limited vocabulary, simply because he or she will not understand the key words on which the correct answer depends. However, having a very large working vocabulary does not guarantee a high verbal score either. One has to be able to draw logical conclusions and relationships from the critical reading selections and analogies to answer some of the questions correctly.

Increased vocabulary will help on sentence completion and critical reading questions. While understanding certain nuances of grammar is important, the critical knowledge needed to understand reading passages and answer the questions is how to make correct inferences and understand the vocabulary used in the passages. The passages are chosen to have some difficult words that average and even advanced students may not have learned. If learning vocabulary enabled a student to correctly answer an additional ten questions on critical reading passages, the increase in verbal score on the SAT would be about sixty or seventy points.

Vocabulary learning has several levels of word mastery. Full mastery gives a person the ability to use the word in writing and speaking. A second level is adequate comprehension of words encountered in reading for one's understanding the context of the passage. Usually, there are a considerable number of words that people have sufficient mastery to understand in reading but do not feel comfortable using in speech and writing. There are also lesser levels of mastery. A person can have a rough idea of the meaning of a word from having encountered it in the course of reading or hearing it but not have an accurate or thoroughly correct understanding of it. Even understanding words at this lowest level can help in taking the SAT.

In this book the vocabulary lists are broken down into groups based on derivation from Indo-European roots. Latin, Greek, or Germanic roots are given. Definitions for the most important words that should be learned are given. They are brief but of sufficient length to convey the primary meanings. Inclusion of the roots and their meanings enables the vocabulary learner to notice relationships and guess the journey that the word took to reach its English meaning.

Knowledge of word origins is often very helpful in learning new words. Knowing the root meaning is the key for many words. Many of the most significant abstract words useful for academic and literary writings have their origins in Latin. Many words have developed significant differences of meaning from the words of their origin, yet the source words from earlier languages may still give considerable insight into the meaning of the English words derived from them. For many English words with Latin origins, the meaning of the Latin ancestor may be of great help for understanding the word. Most of the time, the relationship is quite close. The words 'ascending' and 'descending' come from the Latin verb 'scandeo' meaning 'to climb' with prefixes 'ad' and 'de' indicating 'up' and 'down.' There are many other words that are quite close in meaning to the Latin ancestors. Of course, some words have an association that is purely accidental. For example, the words 'money,' 'monetize,' and 'demonetize,' come from the Latin verb 'mineo' which means "to threaten or warn." Only a person knowing the history of the word could figure out how money is related to threatening or warning: the Temple of Juno Moneo (Moneo is the goddess who saved the Romans by warning them of approaching danger) happened to become the Roman treasury and the place in which the Romans made their coinage.

Vocabulary is learned most efficiently by roots and by grouping many words from the same root. Definitions are given to help students learn quickly. There are a large number of books designed to help students prepare for the SAT. A typical preparatory book for taking the SAT lists either undefined words or short definitions. They are given in alphabetical order. Typically, they give several hundred words that often crop up on the SAT. Although short definitions are sometimes given, it is often left up to the student to look up words.

However, I believe that much more helpful lists of words can be given that will enable students to learn many more words with less effort. The most important words are italicized, but additional words will be learned by association and will be potentially helpful when taking the SAT. The organization of the vocabulary chapters provides additional aids in associating words to their meanings. By organizing words according to roots, many words can be learned together by association with common roots because they have common meanings. By knowing the root and the common sequences of letters associated with the root, the learner can recognize the root and remember the meaning more certainly. By seeing the Latin, Greek, or Germanic roots, the vocabulary learner can in many cases recognize the connection between the root and the English meaning. Thus, the associations with the roots enable vocabulary to be learned in bunches instead of one word at a time, and the associations will enable the words and their meanings to be remembered more readily. The association with roots and the recognition of English-letter sequences associated with roots provide more certain recognition of words. Association with roots will help students recognize words to make intelligent guesses even if the words were not learned well enough to remember their precise meanings.

CHAPTER 2

Improving on the Writing Section of the SAT

The writing section of the SAT tests a student's knowledge of good English grammar and the ability to write, a crucial skill needed to do well in college. The test consists of a multiple-choice section, testing grammatical knowledge; and an essay section, testing writing ability. There are at least four important skills required to do well on this part of the test:

1. A good knowledge of English grammar for doing multiple-choice questions
2. Logical ability to formulate a thesis; select corroborating evidence from literature, nonfiction, or personal experience; and organize an outline for the written essay
3. Ability to write an essay with good style, using varied sentence structures and vocabulary
4. Having a broad vocabulary and an ability to use good diction

IMPROVEMENTS ARE POSSIBLE

In general all four abilities arc acquired over time through having done considerable reading of more difficult fiction and nonfiction works. Through extensive reading of well-written literature, a person picks up the nuances of good English grammar. Studying grammar in a good course or on one's own is also important. Diagramming sentences in a well-written work that one admires and then trying to emulate the style in one's own writing is quite helpful. Seeing logical relationships and knowing how to support arguments with evidence can be improved by taking courses in logic or by studying logic, but it is, again, an ability that is only acquired by doing considerable reading and study. Further, writing well is achieved only through practice. Good writers like to write and usually do quite a lot of writing. Good writing is not easily picked up in a short time. Finally, a broad vocabulary is developed over time as well. However, it is possible to expand vocabulary over a relatively short period, enabling a writer to improve diction by showing greater variety in use of vocabulary.

Some reflection on the four abilities indicates that they are not learned in the short term. It takes reading and practice to develop good knowledge of grammar and to achieve skill in writing. Nevertheless, there are at least four ways to achieve some improvement in the short term:

1. Expand vocabulary by adding important and valuable words. The writer can then use greater variety of words to create more interest, resulting in improved rhetoric and presentation of the argument.
2. Expand the possible literary and personal examples when supporting theses, which may be helpful for the process of selecting a viewpoint for the essay. Some prior thought and reading can help.
3. Study and review grammar, especially if a writer has identified some gaps in grammatical knowledge.
4. Practice writing essays like the kind required on the SAT. Analysis by oneself and others can identify some ways to improve one's writing that will pay off when writing the essay for the SAT.

The four ways to improve in the short term are discussed in more detail in the following sections.

EXPAND VOCABULARY

Expand vocabulary, increasing it by two thousand or more important and valuable words. This can be done by studying chapters 7 through 27. Several approaches have been taken to facilitate vocabulary learning. First, chapters 8 and 9 are organized by important word groups. Many of the most important and useful words for interesting writing belong to one of the twenty-one groups of words and their opposites in the two chapters. Second, over three thousand words have been given with definitions. Third, although space does not permit fully adequate definitions in some cases, the definitions provided are longer and more complete than provided by many self-help books. Fourth, each definition is followed by an indication of the word's origin in Latin, or Greek, or Germanic languages. Fifth, the definitions are organized according to two hundred Indo-European roots. This can bring additional insight, as there are thousands of known Indo-European roots. Two hundred have been selected because they have spawned many English words through the Latin, Greek, or Germanic or because they have spawned several key words that have occurred or are likely to occur on an SAT. The two hundred Indo-European roots yield two thousand defined words (there are, of course, many words from these roots that have not been included among the defined group). An additional twelve hundred words from other roots have been given to cover many important words that could be used on an SAT.

By looking at the definitions and then the root of origin, students can not only get a better sense of the meaning of the words but also will be more likely to remember the words. Moreover, by grouping words from the same Indo-European roots, the student will be able to associate and learn the meanings of many more words in a given period. Placing words from the same root in juxtaposition greatly improves the capacity to remember their meanings.

EXPANDING EXAMPLES

Although the topic for the written essay is not known beforehand, some forethought may help formulate support for the writing sample thesis. By reflecting on one's experiences and by doing some reading of important literary works, one can expand the available examples for use on the SAT essay. With as little as thirty or forty hours of reading, it is possible to read perhaps ten valuable works with perennial literary themes. There are, of course, no guarantees that additional reflection and additional reading will actually offer examples that can be used when taking the SAT. One cannot foresee the topic chosen for the SAT. Nevertheless a person can improve chances of organizing and writing a well-thought-out essay. Measures an essay writer can take are discussed in chapter 6.

REVIEW AND STUDY GRAMMAR

Most students who are well prepared will have taken grammar courses and done considerable reading. They should have sufficient knowledge of the nuances of English grammar to discern the proper answers to the multiple-choice questions. The multiple-choice grammar questions are discussed in chapter 5. Thorough coverage of all aspects of English grammar requires reading a lengthy book and taking a yearlong course. Persons with gaps in their knowledge of English grammar need to consult books on grammar. Students can consult chapter 5 for advice on what to do to remedy deficiencies.

PRACTICE WRITING

Practice writing essays. The only way to improve writing skills is to practice writing. One can take topics like those that might occur on the SAT and write an essay in twenty-five minutes. The essays should then be graded by someone who knows grammar and can give constructive feedback. For a fee, one can submit an essay to www.collegeboard.com for grading. By practicing beforehand, students can determine how they may improve their writing.

There are various measures that can be applied to written material of all kinds to determine its readability. By applying the appropriate measures for short, one-page essays, writers can evaluate how readable their writing is and figure out style changes they can make so that their writing is more readable. There are other methods writers can learn to improve their planning and organizing of essays. Measures that can be taken to improve writing are discussed in chapter 6.

CONCLUSION: WHAT TO DO TO PREPARE FOR THE WRITING SECTION

While there are no quick fixes for improving one's writing, there are a number of activities that can help prepare one for the written essay and some activities that can help achieve a modest improvement on the multiple-choice questions. The actions to take are covered in chapters 5 and 6. Moreover, studying vocabulary in chapters 7 through 27 can help writers increase the variety and clarity of the vocabulary they use in the essay.

CHAPTER 3

Critical Reading

The critical reading passages measure the ability to understand, evaluate, and make inferences about material similar to the kinds of reading encountered in college courses. Before March 2005 the SAT had four long critical reading passages with questions. One of the longer passages had two passages on a related topic for purposes of making comparisons. The new SAT adds short reading passages with questions. Comprehension depends partially on understanding certain nuances of grammar and making good inferences. Much depends on understanding the meaning of the words within their context, which results primarily from having a large vocabulary. To comprehend a passage, it is often not necessary to understand words perfectly. An approximate understanding gleaned from having previously encountered a difficult word in context and having guessed its meaning may be sufficient. Obviously, the more accurately words are known, the greater the confidence and success achieved in taking the test. The better the knowledge of vocabulary, the less delay in trying to decide an answer and move on to the next question.

In this chapter, I first give the basic strategy for reading critical reading passages. Reasons for the strategy are also given to show why it is worth following.

STRATEGY FOR TAKING THE CRITICAL READING SECTION OF THE TEST

Before stating the advocated strategy for reading critical reading passages and answering the questions, one needs to make a distinction between general questions and detail questions. General questions are questions that are based on the information from a number of sentences, whole paragraphs, or even the entire passage. They cannot be answered from reading one or two or even three consecutive sentences in the passage. Detail questions can be answered by reference to several sentences or several lines in the passage. Detail questions often involve merely restating information in the passage. Line numbers refer to the location of the information in the passage so that the student can look for the answer. Vocabulary questions are frequently detail questions. I recommend the following strategy for answering critical reading questions:

1. Read the italicized introduction. This will provide insight concerning what the passage is about. *Optional:* It may sometimes be helpful, especially with unfamiliar material, to take a few seconds before reading a passage to glance over the questions that follow the selection. Of course, the analysis in this chapter will indicate the kinds of general questions that will be asked. Since one should have a good idea of the questions anyway, looking at them beforehand is not likely to be particularly helpful. If you do choose to glance at the questions before reading the passage, don't read every question or try to remember them all. This expends too much time. Skip questions with line references. But what may be helpful is a quick perusal of the questions, trying to notice any that are general (those without line references to the reading selection or those requiring reading the entire passage to answer). This approach can be useful if the reading concerns unfamiliar topics. It may be worth doing particularly for the reading passage that has only about six questions. Spend only a few seconds doing this. When reading the passage, be especially alert to find the answers to those questions. If they can be answered, it will not be necessary to reread the entire passage. The other questions that have line references can be answered by looking back and rereading a few sentences, if necessary.

2. Read the passage carefully. Read carefully, not too slowly, but slowly enough to be able to answer most of the general questions. Don't focus too much on details, but do notice modifying words indicating the author's feelings or attitudes and attitudes of the characters in the passage. Some may find underlining a few important statements in the passage to be helpful. Know the pace you need to take (it is helpful to take a few practice tests to determine the pace needed).

The first third or half of a passage should be read most carefully. You may read remaining paragraphs more cursorily, especially if constrained for time. If you do so, look especially at first and last sentences of the latter paragraphs and look for a summarizing sentence at the end.

Read to be able to answer the following seven types of questions without having to go back to the passage to reread (although sometimes it may be necessary to do so):

- What is the main point or purpose of the selection?
- What is the author's perspective or viewpoint?
- What generalizations are stated, and what is the basis for their support?
- What are the attitudes and beliefs of persons or characters discussed in the selection?
- How does the author support his or her main points?
- What are the authors's main assumptions?
- What comparisons, contrasts, and connections does the author make?

These are especially important for the reading selection that consists of two passages.

When reading double passages, look for similarities and differences. You may find it helpful to use the following procedure: read the first of the two passages and answer its questions; then read the second passage and answer its questions. Finally, answer questions that compare or contrast both paragraphs. You don't need to know scientific terms. The science passages and their questions are written with sufficient context so that one can answer the questions without knowing the scientific terminology.

3. Answer the questions. Read the questions carefully and then try to figure out the answer from reading the passage before looking at the choices. Look back and reread a few sentences in the passage if necessary to answer a question. Refer back to the lines of occurrence and use the context to determine the meaning. After choosing an answer, put the choice in the sentence replacing the vocabulary word in question to see if it works.

3a. Try to answer all the questions you can before moving on. The questions do not go from easy to hard. Answer questions you can answer quickly. Don't get bogged down on difficult questions. One should always be able to eliminate some answers, and one should never leave an answer blank. When some answers can be eliminated, guessing tends to raise scores. High scorers will not need to engage in guessing, except rarely. But others should guess.

3b. Answer questions based only on the reading selection. Don't let your own opinion intrude.

3c. EXCEPT and NOT questions take more time. Skip until the end if necessary.

4. Come back to hard questions if you have time. If you are not sure of a question but have eliminated several answers, mark the remaining possibilities in your booklet and come back to the question after completing other questions on the passage, if you have time. Guess the answer if you can eliminate at least one or two answers and may not have time to come back to the question.

ADVANCE PREPARATION

Read the material in the following section to get an understanding of the kinds of questions that you will encounter. Take some practice tests to develop comfort with taking the SAT and to learn how to pace yourself while taking it. Learn to read faster if needed. Do considerable reading, especially of more difficult material. Expand your vocabulary.

SEVEN QUESTION TYPES

Awareness of the various types of questions is useful for discerning the answers to the questions. Based on my survey of several tests, the following categories describe the kinds of questions asked about critical reading passages (with the percentage of the critical reading questions for the type shown in parenthesis). Of course the percentages will vary from test to test, but the SAT tends to be quite stable.

1. The meaning or interpretation of words, phrases, or sentences (25 percent). A question might ask for the meaning or implication of a word, phrase, or sentence.
2. Questions related to claims or generalizations made by passage authors (18 percent). The questions might ask test takers to identify a claim made in the text or how evidence is used to support or reject claims. The questions may ask for the assumptions behind a principle or statement or for the implications of passage elements. Hypothetical questions may be asked. The test makers may want to know a passage's inferences, an argument's weaknesses, and what additional evidence would support or contradict a passage claim. Questions may seek reasons or explanations for a claim. Finally NOT questions may be asked: What is not answered, qualified, or used as a reason for a claim? These should be saved for last because they take more time to answer.
3. A number of questions concern the main point or purpose of a passage or its parts (15 percent). What is the main point of a passage, quotation, sentence, or phrase? What is a passage's purpose? What is it primarily about? What best summarizes it? What is the main argument? What are the main points or purposes of elements of a passage?
4. Questions about attitudes or beliefs of fictional or nonfictional persons in the passages (11 percent).
5. Questions about the author's viewpoint (11 percent). What represents an author's attitude or belief? What is the author most likely to agree with or disagree with? What does an author assume, stress, or emphasize? What is the tone of the passage?
6. Two-passage comparisons (8 percent). On what are the two writers likely to agree or disagree on? What are common assumptions or ideas of the two passages?
7. Miscellaneous questions (10 percent). A variety of questions may be asked. Various comparisons, contrasts, parallels, and characterizations are possible. Questions may be asked about passage structure, function, or relationships. Questions may also be asked about the authors's methods or techniques.

SUPPORTING ANALYSIS FOR THE CRITICAL READING SELECTIONS AND QUESTIONS

The recommendations are based on my analysis of some past tests looking for tendencies. There is no guarantee that the same tendencies will hold true in future tests, but they are not likely to diverge too greatly. The reader can skip this material, but it provides some insight and understanding of the test that may prove helpful.

KINDS OF READINGS SELECTED FOR LONG PASSAGE READINGS

To understand how best to take the critical reading sections of the SAT, one finds it useful and helpful to note the kind of readings selected by the test makers. Since the test is designed to help predict how students will perform in college, the readings should reflect the kinds of reading that students will encounter in college. The type of material includes argumentative and expository passages and narratives. The subject matter of the readings tends to come from the history of science, general history, writings on social and cultural issues, literary criticism, English literature, biographical writing, and autobiographical material. Some fictional and biographical writings may focus primarily on conveying qualities of character, attitudes, or feelings of fictional and nonfictional characters featured in the writing selection. They may convey various observations by the author about the characters or observations about a topic related to the subject of the selection. But the majority of the selections will make some generalization and provide arguments or evidence for them.

The subject matter of the critical readings falls into three categories. One category of readings includes fictional, biographical, and travel writings that focus primarily on conveying qualities of character, beliefs, attitudes, or feelings of fictional and nonfictional characters. A second category includes history of science, writings on nature, ecology and biology, and general science. The third category includes history, writings on social and cultural issues, political science, art, and language. My analysis of some past tests shows fictional, biographical, and travel critical readings compose about 25 percent of the readings—that is, about one passage per test. The writings on the history of science, on nature, ecology and biology, and general science compose about 33 percent, and those on history, social and cultural issues, political science, art, and language compose about 42 percent.

GENERAL QUESTIONS

As noted, it is useful to make a distinction between general questions and more local questions, which have line number references. The majority of questions (about two-thirds) asked on the critical reading material are directed toward a localized portion of the readings that consists of no more than a few sentences. When this is the case, the question will refer to the several lines (often only one) in the passage. To answer such questions, one only need refer back to the sentence or sentences to get the context. One can reread them and then answer the question. Little time is needed to do this. Consequently, if the reader misses the answer to such questions when initially reading the passage, he or she can get the answer right without having to take much time. In sum, reread the sentences to make sure you get the answer right.

About one-third of the questions do not have such a limited scope. To go back and reread material to find the answer for them would require rereading large sections of the passages, if not the entire passage. To do so would waste time. These questions we have termed *general questions*. It is important for a person seeking a high score to be able to answer most of the general questions from the initial reading of the passage without having to go back and reread major portions of the selection. By glancing at the general questions before reading the selection or through knowing the types of general questions that are likely to be asked, the student will be in a better position to answer the general questions after reading the passage.

My survey of the test's tendencies shows an average of 2.4 general questions per passage reading. For two-passage selections the average number of general questions per selection is much greater at 5.9. So we should look especially for general questions on the two-passage selections. When surveying the kinds of questions asked, I found about one-quarter of the questions were from high difficulty questions.

My analysis of past tests shows that about 75 percent of the general questions fall into one of four types: generalizations and their basis, the main point or purpose, the author's perspective or viewpoint, and two-passage comparisons. Another 10 percent are concerned with a fifth category—namely, attitudes or beliefs of the persons or characters described in the readings. For readings that consist of a single passage, four types include 86 percent of the general questions: the author's viewpoint, the main point or purpose, generalizations and their basis, and attitudes or beliefs of the persons or characters. For readings that consist of two passages, the single type of two-passage comparisons comprises 50 percent of the general questions. Four types add another 39 percent of the general questions: generalizations and their basis, the main point or purpose, the author's viewpoint, and attitudes or beliefs of the persons or characters. The two-passage comparisons generally are comparisons of generalizations, main points and purposes, authors' viewpoints, and character attitudes and beliefs between the two passages.

Four types of the high difficulty questions occur with equal frequency. About one-fifth of the high difficulty questions were based on four categories: generalizations and their basis, the main point or purpose, the author's viewpoint, and two-passage comparisons. Of the general questions, about one-fifth of the high difficulty questions were based on two categories: the author's viewpoint and two passage comparisons. Further, about one-sixth of the high difficulty questions were based on two categories: generalizations and their basis, the main point or purpose.

The conclusion that we can draw is that when reading the critical reading selections, the test taker should be seeking

- the main point or purpose of the reading selection,
- the author's perspective or viewpoint,
- the generalizations stated and the basis for their support, and
- the attitudes and beliefs of the persons or characters discussed in the selection.

These are the things the student should try to discern as he or she reads a selection so that most of the general questions can be answered straight off without referring back to the passage. Of course, there will always be a few general questions for which the test taker will be uncertain and must refer back to the passage. In these cases, I recommend that the test taker either guess or move on and come back later, if there is time.

NEW SHORT READING PASSAGES

The new SAT has some short-paragraph passages with questions to answer. The passages have about four or five sentences—just enough to provide adequate context for the questions. Phrases or words or some other feature of the passage will be selected, and the multiple-choice questions will ask what function or purpose is satisfied by the phrase or feature. The procedure to follow is simple and obvious:

1. Just read the passage to get the meaning and context. It only takes a few seconds.
2. Read the first question. Think what the answer should be. Look back at the phrase or feature in the passage to verify your thought or to figure out what the answer should be if nothing immediately comes to mind.
3. Look at the answers to find one that corresponds to the conclusion you reached in step 2. Quickly look at the other answers to see if any might be even better than the answer you have selected. If you were unable to select an answer straight off, you may have to check each one out and guess, especially if you cannot select one or eliminate four of them.
4. Repeat steps 2 and 3 for any additional questions on the passage.

It is possible that some may want to look at the questions first and then read the passage. This will work, but since it takes only a few seconds to read the passage, reading it first will give a better sense of the context.

CONNECTIVE OR TRANSITION WORDS

To properly make inferences from critical reading passages and to answer questions, one must take connectives or transition words into account. To understand material that gives arguments and makes claims or generalizations, one must also note the role of connective words that signal the role that specific clauses play in the argument of the passage. These connectives also play an important role in determining the correct answers for sentence completion questions. In the course of presenting and arguing for a thesis, an author will use various conjunctions, adverbs, prepositions, and phrases to signal the role or function of the clauses and sentences that precede or follow the author's argument. Knowing the various connective word options is useful for creating variety in vocabulary and sentence structure when writing the essay for the SAT.

Some connective words have a correlative function. They signal that a separate argument or a piece of evidence is being added to the previous argument or piece of evidence. Others may signal denial or a discounting of previous arguments and therefore attempt to offer rebuttal of possible objections. Some are concessive, showing that the author concedes an objection but denies that it is adequate or sufficient to undermine his or her case. Some indicate consequences or implications of previous statements of claims. They may indicate reasons or causes for claims. Other connecting words may show emphasis to alert readers to take special note or an argument, fact, or item of evidence. Some indicate contingency, namely that some result depends on something that may or may not occur. Some key words indicate purpose or results. Others indicate examples. Some indicate comparison or contrast. Finally, key words may signal that the conclusion or summary of the argument follows.

Table 3.1 indicates the most important key words that readers can use for clues to understand the argument and its support. They signal transition points at which new arguments or evidence are introduced or conclusions are stated.

Table 3.1.   Transition Words

Connective Function	Connectives
Correlative	additionally, besides, moreover, furthermore, in fact, likewise, and also, as well as, not only . . . but also, as . . . so, just as . . . so
Disjunctive	or, either . . . or, whether . . . or
Denying/discounting	merely, scarcely, nor, instead, neither . . . nor, but neither, not with . . . but with
Concession/qualification	although, but, granted, however, despite, nevertheless, naturally, notwithstanding, of course, only, still, though, and yet, in spite of, even though, rather than, on the one hand . . . on the other hand, on the contrary, whereas, although it is true that, although you could say that
Implication/consequence	because, since, consequently, hence, then, thus, for, for this reason, on account of, is
Reason/cause–effect	why, as, because of
Emphasis	certainly, chiefly, definitely, especially, indeed, undoubtedly
Contingency/supposition	if, though, unless, provided, barring, including, whether, if . . . then
Purpose/result	that, in order that, lest, so that, is why
Examples	for example, for instance, to illustrate, with reference to, the following . . . example
Comparison/contrast	but, although, yet, however, instead, meanwhile, except, nevertheless, nonetheless, still, though, in contrast, otherwise, else than, other than, rather than, on the one hand . . . on the other hand
Conclusions/summary	consequently, thus, therefore, wherefore, in conclusion, to conclude, in summary, as a result, in other words

GENERAL VERBAL REASONING TIPS

Some general tips for verbal reasoning questions are worth repeating:

- Know the directions beforehand.
- Build your vocabulary. A large part of the score depends on knowing vocabulary. This book provides vocabulary helps that are designed to quickly and efficiently teach the vocabulary needed for the SAT. Set aside some time each day for learning vocabulary. There are eighteen vocabulary chapters in this book. One could peruse a vocabulary chapter a day and repeat several times if started earlier.

For more average students:

- Direct methods are the best and fastest, but if possible, eliminate wrong answers and guess from the remaining.
- Have a system for marking questions that you will skip entirely and those you want to return to answer. When finished with a section, go back to any questions you may still be able to answer. Of course, high scores are not achieved by skipping more than a handful of questions.
- Go through all questions, including the hardest ones—you may know the answer.

ON GUESSING

On the SAT, if some answers can be eliminated, guessing should pay off. Just having some familiarity or recognition of a word can be sufficient to eliminate a couple of possible answers. Suppose Andy was able to eliminate one proposed answer on each of sixteen questions. From the remaining four possible answers, he made a pure random guess. Statistically, he would be likely to get four right and twelve wrong. The test is scored by subtracting 1/4 for each wrong answer, so his net score on the sixteen questions would be $4 - 12/4 = 1$. If he had passed all sixteen questions without making a guess he would have netted zero on them. But if a person has a little familiarity with a word, even just a vague sense of its meaning, he or she will usually be able to eliminate two or three answers. Then, by random guessing, about 40 percent will be answered correctly. If Jack can eliminate two answers on six questions and three answers on ten questions he is likely to get about seven right and nine wrong for a net score of 4 and ¾ ($7 - 9/4$). An additional five correct answers can mean an increase of forty or more points on the verbal section of the SAT. Random guessing therefore pays off if some of the answers can be eliminated.

CHAPTER 4

Sentence Completion Questions

In sentence completion problems one or two blanks are inserted into a sentence to represent missing words or phrases. The missing word or words must be supplied from one of five words or pairs of words given for answers. A reading of the sentence requiring completion will yield clues that dictate one of the five selections. This chapter shows in general how to analyze sentence completion questions.

The sentence completion questions test one's understanding of vocabulary as well as grammatical and logical relationships. The principal approach to doing well is to have a broad vocabulary so that the words are known and one can recognize clues offered by key words. The test uses standard meanings for words. It uses primary definitions found in dictionaries and, sometimes, secondary meanings. Learning vocabulary can help the test taker to answer a number of additional questions correctly. A person who has done considerable reading of difficult (especially argumentative) material will have acquired significant useful vocabulary. A person who has acquired considerable vocabulary in this way can acquire still more by studying the vocabulary chapters in this book.

In addition to strong vocabulary recognition, successful performance on sentence completion questions also requires understanding their patterns and key words. Following the statement of the basic strategy for taking sentence completion questions, the rest of the chapter is devoted to showing how to interpret sentence patterns and key words to determine the meaning of the word or words that could fit in a blank.

STRATEGY FOR TAKING SENTENCE COMPLETION QUESTIONS

The following procedure is recommended:

1. Read the sentence carefully. Notice connective words (words introducing clauses and sentence transitions) and other key words that provide clues about how the blank or blanks should be filled in (especially negation words and prefixes, such as 'not,' 'un,' and 'dis,' which can reverse the meaning). Connective words are sorted by category in table 3.1 (p. 000). Some connective words indicate definitions or examples in the sentence. Others may show comparisons or contrast. Forty-six examples are analyzed in the following to clarify the most important sentence patterns and kinds of clues one must look for.
2. There are two strategies to use. The high scorer will generally take the direct, more efficient, first approach. The second strategy is a fallback strategy. The first strategy uses clues from the structure of the sentence and the indicated synonyms, definitions, and contrasts to determine the meaning of words or phrases that fit the blanks. After having determined what the meaning or approximate meaning is, you can then make a guess. Afterward, look through the answers for an answer that agrees with the guess. Put that answer in the blank and see if it works. Read the whole sentence. If more than one of the answers seems to agree with the guess, try each one to see which works best. It is necessary to find the best answer, not just one that works. Check all the choices, unless you are behind in time. The recommended procedure, or first strategy, is best and most efficient, but if the student has difficulty guessing a word for the blank, he or she should adopt the second strategy, an indirect approach: try each answer choice in the blanks to see which has the best fit.

3. Take one blank at a time. If a two-blank sentence question has one blank that makes a guess possible from the available clues and the other blank is more difficult or quite unclear, the easier blank should be taken first. Look among the answers for those that work for the word to be inserted in the easier blank. After eliminating the answer pairs that do not work for the easier blank—in this way, narrowing down the available answer pairs—then put the remaining answers in the two blanks and see which fits both blanks best.

SOURCES OF DIFFICULTY

There are two factors that can make the sentence completion problems challenging: difficult vocabulary and sentence complexity.

1. The vocabulary may be difficult, as some words may be unfamiliar. The best solution to this problem is to make use of the helps for vocabulary learning provided in this book. By spending some time expanding vocabulary using the lists in chapters 10 through 27 (focusing on italicized words), the student can be confident that very few words encountered will be unfamiliar. Moreover, by gaining knowledge of roots, prefixes, and suffixes from the aids in this book, the student may be able to make better guesses at the meaning of any unfamiliar words encountered.
2. The sentence structure may either be long and complex, or the clues provided may be subtle with minimal help from connective words and other key words. At worst, one may have to resort to the indirect strategy of substitution of each answer to determine which makes the most sense. But there will always be some subtle clues available. One blank may require a word that has positive connotations, and perhaps the other may require a word with a negative connotations. Or, there may be a subtle indication that the words in two blanks are similar or synonymous or that they are contrasting or opposite.

ADVANCE PREPARATION

The best preparation is, first, to expand one's vocabulary using the help provided in this book and, second, to study the examples that follow, which show some of the main clues that will be encountered in an actual test. The student can then determine clues showing definitions, examples, contrasts, comparisons, inferences, and the like. Also, one may wish to practice on past questions from the SAT.

CLUES FOR DETERMINING APPROPRIATE ANSWERS

For solving sentence completion questions, it is helpful to have an intelligent approach for reasoning out answers. The following examples demonstrate grammatical features that give clues for completing the blanks in sentence completion questions. Many single-blank questions could take one of several, roughly synonymous words, but only one of which will be found among the five possible answers given by the test makers. Since some of the possible synonyms may vary in difficulty, the test makers can make the questions easy or difficult by their choice of possible answers. In sentence completions with two blanks, there may be several words in the answer pairs that fit one of the blanks, but only one exists with a word that works in the other blank as well.

There are two basic types of clues: first, definition and synonymy; second, contrast. We will first consider definition and synonymy. There are a variety of ways that an implicit definition or requirement of synonymy determines what fits the blank.

Clues Utilizing Definition or Synonymy

Clues indicating definitions or synonymy with a particular clause or phrase of a sentence completion question are colons, participles, the use of cause and effect, demonstrative pronouns, relative pronouns, indefinite pronouns, and the words 'as,' 'so,' 'is,' and 'are.'

Colon

Frequently, a colon (:) is used in a sentence completion question. Its use often signals that the subsequent phrase is a definition of, and roughly synonymous with, the word or phrase preceding it.

1. John is well known for his _____: he usually acts with great audacity, even recklessness.

Solution: The sentence following the colon indicates that the trait in question involves audacity, a boldness that goes beyond prudence. Synonyms of 'audacity' will fit here. Choose the answer that is synonymous, for example, 'temerity,' 'rashness,' 'boldness,' even 'impudence.'

2. With regard to safety the workers were _____: they seemed careless about following proper procedures.

Solution: It is clear that the adjective 'careless' corresponds and defines the meaning of the word in the blank. We need an adjective synonymous with 'careless,' words such as 'apathetic' and 'unconcerned.'

The object and modifier preceding the colon can be separated by another modifying phrase, as in the following example.

3. The hot, steamy conditions had an _____ impact on the bicyclers: they were becoming exhausted and weak.

Solution: The words "becoming exhausted and weak" determines the meaning of "_____ impact." It indicates that the effect on the hikers is debilitating and weakening. 'Enervating' would be an appropriate choice.

It is possible to have examples with two blanks. In the following example, the blanks on opposite sides of the colon must be filled by words that make the noun and modifier on the left side synonymous with the sentence on the right side.

4. The answer to the math problem in the back of the book was _____: it _____ produces an answer that is ten times larger than the problem allows.

Solution: The sentence following the colon indicates that the answer is erroneous. Hence, words synonymous with 'erroneously' are good choices for the second blank. The first blank will take adjectives like 'spurious,' 'erroneous,' 'wrong,' 'incorrect,' or 'mistaken.'

Semicolons may also function in much the same way as colons. For example,

5. The new theory was _____; only assumed and not proven.

Solution: The adverb 'only' indicates that the word for the blank must be nearly synonymous with 'assumed' and therefore uncertain. The word 'hypothetical' will work.

Participles

Participial phrases in a sentence often function like an adjective. The participial phrase often expands on the meaning of an adjective, further modifying a noun. It therefore acts similar to the sentence following a colon in the preceding section.

Thus the following example uses the participial phrase following the comma to determine the meaning of the adjective that fills in the blank.

6. As one might expect, the diplomats were _____, observing all the rules of protocol in detail.

Solution: The blank is an adjective giving a character trait. The participial phrase "observing all the rules of protocol in detail" modifies the adjective in the blank. The participial phrase determines what can go in the blank since the two must be in agreement, that is, be synonymous. A person who is careful to follow many rules and observe many details is a meticulous person. Other appropriate choices for the blank are 'punctilious,' 'diligent,' 'scrupulous,' 'thorough,' 'sedulous,' and 'persevering.'

Two additional and similar examples are:

7. Smith implemented his plans _____, hiding his plans until it was too late to stop him.

Solution: The participial phrase tells how the plans were implemented. Keeping them hidden until too late indicates an attempt to conceal them. Thus an appropriate choice for the blank is 'surreptitiously.' Words such as 'clandestinely,' 'covertly,' 'secretly,' and 'stealthily' also will work.

8a. Jones's performance of the solo was _____, showing faultless grace and style.

Solution: The participial phrase "showing . . ." determines the adjective in the blank. Suitable answers are 'impeccable,' 'flawless,' 'irreproachable,' and 'perfect.'

The test makers may complicate matters slightly by putting the participial phrase first rather than in its normal order of being last. Thus, for the last example, we might find the following problem:

8b. Showing faultless grace and style, Jones's performance of the solo was _____.

Solution: Nothing is changed except the order of the clauses. The same answers are appropriate here.

A participial phrase can modify the main verb of a sentence or adverb modifying it, adding detail and requiring a verb synonymous with the participle:

9. The math problem was _____, resisting all attempts at solution by distinguished mathematicians.

Solution: The participial phrase indicates the great difficulty of the math problem being well nigh impossible to solve. Possible choices for the blank are 'intractable' and 'unworkable.'

Sentences with two blanks and one subordinate participial phrase are likely to have one blank in the main clause and one in the participial phrase:

10. They were accustomed to living in _____, having never been so unfortunate as to have experienced _____.

Solution: Here the main clause and the subordinate clause with a participle must be roughly parallel. We know that the two clauses must generally be synonymous. The main clause does not give much of a clue to what belongs in the blank. The participial phrase has the adjective 'unfortunate,' which implies experience of bad things or adversity. The test taker should find a word among the second word in the five pairs of potential answers that implies a situation marked by misfortune. Hence, it must refer to hardships, sickness, poverty, pain, or evil. A number of words could satisfy the second blank. For example, 'adversity,' 'setbacks,' 'difficulty,' 'affliction,' 'catastrophe,' 'hardship,' 'poverty,' 'penury,' 'indigence,' 'destitution,' 'hard luck,' and 'tragedy' are all viable candidates for selection. If the people referred to by the subject 'they' have suffered little hardship or misfortune, then the first blank must indicate a lack of familiarity with misfortune. It must be a state that is opposite from the state referred to by the second blank. The words 'living in' restrict the possible choices for the first blank to having wealth or comfortable circumstances. For example, 'living in' works with 'affluence,' 'prosperity,' 'opulence,' 'splendor,' and 'wealth.' Then the second blank must be an opposite state, such as 'poverty,' 'penury,' 'indigence,' and 'destitution.'

Cause and Effect and Purpose

Some sentences state that an action is taken for a purpose; others indicate a cause and effect. In both cases a means may come into play. A person may try to achieve some purpose or goal by means of a chosen action or instrument. Effects are often achieved by a means utilized by the cause. In both cases the word "by" will usually introduce the means used to achieve or to attempt to achieve the effect or purpose.

The phrase following the "by" can provide a definition of a word in the blank. Or it may indicate the cause of an effect that fits the blank.

11. The proposed constitution was made _____ to some opponents by attaching the bill of rights they wanted.

Solution: Attaching a bill of rights desired by opponents will tend to make a constitutional document more acceptable to them. The blank requires a word synonymous with 'acceptable,' such as 'palatable,' 'tolerable,' or 'satisfactory.'

The conjunction "because" introduces a subordinate clause and signals that the clause contains a reason why, or the clause may give the cause of an effect for the state of affairs stated in the main clause.

12. It is clear that Jim has an _____ temperament, because he is so easily angered.

Solution: Some synonyms for being easily angered are 'irascible' and 'volatile.'

Let's change the 'because' clause to 'because he is so changeable':

13. It is clear that Jim has an _____ temperament, because he is so changeable.

Solution: Some synonyms for changeable temperament are 'mercurial,' 'capricious,' 'unpredictable,' and 'volatile.'

14. Because the _____ of evidence seemed to support Jones's argument, the review panel agreed with him.

Solution: From the meaning 'of evidence,' it is clear that the blank represents the amount of evidence in support. Since the review panel agrees, we can conclude that the blank must indicate that it is the majority of the evidence. Possible choices are 'preponderance,' 'weight,' or 'majority.'

15. The new theory is very comprehensive because, though it does not explain one _____, when applied to many other phenomena needing explanation does so satisfactorily and even insightfully.

Solution: The blank must refer to something that is not satisfactorily explained by the theory. Words such as 'anomaly,' 'abnormality,' 'exception,' and 'peculiarity' work.

Demonstrative Pronouns

Demonstrative pronouns such as *that* and *these* often indicate *definitions* or *synonymous* phrases following them.

16. Friends and relatives usually know one's _____, those preferences and tendencies one has to engage in certain activities.

Solution: The word in the blank must be synonymous with 'preferences and tendencies.' Words that work are 'predilections,' 'proclivities,' and 'inclinations.'

17. Jones always excused and aided Smith's lascivious actions, and this _____ to Smith's desires kept Jones in his good graces.

Solution: The pronoun 'this' refers to what Jones was doing when excusing and aiding Smith. Words that fit are 'pandering' and 'catering.' If the 'to Smith's desires' were 'of Smith's desires,' then 'gratification' or 'indulgence' would work.

Relative Pronouns

Relative pronouns such as *who* often give a definition or synonymous phrase that determines the appropriate word for a blank.

18. Jones was annoyed by the _____ behavior of his nephew who kept the focus of the conversation on himself and his interests for the entire evening.

Solution: People who keep the focus on themselves are self-centered. Other synonyms for 'self-centered' that will work in the blank are 'narcissistic,' 'self-centered,' 'egocentric,' 'egotistical,' 'conceited,' 'selfish,' 'vain,' and 'vainglorious.'

The relative pronoun "such" or "such as" give comparisons that dictate the meaning of their antecedents.

19. People tire of reading books they find _____, such as long novels with hackneyed plots.

Solution: Books that tire people and are long with worn-out plots can be characterized as dull or boring. Some words that therefore fit the blank are "prosaic," 'tedious,' 'banal,' 'boring,' 'dull,' 'humdrum,' 'pedestrian,' 'dry,' and 'mundane.'

Indefinite Pronouns

Indefinite pronouns are often used to make two clauses essentially synonymous, as in the following example with "some":

20. By refusing to act reasonably, some people are considered _____.

Solution: The blank calls for words that are synonymous with refusing to behave normally or reasonably: 'recalcitrant,' 'obstinate,' 'contrary,' 'intractable,' 'perverse,' 'refractory,' 'unruly,' 'intransigent,' 'obdurate,' 'stubborn,' 'uncooperative,' and 'willful.'

The indefinite pronoun "one" or "one who" begins a clause that is synonymous with its antecedent phrase as in the following:

21. Jones is a _____ person, one who is always sullen and gloomy.

Solution: A person who is always or nearly always gloomy and sullen is 'morose,' 'melancholy,' 'saturnine,' 'lugubrious,' 'mournful,' or 'depressed.'

The Word "As"

The word "as" is used to indicate similarity, analogy, identity, or comparison. In the following example, the initial "as" has the implication that Smith will disagree with policies that require increased taxes.

22. As a libertarian who seeks smaller government, Congressman Smith tried to prevent _____ of the tax increases on his constituents.

Solution: The word 'as' indicates that the action in the main clause with the blank must be consistent with seeking smaller government. The word 'on' is also very important because it limits the words that will fit in the blank. The words 'imposition' and 'infliction' would work.

The construction "as . . . as . . . ." indicates comparability or equality of the two entities or qualities following the "as" words.

23. Because his essay was poorly edited, it is as _____ today as when Jones wrote it.

Solution: The 'as . . . as . . . .' construction indicates that the condition of the essay today is essentially the same as when it was written. The fact that it was poorly edited indicates that it is still in some poor condition. There are many problems the essay could suffer from. Some possible choices would be 'vague,' 'ambiguous,' 'unclear,' 'confusing,' 'equivocal,' and 'obscure.'

A blank followed by an "as if" clause has the "as if" clause determining and being synonymous with the blank.

24. Jones always gives a _____ appearance, as if he is entirely unaffected by passion or feeling.

Solution: The blank requires a character trait synonymous with 'entirely unaffected by passion or feeling,' for example, 'stoical' or 'phlegmatic.' Some other words would work if the word preceding the blank were 'an,' such as 'imperturbable' or 'impassive.'

The Word "So"

The conjunction "so" can be used to emphasize an extreme quality. In a construction like "P, so _____ . . ." where P is a phrase or clause, the phrase P states that the word in the blank must be synonymous with the word for the blank or essentially provide its definition.

25. Jim was very careful not to share any information, so _____ was he about the topic.

Solution: A person who is extremely reluctant to share information is 'secretive,' 'reticent,' or 'uncommunicative.'

The construction "so _____ that . . ." tends to show causation. So the blank that indicates the cause or a result of the cause must be in agreement or synonymous with the effect. For example,

26. Jim's first novel was so _____ that only a few copies sold.

Solution: A book may not sell because it is poorly promoted. Here the problem is clearly that it is not interesting to read. It must be boring. Some words that fit the blank are 'banal,' 'boring,' 'commonplace,' 'dull,' 'hackneyed,' 'humdrum,' 'pedestrian,' and 'unimaginative.'

The Words "Is" and "Are"

The copulative verb forms "is" and "are" may determine the meaning of the words to be inserted in blanks because they essentially give a definition. Thus in the following example the words following "_____ are" give a definition of the word needed to fill the blank.

27. People characterized as _____ are those who are quite prejudiced.

Solution: Prejudiced people are 'tendentious' or 'biased.'

Comparative

For some sentence completions, the key word that determines the proper choice of fill-in word is a comparative.

28. Particles, the nineteenth-century _____ for subatomic particles was later _____ by a more complex wave-particle model.

Solution: In this example the word "later" indicates that we are comparing what happens or holds first or earlier to what happens or holds at a later time. The "later _____ by (model)" construction requires a word meaning "replaced" in the blank. The first blank could take the word 'paradigm.' The second blank requires a word like 'superseded,' 'replaced,' or 'supplanted.' It is also possible that a second model would augment rather than simply replace the first model. Consequently, words such as 'augmented' or 'supplemented' would also fit the blank.

Comparative adjectives such as "more" and "less" can indicate position on a spectrum over which some quality or trait of character can range. In responding to others, people can range from being subservient, acquiescent, or obsequious to domineering, aggressive, and confrontational. A person who is less confrontational and more conciliatory can expect to experience less confrontation in work or in a political office.

29. Less _____ than Smith, Jones has more _____ relations with people.

Solution: A question like this is sufficiently subtle that one may need to look at the possible answers to determine that the qualities being compared involve conflict or confrontation. The word 'less' implies less of a good thing or less of a bad thing. Which is appropriate depends on the choices the test provides. One blank must convey negative feelings or relations, and the other positive. There are many choices having negative connotations, words such as 'caustic,' 'acrimonious,' belligerent,' 'argumentative,' 'spiteful,' 'bellicose,' 'antagonistic,' 'hostile,' 'pugnacious,' 'truculent,' 'confrontational,' 'quarrelsome,' 'contentious,' 'disagreeable,' 'fractious,' 'querulous,' and 'unfriendly.' If the second blank indicates that Jones has more positive relations with people than Smith, then words such as 'agreeable,' 'friendly,' 'congenial,' 'gratifying,' 'pleasant,' 'amicable,' 'amiable,' 'cordial,' 'genial,' 'peaceful,' 'placid,' and 'serene' will fit the second blank.

Clues Utilizing Contrast

Opposites/Contrast/Range

Although many questions require finding words synonymous with words or phrases in other parts of the sentence, some questions require contrasts or opposites. In most cases words that are polar opposites in meaning reference the opposite ends of a range or spectrum with intermediate positions between the ends of the spectrum. In many cases the question may only require a difference in position on the spectrum; that is, there is a contrast or difference but not entirely opposite. Some words or phrases that indicate an opposite meaning or show some contrast or difference: 'anything but,' 'even more . . . than . . . ,' 'than,' 'far from,' 'first . . . then . . . ,' 'but neither,' 'ranging from,' 'not with . . . but with . . . ,' and 'while . . . others . . .'

The phrase "anything but" requires opposites or near opposites.

30. Although Jones seemed to be behaving with great caution, his actions were anything but _____; actually, he was quite reckless.

Solution: Here the 'anything but' requires that the word in the blank be an opposite to 'reckless.' Words such as 'prudent,' 'cautious,' 'careful,' 'circumspect,' and 'sensible' are appropriate.

The construction "even more . . . than . . ." may just indicate a difference of degree, or it may call for a contrast between two different items or types of items.

31. Even more _____ than the fossils in the exposed layers of limestone rock were the fossils in the underlying layers.

Solution: From knowing that lower levels of rock are formed earlier in time indicates that the blank probably refers to earlier in time. Thus words such as 'primordial,' 'primitive,' 'ancient,' and 'primeval' would work here.

The phrase "far from" calls for opposites or near opposites.

32. Far from _____ the traffic congestion, the new traffic lights had a _____ effect that increased delays.

Solution: Knowing that new traffic lights have been installed tells us that an attempt has undoubtedly been made to reduce traffic congestion. The words 'far from' and 'increased delays' indicate failure. The first blank must be filled by a word such as 'alleviating,' 'diminishing,' 'easing,' 'mitigating,' 'moderating,' 'lessening,' 'palliating,' 'reducing,' or 'relieving.' The second blank can be filled by words indicating the occurrence of an untoward effect that increased rather than reduced delays. Possible words: 'pernicious,' 'deleterious,' 'lamentable,' and 'regrettable.' Other words, such as 'unanticipated,' 'unforeseen,' and 'unenvisaged,' would work if the word 'an' preceded the second blank.

The construction "first . . . then . . ." calls for a contrast. Consider the following:

33. Upon awaking Jack first moved _____, then briskly.

Solution: The adverb 'briskly' following 'then' calls for a word with an opposite meaning for the blank. The word "awaking' gives a clue since upon awaking many people will be a little sluggish in moving about. So we would expect the blank to be filled by words synonymous with 'sluggishly,' for example, 'lethargically,' 'indolently,' 'listlessly,' 'languidly,' and 'torpidly.'

The conjunctive phrase "but neither" indicates a contrast, although it need not consist of polar opposites. In the following example, a contrast in attitudes about one's performance is required.

34. Jones should not be _____ for his acting in the play's leading role, but neither should his performance be ____: his acting is just adequate.

Solution: The sentence following the colon determines what must go into the blanks. The two blanks indicate the degree of merit or commendation Jones's performance should receive. One blank must indicate that the performance is not worthy of high praise. The other blank must indicate that the performance should not be severely criticized. If the first blank then takes a word indicating Jones should not be praised too highly, the word might be 'extolled' or 'lauded.' Some words for the second blank to indicate the performance should not be criticized too severely include 'panned,' 'disparaged,' 'decried,' 'denigrated,' and 'deprecated.'

Some questions may refer to a range of possible types, values, or qualities dictating a particular choice for sentence completion. The phrase "ranging from" might occur in a sentence as in the following example. "Ranging from" is followed by a list of disparate items. The various items listed as being in the range can be important. They can be similar or diverse. The following sentence has a diverse list of items, and the blank must be filled by a word that conveys that notion.

35. The items Jones has bought at garage sales compose an _____ collection ranging from various tools to rock music compact disks.

Solution: A word indicating diversity that can follow 'an' is 'eclectic.' If the word preceding the blank is 'a,' then we could insert 'diverse,' 'heterogeneous,' 'multifarious,' 'miscellaneous,' or 'diversified' in the blank.

Some questions might require opposites if a blank represents one end of a range.

36. Jones's behavior is quite unpredictable, ranging from placid and quiet to quite _____.

Solution: The opposite end of a range beginning with quietness must be noisy and obnoxious. Thus the blank calls for words such as 'belligerent,' 'bellicose,' 'quarrelsome,' and 'truculent.'

The construction 'not with . . . but with . . .' indicates a contrast between two qualities or items. In the following example the blank identifies the kind of person who is designated by the 'but with' option.

37. The concern of a _____ is not with the meritoriousness of an action but with whether it produces pleasure.

Solution: A person who values pleasure most highly is called a hedonist.

The construction "while . . . others . . ." indicates a strong contrast between two options.

38. While some believe the philosophers' works to be _____, others find them to be quite lucid.

Solution: The construction requires the philosophers' works to be the opposite of lucid or clear. They must then be unclear and difficult to understand. Some words that could fit the blank are 'abstruse,' 'obscure,' 'recondite,' 'enigmatic,' 'esoteric,' 'cryptic,' 'nebulous,' and 'vague.'

Concessives/Contrast

Frequently, sentence completion questions depend on concessive conjunctions. Concessive conjunctions are used, first, to concede that a point or argument or an item of evidence has some force in a subordinate clause and; second, in the main clause, to give counteracting reasons for not accepting the arguments that have been conceded to the opposing side. Examples of concessive conjunctions are 'although,' 'but,' 'granted,' 'however,' 'despite,' 'nevertheless,' 'naturally,' 'notwithstanding,' 'of course,' 'only,' 'still,' 'though,' 'and yet,' 'in spite of,' 'even though,' 'rather than,' 'on the one hand . . . on the other hand,' 'on the contrary,' 'whereas,' 'although it is true that,' 'although you could say that.'

The conjunction "although" and its equivalent "though" or "even though" frequently occur and require some kind of contrast between the main and subordinate clauses. Consider the following examples.

39. Although Jones's personal conversation seems quite _____, his journal accounts of his experiences are_____.

Solution: The conjunction 'although' indicates contrast between the journal accounts and Jones's conversations. Several kinds of contrast are possible. One type of contrast is between what is boring and dull and what is interesting and fascinating. Sometimes one may need to discern the contrast from the words in the answers. If Jones's personal conversation is boring, words that fit the first blank are 'tedious,' 'boring,' 'dreary,' 'dull,' 'tiresome,' 'monotonous,' 'uninteresting,' and 'wearisome.' A contrast for the second blank requires words such as 'fascinating,' 'captivating,' 'challenging,' 'enthralling,' 'delightful,' 'transfixing,' and 'riveting.'

Another example:

40. Although his opponents claimed his arguments were _____, closer inspection proved them to be quite _____.

Solution: Since opponents will normally be making criticisms of one's arguments, we can assume that the first blank requires an adjective that negatively assesses the arguments. The main criticism of arguments is that they are 'fallacious.' Other possibilities are 'erroneous,' 'superficial,' 'unconvincing,' 'unpersuasive,' 'misleading,' or 'invalid.' The 'although' indicates a contrast that requires the opposite assessment of the arguments for the second blank, such as 'cogent,' 'compelling,' 'forceful,' 'persuasive,' and 'weighty.'

41. Although the new cosmological theory at first seemed quite_____, a closer analysis showed that it was highly _____.

Solution: The 'although' clause with 'at first' indicates a contrast in credibility or that correctness is involved. Either the first blank must take a synonym for credible or true, and the second blank a synonym for being incorrect or doubtful; or, the first blank must take a synonym for being incorrect or doubtful, and the second blank a synonym for being credible or true. Which case is chosen depends on the available answers. If we take the first blank as a synonym for being incorrect or doubtful and the second blank as a synonym for being credible or true, then the choice for first blank is 'implausible,' 'incredible,' 'inconceivable,' 'doubtful,' 'dubious,' 'improbable,' 'questionable,' 'surprising,' 'untenable,' 'amazing,' 'astonishing,' 'astounding,' and 'unlikely,' and for the second blank 'likely,' 'credible,' 'plausible,' 'passable,' and 'tenable.' One must find a combination in the answers that will fit both blanks. If the meanings for the two blanks are reversed, then the listed words that work for the two blanks must be interchanged. The test makers will choose pairs of proposed answers so that only one will clearly work for both blanks.

Another example:

42. Even though most of his acquaintances thought that Jones had a natural tendency toward laziness, his closest friends thought otherwise: that he had a _____ for diligence.

Solution: Here we find a contrast between two opposite character traits: laziness and diligence. The blank corresponds to the description of a 'tendency.' So words such as 'proclivity' or 'propensity' will fit the blank.

The conjunction "and yet" calls for a contrast. For example:

43. Jones is known for his incisive writings and yet is often quite_____ in his conversation.

Solution: The contrast indicated by 'yet' calls for a word that is an opposite to 'incisive.' Thus we might choose from words such as 'inarticulate,' 'incoherent,' 'disjointed,' 'muddled,' 'rambling,' 'unclear,' 'obscure,' 'vague,' and 'nebulous.'

44. In spite of considerable _____ in their worldviews, the committee was able to achieve _____ in their views on the environment.

Solution: The words 'in spite' require an obstacle. It indicates considerable disagreement in worldviews. Thus words such as 'disagreement,' 'conflict,' 'discord,' 'dissension,' 'difference,' 'dissimilarity,' 'divergence,' 'heterogeneity,' 'incompatibility,' and 'disparity' fit the first blank. The second blank needs a word showing agreement, such as 'accord,' 'concord,' 'agreement,' 'consensus,' 'unanimity,' and 'unity.'

The construction "while . . . once . . . now . . ." requires a contrast between before and after.

45. While Jones was once quite_____ when presented with rational evidence against his position, he is now quite _____ and willing to listen.

Solution: Here the subordinate 'while' clause represents a position "before" and the main clause indicates the situation afterward. The two blanks take words that are opposite. The following words can work in the first blank: 'obdurate,' 'intractable,' 'obstinate,' and 'recalcitrant.' The second blank takes 'agreeable,' 'tractable,' 'accommodating,' and 'amenable.'

In the following example the "as . . . as . . . that . . ." construction can be used to show contrast, especially with a "nevertheless."

46. As _____as Jones's oversight was, that mistake nevertheless had some _____ consequences.

Solution: An oversight may involve negligence. The 'as . . . as . . .' construction tends to imply some personal responsibility and oversight by Jones. So 'negligence' is appropriate for the first blank. The 'nevertheless' indicates that there are positive factors that offset the negative aspects of the oversight. Some words for the second blank are 'constructive,' 'advantageous,' 'beneficial,' 'positive,' 'salutary,' 'useful,' or 'valuable.'

GENERAL VERBAL REASONING TIPS

Some general tips for verbal reasoning questions are:

- Know the directions before you take the test.
- Answer the easy questions before the hard questions—the questions on the sentence completion are arranged from the easiest to the hardest.
- Build your vocabulary. A large part of the score depends on knowing vocabulary. This book provides vocabulary helps that are designed to quickly and efficiently teach the vocabulary needed for the SAT. Set aside some time each day for learning vocabulary. There are eighteen vocabulary chapters in this book. One could peruse a vocabulary chapter each day and repeat doing so several times if sufficient time has been allocated.
- Direct methods are the best and fastest, but if necessary, eliminate known wrong answers and guess from the remaining.
- Have a system for marking questions that you will skip entirely and those you want to return to answer. When finished with a section, go back to any questions you may still be able to answer. Of course, high scores are not achieved by skipping more than a handful of questions.
- Go through all questions including the hardest ones—you may know the answer.

CHAPTER 5

Writing Sample Multiple-Choice Questions

The writing section of the new SAT consists of two parts that must be completed in one hour. One part takes thirty-five minutes and consists of multiple-choice questions. The multiple-choice questions test the student's knowledge of grammar. The twenty-five-minute second part is a written essay on a topic. This chapter discusses ways to improve scores on the multiple-choice part of the writing section. Because proper grammar is covered only in a long book and there is no quick fix for poor grammar, this chapter provides only a brief overview and a few suggestions to remedy identified grammatical deficiencies. Chapter 6 discusses preparations and steps that can be taken to improve a score on the essay.

THE MAIN TYPES OF GRAMMATICAL PROBLEMS

The scope of the writing section of the SAT with multiple choice is to test grammatical sophistication and knowledge of the nuances of good grammar. The range of grammatical problems that can be tested with multiple choice falls into six major categories: (1) lack of clarity due to incomplete thoughts, wordiness, or vagueness, (2) agreement of subjects and verbs, pronouns with antecedents, verb tenses with time and range of action, and the like, (3) word order and proper reference, (4) semantic confusion and association, (5) constructions that are frowned on but may be used in some contexts, and (6) punctuation problems and misspellings.

Students should determine if they need to work on any of these categories of problems. Spelling is not tested in the multiple-choice questions of the SAT, and a few misspellings on the essay will not lower its grade. However, many misspellings on the essay probably would lower the grade. Similarly with punctuation. Good writers know the rules of correct punctuation. A question testing only punctuation is not likely to occur among the multiple-choice questions. A few failures to punctuate properly are not likely to cause the essay to be graded down. Moreover, a short essay supporting a thesis need not contain any punctuation besides periods and commas separating clauses in complex sentences and commas separating parallel constructions. Constructions and expressions that are frowned on but not precluded in all contexts are not likely to be tested with multiple-choice questions. A strongly written essay avoids using them. The primary grammatical problems tested by multiple-choice questions fall in the first four categories and their occurrences on the essay tend to reduce the grade.

Lack of Conciseness and Clarity

Poor grammar is not always an outright breaking of grammatical rules. It may consist in a lack of conciseness and clarity. There are four ways this frequently occurs. Fragments or nonsentences sometimes occur and are not corrected from failure to reread and correct what has been written. Wordiness and redundancy reduce the clarity of writing. Although not grammatical errors in the strictest sense, they reduce persuasiveness of writing. Similarly, avoidable vagueness and abstractness where specificity and concreteness are possible is not a grammatical error but reduces clarity and convincingness. Finally, the passive voice exists because its use is frequently necessary. However, the active voice should be used wherever possible. Use of passive voice instead of the active leads to weak, wishy-washy writing.

Nonsentences

An English sentence must have a subject and predicate. The subject is a noun with optional modifiers, and the predicate is a finite verb with optional modifiers. Putative sentences that lack subject or predicate are incomplete sentences or sentence fragments. Modifiers and modifying clauses may be incomplete in such a way that the supposed sentence does not complete an idea but leaves it dangling. This usually happens as a consequence of an oversight while writing. Sentence fragments are easily recognized and corrected by rereading and checking what one has written. For example, 'Realizing he could not throw the stone across the river' is a subordinate clause but not a sentence. It can be fixed by substituting a subject and finite verb for 'realizing,' as follows: 'He realized he could not throw the stone across the river.' Or, we can add a main clause: 'Realizing he could not throw the stone across the river, he tried skipping it.'

Redundancy and Wordiness

Some words can be added that are redundant. They just repeat what has already been stated by other words in the sentence. Redundant words should be cut. A sentence can use many more words to express an idea than needed. Extra unnecessary words should be excised. For example, consider the sentence "When he turned eighty, Jones wrote the autobiography of his life for his grandchildren." Here the words "of his life" is redundant because this concept is already contained in the meaning of "autobiography." So the sentence should be improved to "When he turned eighty, Jones wrote his autobiography for his grandchildren."

Vagueness

Vagueness is not a grammatical error per se, but good, clear, and concise writing states the details when possible rather than vaguely imply them. It is always better to be specific and concrete when possible. Abstract, non-specific language fails to persuade. Thus, 'Jones grabbed the weapon and held it in a position ready to use it' is quite vague. Much more concrete and specific is 'Jones grabbed the knife and held it up ready to stab Smith.'

Active Voice

Writers should use active voice wherever possible. Passive voice is frequently required for conveying the proper meaning because the subject or object is unknown; however, if active voice can be used, it should be. All too often writers use passive voice when they should use active voice. Thus the passive 'The subject was studied thoroughly by the student' sounds much clearer in the active: 'The student studied the subject thoroughly.'

Agreement

A large part of grammar involves following rules that specify ways in which different parts of speech must be in agreement in number, person, and tense. There are several types of agreement that must be observed in correct English sentences. The most important are as follows.

Parallelism

Parallel constructions with parallel modifiers, phrases, or clauses occur frequently in sentences written in English. Each word or phrase written as a parallelism must agree with other words playing parallel roles. Verbs in parallel phrases and clauses must agree in tense and number. So also must modifying words. Example: "John's goals include earning an MBA, becoming CEO of a large corporation, and election to the U.S. Senate." The objects serving as

John's goals are stated as participial phrases except the last one. Parallelism requires that the third object "election to the U.S. Senate" should also be a participial phrase. Thus the correct sentence is 'John's goals include earning an MBA, becoming CEO of a large corporation, and being elected to the U.S. Senate.'

Verb Tenses

Verb tenses must agree with the context. Actions occurring in the past must be in past tenses (or historical present). Actions to occur in the future must be in a future tense.

Nouns and Verbs

Subject nouns and predicate verbs that modify them must agree in number and person; that is, singular verbs go with singular subject nouns, and plural verbs go with plural subject nouns. Thus 'he' agrees with 'has read,' but 'they' agrees with 'have read.' Sometimes unusual order—for example, the subject follows the verb, or the subject and verb are widely separated—causes writers or speakers to fail to make subject and verb agree in person or number.

Pronouns

Pronouns must agree in number and person; that is, pronouns used to refer to singular subjects (I, he, she, it) must have singular form, and pronouns used to refer to plural subjects must have plural form (we or they).

Pronoun Case

Singular and plural pronouns take different forms depending on their use as subjects or objects. The sentence 'John's socialist principles produced a conflict between he and his friend Jack' uses 'he' as an object. But the objective case form for the pronoun 'he' is 'him,' so the proper form is 'John's socialist principles produced a conflict between him and his friend Jack.'

Comparison

Adjectives in English have a single form except when they are used in comparatives. When two entities are compared in regard to a quality, one may be better or worse in respect to that quality. This can be indicated by use of the comparative form of the adjective. Participles used as adjectives are used with "more." When three or more entities are compared in regard to a quality, some may be better or worse in respect to that quality. One may be the best or most inferior. This can be indicated by use of the superlative form of the adjective. Participles used as adjectives are used with "most" to indicate the superlative.

Adjective vs. Adverb

Sometimes a writer tries to modify a verb using an adjective rather than an adverb. Adverbs usually end in -ly. "He sang sweet" is incorrect. It should be "He sang sweetly."

Problems of Reference

Word order is very important in English since it plays an important role in determining which words modify other words. Placing words in the wrong order can imply something very different. Modifiers can be misplaced.

For example, 'He saw the dead skunk driving on the backroad' tends to cause the action 'driving' to be associated with the skunk rather than with the subject 'he.' The sentence could be fixed either as 'While driving on the backroad, he saw the dead skunk' or 'He saw the dead skunk while driving on the backroad.'

Semantic Confusion

Thus far the types of grammatical incorrectness have resulted from form rather than meaning or content. There are two problems connected primarily to meaning. First, some words sound very much alike and may be confused. Second, there are many specific verbs, infinitives, and gerunds that have an association with particular prepositions. It is necessary to know these relationships to write and speak properly and well.

Word Confusion

Correct usage of terms is important. Some words tend to be confused even by relatively well-educated people because the words are similar in pronunciation. The following words, among many others, are often confused:

accept, except	counsel, council
advice, advise	elicit, illicit
affect, effect	eminent, immanent
assure, ensure	imply, infer
capital, capitol	principal, principle
complement, compliment	

There are also some verb forms that are confusing. Many people fail to use words such as 'may' and 'can' or 'lay' and 'lie' properly. In addition it is also very important to know the proper contexts for using verb–preposition combinations, for example, when to use 'compare to' and when to use 'compare with.'

Proper Prepositions

Certain relationships between verb forms and specific prepositions have idiomatic uses that must be learned from extensive reading. For example, 'differ from' is used to indicate that two or more entities are different. The words 'differ with' or 'differ on' indicate that two or more people disagree in assessment of a situation or who to proceed.

Words That Are Frowned On

There are some constructions that may not be strictly forbidden but are generally frowned on.

Double negatives. Use of double negatives is always incorrect if the double negative is intended to indicate a single negative. Occasionally, if a second negative cancels the first, there are circumstances in which it can be used properly. However, in this case generally the proper course is to make a straightforward statement that does not use negatives at all.

Split infinitives. Use of split infinitives has been considered to be grammatically bad. An infinitive consists of the word "to" and the infinitive form of a verb, for example, "to work." A split infinitive is an infinitive with a modifying adjective or adverb separating the "to" and the verb, for example, "to quickly work" instead of "to work quickly." Avoiding split infinitives is usually proper, although there can be occasions where a split infinitive is appropriate.

Jargon and clichés. Good nonfictional writing avoids use of jargon and clichés. However, an author of fiction while writing dialogue may find jargon and clichés very useful for character development in a novel, play, or story.

Punctuation Problems and Misspellings

Sentences are punctuated by commas, colons, semicolons, apostrophes, quotation marks, hyphens, and dashes. There are a number of rules governing the proper use of these punctuation marks. It is desirable to know the rules and follow them. However, punctuation errors are not tested by the multiple-choice questions, nor will a few mistakes in use of these marks probably reduce the grade given to the essay. Misspellings of words can also detract from writing and should be avoided. However, word misspelling errors are not tested by the multiple-choice questions. A few misspellings on the essay do not by themselves reduce the grade.

MULTIPLE-CHOICE QUESTIONS TEST GRAMMATICAL KNOWLEDGE

The writing section of the SAT has three types of multiple-choice questions that test students' knowledge of English grammar. The test allots thirty-five minutes to answer the questions. The first kind of question tests ability to recognize passages with faulty grammatical constructions. The second and third types of questions test ability not merely to recognize grammatical errors but to improve grammar of sentences and paragraphs. The examples that follow are given as illustrations of the kind of problems encountered for these three kinds of questions.

Recognizing Sentence Errors

The first type of multiple-choice question requires the student taking the SAT merely to recognize grammatical errors. Anyone who has taken a good course in grammar and has done extensive reading of good literature should have developed an ear for good and bad grammar and should be able to recognize words or sentences constituting bad grammar. One set of questions involves identifying sentence errors. A sentence is marked in four places where possible errors may have occurred. The letter E is assigned to cover cases with no grammatical errors occurring in the sentence.

In this form, four words or phrases in a sentence are underlined, and the letters A, B, C, or D are associated in order with the four underlinings. If any underlined word or phrase involves a grammatical error, the letter A, B, C, or D associated with it is the answer. If there is no error, E is the answer.

An example of associated verb and preposition: John and Tom have just agreed with the terms of a contract that will cover the next four years. No error.

Answer: Here, A is associated with the underlined 'have just,' B is associated with the underlined 'agreed with,' and so forth. Agreement on a contract requires "agreed to" rather than "agreed with." So B is the answer.

An example of pronoun agreement: When you write poetry, one must ensure that the words follow the same meter. No error.

Answer: The third person pronoun "one" in the main clause refers to the same person as the second person "you" in the subordinate clause. Good grammar requires that they agree—that is, that they be the same. So "one" should be changed to "you." "You" could be changed to "one," but then the verb "write" must be changed to the third-person form.

An example of redundancy: The student is given a choice of the underlined portion as answer A and four other alternate wordings. No error.

Amswer: Here the word 'alternate' makes the word 'other' redundant. The correct sentence is 'The student is given a choice of the underlined portion as answer A and four alternate wordings.' So C is the answer.

An example of verb agreement: The nonagenarian philanthropist and his wife has given large contributions both to local charities and to national charities. No error.

Answer: The verb here should be 'have given' rather than 'has given.' The philanthropist and his wife are more than one and take a plural verb form.

Fixing Sentences

A second set of questions requires the test taker to improve sentences. A portion of one or sometimes two sentences is underlined. Five sets of words to replace the underlined portion are given as possible answers. A choice of the words that produce the best sentence must be made. The student is given a choice of the underlined portion as answer A and four alternate wordings. The grammatically best wording should be chosen. Here the task is not merely to recognize an error but also to determine how best to fix it.

For example, the sentence 'The boy who is on the left in the picture is the tallest' can be improved to 'The boy on the left in the picture is the tallest' by removing 'who is.'

The sentence 'Cell phones are becoming very popular because they avoid missing calls when away from home or office, can be used almost anywhere, enable the owner to feel safer, and comparable in cost to landline phones' is an example of a sentence needing some fixing to achieve parallelism. It can be corrected by inserting the verb 'are' between 'and' and 'comparable.'

Here is a split-infinitive example: 'So the number of cars built and sold by the automakers is expected to significantly decline' needs to be corrected to 'So the number of cars built and sold by the automakers is expected to decline significantly.'

Fixing Paragraphs

The third type of problem gives an entire paragraph with about a dozen numbered sentences. One or two sentences are singled out and underlined. There are a set of questions that test how to improve the paragraph or paragraphs. For each question, a particular sentence (or portion of it) or two sentences are selected or underlined. Five options are given for how best to modify the selected portion of the paragraph to improve it. The changes may include combining sentences, splitting sentences, or some other option that may improve the grammatical structure of the paragraph. The test taker chooses the answer set of words that produces the best paragraph. Consider the following text:

> Perennially workers, company executives, and voters argue that our industries should be protected so that jobs will not be lost. Unfortunately few understand what economists have understood since the early part of the nineteenth century. Free trade without protectionism is in the best interest of every country and its consumers. It leads to more total trade and better utilization of a country's skills and resources.
>
> Protectionism seems to temporarily benefit industries. In the long term protectionism does not even benefit the industries it was intended to help. Consider the quotas placed on Japanese autos by the Reagan administration in the mideighties. The Big Three automakers and the United Auto Workers Union lobbied for quotas to protect American jobs. What was the result? The quotas limited competition. The Big Three were able to raise auto prices. By imposing quotas, the federal government essentially placed a tax on autos and allowed the Big Three automakers to collect the tax from American consumers. The auto prices were raised. Many people who were planning to buy new cars decided to get by with their old cars. So the number of cars built and sold by the automakers declined significantly. They therefore closed a number of automobile plants and laid off thousands of workers. Costs of production were reduced and profits increased greatly. The very opposite of the purpose of the quotas came about. Moreover, since the auto companies were now making huge profits instead of losses, the top executives of the Big Three were rewarded with large pay increases rather than being fired for incompetence. The only achievement they made was to lobby for and to obtain the protectionist quotas.

For a first example, consider the two sentences: "Protectionism seems to temporarily benefit industries. In the long term protectionism does not even benefit the industries it was intended to help." These can be improved by modifying and combining them to "Protectionism seems to benefit industries temporarily, but in the long term it does not even benefit the very industries it is intended to help." This sentence should be chosen from the candidate answers.

For a second example consider the two sentences: "The auto prices were raised. Many people who were planning to buy new cars decided to get by with their old cars." A better-written sentence combines the two as follows:

"When the auto prices were raised, many people with plans to buy new cars decided to keep their old cars." This sentence should be chosen from the five available selections.

RECOMMENDATIONS FOR THE MULTIPLE-CHOICE QUESTIONS

Anyone who has done much reading of material that is of at least moderate difficulty and has studied grammar or taken a good course in grammar should have acquired the ability to recognize proper grammatical constructions and constructions that are incorrect. Thus well-prepared students should expect to do well on the multiple-choice questions without further study. However, for those who may have major deficiencies in grammatical knowledge because they have not done sufficient reading or study of grammar, it will be very difficult, if not impossible, to remedy even in a few months. If a person planning to take the SAT identifies certain areas of grammatical deficiency, then he or she should study the relevant passages in a good, up-to-date grammar book. Most of the main grammatical problems result from lack of proper agreement of one kind or another. Rules governing agreement of the several parts of speech with one another should be studied with particular care. One of the most useful exercises is to, first, find a grammar book that shows how to diagram sentences and, second, diagram sentences in a book written by a great writer whose writings one admires.

CHAPTER 6

The Writing-Sample Essay

The writing section of the SAT is intended to measure a student's ability to communicate by writing. The advice in this chapter applies primarily to nonfiction writing aimed at arguing for a thesis. This is the kind of writing most college students engage in as they write their papers and exams. Like the eloquence of speech, the excellence of writing is determined by two factors: ideas (or content) and presentation (or rhetoric). The ideas are the content, meaning, logic, and structure conveyed by a forceful argument in writing or speech. The rhetoric covers the way or manner in which the ideas or content are presented. Good choice of words and variety of words and sentence structure can help to persuade without changing the content. Poor choices detract from the argument.

Good writing addresses the subject at hand and effectively conveys an argument or message. When there is excellent content, the reader obtains real insight into the subject matter. When the task requires addressing an issue, the author of a well-written essay states his or her position clearly and concisely. A topical essay must support its thesis in a logical and compelling way, usually with several compelling arguments. The author introduces supporting examples or evidence that is appropriate and buttresses the thesis. In addition the author rebuts the most compelling arguments that can be brought against the thesis. Good writing also shows good organization and development of the argument and evidence supporting the thesis. If evidence and argumentation are poorly organized and developed, the reader will become confused and will not accept the argument even when the ideas and evidence presented are good.

The second aspect of good writing is the presentation of the ideas and evidence. Good rhetoric provides significant variety. It does not repeat the same words for the same ideas but varies the vocabulary using a range of words. The structure of sentences is varied. The use of variety maintains interest. The grammar is correct. Incorrect grammar detracts from an argument. Good writing shows good style and makes use of language in a way that flows smoothly and is pleasing to the reader. Misspellings also mar and detract from the persuasiveness of an essay.

THE NEW ESSAY FOR THE SAT

The new essay for the SAT is intended to measure how well you write. The producers of the test have standards intended to make grading the essays as objective as possible. The readers are trained to apply the standards. The essay topic is designed to give the test taker an opportunity to take one of at least two defensible positions and provide a supporting argument and evidence from personal experience or from literature or other reading. Twenty-five minutes are available to write an essay on an assigned topic.

CHARACTERISTICS OF A GOOD ESSAY

When deciding how to write an essay, one needs to consider the criteria on which that essay is graded. Written essays for the SAT can receive a grade from one to six, with six being the highest possible grade. The essays are graded on content and on presentation. The grading for content depends on (1) how well the essay supports its thesis using reasons, evidence, and examples; and (2) how well it is organized and whether it proceeds logically. The writer may assess how well he or she has done with respect to essay content by asking two questions: How convincing is the essay? and How easy is the essay to follow?

An essay that is convincing because it does an excellent job of using supporting reasons and evidence and is also well organized and therefore easy to follow should earn a score of six in so far as the content is concerned. Essays that are just average or satisfactory should earn a four on content. Inadequate, poor, or very poorly organized essays earn a three, two, and one, respectively.

The grading on the rhetoric, or presentation of the argument, is determined by three factors: the variety of vocabulary used, the variety of sentence structure, and proper grammatical usage. To evaluate presentation, a writer might consider the answers to the following three questions: How good is the diction (range of vocabulary)? Is there a good variety in sentence structure? and How well does the writer use language (good grammar)?

A score of six can be earned if a broad variety of vocabulary is used, if the structure of the sentences shows considerable variety, and if proper grammar is used. A score of six can be earned despite a few minor grammatical errors. A four rewards adequacy on the three factors. Lower scores show various levels of errors.

Based on the system for grading the essays, it is evident that the writer should strive to use good grammar, vary the sentence structure (as long as this is done smoothly), and use a range of vocabulary avoiding repetition.

But more important than the presentation or rhetorical features of the essay are the ideas and content. The best essays have a thesis and supporting examples drawn from literature, science, or the author's experience that do indeed buttress the thesis. The essay also has a good organization. Normally, the thesis should appear in an introductory paragraph and be clearly and concisely stated. If some qualifications are being made, they may be stated as well. The introductory paragraph may also give some indication for the main reason the author holds the thesis. In twenty-five minutes, there is time only to write an essay of three hundred–plus words and three to five paragraphs, including the introductory paragraph. The central paragraphs should be devoted to developing the supporting example or arguments and to rebutting any counterarguments. The final paragraph may be a summarizing and concluding paragraph. Or, the last couple of sentences in the final paragraph can be devoted to stating a conclusion and bringing the essay to a close.

HOW TO PREPARE FOR THE ESSAY

There are no quick fixes to learning to write well. To write well, one must know the nuances of grammar and word meanings. These knowledges are generally acquired through extensive reading and a good course in grammar. As one reads good literature and other well-written works, the reader gradually acquires a good ear for recognizing good and bad grammar and good and bad usage of language.

The second source of learning to write well is to have done considerable writing and to have received feedback on it. Good writers have generally had extensive experience writing and receiving constructive criticism of their writing. Good schools give students frequent writing assignments with constructive feedback.

Writers need to write and evaluate their writing objectively. R. Flesch's *The Art of Readable Writing* (1962) shows how a writer can objectively measure the readability of his or her writing and by so doing learn how to make written work more readable. S. Kaye's *Writing under Pressure* (1989) provides guidelines for allocating time and shows how to plan essays to efficiently produce good results.

Students with extensive reading and writing backgrounds should expect to do well. There are some things good writers can do to prepare for this test to give themselves the opportunity to do even better. The essay assignment does not provide a choice of several topics. There is one topic that everyone must write on. This makes grading the essays fair and relatively objective. Second, students do not have much time to plan their essay. After reading the topic assigned, they have only a few minutes to plan the essay before beginning to write. Different people have read different literature, both fiction and nonfiction, and have had different life experiences. Some preparation for selecting good examples to support the thesis may be helpful. For some well-prepared writers, the topic may happen to be easy. They may readily think of a good example that supports their viewpoint on the topic at issue. For other writers, the topic may seem quite difficult. They may have some trouble thinking of a good example that supports their view on the topic.

Some time spent in thought and preparation beforehand may minimize prospects of having difficulty formulating one's thesis and selecting good supporting evidence when the time to write the essay arrives. Of course, there is no assurance that adequate preparation can be made for all topics. Although a variety of topics for proposed essays is available for test makers, they are likely to choose basic themes that have frequently been treated in great literature. A person who feels well prepared to write, who believes that his or her grammar does not need much reviewing, nor that he or she needs to practice writing with feedback may become better prepared by thinking about possible topics and what supporting evidence could be brought to bear on them. The following preparatory activities could be helpful.

First, try to think of all the life experiences you have had that were most influential. Are there some that come to mind that led to personal growth? Are there others that taught you something important? Some experiences might be so personal that you would not want to write about them in an essay for the SAT. But spending a couple of hours thinking and trying to increase your store of possible examples for the essay could prove very useful. With limited time to state your thesis and to find appropriate supporting examples, it may be very helpful to have spent some time thinking about the possibilities beforehand.

Second, there are a number of basic themes that occur in great literature. There is a significant likelihood that an assigned essay topic for an SAT utilizes a variation on one of these basic themes. It is useful to have read and to be able to use examples from great literature. Since the graders of the writing sample are likely to be English teachers or other persons well versed in good literature, use of literary examples is likely to produce a sympathetic reading. The following section lists some of the most basic literary themes. There are also many variations to some of them. References to great works of literature that utilize the themes are given. They are chosen to cover a broad variety of themes, and most are relatively short. Students preparing for the writing sample should read over the themes and think of examples they could use for each theme. If a theme is identified for which a good example does not come to mind, then one might read one of the recommended works listed for that theme. *Of course, there is no guarantee that this preparation will help for the topic that shows up on the exam.*

Third, try writing an essay on one or more of the themes listed here to practice writing skills. Or just think about supporting examples that could be used in support of the theses.

1. Many of the ills of society will be solved by more technological progress.
2. Conservatives have been too successful holding back needed societal changes.
3. Society as a whole would benefit most if everybody just pursued their own interests.
4. Our society would benefit if more steps were taken to reduce competition and increase cooperation.
5. Society would be better if there were more idealists.
6. Success depends upon overcoming difficulties.
7. Our personal growth depends greatly on others.
8. Selected goals and purposes should guide our actions.

In addition, students should read good literature to have more possible examples and to acquire a better feel for grammar. For those whose knowledge of grammar is weak, study of a good grammar text would be helpful.

Students should also write some essays on several topics and have them graded by someone who knows English very well. By writing and receiving correction, a person who has not developed good writing skills can pinpoint weaknesses and spend some time working on them. Although great improvement in writing over the short term is not realistic, a moderate amount of time spent diagnosing areas needing improvement, writing some practice essays for correction; studying grammar; reading great literature; and thinking about themes and possible examples from literature, nonfiction, and personal experience may produce a significantly better written essay for the SAT.

LITERARY THEMES AND RECOMMENDED LITERATURE

The student-written essay question presents a basic idea that people are likely to disagree about. The assignment is to take a position on the idea, explain it, and support it with reasoning and examples from one's reading and experience. Since the graders are likely to be teachers of English literature or persons knowledgeable of literature, examples drawn from great world literature should be helpful. Of course the writer may have examples from personal experience or from nonfictional writings that are superior.

There are a variety of issues and ideas from which the test makers can choose. Consequently, no matter how one prepares, one cannot be sure that he or she will have experiential or literary examples that are to the point. Nevertheless, it is possible to cover many of the bases and to increase significantly the chances of having appropriate literary examples.

First, there are some basic themes that occur repeatedly in literature and human life. There are many variations on the themes that may serve as springboard ideas for the essay. By considering some of the perennial themes of great works of literature, students can read the works and call on them when writing the essay. Many of the great works are relatively short and can be read in several hours. So what are some of the key themes?

Universal Themes for all Historical Periods

Freedom and the Irrational versus Reason, Order, and Control

The desire for freedom and the desirability of order and control come into conflict. Societies and government must impose order and control, but there will always be differences of opinion concerning whether individuals in a society are given too much freedom or too little or whether there is too much order and control or too little. At a personal level, conflict can come between one's self-discipline and behavior and one's acting irrationally and in response to passion and impulse. One variation of this theme is a comparison of freedom and the existence of slavery. Another variant is the struggle between the rational and irrational. Order and control are associated with what is reasonable and rational and what is opposed by the irrational and emotional side of human nature.

In works of literature a conflict between nature and society or civilization, between uncivilized natural ways of living and civilized life, between the country and the city is often central. There is a fundamental conflict between freedom and law and order. Finally, nature is often associated with, and may be used to symbolize, purity while society and the city are often used to symbolize corruption.

The various themes indicated are central to many important works of literature. For example, Shakespeare's *As You Like It* and *A Midsummer Night's Dream* move back and forth between the forest and the city. Some characters live and operate in only one of the two arenas while some of the principal characters move from one arena to the other. The contrast between nature and civilization is central to these two plays.

A key theme in Mark Twain's *Huckleberry Finn* is the difference between freedom and slavery, as experienced by Huck and Jim. The goal of obtaining Jim's freedom is a fundamental part of the plot. Huck and Jim are free when they are floating in a raft on the river. But they are also rebelling against the control and order imposed by the Widow Douglas and Miss Watson.

The Conflict between Realists and Idealists

Idealism is often believed to result in disillusionment, and yet without it, many useful and good things fail to occur. Idealism can cause much evil when misplaced. The most prominent example is the history of Marxism and communism, which had the idealistic goal of bringing freedom and equality to humankind and eliminating exploitation and control of human being. However, Communism caused the death of many millions. The allegory in George Orwell's *Animal Farm* represents the history of Russian communism and its failures.

The theme of realism versus idealism is prominent in Shakespeare's *Julius Caesar*. Brutus is an idealist who believes the older Roman democratic institutions usurped by Caesar need to be restored and so takes part in the assassination of Caesar. Other actors in the plot to assassinate Caesar act for personal and nonidealistic reasons. In Shakespeare's *Richard II* one finds a contrast between the idealistic and ineffective Richard II and the realistic and pragmatic Henry Bolingbroke, who usurped Richard's throne.

Machiavelli in *The Prince* was first to argue for basing political action on a realistic assessment of human nature. To survive and maintain rule, a ruler must base his approach on the characteristics and foibles of his subjects and opponents. Previously, actions were based on and justified by appeal to a God-ordained order of rule by divinely appointed kings.

Good versus Evil

This is a perennial problem in literature. Because this tends to bring in God and the supernatural to some extent and because those who produce tests such as the SAT generally prefer to avoid issues that involve the supernatural, the essay topic is not very likely to raise the issue of evil. Dickens's *Oliver Twist* remains positive despite so many things going against the main character. In the end, good triumphs over evil. Some important works for which the issue of good and evil is central are Marlowe's *Dr. Faustus*; John Steinbeck's *The Pearl*; and Voltaire's *Candide*, a satire written to ridicule Leibniz's claim that this is the best of all possible worlds.

Several important works are based on the theme, or intended to show, that human nature is the source or main cause of evil. This is the basis for William Golding's *Lord of the Flies*. It is the presupposition of Machiavelli's *The Prince* and implied by John Paul Sartre's *No Exit*.

Modern Themes

Thus far the literary themes covered have been universal because they have been relevant to cultures throughout history. But with eighteenth-century advances in science and the industrial revolution at century's end, great changes occurred. Post-eighteenth-century European and North American societies differ in fundamental ways that have introduced new themes for literature. Societies are no longer primarily agricultural. Standards of living have greatly improved. Advanced countries have changed from monarchies to democracies. A belief in human progress has taken hold. A tendency to believe that the beliefs and actions of individuals are determined by their culture and environment also took hold.

Belief in Human Progress

Those who believe in human progress push for change and encourage innovation. However, many believe that human technological progress has not really brought moral progress. They can cite the two World Wars in the twentieth century. Many people believe in the importance of following traditions, being conservative, and opposing many innovations.

Jonathan Swift's *Gulliver's Travels* is a satire that ridicules scientific speculations made at the beginning of the eighteenth century. It also ridicules the political figures and institutions of the time, the belief in the need for change, and the belief in human progress at the expense of tradition. Swift opposed new, Enlightenment scientific thinking and foresaw abandonment of traditional beliefs. Although widely recognized as the greatest satirical work, much of the satire cannot be understood without detailed knowledge of contemporaneous political figures and scientific speculation. Aldous Huxley's *Brave New World* and George Orwell's *1984* present worlds with totalitarian political institutions in which scientific progress has led to the ability to control people. George Bernard Shaw's *Man and Superman* is predicated on belief in ongoing human progress and evolution.

The Relationship between Self and Society

There are many issues related to the relationship between self and society. Many believe that people's lives are almost entirely determined by their environment. Marxist and socialist thinkers have argued that businesses and those in power exploit working people. The economies of modern successful societies are free market or capitalist. Market economies are efficient and successful to the extent that they utilize competition between buyers and sellers to minimize prices. But many people believe that competition is detrimental to human life, that many people are harmed by it. Competition should be eliminated as far as possible and replaced by cooperation. There is also the issue of whether people should act egoistically or altruistically. Should people act for their own selfish or self-centered goals or for the sake of society even if it is at their own expense?

These interrelated themes are raised in a number of literary works. Ayn Rand's *Anthem* presupposes that people who act egoistically for their own self-interest and development produce the greatest benefit for society. Coversely, Plato in the *Republic*, *Apology*, and *Crito* has Socrates arguing that people should act for the good of their society and not for their own good. Dickens's *Oliver Twist* contrasts the egoistic actions of Fagin with the altruistic actions of Oliver. George Bernard Shaw's *Pygmalion* explores the themes of class and exploitation. Dickens's *Great Expectations* has a protagonist who is unable to change his nature and succeed. Samuel Beckett's *Endgame* presents a hopeless situation for the protagonist that is dictated by outside forces. Dickens's *Hard Times* explores issues of poverty and wealth and the problems of the poor in a capitalist society.

Suffering as Necessary for Success

It is often argued that knowledge and achievement require difficulties. This is a theme in Dostoevsky's *Notes from Underground*, which asserts that truth is only learned through suffering. Correspondingly, Stephen Crane's *Red Badge of Courage* has a protagonist who learns courage through previous failure.

The Responsible Use of Power

Modern conditions offer new understandings of the proper and best use of power and government to rule society. *The Federalist Papers* addresses many issues concerning the viability and operation of a representative democracy as found in the U.S. Constitution. Issues 10 and 51, written by James Madison are of particular importance. (Other important issues are 1, 2, 6, 9, 14, 15, 16, 23, 37, 39, 47, 48, 49, 62, 63, 70, 78, 84, and 85.) Machiavelli's *The Prince* advocates the use of realistic appraisals of human nature to try to maintain rule of society. A primary theme in Shakespeare's *Measure for Measure* is the abuse and responsible use of power.

Culture Clash and Interracial Relationships

This theme has become quite prominent and important in recent years. An early American grcat work that explores this theme is James Fenimore Cooper's *Last of the Mohicans*, in which settlers and American Indian culture interact.

Personal Themes

Some themes are universal in scope but focus primarily on individuals and their character.

Appearance versus Reality

A frequent failing of human beings is the tendency to be more concerned about appearances than the reality or truth. People are often more concerned about how they appear to others, especially if they are concerned about social status.

Putting appearances first tends to produce hypocrisy. It is a characteristic consequence of pride. Proud people want to convince others they are better than they really are. Nearly all societies have a consciousness of classes, a result of a desire to associate and be identified with the higher classes.

A theme of Jane Austen's *Pride and Prejudice* is that some people turn out to be different from first impressions and how they appear to others. A key theme of Shakespeare's *Merchant of Venice* is that the treatment of Shylock the Jew is hypocritical. Arthur Miller's *Death of a Salesman* has a protagonist who always fails to meet his expectations. He has a false opinion of himself that must be corrected if he is to succeed.

War and Courage

Throughout history the conflicts within and between human societies have often led to conflict and war. Wars are fought by young men whose lives are at risk and who must act courageously. There is a theme of learning and gaining self-knowledge and of coming to maturity. Although a theme of Homer's *Iliad* is about winning honor through success in war, the work also raises questions about war. Shakespeare's *Henry V*, the story of perhaps England's greatest king, glorifies war. Another great work, Stephen Crane's *Red Badge of Courage,* has a protagonist who at first fails to act courageously but learns to be courageous in the end.

Love and Hate

Of the many works of literature that explore these themes the best is probably Shakespeare's *Romeo and Juliet*. On one level the play can be viewed as a debate between the various theories about love: (1) Romeo begins the play believing in a fashionable romantic love that is a kind of game as defined by thirteenth-century romances. (2) Mercutio holds a cynical view of romantic love. He is a realist. It is just a game with the goal of obtaining sexual pleasure. (3) The nurse sees love as a physical activity that is inevitable and natural to life. It is useful. Friar Lawrence also sees the love of Romeo and Juliet as useful because it will end the feud between the Capulets and the Montagues. (4) The Capulets have a traditional view. Love is synonymous with a prosperous marriage. Here love is a means to an end. (5) Romeo and Juliet have a pure love. It is a romantic courtly love that makes love an end in itself.

Forgiveness versus Revenge

The need for forgiveness rather than revenge is an important literary theme. Jacques in Shakespeare's *All's Well That Ends Well* experiences betrayal and yet forgives. So do other characters in the play. Forgiveness is also a key theme in Shakespeare's *The Tempest*. The theme of Dumas' *The Count of Monte Christo* is that the protagonist, who has been seeking revenge on those who sent him to prison, discovers that it is not appropriate for him to take punishment for evils into his own hands.

HOW TO WRITE THE ESSAY

Students have twenty-five minutes to write the essay. In writing, it is desirable to use a considerable part of the time for thinking about and planning an essay. Five to seven minutes should be devoted to planning the essay and jotting down an outline to follow while writing. Without some careful thought, it is unlikely that a writer will achieve a well-organized essay with evidence that supports a well-chosen thesis. There should be an introductory paragraph stating the thesis and perhaps a primary reason why the essay writer holds the thesis. An additional three or four paragraphs are desirable. Also the last sentences of the supporting paragraphs could state the conclusion. A short final paragraph stating the conclusion can be added.

For many topics, like those assigned for the written essay, writers could produce long essays using many arguments pro and con and many items of evidence pro and con. However, the written essay for the SAT only allows twenty-five minutes. There is time to write an essay of at most about 350 to 400 words. There is time only to support the thesis chosen with a couple of arguments and items of evidence or examples. It is possible to include the strongest objection the writer envisions against his or her thesis and some rebuttal. Since, to be convincing, each argument or example should be discussed with some expository detail, the arguments and examples should not number more than three.

The following steps should be followed to organize and write the essay:

1. Choose a thesis. Take a position that you believe is correct.
2. Consider the personal, literary, and nonfictional examples that you know are relevant to the thesis.
3. Determine which examples you will use. Perhaps the thesis needs a little revision to accord better with the examples.
4. Jot down a short outline that organizes the arguments and examples to be used to support the thesis. The outline should have sufficient detail to be easily followed. Include the arguments and evidence supporting the thesis and any rebuttals of arguments against the thesis.
5. Review the outline and thesis, and think for a minute to see if any improvements to the argument and examples can be made.
6. Start writing following the outline.
7. Save three or four minutes at the end to read through and make any needed additions or corrections.

The strongest writing is usually done for what one truly believes to be the case. Nevertheless, the point of the essay topic is to provide students with an opportunity to show how well they can write. Some students may be able to write a stronger argument and essay for a position they do not really believe in.

Try to write fairly quickly, concentrating on stating the main ideas in the outline concisely and filling in details. The essay probably needs to be about 350 words in length and needs to be well written to achieve a score of six. This requires writing at a rate of at least twenty words per minute for fifteen to seventeen minutes. However, it is better to spend adequate time planning and organizing the essay and writing a little less than to shortchange the planning stage to produce a longer essay.

It is important to save three or four minutes at the end for rereading and correcting errors. Almost everyone writing a draft makes a few grammatical errors that need correction. An important idea may not be expressed very well and will need some additional explanation.

CHAPTER 7

Learning Vocabulary

If anyone wishes to improve on the verbal section of the SAT, it is certainly desirable to try to expand vocabulary. There are three ways to achieve a comprehensive English vocabulary: engage in broad and extensive reading of serious fiction and nonfiction works, learn Latin, and study vocabulary lists with definitions and look up words in good dictionaries. When the test date for the SAT is only months away, it is too late to accomplish enough through the first two methods. It is time to learn vocabulary from dictionaries and books such as this book, designed especially for learning vocabulary.

To improve vocabulary for taking the SAT sufficiently to achieve a near-perfect score, one could do as I did to prepare for the GRE (a test very much like the SAT) the second time, which resulted in raising my verbal score over one hundred points to a near-perfect 780. Vocabulary expansion was probably responsible for increasing the score by fifty points. It took many days of work. I expended probably three hundred hours of study. I took a large dictionary and went through it, underlining every word not known, excluding medical terms, names of animals, species names for animals and plants, scientific technical terms, geographical place names, names of persons, historical events, and so on. The words underlined tended to be abstract nouns, adjectives, and verbs. After underlining the words, I went through the dictionary studying the words' definitions and their sources, which were usually in Latin.

To fully master words, one should study examples of their use in a good dictionary and try to make sentences with them. Encountering the words in broad reading of fiction and nonfiction helps. The words should be studied until they have been mastered; that is, the student can look at the word and know the meaning without reading it. If a person goes through this very time-consuming process, he or she will have a large vocabulary, which, irrespective of one's performance on the test, will stand him or her in good stead. He or she will also have confidence knowing virtually every word encountered on the test.

To do very well on the SAT, full mastery of words is not necessary. Many questions can be answered with an approximate knowledge of the meaning, with a recognition of the root, or with a knowledge of the context within which it is situated. Often, questions can be answered if one has some sense of a word's meaning, even though unable to offer a dictionary definition of the word. It is helpful to have studied Latin or to have familiarity with it. The ability to recognize Latin cognates is of great help. Nevertheless, mastery of a broad vocabulary can bring confidence and enable the test taker to use his or her time more efficiently.

I have devoted over two thousand hours designing the word lists in the following vocabulary chapters of this book to cover virtually all the words likely to be encountered on the SAT. The emphasis should be on the two thousand *italicized* words. The lists also provide one thousand additional useful words as well. The lists are designed to help the student to pick up many words quickly and retain them better because they are associated with common roots. By investing as little as twenty or thirty hours of study, significant improvement in scores is possible. A modest investment of time could produce better knowledge of vocabulary than I had when I achieved a near-perfect score on the GRE. Had these lists been available to me when I spent three hundred hours studying vocabulary for the GRE, I would have achieved the same score on the verbal section with a fraction of the invested time.

ORGANIZATION OF VOCABULARY

It is evident that efforts to improve on the verbal questions, whether sentence completion or critical reading, will be most useful if one is devoted to increasing vocabulary—that is, to increasing the number of words comprehended. This book has been designed to help the future test taker to expand his or her vocabulary with the right kinds of words, to do so in a manner that minimizes the amount of time required, and to learn in a way that enables better memory and retention of vocabulary so that he or she will recognize, if not master, all the difficult words encountered on an SAT.

In the following chapters, vocabulary is organized by two hundred Indo-European roots out of the six thousand or so Indo-European roots identified in the standard reference work on the subject, J. Pokorny's *Indogermanisches etymologisches worterbuch* (1959). The roots are classified into thirteen categories based on similarity in meaning. Since there are many important words that come from other roots, the thirteen chapters with roots are supplemented by five chapters of miscellaneous additional words from Latin, Greek, Germanic, and other sources. Students interested in investigating Indo-European languages and their relationships more deeply should read F. Bodmer's *The Loom of Language* (1972) or the so-titled sections in *The American Heritage Dictionary* (2000).

This book utilizes several techniques in its design to aid one's learning the kinds of words that could occur on an SAT. Every effort has been made to provide concise but sufficient definitions for over three thousand words selected primarily because they are words that students might encounter during the course of their college reading. Many of these are more important than others because they are more likely to occur on an SAT. These are marked by *italics*. A significant number of the words have been included because they are words that well-educated people ought to know, having the same roots as other important words. They are not in italics. The majority of words, however, are important, and many could occur on an SAT. The italicized words should receive the main focus and attention.

The thirteen chapters with two hundred Indo-European roots begin with a short discussion of the meaning of the roots and features of the roots that may be helpful for learning the words. The roots have been divided into categories with separate chapters and vocabulary lists for each category. Categories of roots for chapters are based on similarities in the meaning of roots. The categories are somewhat arbitrary. For ease of reference, the form in which roots are identified with superscripts follows (based on Calvert Watkins's *The American Heritage Dictionary of Indo-European Roots*, 2000). There are as many as five or six roots that can be represented by an identical spelling. So it is necessary to append superscripts to distinguish individual roots. In some cases some additional Indo-European roots with the same spelling are distinguished as well as other roots not found in the work by Watkins. The additional roots included are based on the standard reference on Indo-European roots, namely, J. Pokorny's *Indogermanisches etymologisches worterbuch*, as are nearly all of the roots distinguished in Watkins's book.

Each root has one or more words from Latin, Greek, or Germanic languages that have spawned English words. The Latin, Greek, or Germanic source words are given for each defined word (and undefined common words as well). *The student should look at the origin and the meaning of the Latin, Greek, or Germanic words and the meaning of the Indo-European root.* For any given English word, knowledge of the root and source usually makes possible a good guess as to how the word came to have its current meaning. This is an aid to remembering the meaning and using the word correctly.

1. The words associated with each Indo-European root are preceded by information such as the following:

1. al-[1] beyond, other
Latin: ALI other —> ALTER another
Greek: ALLO- other

These three lines contain the following type of information:

1. The Indo-European root and its meaning.
2. Syllables or sequences of letters common to English words that have come from the root's Latin or Greek ancestors. When one comes across an unrecognized English word that has one of these sequences, it is a clue that

the word may come from this root and offers a clue concerning its meaning. Brackets [ ] around three or four letters indicate a French form that developed from the Latin.

2. Following the information are one or more words derived from the Indo-European root that are sources of English words are listed with sequential numbering in brackets. They are grouped according to their path to English through Latin, Greek, or Germanic. The numbering—for example, '[3]'—provides a reference for the defined and undefined common words from the Latin source 'alter.' 'L' indicates Latin origin, 'Gk' Greek origin, 'OE' Old English or West Germanic origins, 'ON' indicates Old Norse, 'D' indicates Dutch, and 'LG' Low German. The words are grouped in two columns, such as the following:

[1] L ille that, that yonder   [2] L ultra beyond, further, more
[3] L alter one of two, the other, second   [4] L adulterare commit adultery, corrupt
[5] L alius another, different
[6] Gk allos other
[7] OE other other   [8] OE elles else, otherwise

3. Next follows a list of defined words with a reference to the Latin, Greek, or Germanic source words. These are the part of the three thousand defined words, with the most important words to be learned for the SAT being *italicized*.

adulterate: corrupt; render impure by mixing in other elements [4] L ad to + alter other
alienation: experiencing estrangement from or disaffection with [5] L alienatio < alius other
allegory: story conveying ideas with concrete subjects [6] Gk allos other + agoreuein speak
alteration: the process of changing or modification [3] L alteratio < alter other
altercation: a heated verbal dispute [3] L altercatus pp altercari dispute < alter other
altruism: the trait of seeking the welfare of others [3] Fr altruisme < L alter another
altruistic: seeks the welfare of others [3] Fr altruisme < L alter another
inalienable: not subject to being abandoned or transferred to others [5] L in not + alius other
ulterior: undisclosed or unexpressed; lying beyond [2] L ultra beyond

Many additional words have been included as a bonus because they come from the same root and can be picked up almost by osmosis. *The student should concentrate on learning the italicized words.* These following words, with definitions, might follow the previous information for the root 'al-¹.' Each indicates source words from the Indo-European root indicating the origin.

4. A group of undefined words with minor differences in prefix or suffix that share their meaning with one or more of the words in the defined group of words. These additional words are listed without definition. They are marked by a preceding 'Related:' to indicate that they are just closely related forms to one of the defined words. They are virtually identical in meaning to a defined word and usually are just a different part of speech with the same meaning. Students should be aware that a defined word can be used in slightly altered shapes. The following are related to the words defined here, and their definitions can easily be obtained by examining the corresponding defined word:
Related: alienable alienate altercate

5. A group of undefined words that are held to be common or easier words that should be known. These are marked by a preceding 'Common:' to indicate that they are common words most English speakers should know that come from the same root as the defined words. These words have a number referring back to the list in item 2. to indicate the source. The common words are words that I believe most test takers are likely to know or should know and do not therefore require definition. These are words the student should look at to see whether he or she knows them. If some are not known, they should be looked up. In many cases it may not be necessary to look them

up because they have a number affixed to indicate the Latin, Greek, or Germanic word that is their source. Examples related to the root 'al-[1]' are:

Common: adultery [4] alarm [1] alert [1] alfresco [1] alias [5] alibi [5] alien [5] alienage [5] alienist [5] aliquot [5] alligator [1] allo- [6] allodial [3] alter [3] alterable [3] alternate [3] alternative [3] alternation [3] el nino [1] else [8] hoopla [1] langue d'or [1] lariat [1] other [7] parallel [6] ultimate [2] ultra-[2] utterance [2] voila [1]

HOW TO USE THE VOCABULARY MATERIAL

There are a number of ways to use the materials in the following vocabulary chapters (8 to 27). First everybody should spend a few hours studying the words in the twenty-one word groups found in chapters 8 and 9.

1. Read the introductory material concerning the Indo-European roots at the beginning of each vocabulary chapter.
2. For each of the fifteen to twenty roots in the chapter, peruse the box with root information:
   a. Note the Indo-European root and its meaning.
   b. Note the sequences of letters in the box common to English words that offer clues about Latin or Greek ancestry.
3. Look at each of the Latin, Greek, or Germanic words in the box that are sources of English words.
4. For each root, examine the *defined words*. Glance over the nonitalicized words and focus on the *italicized* words. If you know the word, move on to those you do not know. If you do not know the word, read its definition and think about its meaning. Also look at the reference to the Latin, Greek, or Germanic source that follows the definition. Try to see if you can guess or figure out how the meaning of the English word is related to the source word and how the development from one to the other could have occurred. Sometimes if the meanings are close, this will be straightforward and obvious. In other cases, there will be significant differences in meaning, but one can make a plausible guess concerning the development of meaning. In some cases the path taken will not be clear at all. Where some guess can be made with more or less certainty, this will help to cement the word and its meaning in memory.
5. For each root, examine the group of undefined words marked by 'Related:,' which share their meaning with one or more of the words in the defined group of words. Look back to the defined words to find the word that gives the meaning, and note the possibilities for using the word in these alternate forms.
6. For each root, examine the group of undefined words marked by 'Common:.' If you do not know some of them, take note of the number and of the Latin, Greek, or Germanic source word or words in the preceding box. In some cases you may be satisfied that you have an idea of the meaning, but in general these are words you should know. You should look up the words you do not know in the dictionary.

THREE SUGGESTED PROGRAMS OF VOCABULARY STUDY

I suggest three approaches to studying the vocabulary lists, depending on the time and effort available and the level of achievement or improvement desired. Or, design your own method of use.

Minimal Level

Spend a few hours studying chapters 8 and 9 learning the words in the twenty-one lists of positive and negative words. These are very important to know. Study the definitions of any that are not known.

Ignore the first and fourth tasks. Do not bother to read chapter and introductory information about Indo-European roots. Just look at the lists and read the information in the information preceding the list of words with definitions and then look at the *italicized* words in the lists only. If you know a word, move on to those you do not know. If you do not know the word, read its definition and think about its meaning. Also look at the reference to the Latin, Greek, or Germanic source that follows the definition. Look at the common words. Look up any words in the dictionary that you think could occur on the SAT.

Go through each of the eighteen vocabulary chapters *once*. Schedule a certain number of chapters per day. Estimated total time (spending an average of about thirty seconds per italicized word) is about twenty hours. Time to look up unknown common words has not been included, assuming the average user will not have very many to look up. Nor is the time counted to look up words in a dictionary to find sentences using the words for greater mastery.

Going through the words even one time can give improved recognition of words sufficient to make educated guesses or correctly answer additional questions when taking the SAT.

Moderate Level

Spend a few hours studying chapters 8 and 9 learning the words in the twenty-one lists of positive and negative words. These are very important words to know. Study the definitions of any that are not known.

Read the chapter introductory material on the roots before each chapter. The material points out all the major sound shifts that follow from table 7.1 and the following rules. Study of the table and the rules cited will enable students to notice the sound shifts. Nevertheless, students may appreciate having them pointed out specifically for each root.

Read the information in the information preceding the list of words with definitions and then look at the *italicized* words in the lists only. If you know a word, move on to those you do not know. If you do not know the word, read its definition and think about its meaning. Also look at the reference to the Latin, Greek, or Germanic source that follows the definition. For each root examine the group of undefined words that share their meaning with one or more of the words in the defined group of words. Look back to the defined words to find the word that gives the meaning. Look at the common words. Look up any words in the dictionary that you think could occur on the SAT.

Go through each of the 18 vocabulary chapters *twice*. Schedule a certain number of chapters per day.

Estimated total time (spending an average of about thirty seconds per italicized word) is about thirty-five hours. Time to look up unknown common words is not included (assuming the average user will not have many).

Full Level

Spend a few hours studying chapters 8 and 9 learning the words in the twenty-one lists of positive and negative words. These are very important words to know. Study the definitions of any that are not known.

Read the material on the roots before each chapter. It points out all the major sound shifts that follow from table 7.1 and the following rules. Study of the table and the rules cited will enable students to notice the sound shifts themselves. Nevertheless students may appreciate having them pointed out specifically for each root.

Look at the lists and read the information in the information preceding the list of words with definitions, and then look at the defined words. Peruse the nonitalicized words as well as italicized focusing primarily on *italicized* words in the lists. If you know a word, move on to those you do not know. If you do not know the word, read its definition and think about its meaning. Also look at the reference to the Latin, Greek, or Germanic source that follows the definition. See if you can figure out how the meaning of the English word is related to the source word and how the development from one to the other could have occurred. Sometimes the meanings will be close, and this will be straightforward and obvious. Sometimes they will not be close in meaning, but this process helps for remembering word meanings.

Table 7.1.   Mutes

	I-IE Rough	II-IE Smooth	III-IE/I-OE Middle	II-OE Rough	III-OE Smooth
Labial	bh —> f/ph	p	b	f	p
Palatal	gh —> kh	k	g	h	k
Dental	dh —> th	t	d	th	t

For each root, examine the group of undefined words that share their meaning with one or more of the words in the defined group of words. Look back to the defined words to find the word that gives the meaning. Look at the common words. Look up any in the dictionary you find that you think could occur on the SAT.

Go through each of the 18 vocabulary chapters three times. Schedule a certain number of chapters per day.

Reading and reviewing a couple of times will help to learn words more thoroughly. Looking up definitions in a good dictionary such as the *American Heritage Dictionary,* which includes examples of their use, is helpful and recommended.

Estimated total time is about fifty-five hours. Time to look up unknown common words has not been included (assuming the average user will not have many).

Other Possibilities

Some students may want to do more work and master the words even better if they are looking beyond doing well on the SAT and desire an improved vocabulary for future need and use. Just reading definitions and knowing roots can enable a person to answer questions on a standardized test, but this often does not enable persons to use the words confidently in speech or writing. Mastery will enable words to be used in the written essay in the writing section of the SAT to provide greater variety of vocabulary. To attain greater mastery of the words found in the vocabulary chapters and lists, it is helpful to look up sentences using them in a dictionary. Looking up definitions in a good dictionary such as the *American Heritage Dictionary,* which includes examples of their use, is helpful and recommended. It gives many sample sentences and uses the same spelling of Indo-European roots used here. Further mastery is attained by trying to write sentences with the new words. Finally a person can try using the words in speech.

IMPORTANT BACKGROUND INFORMATION

This section covers some useful information that helps one to understanding the relationship of English words to their Latin, Greek, Germanic, and Indo-European ancestors. For those interested in learning more about Indo-European languages and their grammatical and vocabulary root relationships more deeply should read F. Bodmer's *The Loom of Language* (1972) or Appendix I in *The American Heritage Dictionary* (2000).

There are about a dozen paths followed to generate English words. Some basic sound shifts occurred that, if known, enable the student of word origins to understand common origins. Also it is helpful to know Latin and Greek prefixes and suffixes that occur in many English words. The most important prefixes and suffixes are listed at the end of this chapter.

Paths to English

Study of languages has shown that all of the major European languages, as well as many important languages spoken by people in the Middle East and as far away as India, all have a common origin in a language that has been called Indo-European or Proto-Indo-European. The various Indo-European languages have many words of common origin and share various common grammatical characteristics. The language of English has borrowed words from many languages, but in nearly all cases the languages belong to the Indo-European family. Words have taken about a dozen different routes to enter English:

1. The West Germanic Core. This group includes the most basic words of English that are of most frequent occurrence and are most readily understood even by uneducated English speakers. Most such words come from Anglo-Saxon or Old English and from a West Germanic branch of the Indo-European family. These can be traced back further to common Germanic and yet further back to Indo-European ancestry. Dutch and Low German are related West Germanic languages.

2. From Latin by Way of French. In 1066 England was conquered by the Normans, who were of North Germanic origin having migrated to the Normandy area of France. The Normans spoke French and introduced French into England as the language of the court. Consequently, a large number of words of French origin were brought into the English language. Most French words came from Latin. France was a part of the Roman Empire, and over time the dialect of Latin spoken in the area occupied by the French became the French language. Some French words were picked up by educated Englishmen from French after 1066.

3. From West Germanic or Germanic by way of French. Some Germanic words were picked up directly or came through by Vulgar or Medieval Latin and then were transmitted on through French before and after 1066.

4. From North Germanic. Vikings intermingled with the English and other peoples on the British Isles. Consequently some English words have an origin in Old Norse, a dialect from the North Germanic group of Indo-European languages.

5. Direct from the Latin. Many of the more abstract words in scholarly works and elsewhere found their way into English. Knowledge of classical authors was revived during the Renaissance. Latin was also the language of the church until the Reformation in the sixteenth century. Virtually all theological and scholarly writing was done in Latin up to the sixteenth century and many works were still written in Latin up to the eighteenth century. Consequently, many Latin words provide the basis for coining English words.

6. Direct from the Greek. Knowledge of Greek and Greek science and medicine revived also during the Renaissance. Consequently, the bulk of scientific and medical terms were formed from classical Greek, although many terms also came from the Latin. Ever since, scientists and medical doctors and researchers have coined a vast number of terms from the Greek. There are many interesting words in English with Greek origin. There are a vast number of scientific and medical words that are rather esoteric or limited in scope and not suitable for the SAT that come from Greek.

7. From Celtic, Irish, or Welsh. Since Celtic, Irish, and Welsh peoples have lived on the British Isles with the English since the days of Old English, some words have been picked up from these related Indo-European languages.

8. From other Indo-European languages. These include Slavic, Iranian, Indian, and other languages. Some words have entered during the last two centuries primarily because the languages of origin were spoken in territories of the British Empire.

9. From Semitic languages. Some words have entered English because the Old Testament of the Bible was written in Hebrew. Most such words are names of persons or places, and many were taken directly from the Bible where names are not translated. Some other words were passed on through Latin and Greek from Arabic.

10. From other non-Indo-European and non-Semitic Languages. In the twentieth century there have been many opportunities for words from many countries and languages to find their way into English due to the greater intermingling of peoples and cultures.

11. Creative words. There are a number of words that have not come from other languages but have been created in some fashion. There are many different ways in which words might get coined. Some might be imitative. Others come from names of people or places through association with a characteristic of or practice in a place. There are many other ways in which words can get coined.

12. Unknown. There are a number of words for which we simply do not know their origin.

The majority of words of interest for college level and advanced reading come from one of three sources: Germanic languages (sources 1, 3, 4), Latin (sources 2, 5), or Greek (source 6). These three sources are emphasized in the vocabulary lists.

Indo-European Roots and Sound Shifts

It is helpful to have an understanding of some regularities in sound shifts from the Indo-European roots to the later Germanic forms found in Old English and the Greek and Latin forms. Many of the most important shifts are summarized in table 7.1, on page 48.

Many of the sound shifts from Indo-European roots of interest to speakers of English can be found by reference to table 7.1 of mute consonants. In the table, 'IE' represents the Indo-European form of the root. 'OE' represents Old English (and Western Germanic) forms. The Latin and Greek forms are found in the first three columns of mutes and the West Germanic and Old English in the three columns to the right. Column I-IE represents the rough mutes of Indo-European (bh, gh, and dh) that changed to ph (φ), kh (χ), and th (θ) for ancient Greek. For Latin the bh changed to the f sound as for Greek. The gh sound usually became g or h in Latin, and the dh sound became an f, t, or d since Latin lacks the th sound. The smooth and middle mutes did not change for Greek and Latin but remained the same as for Indo-European. Thus columns I-IE, II-IE, and III-IE indicate the forms for the smooth, middle, and rough mutes for Indo-European, Greek, and Latin.

The corresponding changes that occurred in the development from Indo-European to Western Germanic and Old English forms can be found by moving two columns to the right from the Indo-European form. Thus bh, gh, and dh became b, g, and d in Old English; p, k, and t in Indo-European became f, h, and th; and b, g, and d became p, k, and t in Old English and Western Germanic. When one compares Greek and Latin forms to the English forms that have come through Old English, the Greek and Latin forms in column II-IE will correspond to the consonants in the same row of column II-OE. In some cases root consonants occurring before another consonant will get assimilated or modified in some other fashion. There are several other general rules that can be observed:

1. Liquids (l and r) and nasals (m and n) seldom show any change. The Indo-European root consonants remain the same in Greek, Latin, and Old English or Western Germanic.
2. An initial sibilant or s sound followed by a vowel remains in the Old English or Western Germanic and nearly always in the Latin but is occasionally dropped in the Latin. In the Greek, however, it always becomes an h or in some cases may disappear, although it may affect the form of the following vowel.
3. Initial s sounds conjoined with following consonants usually show no change in Greek, Latin, and Old English. However, they do frequently disappear.
4. The w sound of Indo-European is retained in the Old English forms. In the case of Latin it is pronounced as a w although written as a v and is occasionally dropped. Greek originally had a w sound represented by the digamma letter. However before the classical period of ancient Greece, it disappeared, becoming a rough breathing or h sound. In some cases it is dropped altogether.

These are the main rules that help students understand how the Old English, Germanic, Latin, and Greek words are related to the Indo-European roots and to each other. Of course there are many more exactly stated and detailed rules that can be discovered by the interested student desiring to learn more about the Indo-European background of modern and ancient languages.

Latin and Greek Prefixes

It is very useful to know Latin and Greek prefixes (several Old English prefixes are included here as well). Knowledge of these are important for any student of vocabulary. Many of the different words featured in the vocabulary chapters result from combining these with the basic root. They are helpful to understand and remember better the words being learned. In table 7.2, the first column gives the prefix. The second column gives the meaning. The third column gives the Indo-European root if it is one of the two hundred roots featured in chapters 10 to 22. The number in brackets indicates the number assigned to the root in chapters 10 to 22. The other prefixes and suffixes come from other Indo-European roots. Some of the prefixes just intensify the main root.

Latin and Greek Suffixes

It is also useful to know Latin and Greek suffixes (several Old English prefixes are included here as well). In table 7.3, the first column gives the suffix. The second column gives the meaning. The third column gives the Indo-European root if it is one of the two hundred roots featured in chapters 10 to 22.

Table 7.2.   Latin and Greek Prefixes

Prefix	Meaning	IE Root	
a, ab, abs	from, away	apo-	[3]
ad (a, ac, af, al, an, ap, as, at)	to		
ambi, amphi	around, both	ambhi	[2]
ante, anti	before		
anti	against		
arch	first, chief	arkhein	[72]
auto	self		
ben	good, well	deu-²	[123]
bi	two		
circum	around		
com, con, col, cor, co	together		
contra, contro, counter	against		
de	down, away from, about		
demi	half		
dia	across, through		
dis, di, dif	apart, not		
equi	equal		
ex, e, ef	out of, from		
extra	out of, beyond		
hyper	too much	uper	[20]
hypo	too little, under		
in, il, im, ir	into, in, on	en	[6]
in, il, im, ir	not	ne	[10]
inter, intro	between, among	en	[6]
mal, mis	bad	mel-⁵	[77]
mono	one, single		
neo	new	newo-	[52]
non	not	ne	[10]
ob, of, op	against		
omni	all	op-¹	[192]
ortho	straight		
pan	all		
peri	around	per¹	[12]
poly	many	pele-¹	[194]
post	after	apo-	[3]
pre	before	per¹	[12]
pro	forward, before	per¹	[12]
re	back, again		
retro	backward		
se	apart, away	s(w)c	[81]
semi	half		
sub	under		
super	above, beyond	uper	[20]
syn, sym	with, at the same time		
trans	across	tere-²	[138]
ultra	beyond	al-¹	[1]
un	not	ne-	[10]
uni	one		
vice	instead of		

Table 7.3.   Latin and Greek Suffixes

Suffix	Meaning	IE Root	
-able	able		
-acious, cious	having the quality of		
-age	act, condition		
-al	belonging to		
-ance, -ence	state of		
-ary, -eer, -er	one who, concerning		
-ate	one who		
-cy	state, position of		
-dom	state of	dhe-	[173]
-ence	state of		
-er, -or	one who		
-escent	becoming		
-fy	make	dhe-	[173]
-hood	state of		
-ic, -id	of, like		
-il, -ile	capable of being		
-ion	act of		
-ious	characterized by		
-ish	like		
-ism	belief in or practice of		
-ist	one who practices or is devoted to		
-ive	relating to		
-mony	state of		
-ness	quality of		
-or, -er	one who		
-ory	a place for		
-ous, -ose	full of		
-ship	state of, skill		
-some	characteristic of	sem-[1]	[16]
-tude	state of		
-ward	in the direction of	wer-[3]	[171]
-y	full of		

CHAPTER 8

Vocabulary: Word Groups 1

Many of the most important words students should know belong to groups of words that are roughly synonymous or opposite in meaning. Usually, one set has positive connotations, and the opposite group has negative connotations. Due to the importance of these types of words, two chapters are devoted to them. This chapter and the following outline twenty-one groups of words that those who take the SAT ought to know. For each group there are two subgroups separating the words into positive connotations and negative connotations. These are important words. If a word is not known, it should be looked up. Definitions are given for the more difficult words.

Each word list is headed by a concept. Sometimes it will have an adjectival meaning. In other cases, it will be a noun or verb. The following words in the list have roughly synonymous meanings. Nevertheless, they are different words and cannot always be used in precisely the same contexts. Some lists include words that have negative connotations that the other words in the list do not have. Furthermore, some words in a list may have a different grammatical form, because they occur or are primarily used in a different grammatical form than the word in the heading.

The twenty-one groups can be classified into four categories: characteristics of objects and processes; character and qualities of persons; character traits involved in relating to other people; and qualities of speech or writing. The first two groups are covered in this chapter, the last two groups in the next chapter. The two groups in this chapter include twelve of the twenty-one groups.

Definitions are given for some of the more difficult words as are the sources for the words defined. 'OE' indicates an Old English source, 'OF' an Old French source, 'Fr' a French source, 'L' a Latin source, 'VL' a Vulgar Latin source, 'ML' a Medieval Latin source, 'LL' a Late Latin source, 'Gk' an Ancient Greek source, 'ON' an Old Norse source, 'Ice' an Icelandic source, 'LG' a Low German source, 'MLG' a Middle Low German source, 'OHG' an Old High German source, 'Celt' a Celtic source, 'MD' a Middle Dutch source, and 'D' a Dutch source.

To save space in word definitions, some abbreviations are used 'esp.' for 'especially,' 'rel.' for 'related (to),' 'pert.' for 'pertaining (to),' 'alt.' for 'alteration of,' 'priv.' for 'privative,' 'intens.' for 'intensifier,' 'imit.' for 'imitative,' 'dim.' for diminutive,' 'compar.' for 'comparative,' 'superl.' for 'superlative,' 'pp.' for 'past participle (Latin),' and 'pfp.' for 'perfect participle (Latin).' Parentheses are used for definitions of prefixes and prepositions or to indicate that the preceding Latin form is a participle of a Latin verb. Some prefixes act as privatives; that is, they indicate a lack of an attribute or just act as intensifiers strengthening the meaning of the root to which they are connected.

CHARACTERISTICS OF OBJECTS AND PROCESSES

The category of characteristics of objects and processes includes words indicating whether something is beneficial, harmful, or threatening; whether something is strengthening or weakening; whether there is plenty or scarcity; and whether something is in its beginning and growing stages or is in declining and dying stages.

Beneficial or Harmful

Beneficial	Harmful or threatening
advantageous	baleful
favorable	baneful
profitable	deleterious
rewarding	inimical
salubrious	injurious
salutary	insidious
useful	minatory
wholesome	perfidious
	pernicious

Definitions of words indicating something is beneficial: the words 'salubrious,' 'salutary,' and 'wholesome' tend to emphasize that something is beneficial to health.

advantageous: beneficial; profitable; helpful. OF avant (before) < L abante from before < ab- + ante.
salubrious: conducive to health; healthful; wholesome. L salubris < salus health.
salutary: producing a healthful condition by correcting evil or promoting good. L salutaris < salus health.

Definitions of words indicating harmfulness: The words 'insidious' and 'perfidious' imply evil intent by someone when acting. 'Minatory' indicates harm is threatened. The other words indicating harmfulness can be caused by impersonal forces.

baleful: hurtful; malign; malignant; pernicious; sorrowful; miserable. OE bealu (evil, wickedness).
baneful: harmful; ruinous. OE bana (slayer).
deleterious: hurtful, destructive, detrimental. Gk deleterios < deleomai spoil, harm.
inimical: harmful; hostile. L inimicus < in (not) + amicus friendly.
insidious: proceeding hiddenly with potential lethal effects. L insidiae ambush < in- + sedeo sit.
minatory: threatening as with destruction or punishment. L minatus (pp minor) threaten.
perfidious: treacherous; faithless; disloyal; untrustworthy. L perfidiosus < per (from) + fides faith.
pernicious: tending to kill or hurt; malicious; wicked. L per (through) + neco kill.

Strengthening or Weakening

Strengthening	Weakening
bolstering	enervating
buttressing	obstructing
corroborating	obviating
encouraging	stultifying
enhancing	undermining
fortifying	vitiating
heartening	
reinforcing	
stiffening	
substantiating	
supporting	

Definitions of words indicating something strengthens: The words 'bolstering,' 'buttressing,' 'fortifying,' 'reinforcing,' and 'stiffening' tend to be used primarily in reference to strengthening buildings or physical structures. 'Corroborating,' 'substantiating,' and sometimes 'supporting' and 'reinforcing' are used to indicate that certain evidence strengthens knowledge or belief and can be used in reference to strengthening arguments or positions taken in an argument. 'Enhancing' can be used in many contexts to indicate improvement. 'Encouraging,' 'heartening,' and 'supporting' are used primarily to indicate strengthening of a person.

bolstering: propping up or strengthening. OE bolster (cushion).
buttressing: supporting or reinforcing esp. a wall. OF bouter (strike against).
corroborating: supporting; agreeing with other evidence. L corroborare < com- + roborare < robor strength.
enhancing: improving by adding something, strengthening. L en + altus high.
fortifying: to strengthening; reinforcing. L fortis strong + facere to make.
substantiate: to establish as a position or a truth; verify. L substantia < sub (under) + sto stand.

Definitions of words indicating something weakens: 'Enervating' tends to apply to weakening of a person's ability to act effectively or normally. The other words in the negative group apply more generally with 'obviating,' implying being made irrelevant.

enervating: depriving of nerve, vigor; weakening; rendering ineffective. L e (out) + nervus nerve.
obviate: make anticipated difficulties and objections irrelevant. LL obvio meet < ob + via way.
stultify: show to be absurdly inconsistent or foolish. L stultus foolish + facio (make).
undermine: weaken by removing foundational support. OE (under) + Fr miner < LL mino open a mine.
vitiate: to impair the use or value of; debase; to render defective. L vitiatus (pp vitio) < vitium fault.

Plentiful or Scarce

Plenty	Scarcity
abundant	dearth
affluent	deficit
ample	destitute
bounteous	exiguous
copious	impecunious
luxuriant	impoverished
multifarious	indigent
multitudinous	insolvent
myriad	meager
opulent	needy
pecunious	paltry
plenteous	paucity
plentiful	penniless
plethora	penury/penurious
profuse	poor
prosperous	scanty
superabundant	sparse
surplus	want
teeming	
wealthy	

Definitions of words indicating something is plentiful: Plenty and scarcity may apply to numerical quantity or to quality. We may also distinguish wealth and poverty in possessions. The words may indicate an amount relative to an amount regarded as normal or adequate. Thus 'ample' and 'surplus' indicate having more than adequate. 'Abundant,' 'bounteous,' 'copious,' 'multifarious,' 'multitudinous,' 'myriad,' 'plentiful,' 'plenteous,' 'plethora,' 'profuse,' 'superabundant,' and 'teeming' indicate numerical quantity. 'Luxuriant' indicates plenty in quality. 'Affluent,' 'opulent,' 'paltry,' 'pecunious,' 'prosperous,' and 'wealthy' indicate plenty in possessions.

copious: plentiful. L copiosus < copia abundance.
multifarious: having great diversity or variety. L multifarium in many places < multus (many).
multitudinous: very numerous. L multitudo multitude < multus (many).
pecunious: rich; financial well-off. L pecuniarius < pecunia wealth.
plethora: a great abundance or excess. Gk plethein to be full.
profusion: condition of plenty; supplied in great abundance. L pro (forth) + fundo pour.
teeming: full of; swarming with. OE teman (to beget).

Definitions of words indicating something is scarce: 'Destitute,' 'impecunious,' 'impoverished,' 'indigent,' 'insolvent,' 'needy,' 'penniless,' 'penury,' 'poor,' and 'want' indicate lack or scarcity of possessions. 'Dearth,' 'meager,' 'paucity,' 'scanty,' and 'sparse' indicate scarcity in numerical quantity. 'Exiguous' as well as 'dearth,' 'meager,' and 'scanty' may indicate inadequacy of quality. 'Deficit' indicates inadequacy relative to a normal or required amount.

dearth: scarcity; a great shortage. OE deore (costly).
exiguous: very small; meager, very scanty. L exigere drive out, demand < ex (out) + ago drive.
impecunious: having no money; habitually poor. L im (not) + pecunia money.
indigent: very poor; in want. L indu (<in) + egere lack, want.
insolvent: bankrupt. L in (not) + solvo loosen, solve.
meager: sparse; skimpy; insufficient. L macer thin.
paltry: of little worth. LG palte rag.
paucity: scarcity; meagerness. L paucus few.
penury: extreme poverty. L penuria want.
penurious: destitute; impoverished; poverty-stricken. L penuria want.

Starting/Growing or Declining/Ending

Beginning	Declining
burgeoning	degenerating
callow	deteriorating
inchoate	expiring
incipient	fading
nascent	moribund
	obsolete

Definitions of words indicating something is starting and growing:
burgeoning: sprouting; beginning to grow and flourish. OF burjon a bud < LL burra a garment.
callow: unfledged; not yet feathered; inexperienced; youthful. OE calu bald.
inchoate: in the initial immature or formative stage of development. L inchoatus (pp inchoo) begin.
incipient: belonging to the first stages. L incipiens (pfp incipio) begin.

nascent: beginning to exist or develop. L nascens (pfp nascor) be born.

Definitions of words indicating something is declining or ending:
moribund: dying; at the point of death; coming to an end. L moribundus < morior die.

CHARACTER AND QUALITIES OF PEOPLE

Character and qualities of people include words indicating whether someone is generous or tightfisted and frugal, whether someone is compliant or unswayed and unyielding, whether someone is moral or decadent, whether someone is proud or humble, courageous or timid, whether someone is cheerful or cheerless, lively or sluggish, and whether someone is careful or carefree or careless.

Generosity or Selfishness

Generous	Tightfisted or frugal
altruistic	cheap
beneficent	greedy
benevolent	miserly
charitable	niggardly
eleemosynary	parsimonious
hospitable	skinflinty
humanitarian	sparing
magnanimous	spartan
munificent	thrifty
philanthropic	

Definitions of words indicating someone is generous: 'Charitable' and 'eleemosynary' emphasize charitable giving. 'Magnanimous,' 'munificent,' and 'philanthropic' emphasize giving in very great amounts.

altruistic: seeks the welfare of others. Fr altruisme < L alter (another).
eleemosynary: rel. to charity and giving to the needy. Gk eleemosune pity, charity.
humanitarian: one seeking to promote human welfare. L humanus human.
magnanimous: very generous. L magnus great + animus soul.
munificent: sumptuously generous. L munus gift + facere do.
philanthropic: rel. to contributing large sums of money to benefit others. Gk philia love + anthropos man.

Definitions of words indicating someone is anything but generous: 'Cheap,' 'miserly,' 'niggardly,' 'parsimonious,' 'skinflinty,' 'sparing,' 'spartan,' and 'thrifty' emphasize tightfistedness and frugality. Persons can have the qualities of being 'parsimonious,' 'sparing,' 'spartan,' or 'thrifty' and still be generous toward others even though they are very careful with their own resources. The 'greedy' person wants all that they can get and will not be likely to give much unless expecting to get something equal or greater in return.

miserly: living very frugally and hoarding one's money. L miser wretched.
niggardly: meanly covetous or avaricious; parsimonious; stingy. Ice hnoggr stingy.
spartan: simple; frugal; unadorned; very self-disciplined. Gk Sparta.

Cooperative/Complying or Uncooperative/Stubborn

Compliant	Uncooperative	
accommodating	adamant	pigheaded
amenable	bullheaded	recalcitrant
concede	determined	refractory
deferential	dogged	relentless
docile	froward	renitent
flexible	headstrong	resolute
hospitable	implacable	steadfast
malleable	indisposed	stiff-necked
obliging	inexorable	stubborn
pliable	intractable	tenacious
pliant	intransigent	untoward
submissive	mulish	unyielding
subservient	obdurate	
tractable	obstinate	
yielding	pertinacious	

Definitions of words indicating someone is willing to comply: 'Accommodating,' 'amenable,' 'flexible,' and 'obliging' emphasize willingness to cooperate and comply. A hospitable person is a host who wants to accommodate and serve his or her guests. 'Deferential,' 'docile,' 'malleable,' 'pliable,' 'pliant,' 'submissive,' 'subservient,' 'tractable,' and 'yielding' indicate willingness or tendency to submit to the control of others. 'Concede' indicates a onetime yielding to others, whereas the others indicate general character traits.

amenable: willing and open to follow advice or authority. L minae threats.
deferential: respectfully yielding, submitting. L defero < de (down) + fero bear.
docile: easily led. L docilis teachable < doceo teach.
hospitable: cordial and generous toward guests; agreeable. L hospitare host a guest < hospes guest.
malleable: can be shaped by hammering; influenced easily; able to adapt. L malleus hammer.
pliable: easily bent or twisted; flexible; easily persuaded or controlled. Fr < L plicans (pfp plico) fold.
pliant: easily bent or twisted; flexible; easily persuaded or controlled. Fr < L plicans (pfp plico) fold.
subservient: having a secondary or supporting role or function; servile. L subservire to subserve < servus slave.
tractable: easily led or controlled; manageable; readily handled. L tractabilis < traho draw.

Definitions of words indicating someone is unwilling to comply: The qualities in the 'uncooperative' list exhibit some differences in connotation. 'Determined,' 'dogged,' 'inexorable,' 'pertinacious,' 'relentless,' 'resolute,' 'steadfast,' 'tenacious,' and 'unyielding' indicate perseverance and desire to remain on course despite obstacles. These words are generally commendatory in tone. 'Inexorable' generally applies to forces and processes rather than persons. 'Adamant,' 'headstrong,' 'indisposed,' and 'renitent' tend to suggest mild blame for uncooperativeness when a reasonable person should be willing to change course. However, 'bullheaded,' 'forward,' 'intractable,' 'intransigent,' 'mulish,' 'obdurate,' 'obstinate,' 'pigheaded,' 'recalcitrant,' 'refractory,' 'stiff-necked,' 'stubborn,' and 'untoward' suggest a greater degree of unreasonableness and blame for not cooperating and often indicate willingness to break laws.

adamant: stubbornly inflexible and unbending; (n) extremely hard stone. Gk a- (not) + daman tame.
forward: obstinate; stubbornly resistant. ME fro (away, back) + ward < Ger.

implacable: not willing to be appeased or to yield. L in (not) + placatus (pp placo) appease.

indisposed: slightly ill; disinclined; unwilling. L in- + dis- + ponere to put.

inexorable: not to be moved by entreaty; unyielding. L in (not) + ex (out) + oro pray.

intractable: stubborn; unruly; difficult to treat. L in (not) + tractabilis < tracto handle < traho draw.

intransigence: unwillingness to compromise. L in (not) + transigo come to a settlement.

intransigent: not willing to compromise. L in (not) + transigo come to a settlement.

obdurate: unmoved by feelings of humanity or pity; inexorable. L ob (before) + durus hard.

obstinate: unreasonably resolved in a purpose or opinion; stubborn. L ob (before) + sto stand.

pertinacious: tenacious of purpose; stubbornly maintaining. L per (through) + tenax < teneo hold.

recalcitrant: noncompliant; rebellious; refractory. L recalcitratus < re + calcitro kick < calx heel.

refractory: disobedient; obstinate; resisting normal methods. L re (back) + frango break.

renitent: offering resistance to force or persuasion. OF < L reniter < re (back) + nitor strive.

resolute: maintaining a fixed purpose; determined. L re (again) + solvo loosen.

steadfast: remaining firm, not swerving. OE stede + faest fixed, fast < Ger.

tenacious: unyielding; holding opinions or rights strongly; determined. L tenax < teneo hold.

untoward: vexatious; not yielding readily; refractory; perverse; uncouth. OE un + to + weard ward.

Moral or Decadent

Moral		Decadent	
chaste	righteous	bacchanalian	licentious
decent	seemly	debauched	reprobate
decorous	undefiled	dissipated	ribald
ethical	upright	iniquitous	salacious
proper		lascivious	sordid
pure		libertine	turpitude
respectable		libidinous	

Definitions of words indicating someone is moral: 'Chaste' and 'pure' indicate moral behavior, especially in sexual matters. 'Ethical,' 'pure,' 'righteous,' 'undefiled,' and 'upright' emphasize moral behavior. 'Decent,' 'decorous,' 'proper,' 'respectable,' and 'seemly' indicate correctness of manners and morals as well.

chaste: morally pure; not engaging in sex outside of marriage. L castus pure.

decorous: proper; appropriate. L decor seemliness, beauty.

ethical: morally honorable or correct; rel. to moral values and right conduct. Gk ethos custom.

undefiled: not made dirty, stained, polluted, or corrupted. OF de- + fouler to trample, beat down.

upright: acting in accord with moral principles; standing erect. OE up + riht right, just, correct.

Definitions of words indicating someone does not act morally: For the moral decadence group, 'iniquitous' and 'reprobate' indicate unethical and immoral behavior. 'Sordid' and 'turpitude' emphasize the dirtiness and vileness of immoral behavior. The other words in the list: 'bacchanalian,' 'debauched,' 'dissipated,' 'lascivious,' 'libertine,' 'libidinous,' 'licentious,' 'ribald,' 'salacious' indicate moral impropriety in sexual matters.

bacchanalian: as of a drunken revel or orgy. L Bacchus god of wine.

debauched: corrupted; excessively indulging in sensual pleasure. Fr debaucher < de + OF baucher hew < Ger.

dissipated: dissolute; excessively indulging in sensual pleasure. L dis (apart) + supo throw.

iniquitous: sinful, wicked. L iniquitas < in (not) + aequus equal.

lascivious: lustful; lewd; arousing sexual desire. L lascivus wanton, lustful.
libertine: one showing no restraint in indulging his desires; a rake. L libertinus freedman < liber free.
libidinous: lustful; full of sexual desire. L libidinosus full of lust.
licentious: sexually promiscuous. L licentia freedom < licere to be allowed.
reprobate: strongly disapproving; abandoned in sin; utterly depraved. L re (again) + probo prove.
ribald: showing lewd or vulgar humor. OF riber (to be wanton) < Ger.
salacious: lustful; lascivious. L salax < salio leap.
sordid: dirty; squalid; degraded. L sordidus dirty < sordere to be dirty.
turpitude: baseness; shamefulness; vileness. Fr < L turpitudo < turpis shameful, vile.

Proud or Humble

Proud

			Humble or quiet	
affected	egotistical	ostentatious	demure	taciturn
arrogant	flippant	pompous	diffident	unassuming
aristocratic	haughty	pretentious	plebeian	unostentatious
authoritarian	imperious	supercilious	restrained	unpretentious
autocratic	impertinent	vainglorious	reticent	
condescending	impudent		subdued	
disdainful	insolent		subservient	

Definitions of words indicating someone is proud: Pride is viewed as excessive when a person becomes 'arrogant,' 'condescending,' 'disdainful,' 'egotistical,' 'haughty,' 'imperious,' 'supercilious,' or 'vainglorious.' These qualities show an attitude that is perceived to be offensive. The words 'impertinent,' 'impudent,' 'insolent' show speech that goes beyond bounds and offends. 'Ostentatious,' 'pompous,' and 'pretentious' indicate showing superiority by display and attitude. 'Aristocratic,' 'authoritarian,' 'autocratic,' and 'imperious' emphasize acting in a manner that presupposes superiority in authority or in class. 'Affected' indicates proud behavior that is more humorous than offensive. 'Flippant' indicates speech that shows a sense of superiority and lack of respect for others.

affected: artificial; pretentious; intended to impress. L ad + facio do.
aristocratic: acting as if belonging to an elite or privileged class. Gk aristos best + kratia < krateo rule.
authoritarian: requiring full obedience to authority. L auctoritas < auctor creator.
autocratic: exercising authority in a dictatorial manner. Gk autos self + krateo rule.
condescending: looking down on; patronizing. Fr condescendre < L con- + de + scando climb.
disdain: to regard with proud indifference; reject. L dis (apart) + dignor deem worthy.
egotistical: being conceited, self-centered; selfish. L ego I.
flippant: speaking with inappropriate frivolity. (Imit)
haughty: proud and condescending. OF haut < L altus high.
imperious: proudly domineering. L imperium to command < L in- + parare to prepare, equip.
impertinent: insolent; rude; intrusive; irrelevant; pointless. L in (not) + per (through) + teneo hold.
impudent: insolent; boldly offending. L in- + pudere be ashamed.
insolent: insulting; impertinent and arrogant. L in- + solens < solere to be accustomed.
ostentatious: making a pretentious display; showy; displaying wealth. L ostento (freq ostendo) exhibit.
pompous: self-important; pretentious; bombastic; conceited. L pompa pomp.
pretentious: giving an outward show of importance or intelligence. L prae (before) + tendo stretch.
supercilious: disdaining others; proud; haughty. L superciliosus < super (over) + cilium eyelid.
vainglorious: having great pride and conceit. L vanus empty; evanesco (pfp evanescens) to vanish.

Definitions of words indicating someone is humble or modest: Modesty and lack of pretentiousness are emphasized by 'demure,' 'unassuming,' 'unpretentious,' and 'unostentatious.' Quietness, reserve, and timidity are emphasized by 'diffident,' 'restrained,' 'reticent,' 'subdued,' and 'taciturn.' 'Plebeian' indicates lowliness or commonness as belonging to the lower classes. 'Subservient' indicates a willingness to be under others.

demure: modest or reserved. OF de murs (of manners) < L mora delay.
diffidence: an attitude of distrust, timidity, shyness, or modesty. L dis (apart, asunder) + fides faith.
diffident: having self-distrust; timid; shy; modest; distrustful of others. L dis (apart, asunder) + fides faith.
plebeian: common; inferior; pert. to the common people. L plebeius < plebs the common people.
reticence: quality of being silent, quiet, and reserved. OF < L re (again) + taceo be silent.
reticent: habitually silent or reserved in utterance. OF < L re (again) + taceo be silent.
subservient: having a secondary or supporting role or function; servile. L subservire to subserve < servus slave.
taciturn: habitually silent or reserved; disinclined to conversation. L taciturnus < taceo be silent.
unassuming: modest; not pretentious. L un- + ad- + sumere to take.
unostentatious: unpretentious; modest; plain. OE un- + L ostendere to show.
unpretentious: not giving outward shows of importance. OE un + L prae (before) + tendo stretch.

Courageous or Timid

Courageous	Timid
audacious	craven
bold	diffident
dauntless	indisposed
gallant	pusillanimous
intrepid	recreant
undaunted	reluctant
valiant	reserved
valorous	reticent
	timorous
	trepidation

Definitions of words indicating someone is courageous: 'Dauntless,' 'intrepid,' and 'undaunted' indicate that persons with the quality will press on despite great difficulty. 'Audacious' indicates boldness beyond normal and a willingness to take great risks. 'Gallant' indicates chivalrous action.

audacious: bold; defying dangers or conventional rules of behavior. L audax < audeo dare.
audacity: boldness; willingness to defy danger or conventional rules of behavior. L audax < audeo dare.
dauntless: fearless; cannot be discouraged. L domare to tame + -less.
gallant: brave; chivalrous. OF galer (to rejoice).
intrepid: unshaken in the presence of danger; dauntless. L in (not) + trepidus restless, alarmed.
undaunted: not discouraged; resolute in the face of difficulty. OE un- + L domare to tame.
valiant: brave and courageous. L valere to be strong.
valorous: brave and courageous in battle. L valere to be strong.

Definitions of words indicating someone is timid: 'Craven,' 'pusillanimous,' and 'trepidation' indicate cowardliness and fearfulness. 'Diffident,' 'reserved,' 'reticent,' and 'timorous' show modesty, restraint, and timidity. 'Reluctance' often indicates timidity but need not. A person can have good reasons for being unwilling to do something. So also a 'recreant' may be unfaithful to a cause from cowardice or for other reasons.

craven: cowardly, lacking in courage. ME cravant (conquered, cowardly) < L crepo break.
diffidence: attitude of distrust, timidity, shyness, or modesty. L dis (apart, asunder) + fides faith.
diffident: having self-distrust; timid; shy; modest; distrustful of others. L dis (apart, asunder) + fides faith.
indisposed: slightly ill; disinclined; unwilling. L in- + dis- + ponere to put.
pusillanimous: lacking courage or spirit; cowardly. L pusillus (very little) + animus mind.
recreant: unfaithful to a cause; apostate; a cowardly or faithless person. L re (again) + credo believe.
reluctant: not inclined to; unwilling. L re- luctari to struggle.
reserved: self-restrained; aloof; reticent. L re- + servare to keep.
reticence: quality of being silent, quiet, and reserved. OF < L re (again) + taceo be silent.
reticent: habitually silent or reserved in utterance. OF < L re (again) + taceo be silent.
timorous: afraid to act; fearful. L timor fear.
trepidation: a state of agitation from fear; an involuntary trembling. OF < L trepidatio < trepido tremble.

Cheerful or Sad

Cheerful		**Cheerless**	
animated	jubilant	bad-tempered	gloomy
buoyant	light-hearted	blue	grim
delighted	lively	brooding	hopeless
elated	merry	comfortless	joyless
festive	optimistic	dejected	lugubrious
gay	rapturous	depressed	macabre
glad	spirited	desolate	melancholy
gleeful	sprightly	despairing	miserable
happy	sunny	despondent	morbid
hearty	warm-hearted	disconsolate	morose
hopeful		discouraged	mournful
jaunty		disheartencd	pessimistic
jocund		dispirited	somber
jolly		downcast	sullen
jovial		downhearted	unpleasant
joyful/joyous		forlorn	woeful
			wretched

Definitions of words indicating someone is cheerful or happy: Several comments can be made about the words conveying cheerfulness. The words 'elated,' 'jubilant,' and 'rapturous' indicate a happiness or joy of the greatest degree. The other words convey an attitude of cheerfulness but not necessarily as full. 'Jaunty' suggests confidence. 'Hopeful' and 'optimistic' involve positive feelings and indicate expectations about future events, whereas most of the words just convey a happy feeling or attitude.

buoyant: tending to float or to rise in the air; cheerful. OF boue < Ger.
jaunty: self-confident in manner; dapper in appearance. OF < L gentilis of the same clan.
jocund: cheerful and lighthearted. L iucundus < iuvare to help, delight.
jubilant: rejoicing; feeling and expressing great joy. L jubilo shout for joy.
jubilation: expression of great joy; rejoicing. L jubilo shout for joy.
rapturous: ecstatic; euphoric; intensely delighted. L raptus (pp rapere) to seize.
sprightly: lively; energetic; spirited; animated. L spiritus breath, spirit.

Definitions of words indicating someone is anything but cheerful or happy: We can divide the cheerlessness words into several groups. Several words have disagreeable, blamable, or even gruesome connotations: 'bad-tempered,' 'sullen,' 'macabre,' 'morbid,' 'unpleasant.' Most of the words convey a moderate degree of cheerlessness: 'blue,' 'brooding,' 'depressed,' 'discouraged,' 'disheartened,' 'dispirited,' 'downcast,' 'downhearted,' 'gloomy,' 'grim,' 'joyless,' 'lugubrious,' 'melancholy,' 'miserable,' 'morose,' 'mournful,' 'pessimistic,' 'somber,' and 'woeful.' Finally some of the words convey a much deeper degree of cheerlessness or despair: 'comfortless,' 'dejected,' 'despondent,' 'desolate,' 'despairing,' 'disconsolate,' 'forlorn,' 'hopeless,' 'wretched.'

despondent: dejected in spirit; disheartened. L de (from) + spondeo promise.
disconsolate: destitute of consolation; inconsolable. L con (together) + solor comfort.
dispirited: disheartened; dejected; discouraged. L dis- + spirare to breathe.
downcast: dejected; dispirited. ON kasta.
forlorn: forsaken, lonely, and sad; wretched looking. OE -leosan (to lose), forleosan to forfeit, lose.
lugubrious: exhibiting or producing sadness; doleful; exaggeratedly solemn. L lugubris, lugeo mourn.
macabre: gruesome. Fr macabre < Ar makbara funeral chamber.
melancholy: sadness of spirit; gloom; thoughtful reflection. Gk melas (melan-) black + khole bile.
morbid: diseased; unwholesome; gruesome. L morbidus diseased < morbus disease.
morose: gloomy, melancholic. L morosus peevish < mos caprice.
pessimistic: tending to take unnecessarily unfavorable or gloomier views. L pessimus (worst).
wretched: miserable; pathetic; contemptible; inferior. OE wrecca (exiles, wretch).

Lively or Sluggish

Lively		**Sluggish**	
brisk	scintillating	apathetic	listless
dynamic	stimulating	fatigued	muted
ebullient	titillating	indolent	prostrate
effusive		lackluster	slothful
exhilarated		languid/languor	torpid
exuberant		lazy	weary
inspired		lethargic	

Definitions of words indicating someone is lively: The words conveying liveliness or energy include 'brisk,' which indicates quick and vigorous action. 'Dynamic' indicates forcefulness and energy. 'Scintillating' indicates liveliness and verve that sparkles. 'Ebullient' and 'effusive' indicate liveliness that, as it were, bubbles over. 'Exhilarated' and 'exuberant' indicate great enthusiasm and joy. 'Inspired,' 'stimulating,' and 'titillating' indicate the presence of factors or actions that spur or rouse to feeling or activity. 'Titillating' spurs superficial pleasures.

ebullient: bubbling; enthusiastic. L e (out) + bullio boil.
effusive: gushing; overflowing. L ex (out) + fundo pour.
exuberance: quality of being full of enthusiasm and joy. L ex- + uberare fertile.
inspired: stimulated or motivated to realize a goal. L in (into) + spiro breathe.
scintillate: to produce sparks; to sparkle; to converse brilliantly. L scintilla spark.
stimulating: spurring or rousing to activity. L stimulus goad.
titillating: exciting or stimulating pleasurably (and usually superficially). L titillare to tickle.

Definitions of words indicating someone is sluggish: The words conveying sluggishness exhibit some distinctions. 'Apathetic,' 'lackluster,' and 'listless' suggest indifference and lack of energy. 'Fatigued' and 'weary' indicate sluggishness from exhaustion. A person who is 'prostrate' reaches the extreme in weakness from exhaustion. 'Indolent,' 'languid,' 'languor,' and 'lazy' indicate lack of energy and laziness. 'Lethargic,' 'slothful,' and 'torpid' emphasize sluggishness. Finally, 'muted' indicates being subdued.

apathetic: indifferent. Gk a + pathos.
indolent: lazy; tending to avoid exertion or activity. L indolentia free from pain < in (not) + dolens painful.
languid: showing weak energy, spirit, or force; listless. L languidus < langueo be weak.
languor: laziness; lack of energy; weakness. L langueo be weak.
lethargic: sluggish, drowsy, apathetic. Gk lethargia < lethe forgetfulness + a- not + ergon work.
listless: lacking in effort or energy. OE lystan desire + les less.
muted: subdued; softened; muffled. L mutus silent, dumb.
prostrate: lying face down; extremely weak. L sternere (pp stratus) to stretch, extend.
slothful: sluggish; lazy; indolent. OE slaw (slow).
torpid: sluggish, dull, dormant, numb. L torpidus torpid.

Careful or Careless/Carefree

Careful		**Careless or carefree**
cautious	observant	heedless
chary	provident	improvident
circumspect	prudent	indifferent
conscientious	punctilious	insouciant
discreet	scrupulous	lackadaisical
exacting	scrutinizing	lax
fastidious	wariness	negligent
gingerly	watchfulness	perfunctory
heedful		rash
judicious		remiss
meticulous		reprehensible
mindful		wayward

Definitions of words indicating someone is careful: Words indicating carefulness exhibit some differences in connotation. 'Cautious,' 'circumspect,' and 'gingerly' emphasize exercise of caution and care to avoid unnecessary risk. However, 'conscientious,' 'exacting,' 'fastidious,' 'meticulous,' 'punctilious,' and 'scrupulous' emphasize care to pay attention to and take into account all the relevant details. 'Chary,' 'wariness,' and 'watchfulness' emphasize a wariness and watching out. 'Observant' and 'scrutinize' emphasize care to take notice of events and details. 'Discreet' indicates care to be tactful and unobtrusive. 'Heedful,' 'judicious,' 'mindful,' 'provident,' and 'prudent' indicate thoughtfulness and consideration in handling present matters and in preparing for the future.

chary: careful, wary, stingy. OE cearig (sorrowful, sad) < cearu care, sorrow.
circumspect: cautious; well considered. L circum (around) + specio look.
discreet: tactful, unobtrusive; showing consideration. L discretus < discernere to separate.
fastidious: showing thorough attention to details. L fastidiosus haughtiness < fastus disdain.
gingerly: with great care; very cautiously. L genitus (pp gignere) to beget.
judicious: according to sound judgment; wise. L judicium judgment.
meticulous: extremely precise or concerned with details. L meticulosus timid < metus fear.
provident: saving for the future. L in- (not) + pro (forward) + video to see.

prudent: careful to avoid error; using sound judgment. Fr < L prudens < pro (forward) + video see.

punctilious: very nice or exact in the observance of forms of etiquette. L punctus point.

scrupulous: painstaking; careful. L scrupus scruple.

scrutinizing: observing carefully in detail. L scrutinium < scrutor examine.

Definitions of words indicating someone is careless or carefree: Words showing lack of care have different connotations. 'Heedless,' 'improvident,' 'negligent,' 'rash' indicate different kinds of carelessness. The improvident do not provide for their future. The rash take foolish risks. 'Indifferent,' 'lackadaisical,' and 'perfunctory' suggest indifference more than carelessness. The 'insouciant' has a carefree attitude, and the 'lax' just doesn't care enough to maintain discipline. Yet, 'remiss,' 'reprehensible,' and 'wayward' indicate action that is intentional or careless to the degree of deserving blame for failure to observe duties or to break laws.

improvident: wasteful; not saving for the future. L in- (not) + pro (forward) + video see.

insouciant: nonchalant; carefree lack of concern. OF in- (not) + soucier to trouble < L sollicitus troubled.

lackadaisical: disinterested; without energy and vitality. (alt. of alack the day)

lax: not strict or firm; slack; loose. L laxus loose, slack.

negligent: habitually failing to do the right or required acts or duties. L nec (not) + ligo bind, gather.

perfunctory: done indifferently and routinely. L per (through) + fungor perform.

reprehensible: deserving of blame or rebuke. L re (again) + prehendo seize.

CHAPTER 9

Vocabulary: Word Groups 2

There are groups of words that occur frequently on an SAT that have similar meaning. This chapter and the previous chapter give twenty-one groups of words that test takers ought to know. For each group there are two subgroups separating them into positive connotations and negative connotations. These are important words. If a word is not known, it should be looked up.

Each word group designates a concept. Sometimes it will have an adjectival meaning. In other cases, it will be a noun or verb. The words in the list have roughly synonymous meanings. Nevertheless, they are different words and cannot always be used in precisely the same contexts. Some lists include words that have negative connotations that the other words in the list do not have. Furthermore, some words in a list may have a different grammatical form than that of the heading.

The remaining nine groups not covered in the previous chapter fall into two groups: character traits and qualities of speech or writing. Definitions are given for most of the words, especially the more difficult words.

Definitions are given for some of the more difficult words as are the sources for the words defined. 'OE' indicates an Old English source, 'OF' an Old French source, 'Fr' a French source, 'L' a Latin source, 'Gk' an Ancient Greek source, 'ON' an Old Norse source, 'Ice' an Icelandic source, 'Ger' a German source, 'OItal' an Old Italian source, 'Celt' a Celtic source, and 'MD' a Middle Dutch source.

CHARACTER TRAITS

Character traits include words indicating whether someone is commendatory or criticizing, whether someone is friendly or antagonizing, whether someone is agreeable or disagreeable, whether someone is calming or agitating, and whether someone is genuine or deceptive.

Commending or Critical/Criticizing

Commendatory	Critical or criticizing		
acclaim	(cast) aspersion	denounce	objurgate
accolade	assail	deride/derisive	opprobrium
applaud	belittle	diatribe	pillory
encomium	berate	disparage	rebuke
eulogize	blame	excoriate	remonstrate
exalt	calumniate	execrate	reprehend
extol	castigate	flay	reprimand
flatter	censure	gainsay	reproach
hail	chastise	harangue	reprove

laud/laudatory	chide	impugn	revile
panegyrize	condemn	inveigh against	scold
praise	decry	lambaste	upbraid
venerate	defame	malign	vilify
	denigrate	obloquy	vituperate

Definitions of words indicating someone is commending or commendatory: 'Applaud' and 'praise' designate any ordinary commendation. A higher degree of recognition and commendation are generally expressed by the words 'acclaim,' 'accolade,' 'encomium,' 'exalt,' 'extol,' 'hail,' 'laud,' and 'laudatory.' 'Eulogize' and 'panegyrize' indicate praises given to one upon death, although the latter is not restricted to that occasion. The word 'venerate' indicates high respect and does not imply spoken praises. The word 'flatter' indicates praise given insincerely to gain friendship or favor.

accolade: an expression of praise or high honor. L ad- + collum neck.

encomium: praise; a tribute. Gk enkomion < en (in) + komos celebration, revel.

exalt: raise in status or rank; praise. L ex- + altus high.

extol: give high praise. L ex- + tollere to lift.

eulogize: to speak or write in praise of a dead person. Gk eulogia praise < eu well + lego speak.

laud: to praise. L laus praise.

panegyrize: offer elaborate praise or eulogy. Gk panegyrikos of an assembly.

venerate: to revere. L venerabilis < venerer revere.

Definitions of words indicating someone is critical or criticizing: There are a plethora of words indicating criticism of various kinds and levels. Several words indicate remarks that need not be uttered in the presence of the person criticized and may be relatively mild: 'cast aspersion on,' 'disparage,' and 'impugn.' Other words that also need not be uttered in the presence of the person criticized but indicate strong criticism are 'calumniate,' 'decry,' 'defame,' 'denigrate,' 'denounce,' and 'malign.' The words 'deride,' 'derisive,' and 'pillory' indicate criticism through use of humor and ridicule. Several words may or may not imply direct speech to the person being criticized but also require strong criticism: 'censure,' 'condemn,' 'diatribe,' and 'inveigh against.' Other words imply direct speech to the person being criticized. Some words imply no more than moderate criticism: 'blame,' 'belittle,' 'chastise,' 'chide,' 'rebuke,' 'reprimand,' 'reproach,' 'reprove,' 'scold,' and 'upbraid.' Others imply very strong criticism: 'assail,' 'berate,' 'castigate,' 'excoriate,' 'execrate,' 'flay,' 'lambaste,' 'objurgate,' 'reprehend,' 'revile,' 'vilify,' and 'vituperate.' Two words indicate disagreement with or protest against, but not necessarily criticism of, a person: 'gainsay' and 'remonstrate.' 'Harangue' is applied to speeches that are tedious with the focus more on the person making the criticisms than the target of the criticism. 'Obloquy' and 'opprobrium' refer to the disgrace that may apply to a person.

aspersion: a disparaging or derogatory remark. L ad (to) + spargo sprinkle.

assail: to assault; to attack. L saltus; saliens (pfp salire) to leap, jump.

berate: to scold vehemently. Fr rater (to scold).

calumniate: to slander; make malicious statements against. L calumnia < calvor deceive.

calumny: slander; malicious statements made to damage someone's reputation. L calvor deceive.

castigate: to criticize; punish. L castus pure + ago make.

censure: strong criticism and disapproval. L censere to assess.

chastise: to punish; to severely criticize. ME chasten < L castigate.

chide: to scold or reprimand. OE cidan < cid strife, contention.

decry: denounce publicly; disparage. Fr decrier < de + crier cry < L queri complain.

defame: to slander, libel or attempt to injure a person's reputation. L diffama < dis + fama < for speak.

denigrate: to disparage; defame. L denigrare blacken, defame < de- + niger black.

deride: make fun of; ridicule. L de (intens.) + rideo laugh.

diatribe: a bitter and abusive criticism or denunciation. Gk diatribe lecture < dia + tribein to rub.

disparage: to belittle. OF des + parage (rank) < L dis (not) + par equal.

execrate: to curse or call down evil upon. L ex (out) + sacer sacred.

excoriate: wear or strip off the skin; abrade; denounce. L ex (off) + corium skin.

flay: severely criticize; to whip. OE flean.

gainsay: speak against; contradict; controvert. OE gegn- (against) + secgan say.

harangue: long tedious usually disputatious speech; a tirade. OItal aringo (public square).

impugn: to call in question; gainsay. L in (against) + pugno fight.

inveigh: to utter vehement censure or invective. OF enveir prob < L inveho < invectus scolding.

lambaste: give a beating; thrash; to berate. OE lam + ON beysta beat.

malign: speak evil of; evil in disposition or intent. L malignus malign.

obloquy: state of being in disgrace; infamy; defamation. L ob (against) + loquor speak.

objurgate: berate; rebuke; scold. L ob- + iurgare scold, sue at law < agere do, proceed.

opprobrium: disgrace; ignominy; scorn. L ob- (against) + probum reproach.

rebuke: reprove; reprimand; a strong reproof. Fr re- + bouque (mouth).

remonstrate: present a protest against something; urge in protest. L re (again) + monstro show.

reprehend: to chide sharply; object to forcibly; find fault with; blame. L re (again) + prehendo seize.

reprehensible: deserving of blame or rebuke. L re (again) + prehendo seize.

reprimand: strong rebuke. L reprimere to restrain < re- + premere press.

reproach: criticize or disapprove; (n) blame; disgrace. L re- + prope (near).

reprove: censure; rebuke; express disapproval. L reprobo condemn < re + probo prove.

revile: to scold. Fr re- + avilir cheapen < L vilis worthless.

upbraid: to reproach. OE up (up) + bregdan pull, weave.

vilify: to represent as base, mean or evil; defame; slander. Fr vil < L vilis worthless + facio make.

vituperate: to find fault with abusively; rail at. L vituperatus (pp vitupero) < vitium fault + paro prepare.

Friendly/Agreeable or Antagonizing/Disagreeable

Friendly or agreeable		Disagreeable or antagonizing		
accommodating	(show) favor	acerbic	discourteous	sardonic
affable	genial	acidulous	gruff	spiteful
affectionate	gentle	acrimonious	irascible	surly
agreeable	good-natured	asperity	ireful	testy
amiable	gracious	blunt	malevolent	truculent
amicable	hospitable	brusque	misanthropic	unkind
benevolent	humane	callous	mordant	vexing
benign	kindly	cantankerous	mordacious	vindictive
charitable	lenient	captious	obstinate	
conciliatory	mild	caustic	ornery	
congenial	obliging	churlish	peevish	
considerate	sociable	contentious	perverse	
convivial	sportive	crusty	petulant	
cordial	tolerant	curmudgeon	provocative	
courteous	welcoming	curt	querulous	
decorous		cutting	sarcastic	

Definitions of words indicating someone is friendly or agreeable: Words indicating friendliness or agreeableness can be divided into several groups. Most of the words convey a general friendliness and desire to get along: 'affable,' 'agreeable,' 'amiable,' 'amicable,' 'congenial,' 'convivial,' 'cordial,' 'genial,' 'gentle,' 'good-natured,' 'gracious,' 'hospitable,' 'kindly,' 'mild,' 'obliging,' 'sociable' and 'welcoming.' 'Sportive' indicates a fondness for play. Several words perhaps bring out a greater effort to be accommodating to the interests of others: 'accommodating,' 'considerate,' 'lenient,' 'obliging,' and 'tolerant.' 'Affectionate' brings out the presence of strong feeling for others. The words 'benevolent,' 'benign,' 'charitable,' 'show favor,' and 'humane' indicate a giving nature. 'Acceding' and 'conciliatory' show a willingness to give in to maintain good relations. 'Courteous' and 'decorous' indicate politeness and propriety in behavior.

affable: courteous and mild in manner. L ad- + for speak.
amiable: pleasing in disposition; kind-hearted. L amicabilis < amo love.
amicable: friendly; peaceable. L amicabilis < amo love.
benevolent: kindly; charitable; beneficent. L bene well + volens (pfp volo) wish.
benign: influencing in a favorable or harmless way; of kindly disposition. L benignus kind, generous.
charitable: generous to the needy; lenient; tolerant. L caritas affection < carus dear.
conciliatory: seeking to reduce enmity or hostility; placating; making peace. L concilium council.
congenial: agreeable; pleasant; friendly. L con + genialis of one's tutelary deity.
convivial: sociable; festive; merry. L con (together) + vivo live.
cordial: friendly; warm towards others. L cor, cord- heart.
courteous: polite; showing consideration for others. L cohors courtyard, retinue.
decorous: proper; appropriate. L decor seemliness, beauty.
genial: having a friendly or pleasant manner. L genialis of one's tutelary deity.
gracious: kind and pleasant esp. toward those of lower status. L gratus pleasing, favorable, thankful.
humane: concerned for human welfare and interests. L humanus belonging to a man.
obliging: accommodating; willing and ready to comply. L ob- (to) + ligare to bind.
sportive: rel. to or fond of sport or play; frolicsome; wanton. L de (away) + porto carry.
tolerant: willing to permit and endure. L tolerare (toleratus) to bear, endure.

Definitions of words indicating disagreeableness and even antagonistic action: Words that indicate disagreeableness and antagonizing speech or action divide into several groups. A person may be very abrupt or short in manner. The words 'blunt, 'brusque,' 'curt,' and 'gruff' are then appropriate. Several words emphasize rudeness and ill-humor: 'churlish,' 'crusty,' 'curmudgeon,' 'ornery,' 'surly,' and 'testy.' Others emphasize quarrelsomeness: 'cantankerous,' 'captious,' 'contentious,' and 'querulous.' 'Callous' and 'discourteous' show lack of care about others feelings. 'Obstinate' and 'perverse' imply unreasonableness. 'Vexing' indicates presence of annoyance and irritation. 'Acerbic,' 'acidulous,' and 'acrimonious' indicate expression of sour attitudes. 'Asperity' indicates harshness of attitude. The words 'irascible,' 'ireful,' 'peevish,' and 'petulant' emphasize irritability and expression of anger. Several words convey a corrosive, biting, or derisive quality in attitude and speech: 'caustic,' 'cutting,' 'mordacious,' 'mordant,' 'sarcastic,' and 'sardonic.' 'Provocative' denotes action that incites conflict, and 'truculent' suggests a disposition to engage in conflict. 'Unkind' shows a poor disposition toward others. 'Malevolent' and 'misanthropic' indicate dislike for other people. 'Spiteful' and 'vindictive' imply a desire for revenge.

acerbic: sour, embittered. L acerbus bitter < acer sharp.
acidulous: slightly acid; sour-tempered. L aceo be sour.
acrimonious: full of bitterness; sarcastic; caustic; sharp; morose. L acer sharp.
asperity: roughness or harshness as of temper; hardship; difficulty. L asper rough.
caustic: burning; corrosive. Gk kaustikos < kaio burn.
blunt: frank in speech. ME.
brusque: abrupt and blunt in speech or manner. Fr < LL brucus heather.

callous: hardened; lacking feeling or empathy. L callum hard skin.

cantankerous: quarrelsome and disagreeable. L contactus (pp contingere) to touch.

captious: apt to find fault; hypercritical. L captiosus deceptive.

churlish: rude; boorish; vulgar. OE ceorl (man).

contentious: quarrelsome. Fr < L contentio < contineo < con (together) + teneo hold.

crusty: having a hard outer surface; surly or somewhat disagreeable in manner. L crusta crust, shell.

curmudgeon: crotchety and ill-tempered person. Celt corn + OF muchier hide.

curt: short, terse, or abrupt in manner or speech. L curtus short.

discourteous: impolite; insulting; not considerate of others' feelings. L dis- + cohors courtyard, retinue.

gruff: rough and curt in manner; harsh in tone. MD grof.

irascible: quick to anger. L irasci to be angry < ira anger.

ireful: full of anger; wrathful. L ira anger.

malevolent: having an evil disposition toward others. L malus bad + volo wish.

misanthropic: disliking mankind. Gk misanthropos hating mankind < miseo hate + anthropos man.

mordacious: biting or given to biting; sarcastic. L mordax < mordeo bite.

mordant: biting; pungent. Fr < L mordens (pfp mordeo) bite.

obstinate: unreasonably resolved in a purpose or opinion; stubborn. L ob (before) + sto stand.

ornery: uncooperative; perverse; contrary. Alt of ordinary < L ordo order.

peevish: irritable; bad-tempered. L versatus (pp versare) to turn, twist.

perverse: willfully wrong or erring; unreasonable; refractory. L perversus < per (through) + verto turn.

petulant: displaying capricious fretfulness; peevish; irritable. L petulans < peto attack.

provocative: serving to incite; causing anger. OF provoquer < L pro (forth) + voco call.

querulous: disposed to complain or fret; quarrelsome, complaining. L querulus < queror complain.

sarcastic: exhibiting ridicule by mocking irony. Gk sarkazein to angrily bite the lips < sarx flesh.

sardonic: insincere and derisive; sneering; unnatural or forced as laughter. Gk sardanios bitter.

surly: unfriendly, ill-humored; threatening. ME sirly < L senex old.

testy: disagreeable; irritable; crabby; snappy. LL testa skull.

truculent: disposed to fight, be violent, or bitterly critical. L trux savage, fierce, grim.

vex: to annoy; to frustrate; to irritate. L vexare to agitate, distress.

vexatious: annoying; troublesome. L vexare to agitate, distress.

vindictive: having a revengeful spirit; punitive. L vindicatus (pp vindico) defend.

Calming or Agitating

Calming		Agitating	
abate	mitigate	alienate	nettle
accommodate	mollify	antagonize	oppose
allay	pacify	contradict	oppugn
ameliorate	palliate	dispute	rebuff
appease	placate	embitter	repel
assuage	propitiate	estrange	repulse
concede	quell	incense	snub
conciliate	satiate	infuriate	
gratify	tranquilizing		

Definitions of words indicating a calming effect: Several words emphasize soothing or reducing intensity: 'abate,' 'allay,' 'mitigate,' 'mollify,' 'palliate,' and 'tranquilizing.' Other words emphasize partially or wholly giving in to calm matters: 'accommodate,' 'appease,' 'assuage,' 'concede,' 'conciliate,' 'placate,' and 'propitiate.' 'Pacify' and 'quell' may imply use of force to calm matters. Sometimes calm is brought about by gratifying or satiating some-one. Finally, use of 'ameliorate' indicates improving matters by calming things.

abate: lessen in intensity or degree. L ad- + battere to beat.
accommodate: to service; to allow for; to adjust for. L ad- + com- + modus measure, size, limit.
allay: to calm. OE a + lecgan lay.
ameliorate: to improve; make something bad better. L a- + melior better.
appease: to calm matters esp. by yielding to demands. Fr apaiser < L ad (to) + pax peace.
assuage: to ease; to appease; to calm. L ad (to) + suavis sweet.
conciliate: seek to reduce enmity or hostility; placate; make peace. L concilium council.
mitigate: to lessen in severity or relieve; alleviate. L mitis mild + ago make.
mollify: soothe; appease or calm in temper; soften. L mollis soft + facio do.
pacify: calm down; establish peace. L pax peace + facio make.
palliate: allay fears; excuse partially; reduce the severity or intensity. L pallium cloak.
placate: to turn from a state of enmity or hostility; appease. L placatus (pp placo) appease.
propitiate: to appease. L propitiatus (pp propitio) render favorable, appease.
quell: suppress; pacify. OE cwellan (to kill) < Ger.
satiate: to fill with more than enough; be surfeited. L satiatus (pp satio) < satis enough.

Definitions of words indicating an agitating effect: There are words that instead of calming matters cause more ag-itation. Several words indicate worsening of relations between people: 'alienate,' 'antagonize,' 'embitter,' 'es-trange,' 'incense,' and 'infuriate.' Some indicate minor annoyances in interpersonal relations: 'nettle' and 'snub.' Several words indicate disagreement: 'contradict,' 'dispute,' 'oppose,' and 'oppugn.' Finally, 'rebuff,' 'repel,' and 'repulse' indicate a driving back or away.

alienate: to estrange; become hostile; emotionally isolate. L alienatio < alius other.
antagonize: provoke hostility or enmity. Gk anti (against) + agonizomai contend, strive.
contradict: deny or oppose. L contra (against) + dicere to speak.
embitter: to cause feelings of resentment. OE.
estrange: to alienate; make hostile. L extraneare disown < extraneus foreign < exter (outward).
incense: to enrage or infuriate. L incendere to set fire to, kindle.
infuriate: to make very angry; to enrage. L in- + furiare to enrage.
nettle: to irritate or annoy. OE nett (a net).
oppugn: to oppose; disparage; call into question. L ob (against) + pugno fight.
rebuff: (v) to reject; to repel; (n) a denial or rejection; a repelling. Ital re- + buffo gust, puff.
repulsion: the process of being forced or driven back or away. L repulsus (pp repello) < re (back) + pello drive.
snub: to slight; treat contemptuously. ME snubben (to rebuke).

Genuine or Fake

Genuine	Deceptive or fake
constant	dissembling
faithful	duplicitous
loyal	equivocate/equivocation
reliable	ersatz
sincere	guile
stalwart	mendacious/mendacity
steadfast	prevarication
trustworthy	

Definitions of words indicating someone is genuine: Several words indicate constancy and genuineness: 'constant,' 'faithful,' 'loyal,' 'reliable,' 'sincere,' and 'trustworthy.' They indicate traits of character. 'Stalwart' and 'steadfast' emphasize a tendency to stay firm and on course.

stalwart: strong; firm of resolve; (n) steadfast supporter. OE stathol foundation + weorth valuable.
steadfast: remaining firm, not swerving. OE stede + faest fixed, fast < Ger.

Definitions of words indicating someone is not genuine: Several words indicate characteristics of being inconstant, not genuine, or deceptive or dishonest. 'Dissembling,' 'duplicitous,' 'guile,' 'mendacious,' 'mendacity,' and 'prevarication' indicate lack of genuineness due to dishonesty and deceptiveness. 'Equivocate' and 'equivocation' indicate inconstancy often with intent to deceive but not necessarily. 'Ersatz' refers to lack of genuineness through artificiality.

dissemble: to conceal as by false appearance; pretend; feign. L dissimulo < dis (apart) + similis like.
duplicity: tricky deceitfulness; double-dealing. Fr duplicite < duplex < L duo (two) + plico fold.
equivocate: use ambiguous language to hide the truth or one's intentions. L aequus equal + vox voice.
ersatz: inferior imitation or substitute; artificial. Ger ersetzen replace < ir- (out) + sezzan to set.
guile: craftiness and cunning esp. when used to deceive. OF cunning, deceit < Ger.
mendacious: lying; false. L mendacium lie < mendax lying.
prevaricate: lie; evade the truth; equivocate. L prae (before) + varicus straddling < varus bent.
prevarication: a lie; the act of lying or evading the truth. L prae (before) + varicus straddling.

QUALITIES OF SPEECH OR WRITING

Qualities of speech and writing include words indicating whether spoken or written words are true or false, clear or unclear, concise or inflated, direct or indirect or wandering, interesting or boring or dull. Some of the words can indicate personal characteristics.

True or False

True		False
accurate	unerring	apocryphal
correct	unswerving	erroneous
exact	veracious/veracity	fallacious
factual	verisimilitude	specious
precise	verity	spurious
right		

Definitions of words indicating something is true or correct: Several words indicate correctness of some description or data: 'accurate,' 'correct,' 'exact,' 'factual,' 'precise,' and 'right.' Two words emphasize a tendency to be in accord with the truth: 'unerring' and 'unswerving.' Several words are essentially stand-ins for 'true': 'veracious,' 'veracity,' 'verity,' and 'verisimilitude.'

unerring: not making any mistakes; invariably accurate. OE un- + L errare to wander.
unswerving: not deviating; steadfast, unwavering; constant. OE un- + sweorfan (to rub, scour).
veracious: truthful; true. L verax < verus true.
veracity: habitual regard for the truth; trueness. L verax < verus true.

verisimilitude: appearance of truth; likelihood; realism; resembling truth. L verum truth + similis like.

verity: being a true representation or reality; true statement. L veritas truth < verus true.

Definitions of words indicating something is not true or correct: Several words indicate falsity for different reasons: 'apocryphal' or 'spurious' for poor authority; 'fallacious' for incorrect reasoning; and 'erroneous' or 'specious' for simply being wrong.

apocryphal: of doubtful authority. Gk apo (from) + krypto conceal.

erroneous: marked by error; mistaken. L erro wander.

fallacious: involving incorrect reasoning; deceptive; misleading. L fallacia < fallo deceive.

specious: appearing right, true, and plausible, but false. L speciosus fair < species < specio look.

spurious: not proceeding from the source pretended; not genuine; false. L spurius spurious.

Clarity or Lack of Clarity

Clear		Unclear	
coherent	precise	abstruse	obscure
comprehensible	specific	arcane	opaque
explicit	straightforward	diffuse	rarefied
limpid	transparent	enigmatic	recondite
lucid	unambiguous	esoteric	turbid
pellucid	unequivocal	inscrutable	
perspicuous			

Definitions of words indicating something shows clarity: Several interesting words emphasize clarity of speech or expression. One word indicates logical consistency, namely, 'coherent.' 'Comprehensible' is used to affirm understandability in general. Several words emphasize definiteness: 'explicit,' 'precise,' 'specific,' 'straightforward,' 'unambiguous,' and 'unequivocal.' Several other words emphasize clarity: 'limpid,' 'lucid,' 'pellucid,' 'perspicuous,' and 'transparent.'

coherent: being logically or aesthetically consistent. L co (together) + haereo stick.

comprehensible: can be understood; intelligible. L comprehendo < com (together) + prehendo seize.

explicit: plainly expressed or that plainly expresses; definite; not implied. L ex (out) + plico fold.

limpid: perfectly clear or intelligible. L limpidus clear.

lucid: clear. L lucidus < luceo shine.

pellucid: permitting some passage of light; translucent; transparent; clear. L per (through) + luceo shine.

perspicuous: clear in expression; lucid; transparent. L perspicax < per (through) + specio look.

transparent: can be seen through; clear; apparent; obvious. L trans- (through) + parere to show.

unambiguous: clear; not vague; definite. OE un- + L ambiguus uncertain < ambi around + agere to go.

unequivocal: understandable in only one way; distinct; plain. L aequus equal + vox voice.

Definitions of words indicating something lacks clarity: Some words indicate something is difficult to understand because it known to but a few: 'arcane' and 'esoteric.' Some words indicate things are puzzling: 'enigmatic' and 'inscrutable.' Some words just indicate obscurity: 'abstruse,' 'diffuse,' 'obscure,' 'opaque,' 'rarefied,' 'recondite,' and 'turbid.'

abstruse: difficult to understand; hidden; concealed. L abs (from, away) + trudo thrust, push.

arcane: known by only a very limited group. L arcanus secret.

diffuse: lacking clarity. L dis (apart) + fundo pour.

enigmatic: puzzling; difficult to understand. Gk ainigma < ainos tale.

esoteric: understood only by a limited group of people. Gk esoterikos < eso within.

inscrutable: mysterious; difficult or impossible to understand. L in- + scrutabilis discoverable.

obscure: difficult to perceive; ambiguous; vague; (v) make difficult to understand. L obscurus dark.

opaque: not passing or reflecting light. Fr < L opacus shady.

rarefied: distant from and lacking relevance to ordinary life. L rarus rare + facio make.

recondite: hard to understand; obscure. L reconditus (pp recondere) < re- + condere to preserve.

turbid: with sediments stirred up; cloudy; in confusion; disturbed. L turbidus, turba disturbance.

Short/Concise or Long/Inflated

Concise		Inflated	
brief	pithy	bombastic	overstated
compact	succinct	circumlocution	periphrastic
condensed	terse	exaggerated	profuse
crisp	to the point	extravagant	prolix
incisive	trenchant	flowery	superfluous
laconic		garrulous	turgid
		grandiloquent	verbose
		loquacious	wordy
		overblown	

Definitions of words indicating something is concise: Several words indicate shortness of expression: 'brief,' 'compact,' 'condensed,' and 'laconic.' Others emphasize not only the shortness but also the conciseness of expression: 'crisp,' 'incisive,' 'pithy,' 'succinct,' 'terse,' 'to the point,' and 'trenchant.'

condensed: shortened; reduced in volume. L com- + densare to thicken < densus thick.

incisive: sharp, penetrating thought or action. L in- + caedere to cut.

laconic: using or consisting of few words; concise; pithy. Gk Lakonikos < Lakon a Lacaedemonian.

pithy: brief but packed with meaning. OE pitha.

succinct: clear and concise expression. L sub (below) + cingo gird.

terse: concise; to the point. L tersus (pp tergere) to cleanse.

trenchant: incisive; sharp; clear, vigorous, and effective. OF trenchier (cut) < L truncus trunk.

Definitions of words indicating something is anything but concise: Speech and writing that are not concise but inflated can be described in several ways. It may be very pretentious or pompous: 'bombastic,' 'extravagant,' 'flowery,' 'grandiloquent,' 'overblown,' or 'turgid.' It may 'exaggerated' or 'overstated.' It may be very indirect or roundabout: 'circumlocution' or 'periphrastic.' It may just be excessively wordy: 'garrulous,' 'loquacious,' 'profuse,' 'prolix,' 'superfluous,' 'verbose,' or 'wordy.'

bombastic: pompous in expression. OF bombace (padding) < L bombax cotton.

circumlocution: indirect, roundabout expression. L circumlocutio < circum (around) + loquor speak.

garrulous: very talkative. L garrulus chattering.

grandiloquent: having a pompous or bombastic style. L grandis grand + loquens < loquor speak.

loquacious: extremely talkative. L loquax talkative.

overblown: overdone; pretentious. OE ofer (over) + blawan to blow.

periphrastic: using roundabout inaccurate language. Gk peri (around) + phrazo declare.
profuse: plentiful; occurring in great abundance. L pro (forth) + fundo pour.
prolix: indulging in long and winded discourse; tedious. L prolixus stretched out < liqueo be clear.
superfluous: being more than needed; not needed; extra. L superfluus < super (over) + fluo flow.
turgid: unnaturally distended; swollen; fig. inflated; bombastic. L turgidus < turgeo swell.
verbose: wordy; using more words than are needed. L verbosus < verbum word.

Direct or Indirect/Wandering

Direct

blunt	frank	
candid	open	
categorical	outspoken	
definite	penetrating	
explicit	plain	
express	straightforward	
forthright	unequivocal	

Indirect or wandering

aimless	evasive
circuitous	indirect
circumlocutory	meander
deviate	oblique
devious	ramble/rambling
digress	straying
drifting	tortuous

Definitions of words indicating someone or something is direct: Some direct speech is characterized by openness and frankness: 'blunt,' 'candid,' 'forthright,' 'frank,' 'open,' 'outspoken,' or 'straightforward.' Some discourse is not open to multiple interpretations or is 'categorical' or 'unequivocal.' Some adjectives emphasize definiteness: 'definite,' 'explicit,' 'express,' or 'plain.' Finally, 'penetrating' indicates depth of insight.

blunt: frank in speech; not sharp, but dull. ME.
candid: showing frankness, sincerity, and openness; straightforward. L candidus < candere to shine.
candor: frankness; openness. L candere to shine.
categorical: pert. to a category; without qualification, unequivocal; absolute. Gk kategoria assertion.
explicit: plainly expressed or that plainly expresses; definite; not implied. L ex (out) + plico fold.
express: stated definitely. L ex- + pressus pressure (pp premere) to press, oppress.
forthright: straightforward; without any evasiveness. OE forth + right.
frank: expressing openly; straightforward. LL Francus Frank.
outspoken: blunt, candid, forthright. OE ut (out) + sprecan.
penetrating: astute; keen in insight; very perceptive. L penetrare < penitus deeply.
straightforward: direct; frank; not evasive. ME streccan (to stretch) + OE fore- + weard –ward.
unequivocal: understandable in only one way; distinct; plain. L aequus equal + vox voice.

Definitions of words indicating someone or something is not at all direct: Discourse can be indirect in several ways. It can stray from the direct path: 'deviate,' 'digress,' 'drifting,' or 'straying.' Wandering can occur because purpose is lacking: 'aimless,' 'ramble,' or 'rambling.' Wandering can occur from an intent to deceive. Then it is 'devious' or 'evasive.' 'Indirect' or 'oblique' indicates the indirectness. Other words emphasize multiple twists and turns: 'circuitous,' 'circumlocutory,' 'meander,' or 'tortuous.'

circuitous: roundabout. L circum (around) + eo go.
circumlocutory: using indirect, roundabout expression. L circumlocutio < circum (around) + loquor speak.
deviate: to turn aside, stray. L devius < de (from) + via way.
devious: deceptive; leading away from a straight course; rambling. L devius < de (from) + via way.
digress: to wander. L di (apart) + gradior step.

evasive: tending or seeking to avoid, elude, or escape from. L evado < e (from) + vado go.
meander: take a winding course; move without purpose. Gk Maiandros (winding river in Turkey).
oblique: indirect; not parallel or perpendicular to a line but slanting. L obliquus slanting, indirect.
ramble: move without purpose; speak or write with digressions. MD rammelen (wander about).
tortuous: winding; full of curves, twists, and turns; devious. L tortuosus < tortus twisted.

Interesting or Boring/Dull

Interesting	Boring or dull	
absorbing	arid	mundane
appealing	banal	pedestrian
captivating	clichéd	platitudinous
challenging	colorless	prosaic
compelling	commonplace	repetitious
engaging	drab	soporific
engrossing	dry	stodgy
entertaining	fatuous	tedious
enthralling	flat	trite
fascinating	hackneyed	uninspired
gripping	humdrum	uninteresting
intriguing	insipid	vapid
riveting	lackluster	wearisome
	monotonous	

Definitions of words indicating something is interesting: Ideas or discourse can be moderately interesting. Then it is 'appealing' or 'entertaining.' It may present a challenge and be 'challenging' or 'intriguing.' Intensely interesting discourse is 'absorbing,' 'captivating,' 'compelling,' 'engaging,' 'engrossing,' 'enthralling,' 'fascinating,' 'gripping,' or 'riveting.'

absorbing: engrossing; claiming full attention. L ab (away) + sorbere to suck.
captivating: seizing and holding a person's attention; fascinating. L captivus prisoner < capere to seize.
compelling: forceful; needing urgent action. L compellatio < com (together) + pello drive.
engaging: attractive, appealing. Ger en- + gage pledge.
engrossing: absorbing one's entire attention. L en- + grossa < grossus thick.
enthralling: captivating; holding spellbound. ME en- + thrall slave.
gripping: seizing the interest and attention of. OE gripe (grasp).
riveting: engrossing one's attention; gripping; captivating; spellbinding. OF river (to attach).

Definitions of words indicating something is boring or dull: The emphasis for boring ideas and discourse can be made in different ways. The words or ideas may suffer from overuse. They are then 'banal,' 'clichéd,' 'commonplace,' 'hackneyed,' 'mundane,' 'platitudinous,' or 'trite.' They may just be dull or boring per se: 'humdrum,' 'monotonous,' 'pedestrian,' 'prosaic,' 'repetitious,' or 'uninteresting.' If the dullness comes from stuffiness, it is then 'stodgy.' The emphasis may be on a tendency to put listeners or readers to sleep: 'soporific,' 'tedious,' or 'wearisome.' The lack of interest may be attributed to dryness: 'arid' or 'dry.' Or, it may be attributed to lack of color: 'colorless' or 'drab.' Or, it may be attributed to lack of flavor: 'flat,' 'insipid,' 'lackluster,' or 'vapid.' The discourse may simply be foolish and is 'fatuous,' or it may lack any inspiration and be 'uninspired.'

banal: commonplace; trite. OF banal < ban summons to military service < Ger.

clichéd: worn out from overuse (of expressions). Fr clicher (to stereotype).

commonplace: ordinary; trite. L communis common, public.

drab: dull of color; uninteresting; dreary. LL drappus.

fatuous: stubbornly blind or foolish; idiotic. L fatuus silly.

hackneyed: worn out; trite; clichéd; made commonplace by frequent use. Fr haquenee (ambling horse).

humdrum: uninteresting; dull; boring. (Imit).

insipid: without flavor; unsavory; not qualified to interest; vapid; dull. L in (not) + sapidus savory.

lackluster: dull; insipid; without vigor. MD lac fault + L lustrum purification.

monotonous: lacking variety; repetitious; tedious. Gk mono- one + tonos tone.

mundane: pert. to the world, worldly, ordinary, commonplace. L mundus world.

pedestrian: prosaic or dull; connected with walking; one who walks. L pedester < pes foot.

platitudinous: commonplace; trite; unoriginal. Gk platus flat, broad.

prosaic: belonging to prose; dull. L prosa prose < pro- forward + vertere to turn.

repetitious: done or said many times; reiterated. L re (again) + peto seek.

soporific: causing or tending to produce sleep. L sapor sleep + facio make.

stodgy: dull; lacking imagination; stuffy. ME stodge (to cram).

tedious: lengthy, dull, and boring. L taedium tedium.

trite: used so often as to be made commonplace; worn out. L tritus (pp tero) rub.

vapid: having lost sparkling quality and flavor; flat; dull; insipid. L vapidus insipid.

PART 2

VOCABULARY ORGANIZED BY ROOTS

CHAPTER 10

Roots Indicating Physical, Temporal, or Logical Relations

The categories used in this and the following twelve chapters for classifying the two hundred Indo-European roots that have spawned many of the most useful and interesting English words are somewhat arbitrary. Many of the words that spring from the roots are related only distantly. Nevertheless, we should expect some relatedness from roots with similar meanings. The classification scheme is of relatively little importance in any case. The first category, covered in this chapter, includes roots that have primary emphasis on place, space, time, and logic and the relations between them. Numerical concepts are included here as well. Twenty-two roots are placed in this category. For two of them, only the Latin and Greek forms are cited, since their Indo-European origins are unclear. The form in which roots are identified follows *The American Heritage Dictionary of Indo-European Roots* (second edition), edited by Calvert Watkins, for ease of reference. Sometimes there are as many as five or six roots that can be represented by an identical spelling. So it is necessary to append superscripts to distinguish individual roots. The superscript used follows the reference cited. In some cases, additional Indo-European roots with the same spelling are distinguished, as are roots not found in *The American Heritage Dictionary of Indo-European Roots,* which are based on the standard reference on Indo-European roots, *Indogermanisches Etymologisches Worterbuch* (1959), by Julius Pokorny. Several comments need to be made. Laryngeals in Indo-European are represented by a schwa (e). Labiovelars have a superscripted w—for example, g^w, k^w, and g^wh. A parenthesis ( ) within a root indicates a sound that is optional. Six of the roots are prepositional, indicating relative location or place. These are:

'al-^{1}' meaning "beyond, other"
'ambhi-/m(o)bhi-' meaning "around"
'apo-' meaning "off, away"
'en' meaning "in"
'per^1' meaning "forward, through"
'uper' meaning "over"

The root 'al-^{1}' is the direct source of the English words 'other' and 'else.' The root 'ambhi-' is the source of the English words 'by' and 'be-.' Also 'en' is the source of our words 'in' and 'inner.' The root 'apo-' is the source of the English words 'after' and 'off.' The root 'per^1' is the origin of words including 'forth' and 'far.' One root is negational with a purely logical character:

'ne' meaning "not"

It is the source of the words 'not,' 'none,' 'no,' and 'nothing.' Three roots are concerned with time or sequence:

'at-' meaning "to go"
'CHRON' from Greek 'khronos' meaning "time"
'sek^w-^{1}' meaning "to follow"

While the fundamental meaning of 'at-' is "to go," the words it has spawned all have a temporal significance. The root 'sek^w-1' meaning "to follow" is not limited to following in time but applies to following in action or location. Five roots are essentially numerical, indicating the number of items:

'dekm$_o$-' meaning "ten"
'pau-1' meaning "few, little"
'sem-1' meaning "one, as one, together with"
'trei-' meaning "three"
'EQU' meaning "equal, fair"

EQU involves ideas of much greater breadth than counting but is fundamentally a numerical concept. The root 'dekm$_o$-' is the source of the English words 'ten,' 'tenth, and '-teen.' The root 'pau-1' is the source of the word 'few.' The root 'sem-1' is the source of the English words 'sum' and those ending in '-some.' The root 'trei-' is the source of the English words 'three' and 'third.' Three roots have for their central concept the notion of quantity or size or are directly related:

'me-2' meaning "measure"
'meg-' meaning "great"
'sol-' meaning "whole"

The root 'me-2' is the source of the English words 'moon,' 'month,' and 'meal.' Also 'meg-' is the basis for the archaic English 'mickle' and for 'much.' Finally, four roots have implicit reference to position, lay of the landscape, or position in the land:

'klei-' meaning "to lean"
'pele-2' meaning "flat; to spread"
'plak-1' meaning "to be flat"
'ter-' meaning "peg, post, goal" and the combined root form 'ter-mn-' meaning "boundary post"

The root 'klei-' is the source of the English words 'lean' and 'lid.' The root 'pele-2' is the source of the English words 'field' and 'floor.' The root 'plak-1' is the source of the English word 'flake.'

SOUND SHIFTS

There are several shifts in consonants that show up in some of these roots. Where Indo-European and Latin and Greek have the voiced dental mute 'd,' the corresponding West Germanic and Old English form is generally the smooth dental 't.' Thus 'dekm$_o$-' meaning "ten" produced 'decem-' and 'dec-' in the Latin, but in the English we find 'ten,' 'tenth,' and '-teen.' If Indo-European and Latin and Greek have the smooth palatal mute 'k,' the West Germanic and Old English form is generally the rough palatal 'h.' Thus, 'klei-' meaning "to lean" produced an 'hl' form in Old English from which the initial 'h' sound was lost yielding words like 'lean' and 'lid.'

The Indo-European and Latin and Greek smooth labial mute 'p' shows up in West Germanic and Old English as a rough labial 'f.' This sound change is clearly evident with five of the roots: 'apo-' meaning "off, away," which is the source of the English words 'off' and 'after'; 'pau-1' meaning "few, little," which is the source of the English word 'few'; 'per1,' meaning "forward, through," which is the source of the English words 'for,' 'first,' 'far,' and 'forth'; and 'pele-2' meaning "flat; to spread," which is the source of the English words 'floor' and 'field.' Finally, the root 'plak-1' meaning "to be flat" is the source of the English word 'flake.'

The general third rule cited in chapter 7 concerning sibilants is: "Initial s sounds conjoined with following consonants usually show no change in Greek, Latin, and Old English. However, they do frequently disappear." An initial

Indo-European 's' followed by a vowel tended to become a rough breathing or 'h' in classical Greek. This is illustrated by three of the roots. Thus 'sem-[1]' meaning "one, as one, together with," which is the basis for words like 'same' and 'similar,' is found in Greek in the words 'homos' meaning "same" and 'heis' meaning "one." A second root 'sol-' meaning "whole" is found in Greek in the word 'holos' meaning "whole." In the case of the root 'uper' meaning "over," we find combined forms that produced 'super' in Latin. The corresponding word in Greek is 'huper.'

LIST OF ROOTS IN ORDER OF OCCURRENCE

The following list gives the roots in the order in which they are listed in this chapter. Capital letters show the sequence of letters in English words that generally indicate the root to be the origin. In nearly all cases, if one sees the letters of an English word in capital letters, one can infer that it comes from the Indo-European root in the first column. There may also be some English words from the root that do not accord with the general pattern and some English words that fit the pattern but come from a different root.

1. al-[1] beyond, other	ALI other —> ALTER another
2. ambhi-/m(o)bhi- + al-	AMBUL walk
3. apo- off, away	PON, POS, POSIT, [POUND, POST] put; place
4. at- to go	ANNU, ENNI year ANN/ENN
5. dekm$_o$- ten	DECEM-, DEC- ten DEN CENT hundred
6. en in	IN- in; within; into; on; not INTER- between INTRA- within EN- in ENDO-, ENTO- within
7. klei- lean	CLIN, CLIV lean CLIN lean; lie; incline
8. me-[2] measure	MENS measure
9. meg- great	MAGN- great MEGA, MEGALO large
10. ne not	NEG not NIHIL nothing
11. pau-[1] few, little	PAED, PED child; instruction
12a. per[1] forward, through	PROB good PROB test; prove; PROP, PROX near; PROPR, PROPER one's
12b. per-[3] try, risk (press forward)	PROTO- first PERI- around PRO- before PROS- toward; in addition PARA-, PAR- beside; contrary; amiss; astray
13. pele-[2] flat; to spread	PLAS, PLASM, PLAST mold; shape; substance
14. plak-[1] to be flat	PLAC please; appease
15. sek^w-[1] to follow	SEQU, SECUT, SUE, SUIT follow
16. sem-[1] one, as one, together with	SIMIL, SIMUL, SEMBL together; likeness; pretense HOMO- same HOM/HOMO HOMILOS crowd
17. sol- whole	SALU, SALV, SALUT health; safety; greeting HOLO- whole
18a. ter- peg, post, goal	TERM, TERMIN boundary, limit
18b. ter-mn- boundary post	
19. trei- three	TEST witness
20. uper over	SUPER-, SUPRA- above; more than; over HYPER- over; excessively
21.	CHRON time
22.	EQU equal, fair

Physical, Temporal, and Logical Relations

1. al-[1] beyond, other
Latin: ALI other —> ALTER another
Greek: ALLO- other

[1] L ille that, that yonder   [2] L ultra beyond, further, more
[3] L alter one of two, the other, second   [4] L adulterare (adulteratus) commit adultery, corrupt
[5] L alius another, different
[6] Gk allos other
[7] OE other other   [8] OE elles else, otherwise

adulterate: corrupt; render impure by mixing in other elements. [4] L ad (to) + alter other.
alienate: to estrange; make hostile. [5] L alienatio < alius other.
allegory: a story symbolizing moral, political, or religious concepts. [6] Gk allos other + agoreuein speak.
altercation: a heated verbal dispute. [3] L altercatus (pp altercari) dispute < alter other.
altruism: the trait of seeking the welfare of others. [3] Fr altruisme < L alter another.
inalienable: cannot be taken or given away. [5] L in (not) + alien.
ulterior: undisclosed or unexpressed; deliberately hidden. [2] L ultra beyond.
RELATED: alienable alienation altercate altruistic subalternate subalternating
COMMON: adultery [4] alarm [1] alert [1] alfresco [1] alias [5] alibi [5] alien [5] alienage [5] alienist [5] aliquot [5] alligator [1] allo- [6] allodial [3] alter [3] alterable [3] alteration [3] alternate [3] alternative [3] alternation [3] el nino [1] else [8] hoopla [1] langue d'or [1] lariat [1] other [7] parallel [6] ultimate [2] ultra-[2] utterance [2] voila [1]

2. ambhi-/m(o)bhi- + al-
Latin: AMBUL walk
Greek: AMPHI-, AMPH- around

[1] L ambulare (ambulatus) go about, walk
[2] Gk amphi around, about
[3] ON um(b) about around   [4] OE bi by
[5] OE be- on all sides

ambivalence: having conflicting emotions toward a person or thing. [1] L ambi both + valeo be strong.
amble: stroll or walk unhurriedly. [1] L ambulare to walk.
ambulant: able to walk. [1] L ambulo walk about < ambi- around, about + alare to go.
amphitheater: an open semicircular arena for spectators. [2] Gk amphi- around + theatron theater.
ombudsman: mediator of disputes esp. those with government. [3] ON um(b) about around.
preamble: a document's introductory statement. [1] LL preambulo walk before < ambulo.
RELATED: ambulatory amphi-
COMMON: abaft [4] alley [1] alley-oop [1] ambulance [1] ambulate [1] andante [1] be- [5] but [4] by [4] perambulate [1]

3. apo- off, away
Latin: PON, POS, POSIT, [POUND, POST] put; place
Greek: APO-, AP-, APH- away from, from

[1] L post behind, in the rear, afterwards   [2] L ponere (positus) lay, put, place
[3] Gk apo away from, from
[4] OE oef off   [5] OE aeftan behind
[6] OE aefter after, behind
[7] Russ po at, by, next to

apposite: fitting; appropriate.[2] L appositus (pp appono) place by < ad (to) + pono place.
apropos: fitting; appropriate. [2] L ad- + propos < pro- + ponere put.

component: an ingredient or part. [2] L compono < com (together) + pono place.

composition: the elements of; artistic product; (v) combining; creating an art work. [2] L com + pono place.

composure: having calmness and self-possession. [2] L com (together) + pono place.

decomposition: breaking down a material or entity into its parts. [2] L de (apart) + com- + pono place.

depose: remove from power. [2] L depono < de (down) + pono place, lay.

disposition: temperament; an arrangement; a disposal. [2] Fr < L dis (separately) + pono place.

exponent: person representing a position or set of principles. [2] L expono indicate < ex (out) + pono place.

expository: conveying, containing, or pertaining to explaining. [2] OF exposer < L ex forth + pono place.

exposure: openness to influence or view; making public. [2] L ex- + ponere to place.

expound: give a detailed explanation. [2] L expono indicate < ex forth + pono place.

imposition: an unwanted added burden, demand, or tax. [2] Fr imposer < im + poser.

indisposed: slightly ill; disinclined; unwilling. [2] L in- + dis- + ponere to put.

interpose: put between; step between; intervene; stand between. [2] L inter (between) + pono place.

juxtaposition: a placing close together; contiguity. [2] L juxta (near) + positio < positus (pp pono) place.

malapropism: laughable, confused misuse of a like sounding word. [2] Fr < L pro + pono place.

offal: waste animal parts; any waste or trash. [4] OE oef off + fall.

pogrom: organized massacre. [7] Russ po (at, by).

posterity: succeeding generations. [1] L posterior compar. posterus following.

predispose: to influence toward beforehand.[2] L dis- (apart) + ponere to put.

preposterous: ludicrous; absurd. [1] L prae- + posterus coming behind < post behind.

proponent: one who expounds or supports a position or proposition. [2] L propono < pro (before) + pono place.

proposition: statement proposed for acceptance or consideration. [2] L propositio < pro (before) + pono place.

propound: to propose or offer for consideration. [2] L pro (before) + pono place.

repository: a place for storage; a tomb. [2] L re- + ponere to place.

supposition: what is assumed or believed to be true; conjecture or hypothesis. [2] L sub (under) + pono place.

transpose: to reverse or swap places; to interchange. [2] Fr transposer < L trans (over) + pono place.

RELATED: decompose expose exposition impose juxtapose juxtaposed malapropos preposterousness propose suppose transposition

COMMON: aft [5] abaft [5] after [6] apo- [3] compose [2] composing [2] compost [2] compote [2] compound [2] deposit [2] depositor [2] depository [2] depot [2] dispose [2] expose [2] imposing [2] imposter [2] of [4] offhand [4] oft [4] opponent [2] oppose [2] preposterous [1] position [2] positive [2] post [2] post- [1] posterior [1] postpone [2] posture [2] preposition [2] proposal [2] punt [2] puny [1] purpose [2]

4. at- to go
Latin: ANNU, ENNI year ANN/ENN

[1] L annus year

annals: records narrating events by the year of occurrence. [1] L annus year.

annuity: equal monthly or yearly payments for a given period or until death. [1] L annus year.

biennial: every two years. [1] L bi (two) + annus year.

perennial: continuing or enduring through the year or many years. [1] L per + annus year.

superannuate: to retire or incapacitate by age. [1] L super (over) + annus year.

RELATED: annalist annuitant biennium quadrennium superannuated

COMMON: annual [1] anniversary [1] biannual [1] decennium [1] millenial [1] millenium [1] quadrennial [1] semiannual [1] septennial [1] sexennial [1] triennium [1]

5. dekm$_0$- ten
Latin: DECEM-, DEC- ten DEN CENT hundred

[1] L decem ten   [2] L -ginta ten times
[3] L centum hundred
[4] Gk deka ten   [5] Gk hekaton one hundred
[6] OE teotha tenth   [7] OE tien ten
[8] OE -tene -teen

centurion: Roman army commander of 100 men. [3] L centuria group of a hundred < centum hundred.
decimate: to kill one out of every ten; destroy a large proportion of. [1] L decimus tenth < decem ten.
nonagenarian: person in their nineties. [2] L nonaginta ninety.
tithe: contribution of a tenth part of yearly income. [6] OE teotha.
COMMON: cent [3] centenarian [3] centenary [3] centennial [3] century [3] dean [4] deca- [4] decade [4] decagon [4] deci- [1] decimal [1] decemvir [1] decuple [1] dicker [1] dime [1] December [1] decennium [1] dozen [1] octogenarian [2] percent [3] Septuagint [2] sexagenary [2] -teen [8] ten [7] tenth [6]

6. en in
Latin: IN- in; within; into; on; not INTER- between INTRA- within
Greek: EN- in ENDO-, ENTO- within

[1] L in, in- in, into   [2] L intro inward, within
[3] L intra inside, within   [4] L interim meanwhile
[5] L inter, inter- between, among   [6] L intimus innermost
[7] L industrius diligent   [8] L indigere to be in need
[9] L intus within, inside
[10] Gk en, en- in   [11] Gk enteron intestine
[12] Gk eso within

denizen: citizen; occupant. [1] L de (from) + inius (within) < in (in).
enteric: pert. to the intestine. [11] Gk enteron intestine < entos (within).
esoteric: accessible only to people with special knowledge. [12] Gk esoterikos < eso (within).
indigent: very poor; needy. [8] L indu (<in) in + egere lack, want.
intimate: being closely and deeply acquainted. [6] L intimus innermost.
intrinsic: being essential to something. [3] LL intrinsicus inward.
introspection: reflection on one's thoughts and feelings. [2] L intro- (within) + specere look at.
RELATED: indigence intimacy introspect
COMMON: dysentery [11] enter [3] entrails [5] industry [7] interim [4] interior [5] intern [5] internal [5] intestine [9] introduce [2] introit [2] parenthesis [10]

7. klei- lean
Latin: CLIN, CLIV lean
Greek: CLIN lean; lie; incline

[1] L clinare lean, bend   [2] L clivus slope
[3] L cliens dependent, client   [4] L clemens mild, kind
[5] Gk klinein to lean   [6] Gk klima sloping surface
[7] Gk kline bed   [8] Gk klimax ladder
[9] OE hlid cover   [10] OE hlinian to lean
[11] OE hlaedder ladder

acclimate: become accustomed to new conditions. [6] L ad + clima < Gk klima region.

anticlimax: a trivial event following more significant events. [8] L anti- + Gk klimax ladder.

clemency: showing mercy to enemies or lawbreakers. [4] L clemens mild, kind.

declination: a sloping downward. [1] L declinatio < de (down) + clivus sloping.

declivity: downward slope; descending surface of a hill or mountain. [2] L < de (down) + clivus hill.

disinclination: reluctance, unwillingness. [1] L dis + inclinare lean on; incline.

inclement: rainy or stormy; not merciful. [4] L in- + clemens mild, kind.

inclination: a sloping, leaning or bending. [1] L inclinare lean on; incline.

proclivity: natural tendency; propensity (usually in an unfavorable sense). [2] L pro (before) + clivus sloping.

COMMON: client [3] clientele [3] climax [8] climate [6] clime [6] -cline [5] clinic [7] decline [1] incline [1] inclined [1] ladder [11] lean [10] lid [9] recline [1]

8. me-² measure
Latin: MENS measure
Greek: METER, METR

[1] L metiri (mensus) to measure   [2] L mensis month
[3] Gk metron measure [poss. from med-]
[4] OE moel measure, mark, appointed time   [5] OE mona moon
[6] OE monath month

asymmetric: imbalance and dissimilarity of opposite sides. [3] Gk a- + syn (together) + metron measure.

commensurate: equal; corresponding; proportionate. [1] L com (together) + mensuro measure.

incommensurate: not proportionate or adequate. [1] L in (not) + com (together) + mensuro measure.

isometric: equal in dimension; uses pushing against fixed objects. [3] Gk isos equal + metron measure.

metrical: rel. to poetic meter; rel. to measurement. [3] Gk metrikos < metron measure.

symmetry: correspondence of opposite sides about an axis or plane. [3] Gk syn (with) + metron measure.

RELATED: commensurable commensurability incommensurable incommensurability

COMMON: diameter [3] dimension [1] geometry [3] immense [1] immensity [1] measure [1] menstrual [2] menstruate [2] meter [3] -meter [3] metronome [3] -metry [3] meal [4] Monday [5] month [6] moon [5] piecemeal [4] semester [2] trimester [2]

9. meg- great
Latin: MAGN- great
Greek: MEGA, MEGALO large

[1] L magnus great   [2] L maior greater
[3] L maiestas greatness, authority   [4] L magister master, high official
[5] L maximus greatest   [6] L Maia May
[7] Gk megas (megal-) great
[8] OE micel great   [9] Sans maha- (mahat-) great

magisterial: authoritative. [4] L magister < magnus great.

magnanimous: very generous. [1] L magnus great + animus soul.

magnate: a very powerful and influential businessman. [1] L magnus great.

magniloquent: of bombastic, pompous style; vainglorious. [1] L magnus great + loquens (pfp loquor) speak.

magnitude: greatness in size or importance; measure of size. [1] L magnitudo greatness < magnus great.

megalomania: unwarranted belief in one's greatness. [7] Gk megas large + mania < mainomai rage.

omega: last letter. [7] Gk omega.

RELATED: magnifiable magnanimity magnification magnificent magnifier magniloquence majestic megalomaniac

COMMON: maestro [4] magesterial [4] magistrate [4] magnify [1] maharajah [9] maharishi [9] mahout [9] majesty [3] major [2] majority [2] master [4] maxim [5] maximum [5] May [6] mayor [2] megalo- [7] megaphone [7] mickle [8] mister [4] mistress [4] much [8]

10. ne not

Latin: NEG not NIHIL nothing

[1] L ne- not
[3] L non not
[5] L negare (negatus) to deny
[7] Gk a-, an- not
[8] OE ne not; na no

[2] L nihil nothing
[4] L neg- not
[6] L nullus none

[9] OE un- not

abnegate: renounce or abandon. [8] L ab (away) + negare deny.

annul: to declare invalid or void. [6] L ad- + nullus none.

nefarious: infamous due to wickedness. [1] L nefas crime < ne- (not) + fas divine law.

negate: deny or nullify. [5] L negatio < nego deny.

negligible: not worth considering or of significance. [4] L neglegere neglect < ne- (not) + legere choose + -ible.

nescience: ignorance; lack of awareness. [1] L ne- (not) + scire to know.

nihilism: rejection of morality, religion, political institutions. [2] L nihil nothing.

nullify: to wipe out; to void; to counteract the effects of. [6] L nullus none + -ficare, -fy.

renegade: deserter, rebel. [5] L renegare to deny < re + negare deny.

renege: to fail to carry through with a commitment. [5] L renegere to deny < re + negare to deny.

RELATED: nihilist

COMMON: a- [9] an- [7] annihilate [2] annihilation [2] annul [1] deny [5] naught [8] neglect [4] negligee [4] negotiate [4] neither [8] neuter [1] never [8] nice [1] nil [2] no [8] none [8] non- [3] nonplus [3] nor [8] nothing [8] null [1] nullify [1] renegade [5] un- [9]

11. pau-¹ few, little

Latin: PAUCI- few

Greek: PAED, PED child; instruction

[1] L paucus little, few
[3] L pauper poor
[5] L pusillus dim pullus weak
[7] Gk pais (paid-) child
[8] OE feawe few

[2] L parvus little, small; parum little, rarely
[4] L pullus young of an animal, chicken
[6] L puerilis < puer child

[9] OE fola young horse

impoverish: make poor; remove resources of. [3] en- + L pauper poor.

orthopedics: treatment of diseases of bones and joints. [7] Gk orthos correct + pais child.

paucity: scarcity; meagerness. [1] L paucus few.

pauper: very poor person. [3] L pauper poor.

pedant: one attaching great importance to learned trivia. [9] Gk paidagogos < pais child + ago lead.

pediatrics: branch of medicine concerned with the diseases of children. [7] Gk pais child + iatreia healing.

puerile: juvenile; immature. [6] L puerilis < puer child.
pusillanimous: cowardly. [5] L pusillus weak + animus mind.
RELATED: orthopedia pedagogy pedantic pedantry pediatrician
COMMON: encyclopedic [7] few [8] foal [9] paraffin [2] pedo- [7] pony [4] pool [4] poor [3] poultry [4] poverty [3] pullet [4]

12. per¹ forward, through; per-³ try, risk (press forward)

Latin: PROB good —> PROB test; prove PROP, PROX near PROPR, PROPER one's own; individual PRO-, PER-, POR-

Greek: PROTO- first PERI- around PRO- before PROS- toward; in addition PARA-, PAR- beside; contrary; amiss; astray

[1] L per through, for, by
[2] L pro before, for, instead of
[3] L pronus leaning forward
[4] L reciprocus alternating
[5] L prope near, close to
[6] L proximus nearest
[7] L probus upright, good, virtuous
[8] L prae before, in front of
[9] L praesto at hand, ready
[10] L prior former, higher, superior
[11] L privus single, alone
[12] L proprius one's own, particular
[13] L primus first, foremost
[14] L princeps leader, chief, emporer
[15] L pristinus former, original
[16] L periclum trial, danger
[17] L experiri try, learn by trying
[18] Gk proira forward part of the ship
[19] Gk protos first, foremost
[20] Gk pro before, in front, forward
[21] Gk peira trial, attempt
[22] ON fra forward, away from
[23] OE faer danger
[24] OE feorr far
[25] OE for before, instead of
[26] OE for- pref. ind. destruction, exclusion
[27] OE forth forward
[28] OE furthra farther away
[29] OE formest first; forma first
[30] OE fyrst first
[31] OE fore before; beforen before
[32] OE fram forward
[33] OF founir to supply, provide

approbation: approval; commendation. [7] L approbatus (pp approbo) < ad (to) + probus good.
appropriate: to set apart for one's own use; (adj) fit; proper; relevant. [12] L ad (to) + proprius one's own.
approximate: nearly correct but not exact; (v) derive a close value. [6] L ad (to) + (proximus superl.) prope near.
empirical: pert. to experience. [21] Gk en (in) + peira trial.
expertise: knowledge or skill in a specific area. [17] L experiri to try.
expropriate: to deprive of rights or property; to take for public use. [12] L ex- + proprius one's own.
foreshadow: to suggest or indicate beforehand. [31] OE fore (in front) + sceadu shade, shadow.
foresight: know beforehand; provide for the future. [31] OE fore (in front) + sihth something seen.
forward: obstinate; stubbornly resistant. [22] ME fro away, back + ward < Ger.
impropriety: quality of being unsuitable or not conformed to good usage. [12] L in (not) + proprius one's own.
irreproachable: completely blameless; faultless. [5] L in- (not) + re- + prope near + -able.
misappropriate: to wrongly or dishonestly use or take. [12] L ad (to) + proprius one's own.
primeval: from the earliest stages; original. [13] L primus first.
primogeniture: having the eldest son or child inherit the entire estate. [13] L primus first + genitura birth.
primordial: temporally first; original. [13] L primordium origin < primus first + ordiri begin to weave.
pristine: in its pure natural state uncorrupted by man. [15] L pristinus former, original.
probability: likelihood of an event's occurrence or a statement's truth. [7] Fr < L probabilis < probo prove.

probation: a proceeding designed to test the character or qualifications of someone. [7] L probo prove.

probe: to explore; to investigate; (n) action or device used to detect or obtain information. [7] L probare test.

probity: virtue or integrity tested and confirmed; strict honesty. [7] L probitas < probus good.

prodigal: extravagant and wasteful. [2] L prodigus prodigal < prodigere squander < pro- + agere drive.

prone: having a tendency; lying face downward. [3] L pronus leaning forward.

proprietary: subject to exclusive ownership. [12] L proprietas property.

propriety: being in accord with recognized usage or customs; correctness. [12] L proprietas property.

provincial: not sophisticated; narrow in outlook. [2] L provincia province.

prowess: great strength or skill. [2] OF < L pro (before, for, instead of) + esse to be.

proximity: closeness; nearness. [6] L proximus nearest (superl of prope near).

reciprocal: an identical or interchangeable relationship of two or more things. [4] L reciprocus alternating.

reciprocate: to give back in return. [4] L reciprocus alternating.

reproach: criticize or disapprove; (n) blame; disgrace. [5] L re- + prope near.

reprobate: disapprove with strong dislike; sinful; utterly depraved. [7] L re- (again) + probo prove.

reprove: censure; rebuke; express disapproval. [7] L reprobo condemn < re + probo prove.

RELATED: appropriately appropriation appropriateness approximation empiric expropriation improper probable probate probationary prodigality provincialism reproval

COMMON: afford [27] ampersand [1] approach [5] approve [7] approval [7] approvingly [12] before [31] deprive [11] disproof [7] disprove [7] experience [17] experiment [17] expert [17] far [24] fear [23] first [30] for [25] for- [26] fore [31] fore- [31] forefather [31] foremost [29] former [29] forth [27] frame [32] from [32] furnish [33] furniture [33] further [28] imprest [9] improbable [7] improbability [7] improbity [7] improve [2] para- [18] paramount [1] paramour [1] parvenu [1] per [1] per- [1] peril [16] pirate [21] pre- [8] press [9] presto [9] pride [2] priest [20] prim [13] primary [13] primate [13] prime [13] primitive [13] primavera [13] primogenitor [13] primp [13] prince [14] principal [14] principle [14] prior [10] private [11] privilege [11] privy [11] pro [2] pro- [2] proof [7] proper [12] property [12] protein [19] proto- [19] proton [19] proud [2] prove [7] provable [7] proven [7] prow [18] purchase [2] rapprochement [5] reproof [7] veneer [33]

13. pele-² flat; to spread
Greek: PLAS, PLASM, PLAST mold; shape; substance

[1] L planus flat, level, even, plain, clear   [2] L palma palm of the hand

[3] Gk plassein (pfpass peplasmai) to form, mold, spread out; plastos formed; plastikos fit for molding

[4] Gk planasthai to wander

[5] OE feld field   [6] OE flor floor

plainspoken: blunt; frank in speech. [1] L planus + OE sprecan.

plastic: flexible; any of various non-metallic moldable synthetic compounds. [3] Gk plastikos < plasso form.

plasticity: capacity for being molded. [3] Gk plastikos fit for molding < plastos formed < plasso form.

protoplasm: the essential matter of living cells. [3] Gk protos first + plasma molded < plasso form.

COMMON: explain [1] field [5] floor [6] palm [2] piano [1] pianoforte [1] plain [1] plane [1] planet [4] plano- [1] -plasia [3] plasma [3] -plast [3] plaster [3] -plasty [3]

14. plak-¹ to be flat
Latin: PLAC please; appease

[1] L placere (placitus) to please

[2] L supplex suppliant; supplicare (supplicatus) beg

[3] L placare (placatus) to calm

[4] L plancus flat

[5] L plaga net

[6] Gk plax flat, flat land, surface, plate

[7] Gk pelagos sea

[8] ME flake flake

[9] ON flo

archipelago: a group of many islands. [7] Gk pelagos sea.

complacency: contented and lacking preparation for the future. [1] L com (with) + placeo please.

complaisance: desire to please; politeness. [1] L complaceo < com (together) + placeo please.

implacable: not willing to be appeased or to yield. [3] L in (no)t + placates (pp placo) appease.

placate: to turn from a state of enmity or hostility; appease. [3] L placatus (pp placo) appease.

placebo: a pill lacking medical benefit given to give psychological help. [1] L placere (placitus) to please.

placid: quiet or calm. [1] L placere (placitus) to please.

plagiary: passing off another's ideas or writings as one's own. [5] L plagiarius kidnapper < plaga net.

RELATED: complacent placable plagiarism plagiarize please pleasurable pleasure supplicant

COMMON: flake [8] floe [9] placenta [6] placidity [1] placidly [1] plank [4] plea [1] plead [1] pleasant [1] supple [2]

15. sek^w-^{1} to follow

Latin: SEQU, SECUT, SUE, SUIT follow

[1] L sequi (secutus) to follow

[2] L sequester intermediate, mediating

[3] L secundus following, second

[4] L secus along, beside

[5] L sigmen sign, standard

[6] L socius ally, partner

consecutive: following in uninterrupted succession; successive. [1] L con (with) + sequor follow.

consequential: having significance; having important effects; influential. [1] L com- + sequi to follow.

consign: give over to; entrust; assign to. [5] L com- + signare to mark < signum mark.

dissociate: to separate; to break the association. [6] L dis- + sociare to unite.

execute: carry out; perform; make valid. [1] L executor < exequi carry out < ex + sequi follow.

extrinsic: not inherent to something; extraneous. [4] L exter (outside) + secus (alongside).

inconsequential: of little consequence, unimportant, trivial. [1] L con (together) + sequor follow.

non sequitur: a fallacious argument. [1] L it does not follow < non (not) + sequor follow.

obsequious: servile; sycophantic. [1] L obsequiosus < obsequor follow < ob (upon) + sequor follow.

obsequy: a funeral rite; last office for the dead. [1] L ob (upon) + sequor follow.

resign: accept as unavoidable; give up; relinquish. [5] L re- + signare to seal < signum mark, seal.

sectarian: narrow-minded; from the viewpoint of a faction; rel. to a sect. [1] L secta course < sequi to follow.

sequester: set apart or withdraw; take as security. [2] L sequester depositary, trustee.

subsequent: following in time, place, order, or as a result. [1] L sub (after) + sequor follow.

RELATED: obsequies

COMMON: assign [5] associate [6] consecutiveness [1] consequence [1] consequent [1] consociate [6] designate [5] ensue [1] insignia [5] intrinsic [4] persecute [1] prosecute [1] pursue [1] pursuit [1] resigned [5] scarlet [5] seal [5] second [3] sect [1] segue [1] sequel [1] sequence [1] sign [5] sociable [6] social [6] society [6] socio- [6] sue [1] suit [1] suite [1] suitor [1]

16. sem-^{1} one, as one, together with

Latin: SIMIL, SIMUL, SEMBL together; likeness; pretense

Greek: HOMO- same HOM/HOMO HOMILOS crowd

[1] L simul at the same time   [2] L singulus alone, single
[3] L semper always, ever   [4] L simplus simple
[5] L similis like, of the same kind [6] L simplex plain, simple
[7] L miles, milit- soldier
[8] Gk heis one   [9] Gk homos same
[10] Gk heteros one of two, other
[11] ON samr same   [12] ON soemr fitting
[13] OE sum one, a certain one   [14] OE -some -like

assimilate: to absorb, incorporate. [5] L ad (to) + similis like.

dissemble: to conceal as by false appearance; pretend; feign. [5] L dissimulo < dis (apart) + similis (like).

dissimulation: concealment or disguising of actual intentions and feelings. [5] L dis + simulare to simulate.

semblance: a show without reality; pretense; likeness; image. [5] Fr sembler < L simulo < similis similar.

simile: comparison using "as" or "like." [5] L similis similar.

similitude: similarity; a rhetorical figure using likeness; metaphor. [5] Fr < L similitudo likeness.

simulate: to assume the form or appearance without the reality. [5] L simulatus (pp simulo) < similis similar.

anomaly: irregularity; deviation from the normal rule. [9] Gk an (not) + homalos even < homos same.

heterodox: disagreeing with church doctrines or common beliefs. [10] Gk hetero- (other) + doxa opinion.

heterogeneous: composed of dissimilar elements or parts. [10] Gk hetero- (other) + genos kind.

homogeneous: of the same composition or structure; of same kind. [9] Gk homos same + genos race.

militate: to operate against. [7] L militatus < miles soldier.

seemly: behavior that is proper and suitable; handsome. [12] ON saemr (fitting).

simplistic: superficial; ignoring important complexities. [4] L simplus simple.

singular: designating only one; one of a kind; being remarkable. [2] L singulus single.

RELATED: anomalous assimilation dissimulate homogenize simulation simulator verisimilar

COMMON: assemblage [1] assemble [1] assembly [1] disassemble [1] dissimilar [5] dissimilarity [5] ensemble [1] facsimile [5] hetero- [10] homeo- [9] homo- [9] homonym [9] hyphen [8] militant [7] resemblance [5] resemble [5] same [11] seem [12] semblable [5] semblably [5] semble [5] semblative [5] sempiternal [3] similar [5] similarity [1] simple [4] simplicity [6] simultaneity [1] simultaneous [1] single [2] some [13] -some [14]

17. sol- whole
Latin: SALU, SALV, SALUT health; safety; greeting
Greek: HOLO- whole

[1] L solidus solid   [2] L sollus whole, entire, unbroken
[3] L sollemnis solemn, customary   [4] L salus health, welfare
[5] L salvus whole, safe, healthy
[6] Gk holos whole

catholic: universal. [6] Gk katholikos universal.

consolidation: the process of combining into a whole, securing, or merging together. [1] L com- + solidus solid.

holocaust: wholesale destruction of a population. [6] Gk holos whole + kaustos burnt.

insalubrious: not conducive to health; not healthful; not wholesome. [4] L in- + salubris < salus health.

insouciant: nonchalant; carefree lack of concern. [2] OF in- (not) + soucier to trouble < L sollicitus troubled.

salubrious: conducive to health; healthful; wholesome. [4] L salubris < salus health.

salutary: producing a healthful condition by correcting evil or promoting good. [4] L salutaris < salus health.

salutation: a greeting. [4] L saluto salute.

salvage: to save from destruction; to restore for use; (n) things so rescued or restored. [5] L salvus safe.

salvation: preservation from impending evil; deliverance from penalty of sin. [5] LL salvatio < salvo save.

salvo: simultaneous discharge of guns or projectiles; a verbal outburst. [5] L salvus safe.

solemnity: soberness and seriousness. [3] L sollemnis solemn, customary.

solicitous: evidencing diligent concern for someone. [2] L sollus entire + citus (pfp ciere) set in motion.

RELATED: consolidate salutatorian salutatory salvable salvage solicit

COMMON: holo- [6] safe [5] salute [4] save [5] solder [1] soldier [1] solemn [3] solid [1] sou [1]

18. ter- peg, post, goal / ter-mn- boundary post
Latin: TERM, TERMIN boundary, limit

[1] L terminus boundary, limit

determination: resolve; the act of reaching a decision. [1] L de + termino < terminus boundary.

determinism: belief all voluntary actions are decided by antecedent causes. [1] L de + terminus boundary.

extermination: the process of destroying entirely; annihilation. [1] L ex (out) + terminus boundary.

indeterminate: cannot be made adequately definite. [1] L in (not) + de- + termino < terminus boundary.

interminable: without limit or end; continuing for a very long time. [1] L in (not) + terminus boundary.

predetermine: to fix or decide beforehand. [1] L pre- + de + termino < terminus boundary.

terminate: put an end to or stop to; bring to completion; finish. [1] L terminus boundary.

terminology: the words disciplines use to represent their concepts. [1] L terminus boundary + Gk logos word.

terminus: the final point or goal; end. [1] L termini.

RELATED: determinate determinative determinable determine determinedly determinist exterminable exterminate indeterminism indeterminist interminably terminable termination

COMMON: term [1] terminal [1]

19. trei- three
Latin: TEST witness
Greek: TRI- three

[1] L tres three	[2] L tertius third
[3] L tri- three	[4] L testis witness
[5] L trini three each	[6] L tribuere to pay
[7] Gk tri- three	[8] Gk trias number three
[9] OE thrie three	[10] OE thridda third

attest: bear witness to. [4] L ad (to) + testis witness.

attribute: ascribe; quality or characteristic. [3] L ad + tribuere < tribus tribe.

contest: (v) to dispute; to contend; (n) a competition. [4] L com- + testis witness.

detestable: hated; abhorred; odious. [4] OF detestable < L de (against) + testis witness.

retribution: a punishment or paying back for evil rendered. [6] L retribuere pay back < re- + tribuere grant.

tertiary: third in order or rank. [2] L tertius third.

testify: declare under oath or affirm positively to establish the facts. [4] L testis witness + facio make.

tribute: an acknowledgment of gratitude or achievement; payment made for protection. [6] L tribuere to pay.

RELATED: attestation attribution attributive detest detestation Protestant protestation protester

COMMON: protest [4] testament [4] testicle [4] testimonial [4] testimony [4] third [10] thirteen [9] thirty [9] three [9] thrice [9] trey [1] tri- [3, 7] triad [8] tribe [3] trinity [5] trio [3] triple [3]

20. uper over
Latin: SUPER-, SUPRA- above; more than; over
Greek: HYPER- over; excessively

[1] L super, super- above, over   [2] L superbus superior, excellent, arrogant
[3] L summus highest, topmost   [4] L supra above, beyond
[5] Gk huper over

consummate: to complete. [3] L con (together) + summa sum.
insuperable: insurmountable; cannot be overcome. [1] L in- (not) + superabilis.
sovereign: independent; having supreme power; (n) person or state with supreme power. [1] L super (above).
summation: addition; a sum; conclusion of a speech or argument. [3] L summus highest, topmost.
supercilious: disdaining others; proud; haughty. [1] L superciliosus < super (over) + cilium eyelid.
superficial: near the surface; shallow; cursory; hasty. [1] L superficies < super (over) + facies face.
superfluous: being more than needed; not needed; extra. [1] L superfluus < super (over) + fluo flow.
superimpose: to place something on or over something else. [1] L super + in- (on) + ponere to place.
supervene: follow closely upon, but as extraneous or additional. [1] L super (over) + venio come.
RELATED: superable superciliousness
COMMON: hyper- [5] soprano [4] supra- [4] somersault [4] sum [3] summit [3] super- [1] superb [2] superior [1] supreme [1] supremo [1] sur- [1] sirloin [1]

21. Greek: CHRON time

[1] Gk khronos time

anachronistic: out of date, attributed to the wrong time period. [1] Gk ana (back) + chronos time.
chronic: continuing for a long time; recurring frequently. [1] Gk khronikos of time < khronos time.
chronicle: a narrative of historical events in order of occurrence. [1] Gk khronika annals.
chronology: ordering past events at the correct time of occurrence. [1] Gk chronos time + logos study.
synchronize: assign the same date or time; coordinate clocks. [1] Gk syn (together) + chronos time.
RELATED: anachronism chronological synchronous synchronism

22. Latin: EQU equal, fair

[1] L aequus equal, level; fair

equanimity: calm temper. [1] L aequus equal + animus mind.
equinox: time the sun crosses the equator making day and night equal. [1] L aequus equal + nox night.
equitable: characterized by fairness and just dealing; impartial. [1] L aequitas < aequus equal.
equity: fairness or impartiality; equal justice. [1] Fr equite < L aequitas < aequus equal.
equivocal: open to several interpretations; unclear; uncertain. [1] L aequus equal + vox voice.
equivocate: deceiving or being indefinite with ambiguous language. [1] L aequus equal + vox voice.
iniquity: sin, wickedness. [1] L iniquitas < in (not) + aequus equal.
unequivocal: understandable in only one way; distinct; plain. [1] L aequus equal + vox voice.
RELATED: equableness equinoctial equivocation iniquitous
COMMON: equal [1] equilibrium [1] equality [1] equalize [1] equate [1] equation [1] equator [1] equidistant [1] equivalent [1] inequality [1] unequal [1]

CHAPTER 11

Roots Referring to Actions of Nature and Natural Effects

The second category of roots, covered in this chapter, is primarily concerned with actions of nature or the effects of nature. Twelve roots are placed in this category. Five refer to light, brightness, shining, or burning:

'as-' meaning "burn, glow"
'bha-[1]' meaning "shine"
'bhel-[1]' meaning "shine, flash, burn"
'leuk-' meaning "light, brightness"
'merph-' meaning "form; glitter"

The root 'as-' meaning "burn, glow" is the source of the word 'ash.' The root 'bha-[1]' meaning "shine" is the source of the English words 'beacon' and 'beckon.' The root 'bhel-[1]' meaning "shine, flash, burn" is the source of the English words including 'blaze,' 'bleach,' 'blond,' 'blush,' 'blanch,' 'blue,' 'blind,' and 'black.' The root 'leuk-' meaning "light, brightness" is the source of the English word 'light.' Three roots refer to swelling or flowing:

'bhleu-' meaning "swell, overflow"
'teue-[2]' meaning "to swell"
'wleik-' meaning "flow, run"

The root 'bhleu-' meaning "swell, overflow" is the source of the English word 'bloat.' The root 'teue-[2]' meaning "to swell" is the source of the English words 'thigh,' 'thumb,' 'thimble,' and 'thousand.' Four other roots refer to natural forces or features in some other manner:

'bhel-[3]' meaning "thrive, bloom"
'bhreg-' meaning "break"
'bhreue-' meaning "boil, bubble"
'men-[2]' meaning "project"

The root 'bhel-[3]' meaning "thrive, bloom" is the source of the English words 'bloom,' 'blossom,' and 'blade.' The root 'bhreg-' meaning "break" is the source of the English words 'break' and 'breach.' The root 'bhreue-' meaning "boil, bubble" is the source of the English words 'brew,' 'broth,' and 'bread.' The root 'men-[2]' meaning "project" is the source of the English word 'mouth.'

SOUND SHIFTS

The Indo-European rough labial 'bh' sound appears in Latin and Greek as an 'f' sound (represented as 'ph' in English for words derived from Greek). The corresponding West Germanic and Old English form is generally the voiced labial 'b.' Thus 'bha-¹' meaning "shine" produced 'phaino' in the Greek, but in the English we find 'bea-con' and 'beckon.' The root 'bhel-¹' meaning "shine, flash, burn" yielded 'fulgare,' "to flash, shine," and 'flagrare,' "to blaze," in the Latin and 'phlegein,' "to burn," in Greek. It is the source of the English words including 'blaze,' 'bleach,' 'blond,' 'blush,' 'blanch,' 'blue,' 'blind,' and 'black.' The root 'bhel-³' meaning "thrive, bloom" produced 'folium' or "leaf" in Latin and 'phullon' or "leaf" in Greek and the words 'bloom,' 'blossom,' and 'blade' in English. Another root 'bhleu-' meaning "swell, overflow" is the source of the Latin verb 'fluere,' "to flow." It is also the source of the English word 'bloat.' The root 'bhreg-' meaning "break" is the Indo-European basis for the Latin verb 'frangere' "to break" and is also the source of the English words 'break' and 'breach.' Finally, the root 'bhreue-' meaning "boil, bubble" is the source of the Latin verb 'fervere,' "to be boiling or fermenting," and the English words 'brew,' 'broth,' and 'bread.'

If Indo-European, Latin, and Greek have a smooth dental mute 't,' the corresponding West Germanic and Old English form will be a rough dental 'th.' Thus 'teue-²' meaning "to swell" produced the Latin verb 'tumere' "to swell, be proud," but in the English we find the words 'thigh,' 'thumb,' 'thimble,' and 'thousand.' Where Indo-European and Latin and Greek have the smooth palatal mute 'k,' the corresponding West Germanic and Old English form is generally the rough palatal 'h.' Thus, 'leuk-' meaning "light, brightness" produced 'leoht' and 'liht' meaning "light" in Old English. These were the source of the English word 'light.'

The Indo-European, Latin, and Greek voiced palatal mute 'g' shows up in West Germanic and Old English as a smooth palatal 'k.' For example, the root 'bhreg-' meaning "break" is the source of the Latin verb 'frangere' "to break" and is also the source of the English words 'break' and 'breach.'

LIST OF ROOTS IN ORDER OF OCCURRENCE

The following list gives the roots in order of their occurrence in this chapter. Of course, the capital letters for the sequence of letters in English words generally indicates the root to be the origin. In nearly all cases, if one sees the letters in caps in an English word, one can infer that it comes from the Indo-European root in the first column. There may also be some English words from the root that do not accord with the general pattern and some English words that fit the pattern but come from a different root.

23. as- burn, glow	ARD, ARS burn
24. bha-¹ shine	PHAN, PHEN show; appear; shine PHOT, PHOS light
25. bhel-¹ shine, flash, burn	FULG shine; flash —> FULMIN flash; explode
26. bhel-³ thrive, bloom	FLOR flower
27. bhleu- swell, overflow	FLU, FLUCT, FLUX flow
28. bhreg- break	FRANG, FRING, FRAG, FRACT break FRAG/FRACT
29. bhreue- boil, bubble	FERV boil; bubble
30. leuk- light, brightness	LUC light LUSTR light up; shine LUMEN, LUMIN light; source of light
31. men-² project	MIN, MEN, MOUNT project; threaten MON mountain
32. merph- form; glitter	FORM shape MORPH form
33. teue-² to swell	TUM swell —> TUBER swelling, hump
34. wleik- flow, run	LIQU liquid

Actions of Nature and Effects

23. as- burn, glow
Latin: ARD, ARS burn

[1] L arere to be dry   [2] L ardere burn, be on fire
[3] Gk azaleos dry
[4] OE aesce ash

ardent: passionate; devoted. [2] L ardens (pfp ardere) to burn.
arid: dry, barren; without interest, profitless; boring. [1] L aridus < areo be dry.
ashen: very pale; composed of ashes. [4] OE aesce (ash).
COMMON: arson [1] ash [4] azalea [3]

24. bha-¹ shine
Greek: PHAN, PHEN show; appear; shine   PHOT, PHOS light

[1] LL bandum banner
[2] Gk phainein (fut phano; prpart phainomenon)
    to bring to light; phasis an appearance
[3] Gk phos (phot) light
[4] OE beacen beacon   [5] OE becnan make a sign
[6] OE berie berry   [7] OF boue < Ger

diaphanous: translucent; filmy. [2] Gk dia (through) + phaino show.
epiphany: appearance of the supernatural; moment of insight. [2] Gk epiphaneia < epi (upon) + phaino show.
phenomenon: appraisable, evident, fact or experience. [2] Gk phainomenon (pp phaino) show.
photogenic: artistically suitable for being photographed. [3] Gk photos light + gen produce.
photosynthesis: light induced chemical reaction in plants. [3] Gk photos light + syn (together) + tithemi put.
sycophant: servile flatterer; parasite; informer; accuser. [2] Gk sykophantes < sykon fig + phaino show.
RELATED: phototropic
COMMON: banner [1] banneret [1] beacon [4] beckon [5] berry [6] bouyant [7] fancy [2] mulberry [6] phantom
[2] phenomenal [2] phosphorescence [3] phosphorescent [3] phosphorus [3] photocopy [3] photoelectric [3]
photofinish [3] photograph [3] photographer [3] photometer [3] photosensitive [3] standard [1]

25. bhel-¹ shine, flash, burn
Latin: FULG shine; flash —> FULMIN flash; explode FLAGR blaze FLAM flame

[1] L fulgere flash, shine; fulgur lightening
[2] L fulmen lightning, thunderbolt; fulminare to lighten
[3] L flagrare (pfp flagrans) to blaze   [4] L flamma a flame
[5] Gk phlegein to burn; phlegmatikos abounding in phlegm
[6] ON bleikr shining, white
[7] OF blanc white
[8] OF bleu blue   [9] OF blond blond
[10] OE blencan deceive   [11] OE blaecan to bleach
[12] OE blaese torch, blazing fire [13] OE blind blind
[14] OE blyscan to glow red   [15] OE blaec black

blanch: bleach, whiten, scald [7] OF blanchir (whiten) < Ger.
bleak gloomy; depressing; cold; barren. [6] ON bleikr (white) < Ger.
carte blanche: unrestricted authority. [7] OF carte card + blanc white.

conflagration: a major destructive fire. [3] L com- + flagrare to burn.

emblazon: to adorn or mark prominently. [12] em- + OE blaese torch, blazing fire.

flagrant: conspicuously offensive. [3] L flagrare to burn.

flamboyant: elaborate; colorful; ostentatious; showy. [4] Fr < L flamma a flame.

fulminate: to cause to explode; issue as a threat. [2] L fulminatus (pp fulmino) < fulgeo flash.

inflame: intensify passions. [4] L in- (in) + flammare set on fire < flamma flame.

inflammable: easily ignited and burning quickly. [4] L in- (in) + flammare set on fire < flamma flame.

phlegmatic: calm, even-keeled, unemotional. [5] Gk phlegmatikos < phlegein to burn.

RELATED: conflagrant effulgent fulmination refulgent

COMMON: black [15] blank [7] blanket [7] blaze [12] bleach [11] blind [13] blindfold [13] blond [9] blue [8] blush [14] chemise [4] flambe [4] flame [4] flamingo [4] flammable [4] phlegm [5] purblind [13]

26. bhel-³ thrive, bloom

Latin: FLOR flower FOL

Greek: PHYLL, PHYLLO leaf

[1] L folium leaf

[2] L flos (flor) flower

[3] Gk phullon leaf

[4] ON blom flower, blossom

[5] OE blaed leaf, blade

[6] OE blostm, blostma flower, blossom

flora: the plants that grow in a region. [2] L floridus < flos flower.

foil: a contrast that highlights differences. [1] L folium leaf.

florid: having a bright color; of a lively reddish hue; blooming; flowery. [2] L floridus < flos flower.

flourish: to be thriving or prosperous; to be at one's best. [2] L floresco < floreo blossom.

foliage: the leaves of plants. [1] LL foliates (pp folio) put forth leaves < folium leaf.

portfolio: carrying case; group of investments. [1] L portare to carry + foglio sheet < folium leaf.

RELATED: efflorescence florescent foliaceous

COMMON: blade [5] bloom [4] blossom [6] cauliflower [2] deflower [2] defoliate [1] floral [2] florescence [2] floret [2] Florida [2] florist [2] -florous [2] flour [2] flower [2] flowery [2] folio [1] -phyll [3]

27. bhleu- swell, well up, overflow

Latin: FLU, FLUCT, FLUX flow

[1] L fluere (fluxus; pfp fluens) to flow; -fluus flowing;
    fluctuare (fluctuatus) move like a wave, waver

[2] L flumen river

[3] ON blautr soft, wet

[4] ME blustren rush violently

affluent: wealthy; plentiful. [1] L ad + fluo flow.

bloated: swollen; inflated; (n) an excess. [3] ON blautr (soft, soaked).

bluster: to utter noisily and boisterously; boisterous talk or swagger. [4] ME blustren (rush violently).

confluence: the place where streams meet; a gathering, mingling. [1] L con (together) + fluo flow.

effluence: a flowing out. [1] L ex (out) + fluo flow.

fluctuate: to rise and fall. [1] L fluctuates (pp fluctuo) < fluctus wave.

fluency: easy flow of speech or writing; smoothness. [1] L fluens (pfp fluo) flow.

flux: a flowing; lines of force. [1] L fluo flow.

influx: a continuous flowing in. [1] L influxus < influo flow in < in (in) + fluo flow.

mellifluous: flowing smoothly and sweetly like honey. [1] L mel honey + fluus flowing.

superfluous: being more than needed; not needed; extra. [1] L superfluus < super (over) + fluo flow.

RELATED: affluence blusterous confluent effluent fluctuation fluency fluent frailty

COMMON: afflux [1] bloat [3] efflux [1] fluid [1] flume [2] fluoride [1] flush [1] fluvial [1] influence [1] influenza [1]

28. bhreg- break
Latin: FRANG, FRING, FRAG, FRACT break FRAG/FRACT

[1] L frangere (fractus; pfp frangens) break   [2] L suffragium < suffragari to express support

[3] OE brecan break   [4] OE brec a breaking

breach: an opening; a gap; a violation of an obligation; an estrangement. [4] OE brec (a breaking).

diffraction: breakup of light, sound, or electric waves into interference bands. [1] L dis (priv) + frango break.

fractious: disposed to rebel; restive; unruly. [1] L frango break.

fragmentary: composed of fragments; broken; incomplete. [1] Fr < L fragmentum fragment < frango break.

infraction: the act of breaking or violating. [1] L infractus < infringo break < in (in) + frango break.

infringe: to violate; encroach upon property, rights, or privileges. [1] L infringo break < in (in) + frango break.

refract: to deflect the path of light or sound by changing medium density. [1] L re (back) + frango break.

refractory: disobedient; obstinate; resisting normal methods of reduction. [1] L re (back) + frango break.

suffragist: one seeking voting rights expansion esp. to women. [2] L suffragium < suffragari express support.

RELATED: diffract fragment fragmentation infringement refraction refractive suffrage

COMMON: break [3] defray [1] fractal [1] fraction [1] fracture [1] fragile [1] frail [1] refrain [1] sassafras [1]

29. bhreue- boil, bubble
Latin: FERV boil; bubble

[1] VulgL brodum broth   [2] L fermentum yeast

[3] L fervere (pfp fervens) be boiling or fermenting;
    fervidus hot; fervor heat

[4] OE breowan to brew   [5] OE beorma yeast

[6] OE bread bread

effervescence: quality of bubbling; liveliness. [3] L effervesceo boil up < ex (out) + ferveo boil.

embroil: to involve in a squabble or argument. [1] OF em- en- + brouiller to confuse < Ger breu brew.

ferment: (n) a state of unrest or agitation; (v) convert plant sugar to alcohol. [2] L fermentum yeast.

fervent: showing warmth of feeling; ardent. [3] L ferveo boil.

fervor: strong feeling; ardor; passion. [3] OF < L fervor < ferveo boil.

imbroglio: complicated, difficult situation or entanglement. [1] L in- (in) + brogliare to mix < Ger breu brew.

RELATED: effervesce effervescent fervency fervently fervescent fervid

COMMON: barm [5] barmy [5] bread [6] brew [4] broil [1] ferment [2]

30. leuk- light, brightness
Latin: LUC light LUSTR light up; shine LUMEN, LUMIN light; source of light
Greek: LEUCO- white

[1] L lux light

[2] L lumen light, opening

[3] L luna moon

[4] L lustrum purification

[5] L lustrare to purify, illuminate

[6] L lucere (pfp lucens) to shine; lucidus bright; clear

[7] Gk leukos clear, white

[8] OE leoht, liht light

elucidate: to throw light upon; to clear up. [6] L e (out) + lucidus < luceo shine.

lackluster: dull, average, weak in effort and thought. [4] MD lac fault + L lustrum purification.

limn: to draw or paint as a picture; delineate. [2] ME limnen for enluminen < L illumino < lumen light.

lucent: dispensing light; clear. [6] L lucens < lucere to shine.

lucid: clear. [6] L lucidus < luceo shine.

luminary: body that gives light; person who enlightens and makes subjects clear. [2] L lumen < luceo shine.

luminous: giving or emitting light; full of light. [2] L lumen light < luceo shine.

lunar: rel. to the moon. [3] L luna moon.

luster: brilliancy of beauty, character, or achievements; sheen; splendor. [6] Fr lustre < L luceo shine.

lustration: a purification. [4] L lustrum purification.

pellucid: permitting some passage of light; translucent; transparent; clear. [6] L per (through) + luceo shine.

translucent: allowing diffused light to pass showing indistinct objects. [6] L trans (through) + luceo shine.

RELATED: limner limning lucidity lucubrator lucubratory luminescent lustrous nonluminous

COMMON: illuminate [2] illumination [2] illumine [2] illustrate [5] leuko- [7] light [8] Lucifer [1] lunatic [3] nonluminous [2]

31. men-² project

Latin: MIN, MEN, MOUNT project; threaten MON mountain

[1] L mentum chin

[2] L minae projecting points, threats; minere overhang

[3] L minor (minatus) project, jut, threaten

[4] L mons (mont-) mountain

[5] OE muth mouth

amenable: willing and open to follow advice or authority. [2] L minae threats.

demean: to debase. [3] Fr demener < de (down) + L minor menace.

eminent: distinguished; prominent; noteworthy. [2] L ex- + minere to jut out.

imminent: close at hand; impending; threatening. [3] L immineo overhang < in (on) + mineo project.

insurmountable: cannot be overcome; not climbable. [4] L in- (not) + super (over) + mons mountain.

mien: manner; bearing; appearance. [2] Fr mine < Ital mina < menare conduct < minae threats.

minatory: threatening as with destruction or punishment. [3] L minatus (pp minor) threaten.

paramount: of greatest importance, rank, or power. [4] L per- + amount (above) < ad- (to) + mons hill.

pre-eminent: greater than all others in a class. [3] OF < L prae (before) + emineo stand forth.

prominent: jutting out; conspicuous in position, character, or importance. [3] OF < L promineo project.

promontory: a high point of land or projection into the sea. [4] L pro (forth) + mons mountain.

surmount: to overcome; to climb. [4] L super (over) + mons mountain.

tantamount: equivalent to. [4] L tantum (so) + amunter amount to.

COMMON: amount [4] menace [2] mental [1] montage [4] mount [4] mountain [4] mouth [5] promenade [2]

32. merphe- form, glitter

Latin: FORM shape Greek: MORPH form

[1] L forma shape, contour, appearance
[2] Gk morphe form, appearance

amorphous: without form; vague; characterless. [2] Gk a (priv.) + morphe form.
anthropomorphic: ascribing human attributes to non-human things. [2] Gk anthropos man + morphos form.
conformist: one who agrees and complies with rules and customs. [1] L con (together) + forma form.
formal: rel. to shape or structure; done in or following prescribed procedures. [1] L forma shape.
formality: an established procedure, rule, or custom. [1] L forma shape.
formation: development to final shape or structure; an arrangement esp. of persons. [1] L forma shape.
formative: causing development, growth, or transformation. [1] L forma shape.
formulate: compose a set of symbols or words to direct procedures. [1] L formula < forma shape.
metamorphosis: a transformation in form or substance. [2] Gk metamorphosis < meta (over) + morphe form.
transformation: a distinct and marked change in appearance, nature, or function. [1] L trans + forma shape.
uniformity: characterized by sameness and lack of variation. [1] L uni (one) + forma shape.
RELATED: anthropomorphize conform conformity formalize isomorphic isomorphous metamorphose transform transformer transformative uniform
COMMON: deform [1] form [1] -form [1] format [1] formless [1] formula [1] inform [1] informal [1] information [1] -morph [2] morphic [2] morpho- [2] -morphous [2] multiform [1] platform [1] reform [1] reformation [1]

33. teue-² to swell
Latin: TUM swell —> TUBER swelling, hump
Greek: SOMA, SOMAT body

[1] L tumere to swell, be swollen, be proud; tumescere
(pfp tumescens) to begin to swell
[2] L tuber lump, swelling
[3] L -turare to stop up
[4] L turgeo to swell
[5] Gk turos cheese
[6] Gk soma body
[7] Gk tombos barrow, tomb
[8] OE theoh thigh
[9] OE thusand thousand
[10] OE thuma thumb

obturate: close off or obstruct. [3] L obturare < ob- + turare to stop up.
protuberance: something that protrudes; a bulging. [2] L pro (forth) + tuber swelling.
somatic: concerning or affecting the body. [6] Gk somatikos < soma body.
tuber: a short thickened portion of an underground stem. [2] L tuber a swelling.
tumescent: becoming tumid; forming a tumor. [1] L tumesens (pfp tumesco) swell up < tumeo swell.
tumid: swollen; enlarged; protuberant; bombastic. [1] L tumidus swollen.
tumultuous: noisy and disorderly as of a great crowd. [1] L tumultus commotion.
turgid: bloated; swollen; unduly complex or ornamented (in expression). [4] L turgeo swell.
RELATED: obturation protuberant protuberate tumult
COMMON: butter [5] thigh [8] thimble [10] thousand [9] thumb [10] tomb [7] truffle [1] tuberculosis [2] tumor [1]

34. wleik- to flow, run
Latin: LIQU liquid

[1] L liquere be fluid, liquid; liquescens (pfp liquescere) to become fluid, melt
[2] L prolixus wide, long, stretched out

liquidate: to settle the liabilities of an estate or business and apportion the assets. [1] L liqueo be fluid.
liquidity: being liquid; immediate convertibility of financial assets to cash. [1] L liqueo be fluid.
prolix: indulging in long and winded discourse; tedious. [2] L prolixus stretched out < liqueo be clear.
RELATED: liquefaction prolixious prolixity prolixly prolixness
COMMON: liquefy [1] liquid [1] liquidating [1] liquidation [1] liquor [1]

CHAPTER 12

Roots Naming Objects and Qualities

The third category of roots, covered in this chapter, refers directly to objects or to qualities. Twelve roots are placed in this category. Six roots refer to various objects:

'ge' meaning "the earth"
'kʷrep-' meaning "body, form, appearance"
'man-²' meaning "hand"
'ped-¹' meaning "foot"
'wed-¹' meaning "water, wet"
'CALC, CULC' meaning "heel; pebble" or 'CALC' meaning "lime"

The root 'ge' meaning "the earth" is the source of the Greek word 'ge' for "earth." The second of the six, the root 'kʷrep-' meaning "body, form, appearance," is the source of the Latin word 'corpus' meaning "body" and the English word 'midriff.' The root 'man-²' meaning "hand" is the source of the Latin word 'manus' meaning "hand."

The fourth root, 'ped-¹' meaning "foot," is the source of the Latin word 'pes (ped-)' meaning "foot," the Greek 'pous (pod-)' meaning "foot," and the English words 'foot' and 'fetter.' The fifth root, 'wed-¹' meaning "water, wet," is the source of the Latin 'unda' meaning "wave," the Greek 'hudor' meaning "water," and the English words 'water,' 'wet,' 'wash,' 'winter,' and 'otter.' Finally, 'CALC, CULC' means "heel; pebble; lime" and is found in the Latin word 'calx' for "heel; pebble; lime." Fifteen roots designate attributes:

'ak-' meaning "sharp"
'andho-' meaning "blind, dark"
'del-¹' meaning "long"
'deru-' meaning "hard"
'gʷere-²' meaning "heavy"
'kar-¹' meaning "hard"
'legʷh-' meaning "light"
'lei-/slei-' meaning "slimy"
'mel-¹' meaning "soft"
'meu-' meaning "moist, washed"
'mregh-u-' meaning "short"
'newo-' meaning "new"
'reudh-¹' meaning "red"
'swad-' meaning "sweet"
'sp(h)er-' meaning "twitch, fidget, jerk"

The root 'ak-' meaning "sharp" is the source of the Latin 'acer' meaning "sharp," the Greek 'akme' meaning "point" and 'oxus' meaning "sharp," and the English word 'edge.' The root 'andho-' meaning "blind, dark" is the source of the Latin 'umbra' meaning "shadow."

The root 'del-[1]' meaning "long" is the source of the Latin 'longus' meaning "long" and the English words 'long,' 'along,' 'belong,' 'length,' and 'Lent.' Also 'deru-' meaning "hard" is the source of the Latin 'durus' meaning "hard," the Greek 'dendron' meaning "tree," and the English words 'trust,' 'tree,' 'true,' 'truth,' 'tray,' 'truce,' 'trough,' 'trim,' and 'tar.' The root 'gʷere-[2]' means "heavy" and is the source of the Latin word 'gravis' meaning "heavy" and the Greek 'barus' meaning "heavy." The root 'kar-[1]' meaning "hard" is the source of the Latin 'carina' meaning "ship's keel" and 'cancer' meaning "crab," the Greek 'kratos' meaning "strength or power," and the English word 'hard.' The root 'legʷh-' meaning "light" is the source of the Latin 'levis' meaning "light" and the English words 'light' and 'lighter.' The root 'lei-/slei-' meaning "slimy" is the source of the Latin verb 'linere' meaning "to anoint" and the English words 'slime,' 'slip,' 'slippery,' 'slight,' 'slick,' 'lime,' and 'loam.'

The root 'mel-[1]' meaning "soft" is the source of the Latin 'mollis' meaning "soft," Greek 'malakos' meaning "soft," and the English words 'melt,' 'malt,' 'mild,' 'milt,' and 'mulch.' Also 'meu-' means "moist, washed" and is the source of Latin 'mundus' meaning "world" and Greek 'kosmos' meaning "order, world." The root 'mregh-u-' meaning "short" is the source of the Latin 'brevis' meaning "short," Greek 'brakhion' meaning "shorter," and the English word 'merry.'

The root 'newo-' meaning "new" is the source of the Latin 'novus' meaning "new," Greek 'neos' meaning "new," and the English word 'new.' The root 'reudh-[1]' meaning "red" is the source of the Latin 'ruber' meaning "red" and 'robur' meaning "red oak" and the English words 'red,' 'ruddy,' and 'rust.' The root 'swad-' meaning "sweet" is the source of Latin 'suavis' meaning "delightful" and Greek 'hedone' meaning "pleasure." Finally, 'sp(h)er-' meaning "twitch, fidget, jerk" is the source of the Latin adjective 'asper' meaning "rough."

SOUND SHIFTS

The Indo-European, Latin, and Greek smooth palatal mute 'k' has a corresponding West Germanic and Old English rough palatal 'h.' Two of the roots covered in this chapter show this phenomenon. The root 'kʷrep-' meaning "body, form, appearance" is the source of the Old English word 'hrif' meaning "belly" where the initial k changes to an h. The Old English word is the source of the English word 'midriff.' This phenomenon is also clearly evident by the root 'kar-[1]' meaning "hard," which serves as the source of the English word 'hard.'

When Indo-European and Latin and Greek have a smooth labial mute 'p,' the corresponding West Germanic and Old English form is generally the rough labial 'f.' This sound change is clearly evident with two of the roots: the root 'kʷrep-' meaning "body, form, appearance" is the source of the Old English word 'hrif' meaning "belly," which is formed from the root ending p becoming an f and the source in turn of the English word 'midriff.' It is clear this shift is also found in the root 'ped-[1]' meaning "foot," which is the source of the English words 'foot' and 'fetter.'

The third general rule cited in chapter 7 is that "initial s sounds conjoined with following consonants usually show no change in Greek, Latin, and Old English. However, they do frequently disappear. An initial Indo-European 's' followed by a vowel tended to become a rough breathing or 'h' in classical Greek." The rule applies to one of the roots, namely, 'swad-' meaning "sweet," which is the source of Latin 'suavis' meaning "delightful" and Greek 'hedone' meaning "pleasure."

When Indo-European has a voiced dental mute 'd,' the West Germanic and Old English form is a smooth dental 't.' The change from 'd' to 't' is shown by the root 'wed-[1]' meaning "water, wet," which is the source of the English words 'water,' 'wet,' 'wash,' 'winter,' and 'otter.' It is also shown by the root 'deru-' meaning "hard," which is the source of the English words 'trust,' 'tree,' 'true,' 'truth,' 'tray,' 'truce,' 'trough,' 'trim,' and 'tar.'

The Indo-European had a rough dental 'dh' sound, which in West Germanic and Old English becomes a voiced dental 'd.' Thus 'reudh-[1]' meaning "red" is the source of the English words 'red,' 'ruddy,' and 'rust.'

Several phenomena are noticeable with some of the roots. As noted in the fourth rule in chapter 7 for Indo-European root changes, the w sound of Indo-European is retained in the Old English forms. In the case of Latin, it is occasionally dropped and otherwise represented by the letter 'v,' which, however, was pronounced as a w sound. The original Greek w sound disappeared, becoming a rough breathing or h sound and sometimes was dropped altogether. We see this phenomena with the root 'wed-[1]' meaning "water, wet." We see no change for w for the Germanic words. The root is the source of the English words 'water,' 'wet,' 'wash,' 'winter,' and 'otter.' The Latin word 'unda' meaning "wave" illustrates the case in which the initial 'w' sound gets dropped, and in the Greek, we see the normal change to the rough breathing or h sound with the word 'hudor' meaning "water."

When palatal 'g' or 'k' combine with 'w' in 'g^w' or 'k^w,' the 'g' or 'k' may change to a labial 'b' in Latin or Greek or may get dropped. Two roots show this behavior. For the root 'g^{w}ere-[2]' meaning "heavy," in the Latin the 'w' is dropped yielding 'gravis' meaning "heavy." In the Greek the 'g^w' becomes 'b.' For the root 'leg^{w}h-' meaning "light" in the Latin, the 'g' is dropped leaving the 'w' sound (although spelled with 'v') in the word 'levis' meaning "light." This root produced 'liht' meaning 'light' in the Old English and is the source of the English words 'light' and 'lighter.'

An initial 'mr' can produce 'br' in the Latin and Greek as it does for the root 'mregh-u-' meaning "short." The initial 'mr' does not change for the Germanic and Old English. It is the source of the English words 'mirth' and 'merry.' But the root produces 'brevis' for "short" in the Latin with the 'gh' becoming a 'w' sound. In the Greek the root produces 'brakhus' meaning "short" and 'brakhion' meaning "shorter." (We note here that the rough palatal 'gh' in the Indo-European follows the rule changing to 'kh' as shown in table 7.1 of chapter 7.)

The root 'meu-' meaning "moist, washed" is the basis for the Latin 'mundus' meaning "world, earth." The Greek 'kosmos' meaning "world, order" has been included with it because the two Latin and Greek words are virtually identical in their basic meanings, which identify with cosmetics, order, or the world.

LIST OF ROOTS IN ORDER OF OCCURRENCE

The following list gives the roots in this chapter in order of their occurrence. The syllables in capital letters show sequences of letters in English words that generally indicate the corresponding root to be the origin. In nearly all cases, if one sees the letters in caps in an English word, one can infer that it comes from the Indo-European root in the first column. But there may also be some English words from the root that do not accord with the general pattern and some English words that fit the pattern but come from a different root.

35. ge the earth	GE, GEO earth
36. k^{w}rep- body, form, appearance	CORPOR, CORP body
37. man-[2] hand	MANU hand —> MAND, MEND put in the hands of; entrust; order MAND/MEND
38. ped-[1] foot	PES, PED foot PED PEC sin POD foot
39. wed-[1] water, wet	HUDR water
40.	CALC, CULC heel; pebble CALC lime
41. ak- sharp	ACER, ACR, AC sour; sharp ACERB/ACRI
42. andho- blind, dark	UMBRA shade
43. del-[1] long	LONG- long
44. deru- hard	DUR hard
45. g^{w}ere-[2] heavy	GRAV, GRIEV, GRIEF heavy
46. kar-[1] hard	-CRACY, CRAT rule; government
47. leg^{w}h- light	LEV, LIEV, LIEF light; lift
48. lei-/slei- slimy	
49. mel-[1] soft	MOLL soft
50. meu- moist, washed	MUND world, earth COSM order, world
51. mregh-u- short	BREV-, BRIEF short

52. newo- new	NOV new
53. reudh-[1] red	RUB, RUF red ROBOR strength
54. swad- sweet	SUA sweet
55. sp(h)er-	ASPER rough

Objects

35. ge/gaia the earth
Greek: GE, GEO earth
[1] Gk ge earth

apogee: the highest point, climax. [1] Gk apo (from) + ge earth.
geocentric: taking the earth as the center; measure from the earth's center. [1] Gk ge earth + kentron center.
geode: hollow, spherical rock with internal crystals. [1] Gk ge earth + odes.
geophysics: science dealing with effect of weather on the earth. [1] Gk ge earth + physis nature.
perigee: point nearest earth. [1] Gk peri (near) + ge earth.
RELATED: apogeal apogean geodesy geodetic geotropic
COMMON: geochemistry [1] geographer [1] geographic [1] geography [1] geology [1] geometer [1] geometric [1] geometry [1] geophysical [1] geopolitics [1]

36. kʷrep- body, form, appearance
Latin: CORPOR, CORP body

[1] L corpus body
[2] OE hrif belly

corporeal: having a body; physical. [1] L corporeus < corpus body.
corpulent: very fat. [1] Fr < L corpulentus fleshly < corpus body.
incorporate: merge into; join with. [1] L in + corporatus (pp corporo) make into a body < corpus body.
incorporeal: not having a body. [1] L in (not) + corporeus < corpus body.
RELATED: corpuscular
COMMON: corporate [1] corporation [1] corps [1] corpse [1] corsage [1] corset [1] leprechaun [1] midriff [2]

37. man-[2] hand
Latin: MANU hand —> MAND, MEND put in the hands of; entrust; order MAND/MEND

[1] L manus hand	[2] L manipulus handful
[3] L manceps purchaser	[4] L mandare (mandatus) to entrust, order

commandeer: to confiscate esp. for military use; to force into army service. [4] L com- + mandare entrust.
countermand: revoke or stop an order by a contrary order. [4] L contra (opposite) + mandare command.
emancipation: release from bondage, slavery or any oppressive authority. [3] L e (out) + mancipo give up.
mandate: a specific order. [4] L manus hand + do give.
manifest: clearly apparent; obvious; (v) make evident. [1] L manifestus evident < manus hand + fendo strike.
manifesto: declaration of political principles or policies. [1] L manifestus evident < manus hand + fendo strike.
manipulation: skillful execution; psychological control. [2] L manipulus handful < manus hand + pleo fill.
manumit: to free from bondage as a slave; emancipate; liberate. [1] L manus hand + mitto send.
remand: to send back. [4] L re- + mandare to order.

RELATED: emancipate manifestly manipulate manipulative manipulator manumission
COMMON: command [4] commando [4] commend [4] commendable [4] commendation [4] commodore [4] demand [4] maintain [1] manacle [1] manage [1] mandatory [4] manege [1] maneuver [1] manner [1] manual [1] manufacture [1] manure [1] manuscript [1] Maundy Thursday [4] recommend [4] recommendation [4]

38. ped-¹ foot
Latin: PES, PED foot PEC sin Greek: POD foot

[1] L pes (ped-) foot
[2] L expedire (expeditus; pfp expediens) free from
   a snare
[3] L impedire (impeditus; pfp impediens) fetter,
   entangle, hinder

[4] L pedica fetter, snare	[5] L peior worse
[6] L pessimus worst	[7] L peccare (pfp peccans) to stumble, sin
[8] Gk pous (pod-) foot	[9] Gk pedon ground, soil
[10] Gk pedon rudder	
[11] OE fot foot	[12] OE fetor fetter

expedient: advantageous. [2] OF < L expediens (pfp expedio) < ex (out) + pes foot.
expedite: to hasten the movement or progress of. [2] L expeditus (pp expedio) < ex (out) + pes foot.
fetter: to bind with or cause to be bounded by restrictions. [12] OE fetor fetter.
impair: weaken in strength or usefulness. [5] L in (in) + pejoro make worse < pejor worse.
impeach: bring an accusation; charge. [4] L in- (in) + pedica fetter.
impeccable: faultless. [7] L in (not) + pecco sin.
impede: to hinder, make progress difficult. [3] L in (in) + pes foot.
impediment: a hindrance; an obstacle that makes progress difficult. [3] L in (in) + pes foot.
peccadillo: a slight or trifling sin. [7] Sp peccadillo (dim. peccado) sin < L pecco sin.
pedestrian: prosaic or dull; connected with walking; one who walks. [1] L pedester < pes foot.
pejorative: a word expressing depreciation. [5] L pejor (compar malus) bad.
pessimism: tendency to take unnecessarily unfavorable or gloomier views. [6] L pessimus worst.
podiatrist: doctor who treats diseases of the foot .[8] Gk pous, pod- foot + iatros physician.
podium: a lectern or raised platform for a speaker. [8] Gk podion base < pous, pod- foot.
quadruped: a four-footed animal. [1] L quadri- four + pes foot .
unfettered: not bound by restrictions. [12] un- (not) + OE fetor fetter.
unimpeachable: beyond reproach; cannot be doubted or questioned. [4] L in- (in) + pedica fetter.
RELATED: apod apodal expeditious pejoration pessimistic sesquipedal
COMMON: biped [1] caliber [8] foot [11] millipede [1] octopus [8] Oedipus [8] parallelepiped [9] pawn [1] -ped [1] pedal [1] pedi- [1] pediculous [1] peduncle [1] peon [1] pew [8] pilot [10] pioneer [1] platypus [8] -pod [8] podiatry [8] polyp [8] polypod [8] tripod [8] unfetter [12]

39. wed-1 water, wet
Latin: UND, OUND wave
Greek: HUDR water

[1] L unda wave
[2] Gk hudor water

[3] OE waeter water	[4] OE waet wet

[5] OE waescan to wash   [6] OE winter winter
[7] OE otor otter

dehydrate: remove the water. [2] < de + Gk hydor water.
hydration: chemical combination with water. [2] Gk hydor water.
inundate: flood with water; overwhelm. [1] L in- (in) + undare to surge < unda wave.
redundant: superfluous; unnecessarily repetitive. [1] L re- + undare to surge < unda wave.
superabundant: exceedingly plentiful. [1] L super (over) + abundare to overflow.
undulating: moving with a smooth wavelike motion. [1] LL undula small wave < unda wave.
RELATED: dehydration undulate
COMMON: abundant [1] dehydrated [2] hydroelectric [2] hydrogen [2] hydrophobia [2] hydroponics [2] otter [7] wash [5] water [3] wet [4] winter [6]

40. CALC, CULC heel; pebble CALC lime

[1] L calx lime, small stone   [2] L calcitrare to kick < calx heel

calculable: able to be computed or estimated. [1] L calx small stone.
calculated: done deliberately or after assessing risk; obtained by computation. [1] L calx small stone.
inculcate: to teach, instill, or indoctrinate. [2] L in- (in) + calcare to trample < calx heel.
recalcitrant: non-compliant; rebellious; refractory. [2] L recalcitratus < re + calcitro kick < calx heel.
COMMON: calciferous [1] calciform [1] calcify [1] calcium [1] calculate [1] calculation [1] calculator [1] calculus [1] recalculate [1]

Qualities

41. ak- sharp
Latin: ACER, ACR, AC sour; sharp ACERB/ACRI
Greek: OXY sharp

[1] L acus needle < acuere to sharpen
[2] L acer sharp, bitter   [3] L acerbus bitter, sharp, tart
[4] L acere be sharp, sour
[5] L ocris mountain
[6] Gk akone whetstone
[7] Gk akme point   [8] Gk akros topmost
[9] Gk oxus sharp
[10] OE ecg sharp side

acerbic: sour, embittered. [3] L acerbus bitter < acer sharp.
acerbity: sourness, as of temper; harshness; sharpness. [2] L acer sharp.
acidulous: slightly acid; sour-tempered. [4] L aceo be sour.
acme: the highest point. [7] Gk akme point.
acrid: of a cutting, burning taste; pungent. [2] L acris sharp.
acrimony: sharpness; corrosive; bitterness. [2] L acrimonia sharpness < acer sharp.
acuity: sharpness; keenness esp. of thought. [2] L acer sharp.
acumen: sharpness of mind and judgment. [2] L acer sharp.

exacerbate: make more sharp or bitter; aggravate. [3] L ex (intens.) + acerbus bitter.
mediocre: inferior or ordinary in quality. [5] L medius middle + ocris mountain.
paragon: model of perfection or excellence. [6] Gk para- + akone whetstone.
paroxysm: sudden burst of action or emotion; convulsion. [9] Gk para- + oxunein goad < oxus sharp.
RELATED: acetification acrimonious acute
COMMON: acid [4] acne [7] acro- [8] acrobat [8] acupuncture [1] acuteness [1] eager [2] edge [10] oxygen [9] vinegar [2]

42. andho- blind, dark
Latin: UMBRA shade

[1] L umbra shadow

adumbration: sketching or foreshadowing. [1] L adumbrates (pp adumbrari) to shade < ad + umbra shade.
penumbra: partly shadowed area surrounding a fully shadowed area. [1] L pene (almost) + umbra shade.
somber: gloomy, melancholy. [1] L sub + umbra shadow.
umbra: darkest region of a shadow. [1] L umbra shadow.
umbrage: resentment; sense of injury; act of giving shade. [1] Fr ombrage < L umbraticus < umbra shade.
RELATED: adumbrant adumbrate penumbral
COMMON: sombrero [1] umbrella [1]

43. del-[1] long
Latin: LONG- long

[1] L longus long
[2] OE lengan to prolong
[4] OE gelang along
[6] OE lengten spring, Lent

[3] OE lang long
[5] OE lengthu length

elongate: stretch out; extend; make or grow longer. [1] L e- (out) + longus long.
longevity: length of life or duration; long life. [1] L longus long + aevum age.
lunge: a sudden move forward or thrust. [1] OF alongier < L ad- + longus long.
prolong: to lengthen an activity or process in time. [1] L pro- (forth) + longus long.
purloin: to steal. [1] Fr purloign < L peo- (forth) + longus long.
COMMON: along [3] belong [4] length [5] Lent [6] linger [2] long [3] longitude [1] longshore [3] lounge [1] oblong [1]

44. deru- hard
Latin: DUR hard
Greek: DENDR, DENDER

[1] L durus hard
[3] Gk dendron tree
[4] ON traust confidence, firmness
[6] OE treowe firm, true
[8] OE treg wooden board

[2] L druides druids

[5] OE treow tree; pledge
[7] OE treowth faith, loyalty, truth
[9] OE trog wooden vessel, tray

[10] OE trum firm, strong

[11] OE truma troop

[12] OE teoru resin, pitch

[13] OF triste a waiting place

dour: stern; gloomy. [1] L durus hard.

duress: constraint or fear; compulsion. [1] L durus hard.

indurate: to make hard or hardy; rid of sensibility; grow or become hard or tough. [1] L in (in) + durus hard.

obdurate: unmoved by feelings of humanity or pity; inexorable. [1] L ob (before) + durus hard.

truism: an obvious or trivial truth. [6] OE treowe firm, true.

RELATED: induration obduracy

COMMON: betroth [7] druid [2] endure [1] enduring [1] philodendron [3] rhododendron [3] shelter [11] tar [12] tray [8] tree [5] trim [10] trough [9] truce [5] true [6] trust [4] truth [7] tryst [13]

45. gʷere-² heavy

Latin: GRAV, GRIEV, GRIEF heavy

Greek: BAR heavy

[1] L gravis heavy

[2] Gk barus heavy

[3] OItal briga strife < Celt

[4] OHG kreg stubbornness

aggravate: make worse, greater, or less endurable or excusable. [1] L aggravatus < ad + gravis heavy.

brigand: robber; outlaw. [3] OF < OI < brigare to fight.

grave: serious; weighty; threatening; somber. [1] L gravis heavy, weighty.

gravitate: moving by the force of gravity; tend to move toward. [1] L gravitas heaviness < gravis heavy.

gravity: serious, dangerous; attractive force between bodies. [1] L gravis heavy.

grievance: event believed to justify a complaint or protest. [1] L gravis heavy.

grievous: causing or showing grief or suffering; very serious. [1] L gravis heavy.

RELATED: aggravating aggravation brig brigade gravidity gravitation gravitational

COMMON: barium [2] baritone [2] blitzkrieg [4] brig [3] brigade [3] brigantine [3] brute [1] grave [1] gravel [1] grief [1]

46. kar-¹ hard

Greek: -CRACY, CRAT rule; government

[1] L carina keel of a ship, nutshell

[2] L cancer crab, cancer, constellation

[3] Gk kratos strength, might, power

[4] Gk karkinos crab, cancer

[5] OF hardir make hard < Ger

[6] OE hard hard

aristocracy: government by an elite, privileged, or titled ruling class. [3] Gk aristos best + kratia < krateo rule.

autocratic: exercising authority in a dictatorial manner. [3] Gk autos self + krateo rule.

bureaucracy: unelected government employees or large business organization. [3] Fr bureau + Gk krateo rule.

careen: moving in a lurching or swerving manner. [1] L carina ship's keel, ship.

democracy: direct or indirect government by the people. [3] Gk demos people + krateo rule.

foolhardy: reckless; acting rashly. [5] OF fol hardi <Ger. fool + hardi bold.

hardy: sturdy good health; able to survive harsh weather. [5] OF hardir make hard, embolden.

plutocracy: domain ruled by persons with wealth. [3] Gk ploutos wealth + krateo rule.

theocracy: government by priests claiming divine authority. [3] Gk theos God + krateo rule < kratos strength.

RELATED: aristocrat autocrat democrat plutocrat plutocratic theocrat

COMMON: cancer [2] canker [2] carcinogen [4] carcinoma [4] chancre [2] -cracy [3] -crat [3] hard [6] hardly [6] standard [5]

47. leg^wh- light
Latin: LEV, LIEV, LIEF light; lift

[1] L levis light; levare light on, raise
[2] OE liht light; lihtan to lighten

alleviate: to make lighter or easier to bear; relieve; mitigate. [1] L ad (to) + levis light.
irrelevant: not having a bearing on the matter at hand. [1] L in- (not) + re- + levare to raise.
legerdemain: sleight of hand; clever deception. [1] OF leger de main < L levis light.
levity: lightness of humor or temperament; frivolity. [1] L levitas < levis light.
levy: to tax; to draft for military service; (n) the money or troops levied. [1] OF lever to raise < L levis light.
relevant: having a connection with and some bearing on a matter at hand. [1] L re- + levare to raise.
RELATED: leavening levitate
COMMON: carnival [1] elevate [1] elevation [1] elevator [1] leaven [1] levee [1] lever [1] leverage [1] levitation [1] light [2] lighter [2] relieve [1]

48. lei-/slei- slimy

[1] L obliviscor (oblitus) to forget   [2] L linere (pf levi) to anoint
[3] L deletus pp deleo erase
[4] Gk litaneia < lissomai pray
[5] OE slim slime   [6] OE slipor slippery
[7] OE -slician to make smooth   [8] OE lim cement
[9] OE lam loam   [10] ME slight slender
[11] ME slippen to slip

delete: to erase; remove. [3] L deletus (pp deleo) erase.
litany: a prayer. [4] Gk litaneia < lissomai pray.
obliterate: wipe out, erase completely. [1] L oblitus (pp oblivisci) to forget.
oblivion: condition of being completely forgotten. [1] L oblivisci to forget.
slipshod: careless; sloppy. [11] ME slippen to slip.
COMMON: lime [8] liniment [2] loam [9] oblivious [1] slick [7] slight [10] slime [5] slip [11] slippery [11]

49. mel-¹ soft
Latin: MOLL soft

[1] L mollis soft   [2] L blandus smooth, soft spoken
[3] Gk malakos soft
[4] OE meltan to melt   [5] OE mealt malt
[6] OE milte spleen   [7] MD smelten to smelt
[8] OE milde mild   [9] OE mel(i)sc mild, mellow

bland: affable in manner, gentle, suave; mild, balmy, genial. [2] L blandus mild.
blandishment: soothing, flattering speech or action. [2] L blandus bland.

emollient: softening or relaxing; soothing. [1] L e (out) + mollis soft.
mollify: soothe; calm in temper; to mitigate; grow mild soft or tender. [1] L mollis soft + facio do.
smelt: to melt ore to separate out different metals. [7] MD smelten to smelt.
RELATED: blandish mollifiable mollification mollifier mollifying
COMMON: bonanza [3] malt [5] melt [4] mild [8] milt [6] molten [4] mulch [9] mullusk [1]

50. meu- moist, washed
Latin: MUND world, earth
Greek: COSM order, world

[1] L mundus world
[2] Gk kosmos order, world, universe

cosmology: theory of the nature and principles of the universe. [2] Gk kosmos + lego speak.
cosmopolitan: not national but belonging to the whole world. [2] Gk kosmos world + polites citizen.
cosmos: the universe; the universe as embodying order and harmony. [2] Gk kosmos order, harmony.
microcosm: a little world. [2] Gk mikros small + kosmos world.
mundane: adj. pert. to the world, worldly, ordinary, commonplace. [1] L mundus world.
RELATED: cosmic cosmological cosmopolitanism cosmopolite
COMMON: cosmetic [2] cosmetologist [2] cosmonaut [2]

51. mregh-u- short
Latin: BREV-, BRIEF short

[1] L brevis short
[2] Gk brakhion shorter
[3] OE myrgth pleasure, joy

abbreviate: shorten so that the main content is retained. [1] LL abbreviare < ad- + breviare shorten.
abridge: condense; shorten. [1] LL abbreviare < brevis short.
brevity: of short duration; conciseness. [1] L brevis short.
mirth: gaity and laughter. [3] OE myrgth joy.
RELATED: abbreviation abridgment
COMMON: brace [2] bracero [2] brassiere [2] brief [1] embrace [2] merry [3] pretzel [2]

52. newo- new
Latin: NOV new
Greck: NEO- ncw

[1] L novus new
[2] Gk neos new
[3] OE neowe new

innovation: a novelty, change in something established; new idea. [1] L in (in) + novus new.
nova: star that becomes very bright for a short period of time. *[1] L novus new.*
novelty: something new; new occurrence. [1] L novus new.
novice: beginner in any occupation; inexperienced person. [1] Fr < L novicius new.

renovation: result of repairing, making new [1] L re again) + novus new.
RELATED: innovate innovative innovator renovate
COMMON: neo- [2] neon [2] new [3] novel [1] novella [1]

53. reudh-[1] red
Latin: RUB, RUF red ROBOR strength

[1] L robur red oak, hardness   [2] L rubeus red
[3] L rubicundus red, ruddy   [4] L ruber red
[5] OE read red   [6] OE rudig ruddy
[7] OE rust rust

corroboration: support; agreement with other evidence. [1] L corroborare < com- + robor strength.
rambunctious: boisterous and unruly. [1] L robur red oak, hardness.
robust: strong in health or build. [1] L robur oak, strength.
rubicund: healthy redness; ruddy. [3] L rubicundus red, ruddy.
rubious: red; ruby-colored. [2] L rubeo be red.
ruddy: reddish. [6] OE rudig ruddy.
RELATED: corroborant corroborate robustly
COMMON: red [5] rouge [2] rubella [4] ruby [2] rust [7]

54. swad- sweet
Latin: SUA sweet

[1] L suadere (suasus) to advise, urge   [2] L suavis delightful
[3] Gk hedone pleasure

assuage: to ease; to appease; to calm. [2] L ad to + suavis sweet.
dissuade: to persuade not to follow a proposed course of action. [1] L dis- + suadere to advise, urge.
hedonism: belief that seeking what brings pleasure is the proper goal of action. [3] Gk hedone pleasure.
suasion: persuasion. [1] L suadere to advise, urge.
suave: smooth and pleasant in manner; bland; gracious. [2] Fr < L suavis sweet.
RELATED: hedonist suavity suasive
COMMON: persuade [1] persuasion [1]

55. sp(h)er-
Latin: ASPER rough

[1] L asper rough

asperity: roughness or harshness as of temper; hardship; difficulty. [1] L asper rough.
exasperate: irritate exceedingly; enrage. [1] L ex (out) + asper rough.
RELATED: exasperation

CHAPTER 13

Roots Referring to Life, Death, and Growth

The fourth category of roots, covered in this chapter, refers directly to existence, life, birth, growth, and death. Fifteen roots are placed in this category. Two roots have existence as their central meaning:

'bheue- / bheu-' meaning "be, exist, grow"
'es-' meaning "to be"

The root 'bheue- / bheu-' meaning "be, exist, grow" is the source of the Latin verb 'fieri' meaning "to become" and 'probus' meaning "upright," the Greek 'phuein' meaning "bring forth" and 'phusis' meaning "growth," and the English words 'be,' 'beam,' 'build,' 'building,' 'bower,' 'byre,' and 'forebear.' The other root 'es-' meaning "to be" is the source of the Latin verb 'esse' meaning "to be" and the English words 'is,' 'am,' 'yes,' and 'sin.' Four roots have breathing or living for their main idea:

'ane-mo' meaning "to breathe"
'bhes-²' meaning "to breathe"
'gʷeie-¹' meaning "to live"
'SPIR' meaning "breath"

The first root 'ane-mo' meaning "to breathe" is the source of the Latin 'anima' meaning "soul" and the Greek word 'anemos' meaning "wind." The second root 'bhes-²' meaning "to breathe" is the source of the Greek word 'psuche' meaning "soul." The third root 'gʷeie-¹' meaning "to live" is the source of the Latin verb 'vivere' meaning "to live" and 'vita' meaning "life," the Greek 'bios' meaning "life" and 'zoon' meaning "animal," and the English word 'quick' (as in "the quick [living] and the dead.") The root 'SPIR' meaning "breath" is the source of the Latin 'spiritus' meaning "breath." Two roots have for their primary meaning the idea of bearing and giving birth to children or offspring:

'bher-¹' meaning "carry; bear children"
'gene-' meaning "give birth, beget"

The root 'bher-¹' meaning "carry; bear children" is the source of the Latin verb 'ferre' meaning "to carry" and 'fortuna' meaning "good luck," the Greek 'pherein' meaning "to carry," and the English words 'bear,' 'bring,' 'burden,' and 'forbear.' The other root 'gene-' meaning "give birth, beget" is the source of the Latin verb 'gnascor' meaning "to be born" and 'genus' meaning "kind," the Greek 'genos' meaning "race, family" and 'genesis' meaning "birth" or "beginning," and the English words 'kind,' 'kin,' 'kindred,' and 'king.' Two roots refer to nourishing:

'al-³' meaning "grow, nourish"
'dhe(l)-' meaning "suck"

The root 'al-3' meaning "grow, nourish" is the source of the Latin 'alere' meaning "to nourish" and 'altus' meaning "high" and the English words 'old,' 'elder,' and 'eldest.' The second root 'dhe(l)-' meaning "suck" is the source of the Latin 'felix' meaning "fruitful" and 'filius' meaning "son." Three roots mean "to grow, increase, or thrive":

'aug-1' meaning "to increase"
'ker-3' meaning "to grow"
'spe-1' meaning "to thrive, prosper"

The root 'aug-1' meaning "to increase" is the source of the Latin 'augere' meaning "to increase" and of the English words 'eke,' 'waist,' and 'wax.' The second root 'ker-3' meaning "to grow" is the source of the Latin verbs 'creare' meaning "beget" or "create" and 'crescare' meaning "grow." The third root 'spe-1' meaning "to thrive, prosper" is the source of the Latin verb 'sperare' meaning "to hope" and the English words 'speed' and 'Godspeed.' One root refers to death:

'nek-1' meaning "death"

The root 'nek-1' is the source of the Latin verb 'nocere' meaning "injure" or "harm" and 'noxius' meaning "harmful" and the Greek 'nekros' meaning "corpse." One root was included here because of the importance for living persons of having a name:

'no-mn-' meaning "name"

The root 'no-mn-' is the source of the Latin 'nomen' meaning "name," the Greek 'onoma' meaning "name," and the English word 'name.'

SOUND SHIFTS

There are several shifts in consonants or differences that show up in some of the roots. Where Indo-European had a rough labial 'bh' sound, the Latin and Greek have an 'f' sound (spelled 'ph' for Greek words in English). The corresponding West Germanic and Old English form is generally the voiced labial 'b.' The root 'bher-1' meaning "carry; bear children" is the source of the Latin verb 'ferre' meaning "to carry" and 'fortuna' meaning "good luck," the Greek 'pherein' meaning "to carry," and of the English words 'bear,' 'bring,' 'burden,' and 'forbear.' A second root 'bheue- / bheu-' meaning "be, exist, grow" is the source of the Latin verb 'fieri' meaning "to become" and 'probus' meaning "upright," the Greek 'phuein' meaning "bring forth" and 'phusis' meaning "growth," and the English words 'be,' 'beam,' 'build,' 'building,' 'bower,' 'byre,' and 'forebear.' The root 'dhe(l)-' meaning "suck" does not follow the normal pattern where we would expect a 'th' sound in Greek. But Latin does not have the 'th' sound, and we find that the 'dh' becomes an 'f' as if it were a 'bh.' The root 'dhe(l)- is the source of the Latin 'felix' meaning "fruitful" and 'filius' meaning "son."

If Indo-European, Latin, and Greek have a voiced palatal mute 'g,' the corresponding West Germanic and Old English form is generally a smooth palatal 'k.' The root 'aug-1' meaning "to increase" is the source of the Latin 'augere' meaning "to increase" and the English words 'eke,' 'waist,' and 'wax.' The root 'gene-' meaning "give birth, beget" is the source of the Latin verb 'gnascor' meaning "to be born" and 'genus' meaning "kind." It is also the source of the Greek word 'genos' meaning "race, family" and 'genesis' meaning "birth" or "beginning" and the English words 'kind,' 'kin,' 'kindred,' and 'king.'

When palatal 'g' or 'k' combine with 'w' in 'gw' or 'kw,' the 'g' or 'k' may change to a labial 'b' in Latin or Greek or may get dropped. Thus for the root 'gweie-1' meaning "to live" which is the source of the Latin verb 'vivere' meaning "to live" and 'vita' meaning "life," the 'g' gets dropped leaving 'w.' It changes to 'b' and 'z' in the Greek 'bios' meaning "life" and 'zoon' meaning "animal." For the English word 'quick,' the 'g' changes to 'k' following the normal pattern for Indo-European 'g' yielding 'kʷ' = 'qu.'

For the remaining roots covered here, we do not see any behavior illustrating transformations from the original Indo-European roots. First, 'al-³' meaning "grow, nourish" is the source of the Latin 'alere' meaning "to nourish" and 'altus' meaning "high" and the English words 'old,' 'elder,' and 'eldest.' Second, 'ane-mo' meaning "to breathe" is the source of the Latin 'anima' meaning "soul" and of the Greek word 'anemos' meaning "wind." Third, 'bhes-²' meaning "to breathe" is the source of the Greek word 'psuche' meaning "soul." Fourth, 'es-' meaning "to be" is the source of the Latin verb 'esse' meaning "to be" and the English words 'is,' 'am,' 'yes,' and 'sin.' Fifth, 'ker-³' meaning "to grow" is the source of the Latin verbs 'creare' meaning "beget" or "create" and 'crescare' meaning "grow." Sixth, 'nek-¹' meaning "death" is the source of the Latin verb 'nocere' meaning "injure" or "harm" and 'noxius' meaning "harmful" and the Greek 'nekros' meaning "corpse." Seventh, 'no-mn-' meaning "name" is the source of the Latin 'nomen' meaning "name," the Greek 'onoma' meaning "name," and the English words 'name.' Eighth, 'spe-¹' meaning "to thrive, prosper" is the source of the Latin verb 'sperare' meaning "to hope" and the English words 'speed' and 'Godspeed.' Finally, 'SPIR' meaning "breath" is the source of the Latin 'spiritus' meaning "breath."

LIST OF ROOTS IN ORDER OF OCCURRENCE

The following list gives the roots in the order they are covered in this chapter. The syllables with capital letters indicate sequences of letters in English words that generally indicate the root to be the origin for words containing the sequence. In nearly all cases, if one sees the letters of an English word in caps, one can infer that it comes from the Indo-European root in the first column. There may also be some English words from the root that do not accord with the general pattern and some English words that fit the pattern but come from a different root.

56. al-³ grow, nourish	AL, ALI feed; nourish; support	
57. ane-mo to breathe	ANIM life; spirit; mind; soul	
58. aug-¹ to increase	AUG, AUCT, AUX increase; grow	
59. bher-¹ carry; bear children	-FER, -FEROUS carry; produce FORS chance	
	-PHERY, -PHORIA, -PHOR, -PHER a bearing; a carrying; production	
60. bhes-² to breathe	PSYCH mind; soul; spirit	
61. bheue- / bheu- be, exist, grow	PHYT plant	
62. dhe(l)- suck	FELIC lucky; happy	
63. es- to be	ESSE, ENT be, exist	
64. gene- give birth, beget	GEN, GENER, GEND origin; race; kind GIGN (G)NASC, (G)NAT be born	
	GEN, GON kind; race; origin	
65. gʷeie-¹ to live	VIT, VIV live BIO life ZO animal	
66. ker-³ to grow	CRESC, CRET grow CRE/CRET —> CREA make, create	
67. nek-¹ death	NOC, NOX, NIC, NEC harm; kill NEC/NIC/NOX NECRO dead	
68. no-mn- name	[G]NOMEN, [G]NOMIN name NOM ONOMA, ONYM name	
69. spe-¹ to thrive, prosper	SPER, SPAIR hope	
70. SPIR breath		

56. al-3 grow, nourish
Latin: AL, ALI feed; nourish; support

[1] L alere (altus) to nourish, cherish; alescere to grow up

[2] L almus nurturing   [3] L abolere abolish, destroy

[4] L proles offspring   [5] L altus high, deep
[6] OE eald old   [7] OE ieldra older

abolish: to cancel; to do away with. [3] L abolere abolish, destroy.
alimentary: pert to food, digestion, or nourishment. [1] L alere to nourish; alescere to grow up.
coalesce: to grow or come together. [1] L co- + alescere to grow < alere to nourish.
coalition: an alliance of groups or nations to pursue an objective. [1] L coalescere to grow together.
enhance: improve, strengthen. [5] L en + altus high.
exalt: raise in status or rank; praise. [5] L ex + altus high.
haughty: proud and condescending. [5] OF haut < L altus high.
prolific: abundantly producing works, offspring, or fruit; fertile. [4] L proles offspring.
proletariat: working class; people who live by labor. [4] L proletarius lowest class < proles offspring.
RELATED: exaltation exalted hauteur haughtiness proletarian
COMMON: abolition [3] adolescent [1] adult [1] alderman [6] alimony [1] alma mater [2] alto [5] altimeter [5] altitude [5] alumnus [1] elder [7] eldest [7] old [6]

57. ane-mo to breathe
Latin: ANIM life; spirit; mind; soul

[1] L animus reason, mind, spirit; anima soul, spirit, life, breath
[2] Gk anemos wind

animadversion: criticism or censure; taking notice of an offense. [1] L animus mind + ad (to) + verto turn.
animated: lively; having life. [1] L anima soul.
animosity: active and vehement enmity; ill-will. [1] L animus courage.
equanimity: calm temper. [1] L aequus equal + animus mind.
inanimate: not living or capable of having life; dull. [1] L in- (not) + anima soul.
magnanimity: generosity. [1] L magnus great + animus soul.
pusillanimous: lacking courage or spirit; cowardly. [1] L pusillus very little + animus mind.
RELATED: animadvert magnanimous
COMMON: anemo- [2] anemone [2] animal [1] animate [1] animation [1] animiam [1] unanimous [1]

58. aug-[1] to increase
Latin: AUG, AUCT, AUX increase; grow

[1] L augere to increase   [2] L augur diviner
[3] L augustus majestic   [4] L auxilium aid, support
[5] OE eacan to increase   [6] OE weaxan to grow; waest growth

augment: increase in size or quantity. [1] L augere to increase.
augur: to foretell by omens; one who foretells by omens. [2] L augur diviner.
august: majestic; venerable. [3] L augustus majestic.
authoritarian: requiring full obedience to authority. [1] L auctoritas < auctor creator.
authoritative: generally acknowledged to be reliable; official; commanding. [1] L auctoritas < auctor creator.
auxiliary: supporting; supplementing; backing up; (n) person or group assisting. [4] L auxilium support.
inaugurate: induct into office; officially begin; begin. [2] L augur diviner.
wax: to gradually increase in strength; to grow. [6] OE weaxan to grow; waest growth.

RELATED: augury inaugural inauguration
COMMON: auction [1] author [1] authority [1] authorize [1] eke [5] nickname [5] waist [6]

59. bher-¹ carry; bear children
Latin: -FER, -FEROUS carry; produce FORS, FORTU chance
Greek: -PHERY, -PHORIA, -PHOR, -PHER a bearing; a carrying; production

[1] L ferre (pfp ferens) to carry

[2] L probrum a reproach

[3] L fortuitus happening, by chance

[4] L fortuna chance, good luck, fortune

[5] L fur thief

[6] Gk pherein to carry; phoros a carrying

[7] Gk pherme dowery

[8] OE bringan to bring

[9] OE byrthen burden

[10] OE beran to carry

[11] OE ber bier

[12] ME burlich excellent, exalted

[13] OHG burjan raise

burden: a physical or emotional weight carried; a duty. [9] OE byrthen burden.
burgeon: to put forth buds; sprout as limbs, horns; a bud, a sprout. [13] F < OHG burjan raise.
burly: heavy and muscular. [12] ME burlich.
confer: to grant or bestow; to consult, hold a meeting to discuss a matter. [1] L con (together) + fero bear.
deference: respectful yielding, submission. [1] L defero < de (down) + fero bear.
differentiate: to discriminate specific differences; cause to become different. [1] L dis (apart) + fero carry.
ferret: search for and uncover; weasel-like mammal. [5] L fur thief.
forbearance: the act of refraining or holding back esp. when under provocation. [10] OE forberan to endure.
fortuitous: occurring by chance esp. something desired; accidental. [3] L fortuitus < fors chance.
furtive: stealthy; acting surreptitiously. [5] L furtivus < fur thief.
indifferent: not interested in or partial to; not for or against. [1] L in- + dis (apart) + fero carry.
infer: draw a conclusion from evidence or premises. [1] L inferre bring in, adduce < in- + ferre to bear.
opprobrium: disgrace; ignominy; scorn. [2] L ob- (against) + probum reproach.
proffer: to offer. [1] L pro (forth) + fero bring.
proliferate: to bear frequently or produce rapidly. [1] L proles offspring + fero bear.
vociferous: making a loud outcry; clamorous. [1] L vociferor < vox voice + fero bear.
euphoria: sense of great happiness or well-being. [6] Gk euphoros healthy < eu well + pherein to bear.
metaphor: figure of speech likening one thing to another. [6] Gk metaphora < meta (over) + phero bear.
paraphernalia: equipment. [7] Gk para- (beyond)+ pherne dowry.
peripheral: at the edges or boundary; only indirectly relevant. [6] Gk peri (around) + phero bear.
RELATED: deferential ferriferous forbear indifference inference metaphoric metaphorical periphery proliferation vociferate
COMMON: amphora [6] bear [10] bier [11] bring [8] circumference [1] conference [1] conifer [1] defer [1] deferment [1] differ [1] difference [1] efferent [1] -fer [1] feracious [1] fertile [1] fortune [4] fortunate [4] offer [1] overbearing [10] -phore [6] -phoresis [6] -phorous [6] phosphorus [6] prefer [1] refer [1] reference [1] semaphore [6] suffer [1] transfer [1]

60. bhes-² to breathe
Greek: PSYCH mind; soul; spirit

[1] Gk psuche spirit, soul

psyche: the soul or spirit. [1] Gk psuche spirit, soul.
psychoanalysis: exposing repression to treat mental disorders. [1] Gk psyche mind + ana (back) + lyo loose.

psychoneurosis: emotional disorder. [1] Gk psyche soul, mind + neuron nerve.
psychopathic: emotionally unstable with asocial and criminal behavior. [1] Gk psyche soul + pathos feeling.
psychosis: mental disorder in which the personality is very disorganized. [1] Gk psyche mind.
psychosomatic: symptoms attributable to mental beliefs and processes. [1] Gk psyche mind + soma body.
psychotherapy: use of mental techniques to heal mental disorders. [1] Gk psyche mind + therapeia treatment.
RELATED: psychiatric psychopath psychotic
COMMON: psychiatry [1] psychic [1] psycho- [1] psychology [1]

61. bheue- / bheu- be, exist, grow
Greek: PHYT plant

[1] L fieri to become

[2] L futurus that is to be, future

[3] L dubius doubtful; dubitare to doubt (cf dwo-)

[4] L probus upright (cf per-¹)

[5] L superbus superior, proud

[6] Gk phuein (f phuso) bring forth, make grow;
   phutos, phuton a plant; phusis growth, nature

[7] Gk phulon tribe, class, race; phule tribe, clan

[8] MD gheboer peasant <Ger

[9] MD bodel riches, property

[10] ON bua to live, prepare

[11] OE beon to be

[12] OE byldan to build; bold house

[13] OE bur bower, room

[14] OE byre stall, hut

[15] OE beam beam, tree

approbation: approval; commendation. [4] L approbatus (pp approbo) < ad (to) + probus good.
dubious: arousing questions, doubt, and uncertainty. [3] L dubius doubtful.
fiat: an order or decree. [1] L fiat let it be done (3 pers. sng. pres. subj. of fieri) to become, be done.
indubitable: undeniably true. [3] L in (not) + dubius < duo two.
probability: likelihood of an event's occurrence or a statement's truth. [4] Fr < L probabilis < probo prove.
probation: a proceeding designed to test the character or qualifications of someone. [4] L probo prove.
probative: serving for proof or test. [4] L probo prove.
probity: virtue or integrity tested and confirmed; strict honesty. [4] L probitas < probus good.
reprobate: strongly disapproving; abandoned in sin; utterly depraved. [4] L re (again) + probo prove.
reproof: a rebuke or expression of disapproval. [4] L reprobo condemn < re + probo prove.
boorish: clumsy and rude in behavior. [8] D boer < Ger.
forebears: ancestors. [11] ME fore in front + beer one who is < be be.
husband: conserve; be economical; male spouse. [10] OE hus house + bonda family head < ON bua prepare.
husbandry: occupation of farming. [10] OE hus house + bonda, bunda head of a family < ON bua prepare.
metaphysical: rel. to thought about reality; abstruse; supernatural. [6] Gk meta after + physis nature.
neophyte: a recent convert; a novice; beginner. [6] Gk neos new + phyto produce.
physiological: rel. to the normal functioning of organisms. [6] Gk physis nature + -logy.
phylum: top-level division of a biological taxonomy of plants and animals. [7] Gk phulon class.
physiology: study of the functions of parts of organisms. [6] Gk physis nature + -logy.
RELATED: approbate improbity probable probate probationary reproval
COMMON: approve [4] approval [4] approvingly [4] be [11] beam [15] bondage [10] boodle [9] boor [8] bound [10] bower [13] build [12] building [12] bustle [10] byre [14] disproof [4] disprove [4] doubt [3] future [2] imp [6] improbable [4] improbability [4] neighbor [8] physic [6] physics [6] physio- [6] physique [6] -phyte [6] phyto- [6] proof [4] prove [4] provable [4] proven [4] superb [5]

62. dhe(l)- suck
Latin: FELIC lucky; happy FILI son/daughter

[1] L femina woman   [2] L fetus pregnancy
[3] L fecundus fruitful   [4] L filius son; filia daughter
[5] L felix fruitful, fertile, happy

affiliate: to become a member of; person or organization associated as a member. [4] L ad- + filius son.
effete: lacking vitality; ineffective; decadent; effeminate. [2] L effetus worn out < ex- + fetus pregnant.
fecund: fruitful; intellectually productive. [3] L fecundus fruitful.
felicity: a state of great happiness, comfort, and content; appropriateness. [5] L felicitas < felix happy.
fetus: unborn young of viviparous vertebrates. [2] L fetus offspring.
filial: rel. to a son or daughter. [4] L filius son; filia daughter.
infelicitous: not happy in application, condition, or result. [5] L in + felix happy.
RELATED: affiliation felicitous
COMMON: fawn [2] female [1] feme [1] feminine [1] fetal [2] effeminate [1]

63. es- to be
Latin: ESSE, ENT be, exist
Greek: ONTO- being

[1] L esse (pfp ens) to be
[2] OE is is   [3] OE eam am
[4] OE gese yes   [5] OE synn sin

disinterested: free from self-interest; unselfish; impartial. [1] OF dis + interest < L interest it concerns.
entity: something that exists. [1] L entitas < ens being (pfp esse) to be.
essence: intrinsic nature of an entity; what makes a thing what it is; perfume. [1] Fr < L essentia < esse be.
misrepresent: to portray in a misleading or incorrect manner. [1] ME mis- + L re- + prae + esse to be.
nonentity: something that does not exist. [1] L non (not) + entitas < ens being (pfp esse) to be.
onus: the burden of proof; a burden; a responsibility. [1] L onus burden.
presentment: a report made by a grand jury. [1] OF < L praesens (pfp praesse) be before.
prowess: great strength or skill. [1] OF < L pro (before, for, instead of)+ esse to be.
prude: person excessively concerned with acting properly and modestly. [1] OF prude < L prod- (for) + esse be.
quintessence: purest and most essential part. [1] Fr < L quinta fifth + essentia essence < esse be.
RELATED: disinterest essential interest nonessential
COMMON: absence [1] absent [1] am [3] improve [1] is [2] presence [1] present [1] proud [1] represent [1] sin [5] yes [4]

64. gene- give birth, beget
Latin: GEN, GENER, GEND origin; race; kind GIGN (G)NASC, (G)NAT be born
Greek: GEN, GON kind; race; origin

[1] L genus race, kind; genero (generatus) to beget
[2] L genius innate quality   [3] L ingenuum inborn character
[4] L indigena born in, indigenous   [5] L indigenuus born in, natural, native
[6] L germen shoot, bud   [7] L gens (genti-) race, clan
[8] L gignere (genitus) to beget   [9] L benignus kindly; malignus malevolent
[10] L praegnas pregnant   [11] L gnascor, nascor (natus; pfp nascens) to be born
[12] Gk genos, genea race, family   [13] Gk -genes born

[14] Gk gonos child, seed

[15] Gk genesis birth, beginning

[16] Gk gignomai (aor gegona; pf gegenemai) be born, become

[17] OE cynn family, kin

[18] OE cyning king

[19] OE cynd kind origin, birth, family, kind; cynde natural, fitting

benign: kindly. [9] L benignus benignant, kind.

cognate: related. [11] L co (together) + natus (pp nascor) be born.

congenial: agreeable; pleasant; friendly. [2] L con + genialis of one's tutelary deity.

congenital: dating from birth. [8] L con (together) + gigno bear.

degenerate: to become worse or inferior; deteriorate. [1] L de (down) + generatus (pp genero) beget.

disingenuous: not sincere; deceitful. [5] L ingenuus < in (in) + gigno produce.

engender: to produce. [1] L in (in) + genero beget.

generality: a statement that applies universally or nearly so; a vague statement. [1] L genus, gener- kind.

generate: to produce or bring into being; to cause. [1] L generare to produce < genus birth.

generic: descriptive of a class; general. [1] L genus origin.

genre: a form, style, or type of music, literature, or art. [1] L genus, gener- kind.

gentility: the quality of being well-mannered and polite. [7] OF < L gentilis of the same clan.

gentry: people of good breeding and high social standing, but not nobility. [7] L gens (genti-) race, clan.

genus: a kind or class. [1] L genus origin.

germane: in close relationship; relevant; appropriate; pertinent; akin. [6] L germanus near akin.

gingerly: with great care; very cautiously. [8] L genitus (pp gignere) to beget.

impregnate: make pregnant; fertilize; saturate; imbue with .[10] L in- + praegnatus < praegnas pregnant.

indigenous: native. [4] L indu (< in) + gigno beget.

ingenious: devised with great skill, cleverness, imagination. [3] L ingeniosus < ingenium inborn talent.

ingenuous: free from deceptiveness; artless; high-minded. [5] L ingenuus < in (in) + gigno produce.

innate: inborn; natural. [11] L in (in) + nascor be born.

jaunty: self-confident in manner; dapper in appearance. [7] OF < L gentilis of the same clan.

malign: speak evil of; evil in disposition or intent. [9] L malignus malign.

miscegenation: interbreeding of races. [1] L misceo mix + genus race.

nascent: beginning to exist or develop [11] L nascens pfp nascor be born

preternatural: transcending the natural order; supernatural. [11] L praeter naturam beyond nature.

progeny: offspring. [8] L pro (forth) + gigno produce.

regeneration: produced anew; in Christianity the new birth, conversion. [1] L re (again) + genero generate.

renascence: the state of being reborn; new birth or life. [11] L renascens < re (again) + nascor be born.

unregenerate: remaining unreconciled to God. [1] < un (not) + L re (again) + genero generate.

endogenous: growing from within. [16] Gk endon (within) + gignomai be born.

exogenous: originating or growing from without. [16] Gk exo + genes < gignomai be born.

genesis: creation; origin; beginning. [15] Gk genesis origin.

heterogeneous: of different makeup or composition. [12] Gk heteros other + genos kind.

homogeneous: of the same composition or structure throughout. [12] Gk homos same + genos kind.

pathogenic: pert. to or noting the production of disease. [12] Gk pathos suffering + genos kind.

RELATED: homogenize malignant

COMMON: carcinogenic [1] engine [3] -gen [13] gendarme [7] gender [1] gene [12] genealogy [12] general [1] generous [1] -genesis [15] genetics [15] genial [2] geniality [2] genital [8] genius [2] genocide [12] gent [8] gentle [7] genuine [5] -geny [13] germ [6] germinal [6] germinate [6] gonad [14] gono- [14] -gony [14] kin

[17] kind [19] kindred [17] king [18] naive [11] nation [11] national [11] nationalism [11] nationalist [11] native [11] nativity [11] nature [11] nee [11] Noel [11] pregnant [10] primogeniture [8] puny [11] rejuvenate [11] telegenic [12]

65. g^{w}eie-[1] to live
Latin: VIT, VIV live
Greek: BIO life

[1] L vivus alive	[2] L vipera viper
[3] L vivere to live	[4] L vita life
[5] Gk bios life	[6] Gk zoon living being, animal
[7] Gk hugies healthy	
[8] OE cwic alive, living	[9] OE cwifer

convivial: sociable; festive; merry. [3] L con (together) + vivo live.
devitalize: deprive of the power to sustain life. [4] L de (from) + vita life.
viable: capable of living. [4] Fr < L vita life < vivo live.
vitality: endowed with life and energy; having the power to continue in force. [4] Fr < L vitalis < vita life.
vivacious: full of life and spirits; lively; active. [3] L vivax < vivo live.
vivify: bring to life; enliven. [1] L vivus alive.
abiosis: absence of life; a lifeless state. [5] Gk a (without) + bios life.
amphibian: an animal that can live both on land or in water. [5] Gk amphi- + bios life.
bionic: having electronic systems applying biological principles. [5] Gk bios life + -onics.
biopsy: extraction of tissue samples to aid in diagnosis. [5] Gk bios life + ops eye.
microbe: a microorganism. [5] Gk mikro- small + bios life.
symbiosis: the consorting together or partnership of dissimilar organisms. [5] Gk syn (together) + bios life.
RELATED: viability vital vivacity
COMMON: antibiotic [5] autobiography [5] bio- [5] biochemistry [5] biodegradable [5] biography [5] biology [5] biotic [5] hygiene [7] microbiology [5] quick [8] quicksilver [8] quiver [9] revive [3] survive [3] viand [3] victual [3] viper [2] vitamin [4] viva [3] vivid [3] zodiac [6] -zoic [6] zoo- [6] -zoon [6]

66. ker-[3] to grow
Latin: CRESC,CRET grow CRE/CRET —> CREA make, create

[1] L Ceres goddess of agriculture	[2] L creare (creatus) beget, make, create, produce, elect
[3] L crescare (cretus; pfp crescens) grow, increase	
[4] L sincerus pure, clean	

accretion: growth or formation by external additions. [3] L ad + cresco grow.
accrue: to obtain as a gain or increase; to accumulate from growth or over time. [3] L ad + cresco grow.
concrescence: growing together; increase. [3] L concresco grow together < (con together) + cresco grow.
concrete': embodied in actual existence; relating to a case; particular. [3] L con (together) + cresco grow.
crescendo: slowly increasing in loudness or power. [3] L cresco grow.
decrement: a decreasing; waning. [3] L de (from) + cresco grow.
increment: what is added; increase; the act of increasing. [3] L incrementum < incresco increase.
procreate: produce offspring. [2] L pro- (forward) + creare to create.
RELATED: accrete accruement excrescence
COMMON: cereal [1] create [2] Creole [2] crescent [3] crew [3] decrease [3] increase [3] insincere [4] recreation [2] recruit [3] sincere [4] sincerity [4]

67. nek-¹ death
Latin: NOC, NOX, NIC, NEC harm; kill NEC/NIC/NOX
Greek: NECRO dead

[1] L nex death

[2] L nocere injure, harm

[3] L noxa injury; noxius harmful

[4] Gk nekros corpse

[5] Gk nektar food of the gods

innocuous: harmless. [2] L innocuus < in (not) + nocuus harmful.
internecine: destructive and deadly to both sides. [1] L internecinus deadly < inter (between) + neco kill.
necrology: list of deaths from a certain place or time; account of the dead. [4] Gk nekros corpse + logy.
necromancy: divination by communication with the dead. [4] Gk nekros dead body + mantis prophet.
noisome: very offensive; particularly to the sense of smell; noxious. [3] Fr noise quarrel < L noxia injury.
noxious: harmful. [3] L noxius < noceo hurt.
obnoxious: of a character to give offense or excite aversion; odious. [3] L obnoxius liable.
pernicious: tending to kill or hurt; malicious; wicked. [1] L per (through) + neco kill.
RELATED: innoxious
COMMON: innocent [2] necro- [4] necropolis [4] nectar [5] nectarine [5] nuisance [2]

68. no-mn- name
Latin:[G]NOMEN, [G]NOMIN name NOM
Greek: ONOMA, ONYM name

[1] L nomen name, reputation
[2] Gk onoma, onuma name
[3] OE nama name

ignominy: a state of shame, dishonor, or contemptibility. [1] L ignominia < in (not) + nomen name.
misnomer: a wrong name or epithet for something. [1] OF mesnomer misname < L nomen name.
nomenclature: names of things. [1] L nomenclatura list of names.
nominative: ascribing a person's name; case of subjects of finite verbs. [1] L nominativus < nomen name.
nominal: consisting of giving a name; in name only; hardly worth mention. [1] L nominalis < nomen name.
renown: wide acclaim and fame. [1] L re- + nomen name, reputation.
acronym: a word made from the first letter of a series of words. [2] Gk akros highest + omyma name.
anonymous: nameless, without a disclosed identity. [2] Gk an (priv.) + onyma name.
eponym: person thought to be a basis for the name of something else. [2] Gk epi- + onoma name.
onomatopoeia: use of words which imitate the objects they refer to. [2] Gk onoma name + poiein to make.
pseudonym: fictitious name esp. a pen name. [2] Gk pseudes false + onoma name.
RELATED: anonymity eponymous ignominious nominalist patronymous synonym synonymous
COMMON: antonym [2] binomial [1] denominate [1] homonym [2] name [3] nominate [1] nominee [1] noun [1] -onym [2] -onymy [2] pronoun [1] synonymy [2]

69. spe-¹ to thrive, prosper
Latin: SPER, SPAIR hope

[1] L sperare (pfp sperans) to hope

[2] L prosperus favorable, prosperous

[3] OE sped success

despair: to abandon all hope; (n) utter hopelessness. [1] L despero < de (from) + spes hope.
prosperity: success or wealth. [2] L pro (for) + spes hope.
RELATED: prosper prosperous
COMMON: Godspeed [3] speed [3]

70. SPIR breath

[1] L spiro (spiratus; pfp spirans) breathe; spiritus breath

aspire: eagerly desire to obtain status, honor, or achievement. [1] Fr aspirer < L ad (to) + spiro breathe.
conspiracy: secret plot with unlawful or treasonous purposes. [1] L conspiro < com (together) + spiro breathe.
dispirited: disheartened; dejected; discouraged. [1] L dis- + spirare to breathe.
expiring: dying; coming to an end; ceasing to be valid; exhaling. [1] L ex- + spiro to breathe.
inspire: to stimulate or motivate to realize a goal; to cause a feeling or thought. [1] L in (into) + spiro breathe.
respire: breathe. [1] L re (back) + spiro breathe.
spiritual: having to do with the spirit or soul. [1] Fr spirituel < L spiritualis < spiro breathe.
transpire: send off through skin and lungs; come gradually to publicity. [1] L trans (through) + spiro breathe.
uninspired: not stimulating, raising interest, or exciting; dull. [1] un + L in (into) + spiro breathe.
RELATED: aspirant aspiration conspire conspirator conspiratorial inspiration respiration respiratory spirit spirituality spiritualize
COMMON: perspiration [1]

CHAPTER 14

Roots Referring to Power, Religion, and Social Relations

The fifth category of roots, covered in this chapter, refers directly to religion, human beings, and their political and social relations. Fourteen roots are placed in this category. Five roots have spawned many words that fall within this category and were included here even though the central meaning of the root does not quite fit:

'andher-/ndher-' meaning "point, stalk"
'kerd-[1]' meaning "heart"
'(s)twer-[1]' meaning "turn, whirl"
's(w)e-' is the source of personal and reflexive pronouns
'wal-' meaning "be strong"

The root 'andher-/ndher-' meaning "point, stalk" is the source of the Greek word 'anthropos' meaning "man." Also 'kerd-[1]' meaning "heart" is the source of the Latin 'credere' meaning "to believe" and 'cors (cord-)' meaning "heart," Greek 'kardia' meaning "heart," and of the English word 'heart.' Next '(s)twer-[1]' meaning "turn, whirl" is the source of the Latin 'turba' meaning "crowd" or "tumult" and English words 'stir' and 'storm.' The root 's(w)e-' is the source of personal and reflexive pronouns. It is the source of the Latin 'sui' meaning "of oneself," Greek 'ethos' meaning "custom," and of the English word 'self. Finally 'wal-' meaning "be strong" is the source of the Latin verb 'valere' meaning "to be strong" and of the English word 'wield.' Two roots have reference to ruling or leading:

'arkein' meaning "begin; rule"
'reg-[1]' meaning "move in a straight line, lead, rule"

The root 'arkein' meaning "begin; rule" is the source of the Greek word 'arche' meaning "beginning" or "rule." Second, 'reg-[1]' meaning "move in a straight line, lead, rule" is the source of the Latin 'regere' meaning "rule" and 'rex' meaning "king," the Greek 'orexis' meaning "desire," the Old English 'riht' meaning "right," and the English words 'rich,' 'rake,' 'rank,' 'reckon,' and 'reckless.' Three roots are the basis for many religious concepts:

'dhes-' refers to religious concepts
'dyeu-' meaning "to shine (sky, heaven, god)"
'sak-' meaning "sanctify"

The root 'dhes-' has religious overtones and is the source of the Latin 'festus' meaning "festive" and 'fanum' meaning "temple" and Greek 'theos' meaning "god." Also 'dyeu-' meaning "to shine (sky, heaven, god)" is the source of the Latin 'deus' meaning "god" and 'dies' meaning "day." The root 'sak-' meaning "sanctify" is the source of the Latin 'sacer' meaning "sacred." Four roots refer to desire or have moral connotations:

'ghwel-' meaning "to will, want"
'mel-[5]' meaning "false, bad, wrong"
'were-o-' meaning "true, trustworthy"
'CULP' meaning "blame, fault"

The root 'ghwel-' meaning "to will, want" is the source of the Latin word 'fallax' meaning "false." The root 'mel-[5]' meaning "false, bad, wrong" is the source of the Latin 'malus' meaning "bad" and Greek 'blasphemos' meaning "blasphemous." The root 'were-o-' meaning "true, trustworthy" is the source of the Latin word 'verus' meaning "true" and the Old English word 'waer' meaning "faith" or "pledge." The root 'CULP' meaning "blame, fault" of the Latin word 'culpa' meaning "fault."

SOUND SHIFTS

As indicated in the first table in chapter 7, if Indo-European, Latin, and Greek have a smooth palatal mute 'k,' the West Germanic and Old English form is a rough palatal 'h.' Hence, 'kerd-[1]' meaning "heart" is the source of the Latin 'credere' meaning "to believe" and 'cors (cord-)' meaning "heart," the Greek 'kardia' meaning "heart," and the English word 'heart.'

Table 7.1 also shows that the Indo-European, Latin, and Greek voiced palatal mute 'g' has a corresponding West Germanic and Old English smooth palatal 'k.' Thus, 'reg-[1]' meaning "move in a straight line, lead, rule" is the source of the Latin 'regere' meaning "rule" and 'rex' meaning "king." It is the root for Greek 'orexis' meaning "desire" and the Old English 'riht' meaning "right" and English words 'rich,' 'rake,' 'rank,' 'reckon,' and 'reckless.'

Indo-European had a rough dental 'dh' sound that in Greek becomes a 'th' sound. But Latin does not have the 'th' sound, and we find that the 'dh' becomes an 'f' as if it were a 'bh.' The root 'dhes-' meaning "(religious concepts)" is the source of the Latin 'festus' meaning "festive" and 'fanum' meaning "temple" and the Greek 'theos' meaning "god."

As noted by the fourth rule in chapter 7, Indo-European roots with a w sound retain it in the Old English forms. In the case of Latin, it is occasionally dropped and otherwise represented by the letter 'v,' which, however, was pronounced as a w sound. We see this phenomena with the root 'wal-' meaning "be strong" as the source of the Latin verb 'valere' meaning "to be strong" and the English word 'wield.' The root 'were-o-' meaning "true, trustworthy" is the source of the Latin word 'verus' meaning "true" and the Old English word 'waer' meaning "faith" or "pledge."

When palatal 'g' or 'k' combine with 'w' in 'g[w]' or 'k[w],' the 'g' or 'k' may take different forms, including a rough labial 'f' in Latin, or may get dropped. Thus 'ghwel-' meaning "to will, want" is the source of the Latin word 'fallax' meaning "false."

The other roots do not show any basic shifts in sound as covered in chapter 7 from the Indo-European root to the Latin, Greek, or Germanic. First, 'andher-/ndher-' meaning "point, stalk" is the source of the Greek word 'anthropos' meaning "man." Second, 'arkein' meaning "begin, rule" is the source of the Greek word 'arche' meaning "beginning" or "rule." Third, 'dyeu-' meaning "to shine (sky, heaven, god)" is the source of the Latin 'deus' meaning "god" and 'dies' meaning "day." Fourth, 'mel-[5]' meaning "false, bad, wrong" is the source of the Latin 'malus' meaning "bad" and Greek 'blasphemos' meaning "blasphemous." Fifth 'sak-' meaning "sanctify" is the source of the Latin 'sacer' meaning "sacred." Sixth '(s)twer-[1]' meaning "turn, whirl" is the source of the Latin 'turba' meaning "crowd" or "tumult" and English words 'stir' and 'storm.' The root 's(w)e-' is the source of personal and reflexive pronouns. It is the source of the Latin 'sui' meaning "of oneself," the Greek 'ethos' meaning "custom," and the English word 'self.'

LIST OF ROOTS IN ORDER OF OCCURRENCE

The following list gives the roots in order that they are covered in this chapter. The syllables in capital letters show sequences of letters in English words that generally indicate the root of its origin. In nearly all cases, if one sees the letters in caps in an English word, one can infer that it comes from the Indo-European root in the first column. There may also be some English words from the root that do not accord with the general pattern and some English words that fit the pattern but come from a different root.

71. andher-/ndher-   ANTHROP man; mankind
72. arkein begin, rule   ARCH, ARCHI rule; govern
73. dhes- (religious concepts)   THEO god
74. dyeu- to shine   DIA, DIURN, JOURN day (sky, heaven, god)
75. ghwel-   FALL, FALS, FAIL deceive; fail
76. kerd-[1] heart   CRED believe, trust
77. mel-[5] false, bad, wrong   MAL- bad; ill
78. reg-[1] move in a   REG, RIG, RECT rule; straight; right ROGA ask,
    straight line   lead, rule
79. sak- sanctify   SACER, SACR, SECR sacred SANCT holy
80. (s)twer-[1] turn, whirl   TURB, TURBIN commotion; crowd; disorder; whirlwind;
                                   spiral
81. s(w)e- personal and reflexive pronoun   ETHN nation ETH/ETHN
82. wal- be strong   VAL, [VAIL] strong, well, farewell
83. were-o- true, trustworthy   VER truth
84.   CULP blame, fault

71. andher-/ndher-
Greek: ANTHROP man; mankind

[1] Gk anthropos man

anthropocentric: believing human beings have greatest importance. [1] Gk anthropos man + kentron center.
anthropoid: resembling man. [1] Gk anthropos man.
anthropology: the science of man. [1] Gk anthropos man + logy.
misanthropic: disliking mankind. [1] Gk misanthropos hating mankind < miseo hate + anthropos man.
philanthropist: contributor of large sums of money to benefit others. [1] Gk philia love + anthropos man.
RELATED: anthropologist misanthrope misanthropy philanthropic philanthropy

72. arkhein begin, rule
Greek: ARCH, ARCHI rule; govern

[1] Gk arche beginning, rule; archos ruler; archein begin, rule

anarchist: one advocating lawlessness and the absence of government. [1] Gk a (priv.) + archo rule.
archaic: out of date; of an earlier or more primitive time. [1] Gk arkein to begin.
archeology: study of human life and culture by excavating sites. [1] Gk arkein to begin + logos study.
archives: records; depository for records. [1] Gk archeion public office < archo rule.
hierarchy: persons or things arranged in ranks and grades. [1] Gk hieros sacred + archos ruler.
monarchy: rule by one ruler. [1] Gk monos alone + archos rule.
oligarchy: rule by a few. [1] Gk oligos few + archo rule.
patriarch: leader of a tribe. [1] Gk patria race + archo rule.

RELATED: anarchy hierarch hierarchical monarch monarchist oligarch patriarchal
COMMON: arch- [1] -arch [1] archaeo- [1] archi- [1] -archy [1]

73. dhes- (religious concepts)
Greek: THEO god

[1] L feriae holidays   [2] L festus festive
[3] L fanum temple
[4] Gk theos (thes-os) god

fanaticism: excessive unreasoned zeal for a cause. [3] L fanaticus < fanum temple.
festive: joyous as for a feast. [2] L festivus < festus festive.
festoon: suspend decorations or flowers on strings. [2] L festus festive.
fete: honor or entertain with a feast .[2] L festus festive.
profane: secular; not religious; irreverent; (v) treat irreverently. [3] L pro (outside) + fanum temple.
profanation: the act of desecrating or treating sacred things irreverently [3] L pro (outside) + fanum temple.
atheist: person who believes the nonexistence of God or a supreme being. [4] Gk a (priv.) + theos god.
apotheosis: exaltation to divine honors; deification. [4] Gk apo (from) + theos god.
monotheist: person who believes one God or a supreme being exists. [4] Gk mono single + theos god.
pantheism: belief of God-nature unity. [4] Gk pas (all) + theos God.
pantheon: temple honoring all gods or heroes. [4] Gk pantheios of all gods < pan (all) + theos god.
polytheism: belief in the existence of many gods. [4] Gk poly many + theos god.
theocentric: holding God as its center or center of interest. [4] Gk theos God + kentron center.
theology: study of God, his attributes, and religious doctrines. [4] Gk theos God + logos discourse.
RELATED: atheism atheistic festal monotheism pantheist pantheistic polytheist theurgic theurgical theurgically theocrat theocratic theologian theological
COMMON: enthusiasm [4] fair [1] feast [2] -fest [2] festival [2] fiesta [2] theo- [4] theocracy [4] tiffany [4]

74. dyeu- to shine (sky, heaven, god)
Latin: DIA, DIURN, JOURN day

[1] L Iovis Jupiter   [2] L deus god
[3] L divus divine, god   [4] L dies day

adjournment: postponement of a session for a time. [4] L ad (to) + diurnus daily < dies day.
circadian: having a period of 24 hours. [4] L circa (around) + dies day.
deify: exalt to a the status of a god. [2] L deificus < deus god.
deism: belief in a creator God who has not intervened after creation. [2] L deus god.
diurnal: daily; done in the daytime. [4] L diurnalis < diurnus daily < dies day.
diva: highly successful female singer esp. operatic. [3] L diva goddess.
divine: being or having the qualities of a deity; sacred; delightful. [3] L diva goddess.
jovial: convivial; fun-loving; cheerful. [1] L Iovis Jupiter.
meridian: circle of points on the earth with the same longitude. [4] L medius middle + dies day.
quotidian: daily. [4] L quot (how many) + dies day.
sojourn: reside or dwell temporarily; abide for a time. [4] Fr sejourner < L sub (under) + diurnus daily.
RELATED: adjourn deity
COMMON: adieu [2] Deus [2] dial [4] diary [4] diet [4] dismal [4] journal [4] journey [4] journeyman [4] Jove [1]

75. ghwel-
Latin: FALL, FALS, FAIL deceive; fail

[1] L fallo (falsus) to deceive, fail; fallax false

default: a failure in or neglect of an obligation or duty. [1] L de (away) + fallo deceive.
fallacious: involving incorrect reasoning; deceptive; misleading. [1] L fallacia < fallo deceive.
fallible: liable to error or mistake. [1] L fallo deceive.
falter: to hesitate; stumble. [1] L fallo deceive.
infallible: exempt from error or mistake. [1] L in (not) + fallo deceive.
COMMON: false [1] fault [1] falsify [1] falsetto [1]

76. kerd-[1] heart
Latin: CRED believe, trust
Greek: CARDI- heart

[1] L cor (stem cord-) heart; concordare (concordatus) to agree, be in harmony
[2] L credere (creditus; pfp credens) to believe; credulus trusting
[3] Gk kardia heart
[4] OE heorte heart

accord: agreement; concurrence; harmony; a settlement; (v) to grant or bestow. [1] L ad- + cor, cord- heart.
cardiologist: medical doctor specializing in heart disorders. [3] Gk kardia heart.
concord: agreement; harmonious sounds. [1] L concordare to agree.
cordial: friendly; warm towards others. [1] L cor, cord- heart.
credence: confidence based on external evidence; belief. [2] L credens (pfp credo) believe
credible: worthy of belief, credit, confidence, or acceptance. [2] L credibilis < credo believe.
creditable: deserving or reflecting credit; praiseworthy; meritorious. [2] L creditum < credo believe.
credo: a creed; a set of beliefs one tries to live by. [2] L credo believe.
credulity: tendency to believe on insufficient evidence. [2] L credulus < credo believe.
discordant: conflicting, disagreeable sound. [1] Fr < L discordia < dis (apart) + cor heart.
discredit: to injure the credit or reputation of; dishonor. [2] L creditum < credo believe, trust.
dishearten: to degrade someone's resolution or courage; to demoralize. [4] OE dis- + heorte heart.
incredulous: not believing. [2] L credulus < credo believe.
miscreant: a vile wretch; evil-doer; misbeliever; infidel. [2] OF mescreant unbelieving < L credo believe.
recreant: unfaithful to a cause; false; a cowardly or faithless person. [2] L re (again) + credo believe.
RELATED: cardiology credent credibility credulous discord
COMMON: cardiac [3] courage [1] credential [2] credit [2] creed [2] grant [2] heart [4] incredible [2] quarry [1] record [1]

77. mel-[5] false, bad, wrong
Latin: MAL- bad; ill

[1] L malus bad
[2] Gk blasphemos blasphemous

blasphemy: speaking impiously or revilingly of God or sacred beings. [2] Gk blapto hurt + phemi speak.
malaise: sense of unease, depression, or discomfort. [1] Fr mal + aise ease.

malefactor: a wrongdoer; a criminal. [1] L male ill + facere do.
malevolence: the attribute of having an evil disposition toward others. [1] L malus bad + volo wish.
malfeasance: unlawful or wrongful action; wrongdoing in general. [1] Fr < L malus bad + facio do.
malicious: acting deliberately or spitefully to harm. [1] L malus bad.
malingerer: one pretending to be ill to avoid work. [1] Fr malingre sickly < L mal- + aeger.
RELATED: blaspheme blasphemer blasphemous malediction maleficence maleficent malevolent maliciousness
COMMON: blame [2] dismal [1] mal- [1] maladroit [1] malady [1] malaria [1] maledict [1] malfeasance [1] malice [1] malign [1]

78. reg-¹ move in a straight line, lead, rule

Latin: REG, RIG, RECT rule; straight; right   ROGA ask

[1] L regere (rectus; pfp regens) to lead
    straight, guide, rule; corrigo to correct;
    surgo to stand up

[2] L rex king   [3] L regula straight piece of wood, rod
[4] L rogare (rogatus) to ask, beg   [5] L ergo therefore
[6] Gk oregein (aor orexa) to stretch out,
    reach out for; orexis desire
[7] OE riht right, just, correct   [8] OE rice strong, powerful; realm
[9] OE raca rake   [10] OE ranc straight, strong, overbearing
[11] OE gerecnian arrange in order, recount   [12] OE receleas careless

abrogate: to annul, abolish. [4] L ab + rogo propose a law.
adroit: having dexterity or deftness. [1] Fr a droit < L ad-+ directus.
anorectic: lacking appetite. [6] Gk ana (without) + oregein to stretch out, reach out for.
arrogance: showing haughtiness and unjustified pride. [4] OF arrogance < L ad (to) + rogo ask.
arrogate: to take, demand, or claim unreasonably or presumptuously; assume; usurp. [4] L ad + rogo ask.
derogatory: disparaging. [4] L derogatus < de (from) + rogo propose a law.
dirge: funeral song or hymn expressing mourning. [1] L dirigo direct.
ergo: therefore. [5] L ergo therefore.
forthright: straightforward; without any evasiveness. [7] OE forth + right.
incorrigible: beyond reform. [1] L in (not) + corrigo < con (together) + rego rule.
insurrection: revolt against civil authorities. [1] L insurrectus (pp insurgere) to rise up.
interregnum: a time of vacancy of the throne; period of abeyance. [1] L inter (between) + regnum reign.
interrogate: to formally ask questions of. [4] L inter (between, among) + rogo ask.
maladroit: clumsy; inept. [1] Fr mal- + adroit adroit < a + L directus < dis + regere to guide.
orectic: of or pert. to the appetites or desires; appetent. [6] Gr orektikos < orexis desire.
prerogative: privilege. [4] L prae (before) + rogo ask.
rectitude: uprightness. [1] Fr < L rectitudo < rectus straight, right.
rectify: make right; correct. [1] L rectus right + facio make.
rectilinear: pert. to, consisting of, movement in a straight line. [1] L rectus straight, right + linea line.
regal: belonging to or fit for a king; royal; stately. [2] OF < L regalis royal.
regime: a current or former ruling government; a regimen. [1] OF < L regimen government < regere to rule.
regimen: systematized course of living. [1] OF < L rego rule.
regimentation: organized and systematic control and direction as in a military corps. [1] OF < L rego rule.
regicide: killing of a king or sovereign. [2] L rex king + caedo kill.

resurge: to rise again; to renew former influence. [1] L re- (again) + surgere to rise.
surrogate: a substitute. [4] L surrogatus (pp surrogo) substitute.
unruly: difficult, if not impossible, to control. [3] OE un- + L regula rule, principle.
RELATED: anorexia arrogant arrogation corrigible derogate derogation insurrectionary interrogation interrogator interrogatory maladroitness prorogation orective orexis rectification rectitude resurgent regiment
COMMON: address [1] alert [1] bishopric [8] correct [1] correction [1] corrective [1] correctness [1] direct [1] direction [1] directive [1] director [1] directory [1] dirigible [1] erect [1] erection [1] incorrect [1] indirect [1] insurgent [1] interrogative [4] irregular [3] irregularity [3] misrule [3] rail [3] rake [9] rank [10] real [2] realm [4] reckless [12] reckon [11] rectangle [1] rector [1] rectum [1] regale [2] regalia [2] regency [1] regent [1] regina [1] region [1] regnant [2] regular [3] regularity [3] regulate [3] regulator [3] regulatory [3] reign [2] rich [8] right [7] royal [2] rule [3] ruler [3] source [1] surge [1] viceroy [2]

79. sak- sanctify
Latin: SACER, SACR, SECR sacred   SANCT holy

[1] L sacer holy, sacred, dedicated   [2] L sacerdos priest
[3] L sancire (sanctus) make sacred, consecrate

consecrate: declare to be holy or sacred. [1] L con (together) + sacer sacred.
desecrate: violate or profane something sacred. [1] L de + sacro make sacred.
execrable: abominable; accursed. [1] L ex (out) + sacer sacred.
execrate: to curse or call down evil upon. [1] L ex (out) + sacer sacred.
sacrilegious: profaning or ready to profane anything sacred. [1] OF < L sacer sacred + lego choose.
sacrosanct: peculiarly and exceedingly sacred. [3] L sacer sacred + sanctus (pp sancto) render sacred.
sanctification: the act of making holy, purifying. [3] Fr sanctifier make holy < L sanctio make holy.
sanctimonious: acting in a very pious manner. [3] L sanctio make holy.
sanction: ratification; a coercive measure used to penalize a violation of law. [3] Fr < L sanctio decree.
sanctity: sacredness; being worthy of protection. [3] L sancire (sanctus) make sacred, consecrate.
sanctuary: a holy place; a place of refuge; an area reserved for protection of wildlife. [2] L sacerdos priest.
RELATED: consecration desecration execration sacrilege sanctify sanctimony
COMMON: sacred [1] sacrifice [1] sacrificial [1] sacristan [1] sexton [1]

80. (s)twer-[1] turn, whirl
Latin: TURB, TURBIN commotion; crowd; disorder; whirlwind; spiral

[1] L turba crowd, tumult; turbare confuse,
    disorder < Gk turbe disorder, tumult
[2] OE storm storm   [3] OE styrian move, agitate

disturbance: event having disorder or abnormal amounts of noise. [1] L disturbo < dis (apart) + turba tumult.
imperturbable: incapable of being agitated. [1] L in- (not) + per (through) + turba crowd.
perturb: to cause agitation or alarm; unsettle. [1] L per (through) + turba tumult.
perturbation: disturbance; disorder; irregularity in motion of a planet. [1] L per (through) + turba tumult.
turbid: with sediments stirred up; cloudy; in confusion; disturbed. [1] L turbidus, turba disturbance.
turbulence: violent agitation or commotion. [1] L turbulentus turbulent.
RELATED: disturb disturbing imperturbability
COMMON: stir [3] storm [2] trouble [1] turbine [1]

81. s(w)e- personal and reflexive pronoun
Greek: ETHN nation ETH/ETHN

[1] L sui of oneself

[3] L sobrius not drunk

[5] L suescere (suetus) to accustom, get accustomed

[6] Gk ethos custom

[8] Gk idios personal, private

[9] OE self self, same

[2] L sed, se, se- without, apart

[4] L solus by oneself alone

[7] Gk ethnos nation, people

[10] OE sibb relative

desolate: lacking or unsuited for life. [4] L de- + solus by oneself alone.

insolence: arrogance, rudeness, and disrespect. [5] L in- (not) + solens (pp solere) to be accustomed.

sedition: rebelling or inciting rebellion against the state. [2] L sed, se, se- (without, apart).

seduction: inducing to violate proper conduct esp. in sexual activity. [2] L se- (apart) + ducere lead.

segregate: isolate or make into isolated groups. [2] L se (aside) + grex flock.

sobriety: abstinence from drugs or alcohol; seriousness and solemnity of manner. [3] L sobrius not drunk.

soliloquy: a speech revealing thoughts by a person when alone. [4] L solus (alone) + loqui to speak.

solipsism: belief that the self is the only reality or only thing knowable. [4] L solus by oneself alone.

solitary: being alone or apart from others. [4] L solus by oneself alone.

solitude: state of being apart from others. [4] L solus by oneself alone.

sullen: resentful; somber; morose. [4] L solus by oneself alone.

ethnology: study of human cultures and origin of races. [7] Gk ethnos race + logy.

idiomatic: characteristic of expressions that are peculiar to a language. [8] Gk idios personal, private.

sibling: a brother or sister. [10] OE sibb relative.

RELATED: ethnological ethnologist idiom seclusion

COMMON: custom [5] ethic [6] ethnic [7] ethno- [7] gossip [10] mastiff [5] obsolete [5] secede [2] seclude [2] secret [2] secure [2] select [2] self [9] separate [2] sever [2] sober [3] sole [4] solo [4] suicide [1] sure [2]

82. wal- be strong
Latin: VAL, [VAIL] strong, well, farewell

[1] L valere (pfp. valens) to be strong; validus strong

[2] OE wealdan to rule; wieldan to govern

ambivalence: having conflicting emotions toward a person or thing. [1] L ambi both + valeo be strong.

countervail: oppose with equal power; counteract; offset. [1] L contra (against) + valeo be strong.

invalidate: to cancel or nullify. [1] L in- + validus strong < valere to be strong.

invaluable: of a value beyond estimation; very precious. [1] L in (not) + valeo be strong.

prevail: to win; to prove stronger; to predominate; to be in effect. [1] L prae + valere to be strong.

prevalent: predominant; common; of wide extent; frequent. [1] L prae (before) + valeo be strong.

unwieldy: hard to move or direct due to size, shape, or complexity. [2] OE un- + wealdan to rule.

valedictory: a farewell address. [1] L vale (imper valeo be well) farewell + dico say.

valid: the quality of holding or being true. [1] L valeo be strong.

validate: ratify and confirm. [1] L validus < valeo be strong.

RELATED: ambivalent prevailing prevalence valediction valedictorian valedictory valetudinary validity valuable value

COMMON: avail [1] available [1] convalesce [1] convalescent [1] devaluate [1] equivalent [1] evaluate [1] invalid [1] revalidate [1] unavailing [1] valance [1] vale [1] valence [1] valentine [1] valiance [1] valiant [1] valor [1] valorous [1] valueless [1] wield [2]

83. were-o- true, trustworthy
Latin: VER truth

[1] L verus true
[2] OE waer faith, pledge

aver: affirm; assert. [1] L ad (to) + verus true.
veracious: truthful; true. [1] L verax < verus true.
veridical: true. [1] L verus true + dicere to say.
verisimilitude: appearance of truth; liklihood; realism; resembling truth .[1] L verum truth + similis like.
verity: being a true representation or reality; true statement. [1] L veritas truth < verus true.
RELATED: veracity verisimilar
COMMON: verdict [1] verifiable [1] verification [1] verify [1] veritable [1] warlock [2]

84. CULP blame, fault

[1] L culpa fault

culpable: deserving of blame or censure. [1] OF < L culpabilis < culpa fault.
exculpate: to exonerate; excuse. [1] L ex + culpo blame < culpa fault.
inculpate: to charge with wrong-doing; implicate. [1] L in (in) + culpa fault.
RELATED: culpability
COMMON: culprit [1]

CHAPTER 15

Roots Referring to Speech and Writing

The sixth category of roots, covered in this chapter, refers directly to speaking, shouting, and writing. Twelve roots fall into this category. Seven roots involve the meaning of speaking. Five mean speaking; one refers to the mouth but has spawned words involving speaking; and one involves shouting:

'bha-²' meaning "speak"
'kele-²' meaning "shout"
'os-¹' meaning "mouth"
'tolkʷ-' meaning "to speak"
'wed-²' meaning "speak"
'wekʷ-' meaning "speak"
'were-³' meaning "to speak"

The root 'bha-²' meaning "speak" is the source of the Latin verb 'fari' meaning "to speak" and 'fama' meaning "talk" or "fame," the Greek 'phone' meaning "voice" or "sound," and the English words 'ban,' 'banish,' and 'abandon.' A second root 'kele-²' meaning "shout" is the source of the Latin verb 'calere' meaning "call" or "summon" and 'clamare' meaning "call," for the Greek 'kalein' meaning "to call," for the Old English 'hlowan' meaning "to low" or "to roar," and the English words 'low,' 'haul,' and 'halyard.' The root 'os-¹' meaning "mouth" is the source of the Latin word 'os' meaning "mouth" or "opening." Another root 'tolkʷ-' meaning "to speak" is the source of the Latin verb 'loqui' meaning "to speak." The root 'wed-²' meaning "speak" is the source of the Greek 'oide' meaning "song." The root 'wekʷ-' meaning "speak" is the source of the Latin verb 'vocare' meaning "to call" and 'vox' meaning "voice." It is also the source of the Greek word 'ops' meaning "voice." Finally the root 'were-³' meaning "to speak" is the source of the Latin verb 'verbum' meaning "word." It is also the source of the Greek 'eirein' meaning "to speak" or "to say" and the English word 'word.' Five other roots have spawned many words related to speech, writing, and written matter:

'deik-' meaning "show, indicate, point"
'gerbh-' meaning "scratch"
'leg-¹' meaning "to collect"
'dheie-' meaning "see, look"
'yewes-' meaning "law"

The root 'deik-' meaning "show, indicate, point" is the source of the Latin verb 'dicere' meaning "say" and 'dicare' meaning "proclaim," the Greek 'deiknumi' meaning "to show," and the English words 'toe,' 'teach,' and 'token.' The root 'gerbh-' meaning "scratch" is the source of the Greek verb 'graphein' meaning "to write" and the English words 'carve,' 'crab,' and 'crawl.' The root 'leg-¹' meaning "to collect" is the source of the Latin verb 'legere' meaning "to choose" or "to read" and 'lex' meaning "law," the Greek 'legein' meaning "to gather" or "to speak" and 'logos' meaning "speech" and "reason," and the English word 'leech.' The root 'dheie-' meaning "see, look" is the source of the Greek 'thauma' meaning "wonder" and 'sema' meaning "sign." The root 'yewes-' meaning "law" is the source of the Latin verb 'ius, iuris' meaning "right" or "law."

SOUND SHIFTS

There are several shifts in consonants that show up in some of the roots. The Indo-European rough labial 'bh' sound becomes an 'f' sound (represented in English as a 'ph' showing the Greek origin) in Latin and Greek. The corresponding West Germanic and Old English form is the voiced labial 'b.' The root 'bha-2' meaning "speak" is the source of the Latin verb 'fari' meaning "to speak" and 'fama' meaning "talk" or "fame" and the Greek 'phone' meaning "voice" or "sound." It is the source of the English words 'ban,' 'banish,' and 'abandon.' Second, the root 'gerbh-' meaning "scratch" is the source of the Greek verb 'graphein' meaning "to write" and the English words 'carve,' 'crab,' and 'crawl.'

If Indo-European and Latin and Greek have the smooth palatal mute 'k,' the corresponding West Germanic and Old English form becomes a rough palatal 'h.' Thus 'deik-' meaning "show, indicate, point" is the source of the Latin verb 'dicere' meaning "say" and 'dicare' meaning "proclaim" and of the Greek 'deiknumi' meaning "to show." It is also the source of the English words 'toe,' 'teach,' and 'token.' A second root 'kele-2' meaning "shout" is the source of the Latin verb 'calere' meaning "call" or "summon" and 'clamare' meaning "call," the Greek 'kalein' meaning "to call," the Old English 'hlowan' meaning "to low" or "to roar," and the English words 'low,' 'haul,' and 'halyard.'

Table 7.1 (p. 000) shows that where Indo-European and Latin and Greek have the voiced palatal mute 'g,' the corresponding West Germanic and Old English form is the smooth palatal 'k.' Hence 'gerbh-' meaning "scratch" is the source of the Greek verb 'graphein' meaning "to write" and the English words 'carve,' 'crab,' and 'crawl.' The root 'leg-1' meaning "to collect" is the source of the Latin verb 'legere' meaning "to choose" or "to read" and 'lex' meaning "law," the Greek 'legein' meaning "to gather" or "to speak" and 'logos' meaning "speech" and "reason," and the English word 'leech.'

When Indo-European and Latin and Greek have a voiced dental mute 'd,' the corresponding West Germanic and Old English form will show a smooth dental 't.' Consequently 'deik-' means "show, indicate, point," which is the source of the Latin verb 'dicere' meaning "say" and 'dicare' meaning "proclaim," the Greek 'deiknumi' meaning "to show," and the English words 'toe,' 'teach,' and 'token.'

Where Indo-European had a rough dental 'dh' sound, Greek has a 'th' sound. Thus 'dheie-' meaning "see, look" is the source of the Greek 'thauma' meaning "wonder" and 'sema' meaning "sign."

The fourth rule in chapter 7 shows that the w sound of Indo-European is retained in the Old English forms. In the case of Latin it is occasionally dropped and otherwise represented by the letter 'v,' which, however, was pronounced as a w sound. The original w sound in Greek disappeared becoming a rough breathing or h sound or in many cases was dropped altogether. We see this phenomena with the root 'wed-2' meaning "speak," which is the source of the Greek 'oide' meaning "song." The root 'wekʷ-' meaning "speak" is the source of the Latin verb 'vocare' meaning "to call" and 'vox' meaning "voice" and the Greek 'ops' meaning "voice." Finally 'were-3' meaning "to speak" is the source of the Latin verb 'verbum' meaning "word," the Greek 'eirein' meaning "to speak" or "to say," and the English word 'word.'

For Indo-European labiovelar 'gʷ' or 'kʷ,' the 'g,' 'k,' or the 'w' may get dropped. It does not change for the root 'tolkʷ-' meaning "to speak," which is the source of the Latin verb 'loqui' meaning "to speak." The root 'wekʷ-' meaning "speak" is the source of the Latin verb 'vocare' meaning "to call" and 'vox' meaning "voice" and the Greek 'ops' meaning "voice."

Two of the roots covered do not show the sound shift changes covered in chapter 7, namely, 'os-1' meaning "mouth," which is the source of the Latin word 'os' meaning "mouth" or "opening," and 'yewes-' meaning "law," which is the source of the Latin verb 'ius, iuris' meaning "right" or "law."

LIST OF ROOTS IN ORDER OF OCCURRENCE

The following list gives the roots in the order found in this chapter. Syllables with capital letters show sequences of letters in English words generally indicating the root as the origin of the word containing them. In nearly all cases, if one sees the letters in capital letters in an English word, one can infer that it comes from the Indo-European root in the first column. However, there may also be some English words from the root that do not accord with the general pattern and some English words that fit the pattern but come from a different root.

85.	bha-^{2} speak	FA, FAT, FESS speak —> FAR divine law
		PHEMI PHON sound
86.	deik- show, indicate, point	DIC, DICT say, speak, assert VINDIC defend; justify DEIKN show
87.	gerbh- scratch	GRAPH, GRAM write; draw; describe; record
88.	kele-^{2} shout	CIL, (CAL) call; summon —> CLAM, [CLAIM] call out; shout
89.	leg-^{1} to collect	LEG, LIG, LECT choose, gather —> LEG, LECT read —> LEG
		law LEGA
		LEG, LOG idea; word; speech; discussion; reason; study, choose, pick
90.	os-^{1} mouth	ORA mouth, speech, prayer
91.	dheie- see, look	SEMA, SEMAT sign
92.	tolk^w- to speak	LOQU, LOCUT speak
93.	wed-^{2} speak	OD song
94.	wek^w- speak	VOC, VOK voice, call EP word
95.	were-^{3} to speak	VERB word
96.	yewes- law	JUR just, right, justice, oath —> JUDIC judge, decide

85. bha-^{2} speak

Latin: FA, FAT, FESS speak —> FAR divine law
Greek: PHEMI speech PHON sound

[1] L fari (fatus) to speak; fabula story	[2] LL bannus, bannum proclamation
[3] L fama talk, reputation, fame	[4] L fateri (fassus) acknowledge, admit
[5] Gk phanai to speak	[6] Gk pheme saying, speech
[7] Gk blasphemes evil speaking	[8] Gk phone voice, sound; phonein to speak
[9] OF ban summons, proclamation < Ger	[10] OE bannan to summon, proclaim
[11] OF banir to banish	[12] ON bon prayer, request

affable: courteous and mild in manner. [1] L ad + for speak.
confabulate: to chat; gossip; converse. [1] L con + fabula conversation < fari to speak.
contraband: goods illegally imported or exported. [2] L contra- (against) + bando legal proclamation.
defame: to slander, libel or attempt to injure a person's reputation. [3] L diffama < dis + fama < for speak.
fabulous: fictitious, mythical; incredible; beyond belief. [1] L fabula < for speak.
fatalism: the belief that every event is predetermined and inevitable. [1] OF < L fatalis < for speak.
ineffable: inexpressible; too awesome or sacred to be expressed. [1] L in (not) + ex (out) + for speak.
infamous: having a very bad or evil reputation. [3] L in- + fama fame.
infantile: rel. to babies; showing very childish behavior. [1] L in- + fans (prp fari) to speak.
aphasia: loss of ability to speak or write and understand the same. [5] Gk a- (not) + phanai speak.
banal: commonplace; trite. [9] OF banal < ban summons to military service < Ger.
blasphemy: speaking impiously or revilingly of God or sacred beings. [7] Gk blapto hurt + phemi speak.
cacophonous: having an unpleasant or discordant sound. [8] Gk kakos bad + phone voice.

euphemism: mild expression. [6] Gk euphemismos < eu well + phemi speak.
euphonious: pleasant sounding. [8] Gk eu well + phone voic, sound.
polyphonic: making or representing more than one sound. [8] Gk poly many + phone voice, sound.
prophetic: foretelling events; rel to foretelling of events. [5] Gk pro (before) + phanein to speak.
RELATED: affability blaspheme cacophony confab confabulation confabulatory defamation euphony fable fatalist fate Fates
COMMON: abandon [9] anthem [8] antiphon [8] ban [9,10] bandit [9] banish [11] blame [7] boon [12] confess [4] contraband [9] fairy [1] fame [3] famous [3] infant [1] infantry [1] megaphone [8] -phasia [5] phone [8] -phone [8] phonetic [8] phonics [8] -phono [8] phonograph [8] -phony [8] preface [1] profess [4] profession [4] professional [4] professor [4] prophet [5] symphony [8] xylophone [8]

86. deik- show, indicate, point; pronounce
Latin: DIC, DICT say, speak, assert VINDIC defend; justify; avenge
Greek: DEIKN show

[1] L digitus finger
[3] L dicare (dicatus) consecrate, proclaim
[5] L iudex judge
[7] L vindico (vindicatus) defend
[8] Gk deiknumi (pfm dedeigmai; aorp edeikthen) to show
[9] OE ta toe
[11] OE taecan show, instruct

[2] L dicere (dictus) say, tell
[4] L index indicator, forefinger
[6] L vindex surety, claimant, avenger
[10] OE tacan sign, mark

abdicate: to renounce or abandon an office or power esp. the office of king. [3] L ab (from) + dico say.
addiction: a compulsive need for some substance or practice. [2] L ad- + dicere (dictus) say, tell.
avenge: to get revenge; to punish in return. [7] L ad- + vindicare to claim.
benediction: blessing. [2] L bene well + dico say.
conditional: expressing conditions; not absolute. [2] Fr < L condicio < con (together) + dico mention.
contradiction: assertion of two claims that cannot both be true. [2] L contra (against) + dicere to speak.
dictator: person invested with absolute power. [2] L dictatus (pp dicto freq dico) say.
dictum: an authoritative or positive utterance. [2] L dico say.
edict: public notice. [2] L e (out) + dico say.
juridical: legal. [2] L juridicus < jus law + dico declare.
jurisdiction: having authority to decide legal cases. [2] L jurisdictio < juris right, law + dico speak.
indicative: pointing out; showing something; stating an idea or fact. [4] L in- + dicare to say.
indict. to charge or accuse of wrongdoing or crimes. [2] L indicto < in (in) + dico say.
indite: to put into words or writing; frame an expression or composition. [2] L indicto < in (in) + dico say.
interdict: prohibit by legal sanction; cut off activities, trade, or communication. [2] L inter + dicere to say.
paradigm: a model or pattern to follow. [8] Gk para (beside) + deiknymi show.
predicament: situation from which extrication is very difficult. [3] L prae + dicare to speak.
vindicate: to defend against attacks; maintain successfully; justify. [6] L vindicatus (pp vindico) defend.
vindictive: having a revengeful spirit; punitive. [6] L vindicatus (pp vindico) defend.
RELATED: abdication addict condition contradict interdiction malediction valedictory vindicative
COMMON: betoken [10] dedicate [3] dictate [2] diction [2] digit [1] disk [8] ditto [2] ditty [2] index [4] indicate [4] indiction [2] judge [5] judicial [5] maledict [2] malediction [2] policy [7] preach [3] predicate [3] predict [2] prediction [2] prejudice [5] revenge [6] teach [11] toe [9] token [10] valedictorian [2] vendetta [6] verdict [2] veridical [2]

87. gerbh- scratch
Greek: GRAPH, GRAM write; draw; describe; record

[1] Gk graphein (pfm gegrammai) scratch, write; gramma picture,
    written letter; gramme a line

[2] OE ceorfan to cut   [3] OE crabba a crab

[4] ON krafla to crawl

anagram: a word or phrase made from another by rearranging its letters. [1] Gk ana back + grapho write.
cartographer: a mapmaker. [1] L charta paper (papyrus) + graphein to write.
choreography: the arrangement of the movements of a ballet. [1] Gk choreia dance + grapho write.
epigram: witty thought. [1] Gk epi (on) + grapho write.
epigraph: carved inscription on a tomb; superscription prefixed to a book. [1] Gk epi (upon) + grapho write.
graphology: study of handwriting esp. to analyze character. [1] Gk graphos writing + ology.
holograph: document handwritten solely by its signer. [1] Gk holos whole + grapho write.
monograph: a book, article, or paper written about a single subject. [1] Gk monos single + grapho write.
orthography: science of spelling. [1] Gk orthos straight + grapho write.
pictograph: a picture representing an idea, as in primitive writing. [1] L pictor painter + Gk grapho write.
seismograph: instrument measuring earthquake intensity. [1] Gk seismos earthquake + grapho write.
stenography: process of writing in or taking dictation in shorthand. [1] Gk stenos narrow + grapho write.
topography: representation of surface features of regions of land. [1] Gk topos place + grapho write.
RELATED: cacography choreographer lithograph stenographer
COMMON: autobiography [1] bibliography [1] biography [1] calligraphy [1] carve [2] crab [3] crabbed [3] crawl
[4] cryptogram [1] demography [1] diagram [1] geographer [1] geography [1] glamour [1] graft [1] gram [1] -gram
[1] grammar [1] grammarian [1] grammatical [1] graph [1] -graph [1] -grapher [1] graphic [1] graphite [1] -graphy
[1] kilogram [1] lithography [1] monogram [1] oceanography [1] paragraph [1] parallelogram [1] phonograph [1]
photograph [1] program [1] telegram [1] telegraph [1] telegraphy [1]

88. kele-² shout
Latin: CIL, (CAL) call; summon —> CLAM, [CLAIM] call out; shout

[1] L clamare (clamatus) call, cry out   [2] L concilium meeting
[3] L calendae the calends   [4] L calare (calatus) call, summon
[5] L clarus bright, clear   [6] L classis summons
[7] Gk kalein (aorp eklethein) to call; ekklesia assembly
[8] OE hlowan to roar, low   [9] OF haler to haul

acclaim: give enthusiastic approval; praise. [1] L acclamare shout at < ad (to) + clamare call.
clairvoyant: intuitive perceiver of unsensed events. [5] Fr clair clear + voyant seeing < L videre see.
clamor: loud repeated outcry or noisy confusion of voices. [1] L clamor < clamo cry out.
conciliatory: seeking to reduce enmity or hostility; placating; making peace. [2] L concilium council.
declamation: speech recited from memory; bombastic rhetoric. [1] L de (intens.) + clamo cry out.
disclaim: disavow any connection with or responsibility for; disown; reject. [1] L dis + clamo cry out.
ecclesiastical: rel. to the nature and functions of a church. [7] Gk ekklesia assembly.
exclaim: to utter suddenly and forcefully. [1] L ex- + clamare to call.
intercalate: insert or interpolate esp. a day or month in a calendar. [4] L inter (between) + calare proclaim.
irreconcilable: not able to be restored to friendship after an estrangement. [2] L re- + concilium council.
proclamation: a public authoritative announcement. [1] L pro (forth) + clamo call.

reclamation: an obtaining the return or restoration of. [1] L re (again) + clamo call.
reconcile: restore to friendship after an estrangement. [2] L re (again) + concilium council.
RELATED: acclamation clamorous conciliate conciliation declaim ecclesiastic intercalary proclaim reclaim reconciliation
COMMON: acclaim [1] calendar [3] claim [1] claimant [1] clamor [1] clear [5] council [2] class [6] classify [6] classification [6] declare [5] eclair [5] exclamation [1] halyard [9] haul [9] keelhaul [9] low [8]

89. leg-¹ to collect
Latin: LEG, LIG, LECT choose, gather —> LEG, LECT read —> LEG law LEGA
Greek: LEG, LOG idea; word; speech; discussion; reason; study, choose, pick

[1] L legere (lectus) to gather, choose, read

[2] L lignum wood, firewood

[3] L lex law

[4] L legare (legatus) to commission, charge

[5] Gk legein (pfm eilegmai; aorp elekthen) to gather, speak; lexikos of words

[6] Gk logos speech, word, reason

[7] OE laece physician

colleague: fellow member or associate of a profession or organization. [4] L com (with) + legare to depute.
diligent: industrious, painstaking. [1] Fr < L diligens careful.
electorate: those who elect; mass of voters. [1] L electus (pp eligo) < e (out) + lego choose.
electors: those qualified to vote in an election. [1] L electus (pp eligo) < e (out) + lego choose.
eligible: qualified; fit for selection. [1] OF eligible < L eligo select < e (out) + lego choose.
intelligentsia: the class of highly educated and thinkers in a society. [1] L inter- + legere to choose.
intellect: the ability to reason and think abstractly and deeply. [1] L intellectus intellect.
legacy: something left by will; something derived from an ancestor. [4] L legatum < lego bequeath.
relegate: to consign to a lower position, class, or place; exile. [4] L re (back) + lego send.
analogous: corresponding or similar to. [6] Gk ana (according) + logos speech.
analogy: a comparison showing a correspondence or similarity. [6] Gk analogous proportion < lego speak.
anthology: a collection of poems or stories. [5] Gk anthos flower + lego speak.
apologist: person who argues in defense of a doctrine or institution. [5] Gk apologos < apo (from) + lego speak.
apologue: a fable or moral tale. [5] Gk apologos < apo (from) + lego speak.
dialectic: testing validity by question and answer; resolving contradictions. [5] Gk dia (between) + lego talk.
dialogue: conversation discussing ideas; speech in a written work. [5] Gk dia (between) + lego talk.
doxology: hymn praising God. [5] Gk doxa praise + lego speak.
eclectic: selecting from various systems and doctrines. [5] Gk ek (out) + lego select.
ecology: study of organisms and their environment. [5] Gk oikos house + -logy study.
epilogue: concluding literary portion. [5] Gk epi (upon) + lego say.
eschatological: rel. to the end of history and Christ's Second Coming. [6] Gk eskhatos last + logos speech.
etymology: the origin and evolution of a word. [6] Gk etymos true + logos word < lego speak.
eulogy: a speech or writing in praise of a dead person. [6] Gk eulogia praise < eu well + lego speak.
homologous: same in relative position, structure, and character. [6] Gk homos same + lego speak.
ideology: doctrines and way of thinking of an individual or group. [6] Gk idea an idea + lego speak.
lexicon: dictionary. [5] Gk lexicon < lexikos of words.
ornithology: the study of birds. [6] Gk ornis, ornith-, bird + logos study.
paleontology: study of life in prehistoric times. [6] Gk palaios ancient + logos study.
philology: study of words. [6] Gk philo- love + logos reason, speech.

prologue: introduction to a poem or play. [5] Gk pro (before) + logos discourse.

syllogism: deductive reasoning with two premises and inferred conclusion. [6] Gk syn (with) + logos.

tautology: a statement redundant or true without reference to facts. [6] Gk tauto the same + lego speak.

RELATED: analectic analogue dialectician dialectical dialectics diligence ecologist elect electoral etymologist eulogize legation

COMMON: anthropology [6] apology [6] archeology [6] astrology [6] catalog [5] coil [1] collect [1] collection [1] collective [1] collector [1] college [4] collegial [4] cosmology [6] cull [1] Decalogue [6] delegate [4] delegation [4] dermatology [6] dialect [5] dyslexia [5] entomology [6] genealogy [6] intelligent [1] lectern [1] lector lecture [1] leech [7] legal [3] legend [1] legible [1] legion [1] legislation [3] legislator [3] legitimate [3] lesson [1] ligne- [2] ligneous [2] logarithm [6] logic [6] logical [6] logistic [6] logo- [6] logos [6] loyal [3] monologue [5] morphology [6] necrology [6] neglect [1] pathology [6] philologist [6] privilege [3] psychology [6] sacrilege [1] select [1] technology [6] tetralogy [6] trilogy [6] zoology [6]

90. os-[1] mouth

Latin: ORA mouth, speech, prayer

[1] L os (or-) mouth, face, opening

adoration: utmost love or devotion; worship; deep admiration. [1] Fr < L ad (to) + oro pray < os mouth.

inexorable: not to be moved by entreaty; unyielding. [1] L in (not) + ex (out) + oro pray.

oracular: prophetic. [1] Fr < L oraculum < oro pray.

orator: eloquent public speaker. [1] L orator < oratus (pp oro pray, plead).

orifice: opening. [1] Fr < L os mouth + facio make.

oscillate: swinging back and forth with regularity. [1] L oscillo < oscillum swing.

peroration: an harangue; the conclusion or summing up of a speech. [1] L per + oro speak.

RELATED: adorable adore adoring oration oratorical oratory perorate

COMMON: oral [1] usher [1]

91. dheie- see, look

Greek: SEMA, SEMAT sign THAUM, THAUMAT wonder

[1] Gk sema sign   [2] Gk thauma wonder
[3] Gk theorein look at

semantic: pert. to meaning. [1] Gk semantikos significant < sema sign.

sememe: meaning of the smallest unit carrying meaning in words. [1] Gk sema sign + -eme.

theoretical: conceptual and hypothetical as opposed to practical action. [3] Gk theorein look at.

COMMON: semaphore [1] theory [3]

92. tolk^w- to speak

Latin: LOQU, LOCUT speak

[1] L loqui (locutus; pfp loquens) to speak; loquax, -acis talkative

circumlocution: indirect, roundabout expression. [1] L circumlocutio < circum (around) + loquor speak.

colloquial: relating to informal conversational speech. [1] L col (together) + loquor speak.

colloquy: a conference. [1] L col (together) + loquor speak.

elocution: public speaking emphasizing delivery. [1] L eloqui to speak out < ex- + loqui to speak.

eloquence: persuasive moving speech. [1] L ex-(out) + loquor speak.

grandiloquent: having a pompous or bombastic style. [1] L grandis grand + loquens < loquor speak.

interlocutor: one who takes part in a conversation; an interpreter; questioner. [1] L inter + loquor speak.

locution: mode of speech; idiom; phrase; discourse. [1] L locutio < loquor speak.

loquacious: extremely talkative. [1] L loquax talkative.

obloquy: state of being in disgrace; infamy; defamation. [1] L ob (against) + loquor speak.

soliloquy: a monologue. [1] L solus alone + loquor talk.

RELATED: circumlocutory colloquialism colloquium grandiloquence loquaciousness loquacity soliloquize

COMMON: eloquent [1] ventriloquism [1]

93. wed-² speak
Greek: OD song

[1] Gk oide song, ode

parody: imitation of a work in a fashion that ridicules it. [1] Gk para + oide song.

rhapsody: expression of great feeling; bliss. [1] Gk rhapsoidein recite poems < rhaptein sew + oide song.

threnody: an ode or song of lamentation; dirge. [1] Gk threnodia < threnos lament + ode song.

RELATED: rhapsodize

COMMON: comedy [1] melody [1] ode [1] tragedy [1]

94. wekʷ- speak
Latin: VOC, VOK voice, call
Greek: EP word

[1] L vox voice; vocalis of the voice

[2] L vocare (vocatus) to call; vocabulum name

[3] Gk ops voice

[4] Gk epos song, word

advocate: defend; plead for; (n) one pleading another's cause. [2] L advoco call to < ad (to) + vox voice.

avocation: hobby. [2] L ab (away) + voco call.

avouch: to affirm positively; proclaim; vouch for. [2] L ad + voco call.

convoke: to call together. [2] L con (together) + voco call.

disavowal: a denial of knowledge about or responsibility for. [2] L dis- + ad- + vocare to call.

epic: long poem of grandeur. [4] Gk epikos < epos word.

equivocal: susceptible of different interpretations; questionable. [2] L aequus equal + vox voice.

equivocate: to use ambiguous language with intent to deceive. [2] L aequus equal + vox voice.

evoke: to call forth. [2] L e (out) + voco call.

invoke: to call on supernatural beings for help; set in motion fixed procedures. [2] L in (on) + voco call.

irrevocable: unalterable; cannot be repealed or prevented. [2] L in (not) + re (again) + voco call.

provocative: serving to incite; causing anger. [2] OF provoquer < L pro (forth) + voco call.

revoke: to cancel, annul, or make void; failure to follow suit when required in cards [2] L re (again) + voco call.

unequivocal: understandable in only one way; distinct; plain. [2] L aequus equal + vox voice.

vocable: a word or a vocal sound. [2] Fr < L vocabulum < voco call.

vociferate: utter with a loud, vehement voice; exclaim noisily. [2] L vociferatus < vox voice + fero bear.

vouchsafe: to grant a privilege. [2] ME vouchen warrant + OF sauf safe < L vocare to call + salvus healthy.

RELATED: advocacy evocation evocative provoke revocable vociferous

COMMON: avow [2] calliope [3] invocation [2] vocabulary [2] vocal [1] vocation [2] voice [1] vouch [2] vowel [1]

95. were-[3] to speak
Latin: VERB word

[1] L verbum word
[2] Gk eirein say, speak   [3] Gk rhetor public speaker
[4] OE word word

irony: incongruity between an expression's meaning and its context. [2] Gk eiron dissembler < eirein say.
rhetoric: the art of speaking or writing persuasively. [3] Gk rhetor rhetor.
rhetorical: characterized by use of techniques of persuasive speech or writing. [3] Gk rhetor rhetorician.
verbalize: to state in words. [1] L verbum a word.
verbatim: repeating word for word. [1] L verbum a word.
verbiage: wordiness; excessive use of words. [1] Fr < L verbum word.
verbose: wordy; using more words than are needed. [1] L verbosus < verbum word.
verve: enthusiasm and liveliness of expression. [1] L verbum word.
RELATED: ironic ironist ironize verboseness verbosity
COMMON: adverb [1] proverb [1] verb [1] verbal [1] word [4]

96. yewes- law
Latin: JUR just, right, justice, oath —> JUDIC judge, decide

[1] L ius, iuris right, law; iurare swear; iurgare
    (iurgatus) to scold
[2] L iudex judge   [3] L iustus just

abjure: to renounce under oath; recant; repudiate. [1] L ab + juro swear.
adjudicate: act or process of deciding by a court of law or appointed arbiter. [2] L ad (to) + judicare judge.
adjure: to charge or entreat solemnly as under oath. [1] L ad + juro swear.
conjure: to produce by magic. [1] L con (together) + juro swear.
injudicious: having poor judgment; showing lack of discretion or wisdom. [2] L in (not) + judicium judgment.
injurious: harmful; detrimental. [1] OF injurer < L injuriosus < injuria wrong < in (not) + juris right.
judicious: according to sound judgment; wise. [2] L judicium judgment.
jurisdiction: having authority to decide legal cases. [1] L jurisdictio < juris right, law + dico speak.
jurisprudence: the science or philosophy of law; system of laws. [1] L juris right + prudentia foreseeing.
justifiable: that can be vindicated or defended. [3] OF justifier < L justus just + facio make.
justification: act of being vindicated; evidence or fact providing vindication. [3] L justus just + facio make.
objurgate: berate; rebuke; scold. [1] L ob- + iurgare scold, sue at law < agere do, proceed.
perjury: willful telling of a lie while under oath. [1] L per (through) + juris right, justice.
RELATED: justify injury objurgation
COMMON: injustice [3] judge [2] judicial [2] judiciary [2] jurist [1] juror [1] jury [1] just [3] justice [3] nonjuror [1] perjure [1] prejudice [2]

CHAPTER 16

Roots Referring to Perception and Thought

The seventh category of roots, presented in this chapter, refers primarily to perception, thinking, discovery, and knowledge. One root referring to will is included here as well. Fifteen roots fall into this category. Two roots specifically designate thought:

'gʷhren-' meaning "think"
and 'men-¹' meaning "to think"

The root 'gʷhren-' meaning "think" is the source of the Latin verb 'dicere' meaning "say" and 'dicare' meaning "proclaim" and the Greek 'phrazein' meaning "to show." The second root 'men-¹' meaning "to think" is the source of the Latin verb 'monere' meaning "to warn" and 'mens (ment-)' meaning "mind," the Greek 'mnemon' meaning "mindful," and the English word 'mind.' Four roots designate activity involving discovery, blocking discovery, or willing:

'krei-' meaning "sieve, discriminate, distinguish"
'krau-' meaning "conceal, hide"
'sag-' meaning "seek out"
'wel-²' meaning "wish, will"

The root 'krei-' meaning "sieve, discriminate, distinguish" is the source of the Latin verb 'cernere' meaning "sift" or "discern" and 'crimin' meaning "crime," Greek 'krinein' meaning "to decide" or "judge," Old English 'hridder' meaning "sieve," and the English word 'riddle.' The second root 'krau-' meaning "conceal, hide" is the source of the Greek verb 'kryptein' meaning "to conceal." The root 'sag-' meaning "seek out" is the source of the Latin verb 'sagire' meaning "to perceive," the Greek 'hegeisthai' meaning "to lead," and the English words 'seek,' 'sake,' and 'forsake.' Finally, 'wel-²' meaning "wish, will" is the source of the Latin 'velle' meaning "to wish" or "to will" and 'voluptus' meaning "pleasure," and the English words 'will,' 'well,' 'wealth,' and 'weal.' Two roots refer to knowledge or wisdom:

'gno-' meaning "know"
'SOPH' meaning "wise"

The root 'gno-' meaning "know" is the source of the Latin verb 'gnoscere' meaning "get to know" and 'nota' meaning "mark," the Greek 'gnosis' meaning "knowledge," and the English words 'can,' 'ken,' 'cunning,' 'know,' and 'knowledge.' The root 'SOPH' meaning "wise" is the source of the Greek word 'sophia' meaning "wisdom." Four roots refer to visual perception, one making a more general reference to perception but implying sight:

'okʷ-' meaning "to see"
'spek-' meaning "to observe"

'weid-' meaning "to see"
'wer-[4]' meaning "to perceive, watch out for"

The root 'ok^w-' meaning "to see" is the source of the Latin verb 'oculus' meaning "eye," the Greek 'ops' meaning "eye" and 'optos' meaning "visible," and the English words 'eye' and 'daisy.' The second root 'spek-' meaning "to observe" is the source of the Latin verb 'specere' meaning "to look at" and the Greek verb 'skopein' meaning "to view." The third root 'weid-' meaning "to see" is the source of the Latin verb 'videre' meaning "to see" and 'dividare' meaning "to separate," the Greek 'eidos' meaning "form," 'idea' meaning "appearance" or "form," and 'histor' meaning "wise," and the English words 'wit,' 'witticism,' 'twit,' 'wise,' and 'wisdom.' And the root 'wer-[4]' meaning "to perceive, watch out for" is the source of the Latin verb 'vereri' meaning "to respect," the Greek 'horan' meaning "to see," and the English word 'wary.' Finally, three roots refer to nonvisual perception:

'sep-[1]' meaning "taste, perceive"
'swen-' meaning "to sound"
'tag-' meaning "touch, handle"

The root 'sep-[1]' meaning "taste, perceive" is the source of the Latin verb 'sapere' meaning "to taste." The root 'swen-' meaning "to sound" is the source of the Latin word 'sonus' meaning "sound" and the English word 'swan.' Finally, 'tag-' meaning "touch, handle" is the source of the Latin verb 'tangere' meaning "to touch."

SOUND SHIFTS

The Indo-European, Latin, and Greek smooth palatal mute 'k' surfaces in West Germanic and Old English as a rough palatal 'h.' The root 'krei-' meaning "sieve, discriminate, distinguish" is the source of the Latin verb 'cernere' meaning "sift" or "discern" and 'crimin' meaning "crime," the Greek 'krinein' meaning "to decide" or "judge," the Old English 'hridder' meaning "sieve," and the English word 'riddle.'

If Indo-European and Latin and Greek show a voiced palatal mute 'g,' the corresponding West Germanic and Old English form is generally the smooth palatal 'k.' The root 'gno-' meaning "know" is the source of the Latin verb 'gnoscere' meaning "get to know" and 'nota' meaning "mark," the Greek 'gnosis' meaning "knowledge," and the English words 'can,' 'ken,' 'cunning,' 'know,' and 'knowledge.' Also, the root 'sag-' meaning "seek out" is the source of the Latin verb 'sagire' meaning "to perceive," the Greek 'hegeisthai' meaning "to lead," and the English words 'seek,' 'sake,' and 'forsake.'

The third general rule cited in chapter 7 applies to one root. (As you will recall, initial s sounds conjoined with following consonants usually show no change in Greek, Latin, and Old English. However, they do frequently disappear. An initial Indo-European 's' followed by a vowel tended to become a rough breathing or 'h' in classical Greek.) The root 'sag-' meaning "seek out" is the source of the Latin verb 'sagire' meaning "to perceive," the Greek 'hegeisthai' meaning "to lead," and the English words 'seek,' 'sake,' and 'forsake.'

When Indo-European and Latin and Greek have a voiced dental mute 'd,' West Germanic and Old English have a smooth dental 't.' We observe this phenomenon for 'weid-' meaning "to see," which is the source of the Latin verb 'videre' meaning "to see" and 'dividare' meaning "to separate" and the Greek 'eidos' meaning "form," 'idea' meaning "appearance" or "form," and 'histor' meaning "wise." Several English words 'wit,' 'witticism,' 'twit,' 'wise,' and 'wisdom' show the 't.'

The fourth rule from chapter 7 indicates that the w sound of Indo-European is retained in the Old English forms. In the case of Latin it is occasionally dropped and otherwise represented by the letter 'v,' which, however, was pronounced as a w sound. The original Greek w sound disappeared becoming a rough breathing or h sound and often was dropped altogether. We see this phenomenon with the root 'wer-[4]' meaning "to perceive, watch out for," which is the source of the Latin verb 'vereri' meaning "to respect," the Greek 'horan' meaning "to see," and the English word 'wary.' The root 'swen-' meaning "to sound" is the source of the Latin word 'sonus' meaning "sound" and the English word 'swan.' The 'w' is retained for the root in Latin and dropped in Greek for the root 'weid-' meaning "to see." It is the source of the Latin verb 'videre' meaning "to see" and 'dividare' meaning "to separate" and the Greek 'eidos' meaning "form," 'idea' meaning "appearance" or "form," and 'histor' meaning "wise." The 'w' is retained for the English words 'wit,' 'witticism,' 'twit,' 'wise,' and 'wisdom.'

The Indo-European labiovelar 'g^w' or 'k^w' may take different forms in Latin or Greek and may drop 'g,' 'k,' or 'w.' The root 'g^{w}hren-' meaning "think" is the source of the Latin verb 'dicere' meaning "say" and 'dicare' meaning "proclaim" and the Greek 'phrazein' meaning "to show." The root 'ok^w-' meaning "to see" is the source of the Latin verb 'oculus' meaning "eye." It is also the source of Greek 'ops' meaning "eye" and 'optos' meaning "visible" and the English words 'eye' and 'daisy.'

A number of the roots covered in this chapter do not show the sound shift changes covered in chapter 7. The root 'krau-' meaning "conceal, hide" is the source of the Greek verb 'kryptein' meaning "to conceal." 'Men-[1]' meaning "to think" is the source of the Latin verb 'monere' meaning "to warn" and 'mens (ment-)' meaning "mind," the Greek 'mnemon' meaning "mindful," and the English word 'mind.' 'Sep-[1]' meaning "taste, perceive" is the source of the Latin verb 'sapere' meaning "to taste." 'Spek-' meaning "to observe" is the source of the Latin verb 'specere' meaning "to look at" and the Greek verb 'skopein' meaning "to view." 'Tag-' meaning "touch, handle" is the source of the Latin verb 'tangere' meaning "to touch." And 'wel-[2]' meaning "wish, will" is the source of the Latin verb 'velle' meaning "to wish" or "to will" and 'voluptus' meaning "pleasure," and the English words 'will,' 'well,' 'wealth,' and 'weal.'

LIST OF ROOTS IN ORDER OF OCCURRENCE

The following list gives the roots in the order they are covered in this chapter. The syllables in capital letters indicate sequences of letters in English words that usually indicate the root as the origin of the word. In nearly all cases, if one sees the letters in caps in an English word, one can infer that it comes from the Indo-European root in the first column. However, there may also be some English words from the root that do not accord with the general pattern and some English words that fit the pattern but come from a different root.

97. g^{w}hren- think	PHRAS speak
98. gno- know	[G]NO, [G]NOSC come to know; note; recognize GNI/GNO GNO, GNOS know
99. krei- sieve, discriminate, distinguish	CERN separate CRIT, CRIS separate; judge; discern
100. krau- conceal, hide	CRYPT hide
101. men-[1] to think	MON, MEN, MIN, MENT think; remind; advise; warn MONI MNEM, MNE, MNES memory
102. ok^w- to see	OPS, OPT, OP sight; view; eye → OPHTHALM eye
103. sag- seek out	SAG shrewd, wise
104. sep-[1] taste, perceive	SAP, SIP taste, discern, be wise
105. wer-[4] to perceive, watch out for	
106.	SOPH wise
107. spek- to observe	SPEC, SPIC, SPECT look at; examine SCOP, SCEPT, SKEPT look at; examine
108. swen- to sound	SON sound

109. tag- touch, handle   TANG, TING, TAG, TIG, TACT touch
110. weid- to see   VID, VIS see -IDEO, -IDEA idea, form
111. wel-² wish, will   VOL, VOLI, VOLUNT wish; will

97. gʷhren- think
Greek: PHRAS speak

[1] Gk phren the mind   [2] Gk phrazein (aor ephrasa) to point, show

frenetic: frenzied; frantic. [1] Gk phrenitis < phren mind.
frenzied: marked by wild excitement or mental agitation; madness. [1] Gk phren the mind.
paraphrase: a restatement of a passage in different words. [2] Gk para- (alongside) + phrazein to show.
periphrastic: using roundabout inaccurate language. [2] Gk peri (around) + phrazo declare.
RELATED: frenetical paraphrasis
COMMON: frantic [1] frenzy [1] paraphrase [2] phrase [2] -phrenia [1] phreno- [1]

98. gno- know
Latin: [G]NO, [G]NOSC come to know; note; recognize GNI/GNO
Greek: GNO, GNOS know

[1] L (g)noscere (notus) get to know, get acquainted with;
    cognoscere (cognitus; pfp cognoscens) to learn
[2] L ignorare (pfp ignorans) not to know, disregard
[3] L nobilis knowable, famous, noble   [4] L narrare (narratus) to tell, relate
[5] L nota mark, note   [6] L norma carpenter's square, rule, pattern
[7] Gk gignoskein to know, think, judge; gnosis
    knowledge, inquiry; gnomon judge, interpreter
[8] OE cnawan to know < Ger   [9] OE cyth knowledge, friendship, kinfolk
[10] OE cennan to declare   [11] OE cunnan to know, be able to
[12] OE cuth known, usual, excellent   [13] OE cene brave

annotate: to add explanatory notes to a text. [5] L annotare to note down < ad- + notare to write < nota note.
cognition: the process of knowing or perceiving; perception. [1] L co (together) + nosco know.
cognitive: rel. to the process of knowing, reasoning, and judging. [1] L co (together) + nosco know.
cognizant: being aware of; informed. [1] L co (together) + nosco know.
connoisseur: one who has fine and discriminating taste. [1] Fr connaisseur < L cognoscere to know.
ennobling: make noble and honorable. [3] Fr en- + noble < L nobilis well known.
ignoble: dishonorable; of mean estate. [3] Fr < L ignobilis unknown < in (not) + nobilis well known.
norm: a standard representing typical behavior or results. [6] L norma carpenter's square, norm.
notoriety: well-known; unfavorable reputation; ill fame. [1] L notus known < noscere get to know.
recognizance: recognition; court obligation requiring action. [1] L re (again) + co (together) + nosco know.
quaint: odd or strange but in a charming way. [1] OF queinte < L co (together) + nosco know.
acknowledge: admit to be true; expressly recognize. [8] OE on + cnawan to know < Ger.
agnostic: one skeptical about something esp. the existence of God. [7] Gk a + gnosis know.
canny: shrewd and clever. [11] OE cunnan to know how.
gnome: a pithy proverbial saying; maxim. [7] Gk gnome thought, maxim < gignosko know.
gnostic: possessing knowledge; claiming esoteric wisdom. [7] Gk gnostikos knowing < gignosko know.

prognosis: a prediction esp. about recovery from a disease. [7] L < Gk pro (before) + gignosko know.
uncanny: weird; strange; seemingly supernatural. [11] OE un + cunnan.
uncouth: clumsy or crude. [12] OE uncuth < un- (not) + cuth known.
RELATED: agnosticism cognizance cognize diagnose diagnostic enormous note notable noted notorious prognosis prognosticate
COMMON: abnormal [6] acquaint [1] can [11] con [11] cunning [11] diagnosis [7] enormity [6] ignorant [2] ignore [2] incognito [1] keen [13] ken [10] kith and kin [9] know [8] knowledge [8] narrate [4] narrative [4] noble [3] normal [6] notable [5] notice [1] notify [1] notion [1] recognition [1] recognize [1] reconnaissance [1] reconnoiter [1]

99. krei- sieve, discriminate, distinguish
Latin: CERN, CERT, CRET, CRIM, CRIMIN separate
Greek: CRIN, CRIT, CRIS separate; judge; discern

[1] L cribrum sieve
[3] L discrimen distinction
[5] Gk krinein (aorp ekrithen) to separate, decide, judge; krinesthai to explain
[6] OE hridder sieve

[2] L crimen judgment, crime
[4] L cernere (cretus or certus) sift, discern, decide

ascertain: determining to be true by checking evidence. [4] L ad- + certain certain < cernere to determine.
certain: fixed; inevitable; indisputable; holding confidently. [4] L certus (pfp cernere) to determine.
certitude: belief that something is definite, inevitable, or indisputable. [4] L certus < cernere discern.
concerted: action made in harmony through agreement or planning. [4] L cernere (certus) sift, discern, decide.
discernible: capable of being distinguished from other objects. [4] L discerno < dis (apart) + cerno separate.
discerning: making distinctions between things. [4] L discerno < dis (apart) + cerno separate.
disconcert: ruffle; confuse; upset. [4] OF desconcerter < L discerno < dis (apart) + cerno separate.
discrete: distinct or separate; made of distinct parts or separate units. [4] L dis (apart) + cerno separate.
discriminating: detect fine differences; showing fine taste; analytical. [3] L discrimin distinction.
excretion: the process of eliminating body waste products. [4] L cernere (cretus or certus) discern.
incriminate: to accuse of wrongdoing or crimes; to implicate. [2] L in- + crimen crime.
indiscretion: lack of good judgment; a foolish or unwise act or remark. [4] L in- + dis (apart) + cerno separate.
indiscriminate: failing to make distinctions; not selective; haphazard. [3] L in- + discrimin distinction.
recrimination: a countercharge [2] L re- + crimen accusation, crime.
secrete: remove from observation; exude apart from blood. [4] L secretus < se aside + cerno separate.
criterion: standard of judging. [5] Gk kriterion < krino judge.
hypercritical: given to excessive criticism; unduly exact. [5] Gk hyper (over, above) + kritikos < krino judge.
hypocritical: pretending to have virtue. [5] Gk hypokrinesthai play a part < hypo + krinesthai dispute.
riddle: pierce with many holes; to occur with wide extent. [6] OE hriddel.
RELATED: discriminate discriminatory discriminative excrete garbled hypocrisy incertitude indiscriminating recriminate recriminatory
COMMON: concern [4] concert [4] crime [2] criminal [2] crisis [5] critic [5] critical [5] criticize [5] critique [5] decree [4] excrement [4] garble [1] secret [4] secretary [4]

100. krau- conceal, hide
Greek: CRYPT hide

[1] Gk kryptein (pf kekrupha) to hide, conceal

apocryphal: of doubtful authority. [1] Gk apo from + krypto conceal.
cryptic: mysterious; hidden in meaning. [1] Gk krypto hide.
grotesque: bizarre or incongruous manner or appearance. [1] L crypta vault < Gk kryptein to conceal.
RELATED: grotesquerie
COMMON: crypt [1] crypto- [1] cryptographer [1] grotto [1] krypton [1]

101. men-¹ to think
Latin: MON, MEN, MIN, MENT think; remind; advise; warn MONI
Greek: MNEM,MNE,MNES memory

[1] L mens (ment-) mind
[3] L meminisse to remember; memor mindful
[5] L reminisci recall, recollect
[6] L monere (monitus) to warn, advise; monitio
   warning; monitor prompter; monumentum monument
[7] Gk mimneskein (f mneso) to remember
[9] Gk -matos willing
[11] Gk mantis seer
[13] Gk Mentor
[14] OE gemynd mind, memory

[2] L mentio remembrance, mention
[4] L comminisci contrive by thought

[8] Gk mnemon mindful
[10] Gk mania madness
[12] Gk Mousa a Muse

admonition: a warning or reproof. [6] L ad (to) + moneo advise.
demented: insane; mentally ill. [1] L demens senseless < de- + mens mind.
monitor: to collect information to keep track of something; a device used for checking. [6] L monere warn.
monumental: magnificently large and enduring; astounding; serving as a memorial. [6] L monere to remind.
muster: to summon esp. for battle; to gather. [6] L monstrare to show < monere to warn.
premonition: an instinctive foreboding of something yet to occur. [6] OF < L prae (before) + moneo warn.
reminiscence: the recollection of past experiences. [5] L reminisci to recollect.
remonstrance: a reproof, complaint, or protest. [6] L re (again) + monstro show.
remonstrate: present a protest against something; urge in protest. [6] L re (again) + monstro show.
amnesia: partial or total loss of memory. [7] Gk a (priv.) + mnasthai to remember.
amnesty: a general pardon for or overlooking of an offense. [7] Gk a + mnaomai remember.
automaton: a robot or other self-operating device. [9] Gk automatos self-acting.
bemused: bewildered; confused; absorbed in thought. [12] OE be + Gk Mousa a Muse.
dipsomaniac: an alcoholic. [10] Gk dipso thirst + mania mania.
mentor: a counselor or teacher esp. to those of lower rank; (v) to serve as a counselor. [13] Gk Mentor.
mnemonic: memory device. [8] Gk mnemonikos < mnaomai remember.
mosaic: design composed of small pieces of tile placed adjacently together. [12] Gk Mousa muse.
muse: to meditate on or consider thoughtfully. [12] Gk Mousa a Muse.
RELATED: admonish admonitory mnemonic monitory
COMMON: automatic [9] comment [4] demented [1] demonstrate [6] kleptomaniac [10] -mancy [11] mania [10]
maniac [10] maniacal [10] manic [10] mantic [11] memento [3] mental [1] mention [2] mind [14] monetary [6]
monetize [6] money [6] monster [6] monument [6] monumental [6] Muse [12] museum [12] music [12] muster [6]
reminisce [5] reminiscent [5] summon [6]

102. okʷ- to see
Latin: OCUL eye
Greek: OPS, OPT, OP sight; view; eye —> OPHTHALM eye

[1] L oculus eye
[2] L (with ant- front, forehead) antiquus former, antique
[3] L (with ater- fire) atrox frightful
[4] L (with gwher- wild beast) ferox (feroc-) fierce
[5] Gk ops eye
[6] Gk opsis sight, appearance
[7] Gk optos seen, visible
[8] Gk opthalmos eye
[9] OE eage eye
[10] ON auga eye
[11] LG oog eye

antiquated: out of date; no longer useful. [2] L antiquus former, antique.
atrocity: an extremely cruel, bad, or evil action. [3] L atrox frightful, cruel.
inoculate: insert an immunizing body into an organism to protect from disease. [1] L in- (in) + oculus eye.
inveigle: to persuade by artful talk. [1] OF aveugle blind < L ab- (away from) + oculus eye.
ocellated: having spots or markings resembling the eye. [1] L ocellus < oculus eye.
ocular: rel. to the eye [1] L oculus eye.
autopsy: inspection of a corpse. [7] Gk autos self + optos seen.
myopia: nearsightedness. [5] Gk myops short-sighted < myo close + ops eye.
ogle: to stare at in a flirtatious manner. [11] LG oghelen < oghe eye.
optician: maker and seller of lenses and eyeglasses. [7] Gk optikos < optos visible.
synopsis: summary giving a general review or condensation. [6] Gk syn (together) + opsis sight.
RELATED: antiquate myopic ophthalmologist synoptic
COMMON: antic [2] antique [2] antler [1] atrocious [3] daisy [9] eye [9] eyelet [1] ferocious[4] oculist [1] ophthalmo- [8] -opsis [6] -opsy [6] optic [7] optical [7] optics [7] optoelectrics [7] optometry [7] Pelops [5] pinochle [1] walleyed [10] window [10]

103. sag- seek out
Latin: SAG shrewd, wise

[1] L sagire to perceive
[2] L sagax of keen perception
[3] Gk hegeisthai to lead; hegemon leader
[4] ON saka to seek
[5] OE saecan to seek
[6] OE sacu lawsuit, case
[7] OE forsacan to renounce, refuse

beseech: to implore; beg for. [5] OE be- + secan to seek.
forsake: to give up, abandon, or renounce. [7] OE forsacan.
hegemony: exercising dominance over a state or region. [3] Gk hegemon leader.
presage: portend; foretell. [1] L prae (before) + sagio perceive.
sagacious: wise; discerning, and shrewd. [2] L sagio perceive quickly.
RELATED: hegemonic sagacity
COMMON: ramshackle [4] ransack [4] sake [6] seek [5]

104. sep-¹ taste, perceive
Latin: SAP, SIP taste, discern, be wise

[1] L sapere (pfp sapiens) taste, suggest, be wise; sapor, -is flavor

insipid: without flavor; unsavory; not qualified to interest; vapid; dull. [1] L in (not) + sapidus savory.
sage: person of recognized foresight; (adj) having wisdom; profound. [1] L sapere be wise.
sapience: wisdom; learning often ironical. [1] Fr < L sapientia wisdom.

savant: a wise or learned person. [1] L sapere to be wise.
savory: appetizing; tasty. [1] Fr savourer < L sapor taste.
RELATED: sapient sapiential savor savorless
COMMON: savvy [1]

105. wer-[4] to perceive, watch out for

[1] L vereri (pfp verens) to respect, feel awe for
[2] Gk horan to see
[3] OE waer watchful
[4] OF guarder to guard

irreverence: disrespectfulness esp. toward God and what is holy. [1] L re- + vereri to respect.
panoramic: giving a sweeping view to the horizon in all directions. [2] Gk pan all + horan to see.
reverence: feeling of deep respect, veneration, worship. [1] L re (again) + vereor fear.
vanguard: front-most troops in battle; movement leaders. [4] Fr avaunt before (< L ante) + garde guard.
wary: watchful; not trusting. [3] OE waer watchful.
RELATED: irreverent panorama revere reverent wariness
COMMON: guard [4] panorama [2] regard [4]

106. Greek: SOPH wise

[1] Gk sophia wisdom

philosophy: investigation of principles and truths that underlie all reality. [1] Gk philia love + sophia wisdom.
sophisticated: worldly-wise, knowing person; highly refined. [1] L sophisticus < Gk sophistes wise man.
sophism: clever quibble or fallacious argument often intended to deceive. [1] Gk sophos clever, wise.
sophistry: deceptive reasoning that appears sound but is fallacious. [1] Gk sophistes sophist, wise man.
sophomoric: self-assured and opinionated but immature. [1] Gk sophos wise + moros foolish.
RELATED: philosopher philosophical sophist sophistical sophisticate sophistication sophomore

107. spek- to observe
Latin: SPEC, SPIC, SPECT look at; examine
Greek: SCOP, SCEPT, SKEPT look at; examine

[1] L specere (spectus) to look at; spectare (spectatus) to look at, test,
    examine; speciosus showy
[2] L despicari to despise   [3] L auspex a diviner
[4] Gk skeptesthai to examine, consider; skeptikos thoughtful
[5] Gk skopos a watcher, goal; skopein view
[6] OF espier to watch

aspect: appearance or expression; a given side, exposure, view, or phase. [1] L ad (to) + specio look.
auspicious: favorable; propitious. [3] L auspex a diviner < avis bird + specio view.
circumspect: cautious; well considered. [1] L circum (around) + specio look.
conspicuous: clearly visible; prominent; striking; notable. [1] L con (together) + specio see.
despicable: contemptible. [2] L despicio < de (down) + specio look at.

despise: to view with scorn or contempt; to loathe. [1] L despicere < de- + specere to look.

espionage: the use of spies to obtain secret military or business information. [6] OF espion spy.

expectation: perceiving an event as about to happen; degree of probability of. [1] L ex (out) + specio look.

introspection: reflection on one's thoughts and feelings. [1] L intro- (within) + specere look at.

irrespective: lacking respect or relation; regardless. [1] L in (not) + re (back) + specio look.

kaleidoscope: tube giving views of symmetrical designs. [5] Gk kalos beautiful + eidos form + skopos see.

perspective: the effect of distance. [1] Fr < L per (through) + specio look.

perspicacious: keen in judgment or understanding. [1] L perspicacitas < per (through) + specio look.

perspicuity: clearness of expression; lucidity; transparency. [1] L perspicax < per (through) + specio look.

prospective: anticipated; looking to the future. [1] Fr < L pro (forward) + specio look.

respite: pause or rest. [1] OF respit < L re (back) + specio look.

retrospective: thinking of the past; looking back to the past. [1] L retrospectus < retro (back) + specio look.

skeptic: person who questions generally accepted beliefs. [4] Gk skeptikos < skopeo view.

specific: distinctly set forth; definite; determinate; particular. [1] L species look, kind + facio make.

specious: appearing right and true; plausible. [1] L speciosus fair < species < specio look.

specter: apparition; phantom. [1] L spectrum appearance, apparition.

spectrum: range of radiation of differing wavelengths esp. the range of visible light. [1] L spectrum vision.

speculation: act of theorizing; theory; risky investment. [1] L speculatus (pp speculor) behold < specio see.

RELATED: circumspection expect expectancy introspect introspective perspicacity perspicuous prospect retrospect retrospection skeptical specification specificity specify speciosity speciousness speculate speculative

COMMON: bishop [5] disrespect [1] especially [1] espy [6] frontispiece [1] horoscope [5] inspect [1] inspection [1] inspector [1] microscopic [5] periscope [5] prospector [1] respect [1] respectable [1] respectful [1] respective [1] respecting [1] respectively [1] scope [5] -scope [5] -scopy [5] special [1] specialist [1] speciality [1] specialize [1] specialization [1] specialty [1] specie [1] species [1] specimen [1] spectacle [1] spectacular [1] spectator [1] speculate [1] speculator [1] spice [1] spiteful [2] spy [6] suspect [1] suspicion [1] suspicious [1] telescope [5] telescopic [5]

108. swen- to sound
Latin: SON sound

[1] L sonus sound   [2] L sonare (pfp sonans) to sound; sonorus resonant
[3] OE swan swan

consonance: agreement or harmony; consistency with. [2] L consonans < con (together) + sono sound.

dissonant: inharmonious. [2] L dis (apart) + sono sound.

resonance: the quality of sending back or prolonging sound. [2] L re (again) + sono sound.

sonorous: producing a full, rich sound. [2] L sonorus < sono sound.

RELATED: inconsonant resonant resonate resonator

COMMON: resound [2] sonata [2] sonic [1] sonnet [1] sound [1] supersonic [1] swan [3] transonic [1] ultrasonic [1] unison [1]

109. tag- touch, handle
Latin: TANG,TING,TAG,TIG,TACT touch

[1] L tangere (tactus; pfp tangens) to touch; tactilis that can be touched; taxare to touch, assess
[2] L integer intact, whole, honest
[3] L contaminare (contaminatus) to corrupt by mixing or contact

contagion: transmitting of disease by contact; rapidly spreading harmful influences. [1] L contingere to touch.

cantankerous: quarrelsome and disagreeable. [1] L contactus (pp contingere) to touch.

contaminate: render impure or unclean through contact or mixing. [3] L contaminare to corrupt.

contiguous: next to. [1] L contiguus < contingo < con (together) + tango touch.

contingent: conditional. [1] L contingens (pfp contingo) < con together + tango touch.

intact: unimpaired; remaining complete. [1] L intactus untouched < in (not) + tactus (pp tango) touch.

intangible: not touchable. [1] L in (not) + tango touch.

integrity: uprightness of character; probity; honesty. [2] L integritas < in (not) + tango touch.

tactful: apt to do what is proper; considerate; skilled in avoiding offense. [1] L tactus (pp tango) touch.

tactile: pert. to the organs or sense of touch. [1] Fr < L tactilis < tactus touch.

tactless: showing lack of consideration; tending to cause offense. [1] L tactus (pp tango) touch.

tangential: just touching; barely relevant, not directly addressing an issue. [1] L tango touch.

tangible: perceptible by touch; within reach by touch; not elusive or unreal. [1] Fr < L tango touch.

RELATED: cotangent tact tactual tangent

COMMON: attain [1] contact [1] contagious [1] entire [2] integrate [2] integer [2] task [1] taste [1] tax [1]

110. weid- to see/ weidh- divide, separate
Latin: VID, VIS see
Greek: -IDEO,-IDEA idea, form

[1] L videre (visus; pfp videns) to see, look	[2] L dividere (divusus; pfp dividens) to divide, separate
[3] Gk eidos form, shape	[4] Gk idea appearance, form, idea
[5] Gk histor wise, learned	[6] Gk Haides the underworld
[7] OE witan to reproach	[8] OE wit knowledge; witan to know
[9] OE wis wise	[10] OE wisdom learning, wisdom
[11] OF guidar to guide m	[12] OF guise manner

clairvoyant: intuitively perceiving the unsensed. [1] Fr clair clear + voyant seeing < L videre see.

devise: form a plan or design a device or approach. [2] L dividere to separate.

envisage: to conceive or have an idea of a future possibility. [1] L en + videre (visus; pfp videns) to see, look.

evident: plain or manifest as to the mind or the senses; obvious. [1] L evidentia clearness < video see.

improvident: wasteful; not saving for the future. [1] L in- (not) + pro (forward) + video see.

improvise: to make up or invent as one acts or performs. [1] L in- (not) + pro (forward) + video see.

imprudent: not careful to avoid error; not using sound judgment. [1] Fr < L prudens < pro (forward) + video see.

invidious: producing ill will or resentment. [1] L invidiosus envious, hostile < invidia envy.

Providence: Supreme Being who controls, furnishes, and provides all things. [1] L pro (forward) + video see

providential: opportune as if from divine intervention. [1] L pro (forward) + video see.

provisional: holding or applying temporarily. [1] L proviso < pro (forward) + video see.

proviso: a conditional stipulation or clause in a contract or statute. [1] L proviso < pro (forward) + video see.

prudent: careful to avoid error; using sound judgment. [1] Fr < L prudens < pro (forward) + video see.

purveyor: one furnishing food or other goods or offering ideas. [1] L pro + videre to see.

purview: scope; range; extent. [1] Fr purveier to provide < L providere to provide < pro- + videre to see.

visage: form and features of the face; appearance. [1] L visus a look < video see.

visibility: condition or quality of being perceivable by sight. [1] Fr < L visibilis < visus (pp video) see.

visionary: showing foresight. [1] Fr < L visio < visus (pp video) see.

vista: a view or prospect; an outlook. [1] Ital. < L video see.

voyeur: one who is given to secretly observing nakedness or sexual acts. [1] L videre to see.

aneroid: not employing a fluid. [3] Gk a- (priv.) + neros wet + eidos form.

guise: appearance esp. false or pretended. [12] OF guise manner.

ideal: existing in ideas; conceived as perfect or supremely excellent. [4] Gk idea form < idein to see.

ideology: body of ideas. [4] Gk idea form, idea < idein to see + ology.

idolatry: worship of images. [3] Gk eidolon < eidomai appear + latry worship.

idyllic: simple or poetic. [3] Gk eidyllion < eidos form.

unwitting: lacking awareness of what one is doing; unintentional. [8] OE un- + witan know < Ger.

witless: stupid; without understanding. [8] OE witan know < Ger.

witticism: clever and humorous remark. [8] OE witan know < Ger.

RELATED: evidence evidential evidentiary ideologize invidiously invisible provide provident provider

COMMON: advice [1] advise [1] device [2] divide [2] division [2] envy [1] guide [11] guidon [11] Hades [6] history [5] idea [4] ideo- [4] idol [3] interview [1] kaleidoscope [3] -oid [3] outwit [8] review [1] revise [1] story [5] supervise [1] supervision [1] supervisor [1] survey [1] twit [7] view [1] visa [1] visible [1] vision [1] visor [1] visual [1] visualize [1] visualization [1] wisdom [10] wise [9] wit [8] wizardry [9]

111. wel-² wish, will

Latin: VOL, VOLI, VOLUNT wish; will

[1] L velle (pfp volens) wish, will; voluntas, -tatis will

[2] L voluptus pleasure; voluptarius pleasant, pleasure seeking

[3] OE wel well

[4] OE wela well-being, riches

[5] OE willa desire, will-power; willan to desire

[6] OF galoper to gallop

[7] OF galer to rejoice

benevolent: kindly; charitable; beneficent. [1] L bene well + volens (pfp volo) wish.

commonweal: the public good or well-being. [4] OE wela well-being, riches.

involuntary: not under the will's control; contrary to one's will. [1] L in (not) + voluntarius < voluntas will.

malevolent: having an evil disposition toward others. [1] L malus bad + volo wish.

volition: exercise of the will. [1] Fr < L volo will.

voluntary: proceeding from the will; intentionally done; not constrained. [1] L voluntarius < voluntas will.

voluptuary: one living for sensual pleasures. [2] L voluptarius devoted to pleasure < voluptas pleasure.

willful: deliberate; done on purpose. [5] OE willa desire, will-power; willan to desire.

RELATED: benevolence volitive voluptuarian voluptuous voluptuously

COMMON: gallant [7] gallop [6] nill [5] weal [4] wealth [4] well [3] will [5] willy-nilly [5]

CHAPTER 17

Roots Referring to Attitudes, Feeling, and Emotion

The eighth category of roots, covered in this chapter, refers directly to human attitudes, feelings, and emotion. Ten roots fall into this category. Three roots refer to love and desire:

'am-' is a source of words for love
'PHIL' means "love"
'wen-[1]' means "desire, strive for"

The root 'am-' is a source of words for love. It is the source of the Latin verb 'amor' meaning "love" and 'amicus' meaning "friend." The root 'PHIL' meaning "love" is the source of the Greek 'philia' meaning "love" or "friendship." Third, 'wen-[1]' meaning "desire, strive for" is the source of the Latin verb 'venerer' meaning "to revere" and 'venus' meaning "love" and the English words 'wean,' 'wont,' 'win,' and 'wish.' Two roots refer to suffering:

'k^{w}ent(h)-' means "to suffer"
'pe(i)- ' means "to hurt"

The root 'k^{w}ent(h)-' meaning "to suffer" is the source of the Greek word 'pathos' meaning "suffering." Also 'pe(i)-' meaning "to hurt" is the source of the Latin verb 'pati' meaning "to suffer" and the English word 'fiend.' Five roots refer to various other attitudes, feelings, or emotions:

'bheidh-' meaning "to trust, confide, persuade"
'eis-[1]' is a source of words indicating passion
'g^{w}ere-[3]' meaning "to favor"
'kwes-' meaning "to pant, wheeze"
'sa-' meaning "to satisfy"

The root 'bheidh-' meaning "to trust, confide, persuade" is the source of the Latin word 'fides' meaning "trust" or "faith" and the English words 'bide,' 'abide,' and 'abode.' The root 'eis-[1]' is a source of words indicating passion. It is the source of the Latin word 'ira' meaning "anger," the Greek 'hieros' meaning "holy," and the English word 'iron.' Another root 'g^{w}ere-[3]' meaning "to favor" is the source of the Latin word 'gratus' meaning "favorable" or "thankful" and the English word 'bard.' The root 'kwes-' meaning "to pant, wheeze" is the source of the Latin verb 'queri' meaning "to complain" and 'quero' meaning "to seek," the Greek 'kustis' meaning "bladder," and the English word 'wheeze' (from the Old Norse 'hvaesa' meaning "to hiss.") Finally, 'sa-' meaning "to satisfy" is the source of the Latin word 'satis' meaning "enough" and the English words 'sad' and 'sate.'

SOUND SHIFTS

The Indo-European rough labial 'bh' sound becomes an 'f' sound (represented by 'ph' in English, showing Greek origin) in Latin and Greek. The corresponding West Germanic and Old English form is generally the voiced labial 'b.' The root 'bheidh-' meaning "to trust, confide, persuade" is the source of the Latin word 'fides' meaning "trust" or "faith" and the English words 'bide,' 'abide,' and 'abode.'

If Indo-European, Latin, and Greek have a smooth palatal mute 'k,' the West Germanic and Old English form will generally be a rough palatal 'h.' Hence, 'kwes-' meaning "to pant, wheeze" is the source of the Latin verb 'queri' meaning "to complain" and 'quero' meaning "to seek," the Greek 'kustis' meaning "bladder," and the English word 'wheeze' (from the Old Norse 'hvaesa' meaning "to hiss.")

When Indo-European and Latin and Greek show a smooth labial mute 'p,' West Germanic and Old English show a rough labial 'f.' This sound change is clearly evident in the root 'pe(i)-' meaning "to hurt," which is the source of the Latin verb 'pati' meaning "to suffer" and the English word 'fiend.'

The Indo-European rough dental 'dh' sound becomes a 'th' sound Greek, but since Latin does not have a 'th' sound, it takes other forms in Latin. The corresponding West Germanic and Old English form is a voiced dental 'd.' Hence, 'bheidh-' meaning "to trust, confide, persuade" is the source of the Latin word 'fides' meaning "trust" or "faith" and the English words 'bide,' 'abide,' and 'abode.'

The w sound of Indo-European is retained in the Old English forms. In the case of Latin, it is occasionally dropped and otherwise represented by the letter 'v,' which, however, was pronounced as a w sound. We see this phenomena with the root 'wen-¹' meaning "desire, strive for," which is the source of the Latin verb 'venerer' meaning "to revere" and 'venus' meaning "love" and the English words 'wean,' 'wont,' 'win,' and 'wish.'

For the Indo-European labiovelar 'gʷ' or 'kʷ,' the 'g' or 'k' may take several forms (e.g. change to a labial 'b' or 'f') in Latin or Greek or may drop the 'g,' 'k,' or 'w.' Thus, 'gʷere-³' meaning "to favor" is the source of the Latin word 'gratus' meaning "favorable" or "thankful" and the English word 'bard,' while 'kʷent(h)-' meaning "to suffer" is the source of the Greek word 'pathos' meaning "suffering."

Three roots do not show any of the sound shift changes covered in chapter 7. These include 'am-,' which is a source of words for love. It is the source of the Latin verb 'amor' meaning "love" and 'amicus' meaning "friend." They include also 'sa-' meaning "to satisfy," which is the source of the Latin word 'satis' meaning "enough" and the English words 'sad' and 'sate,' as well as 'eis-¹,' which is a source of words indicating passion. It is the source of the Latin word 'ira' meaning "anger," the Greek 'hieros' meaning "holy," and the English word 'iron.'

LIST OF ROOTS IN ORDER OF OCCURRENCE

The following list gives the roots in order of occurrence in this chapter. The syllables in capital letters indicate sequences of letters in English words that generally indicate the root to be the origin of the word. In nearly all cases, if one sees the letters in caps in an English word, one can infer that it comes from the Indo-European root in the first column. However, there may also be some English words from the root that do not accord with the general pattern and some English words that fit the pattern but come from a different root.

112. bheidh- to trust, confide, persuade   FID faith, trust
113. eis-¹ words of passion   HIER- sacred
114. gʷere-³ to favor   GRAT, GRAC pleasing GRAT
115. kʷent(h)- to suffer   PATH feeling; disease
116. kwes- to pant, wheeze   QUER, QUEST, QUIR, QUIS seek, ask → QUERI, QUERU complain
117. pe(i)- to hurt   PATI, PASS suffer, feel, endure

118.	PHIL love
119. sa- to satisfy	SAT enough
120. wen-[1] desire, strive for	VEN
121. am- (nursery)	AMO love AM/IM

112. bheidh- to trust, confide, persuade
Latin: FID faith, trust

[1] L fidere (pfp fidens) trust confide; fidus faithful;
    fidelis, -e faithful; fiducia confidence
[2] L foedus (foeder-) treaty, league   [3] L fides faith, trust
[4] OE bidan await, stay

affidavit: sworn statement in writing. [1] L affido < ad + fides faith.
confidant: a person to whom secrets are entrusted. [1] Fr < L con (with) + fido trust.
confidential: privately held; entrusted to a limited circle of associates. [1] L con (with) + fido trust.
diffidence: attitude of distrust, timidity, shyness, or modesty. [1] L dis (apart, asunder) + fides faith.
fidelity: faithfulness to do a duty or obligation; loyalty; strict adherence to truth. [3] L fidelitas < fides faith.
infidel: lacking the true faith; an unbeliever (religious). [3] L in (not) + fidelis faithful < fides faith.
perfidy: treachery; faithlessness. [3] L perfidia < per (from) + fides faith.
RELATED: confide diffident fiducial perfidious
COMMON: abide [4] abode [4] confederate [2] confident [1] defiance [1] defy [1] faith [3] federal [2] federate [2] fiance [1]

113. eis-[1] words indicating passion
Latin: IRA anger
Greek: HIER- sacred

[1] L ira anger
[2] Gk hieros holy   [3] Gk oistos gadfly, goad
[4] OE ise(r)n iron

hierarchy: persons or things arranged in ranks and grades. [2] Gk hieros sacred + archos ruler.
hieratic: pert to priests; consecrated. [2] L hieraticus < Gk hieratikos < hieros sacred.
hieroglyphic: picture symbol representing words; hard to read. [2] Gk hieros sacred + glypho carve.
irascible: quick to anger. [1] L irasci to be angry < ira anger.
irate: very angry. [1] L irasci to be angry < ira anger.
RELATED: hierarchical hieroglyph
COMMON: andiron [4] estrogen [3] hiero- [2] irascibility [1] ire [1] iron [4]

114. gʷere-[3] to favor
Latin: GRAT, GRAC pleasing GRAT

[1] L gratus pleasing, favorable, thankful
[2] Welsh bardd bard

gratify: to please, satisfy. [1] L gratia favor + facio do.
gratis: free; not requiring recompense. [1] L gratia favor.

gratuitous: given freely without claim or consideration; voluntary. [1] L gratuitus < gratia favor.

ingrate: ungrateful person. [1] OF ingrat < L in (not)+ gratus grateful, pleasing.

ingratiate: acting to curry the favor of another. [1] L in gratiam for the favor of < in (in) + gratia favor.

RELATED: gratuitously gratuity ingratiation

COMMON: agree [1] bard [2] congratulate [1] disgrace [1] grace [1] gracious [1] grateful [1] gratitude [1] ingrateful [1] ingratitude [1]

115. kʷent(h)- to suffer
Greek: PATH feeling; disease

[1] Gk pathos suffering, passion

antipathy: an instinctive feeling of aversion or dislike. [1] Gk anti (against) + pathos feeling.

apathy: indifference [1] Gk a + pathos.

empathy: identification with the feelings of others. [1] Gk en (in) + pathos feeling.

homeopathy: system of medicine based on "like cures like." [1] Gk homoios like + pathos suffering.

pathetic: arousing compassion or pity. [1] Gk pathos suffering.

pathological: deviant behavior; related to the study of disease. [1] Gk pathos suffering + logos study.

pathos: suffering, disease. [1] Gk pathos suffering.

sociopath: person given to antisocial behavior. [1] L socius companion + Gk pathos passion.

RELATED: apathetic empathetic pathology sympathize sympathizer sympathy

COMMON: patho- [1] -pathy [1] psychopathic [1] sympathetic [1] telepathy [1]

116. kwes- to pant, wheeze
Latin: QUER, QUEST, QUIR, QUIS seek, ask —> QUERI, QUERU complain

[1] L queri (questus) to complain; querulus complaining

[2] L quaero (quacsitus) to seek

[3] Gk kustis bladder, bag

[4] ON hvaesa to hiss

decry: disparage; traduce. [1] Fr decrier < de + crier cry < L queri complain.

disquisition: discussion of a subject [2] L dis (apart, about) + quaero seek.

exquisite: characterized by fineness and delicacy; refined; delicately beautiful. [2] L ex (out) + quaero seek.

inquest: a judicial investigation into a matter. [2] OF enqueste < L inquisitas < in (into) + quaero seek.

inquisition: an investigation; suppression of those thought dangerous. [2] L in (into) + quaero seek.

perquisite: incidental profit beyond salary or wages; any claimed benefit. [2] L per (through) + quaero seek.

prerequisite: necessary antecedent condition. [2] L prae (before) + re (again) + quero ask.

querulous: disposed to complain or fret; quarrelsome, complaining. [1] L querulus < queror complain.

querimonious: apt to complain; querulous; fretful. [1] L queror complain.

RELATED: inquisitor querimony

COMMON: acquire [2] conquest [2] cyst [3] cysto- [3] descry [1] inquiry [2] inquisitive [2] quarrel [1] query [2] quest [2] request [2] requisition [2] wheeze [4]

117. pe(i)- to hurt
Latin: PATI, PASS suffer, feel, endure

[1] L pati (passus) to suffer; patibilis endurable;
    patientia endurance

[2] L paenitere to repent   [3] L penuria want

[4] OE feond enemy, devil

compassion: pity for suffering with desire to help; sympathy. [1] Fr < L com- (together) + patior suffer.
compatible: working harmoniously; consistent; in agreement. [1] Fr compatible < L com (with) + patior suffer.
dispassionate: free from passion; unprejudiced. [1] Fr < L dis + patior suffer.
impassioned: animated; excited. [1] Fr < L in (in) + passus (pp patior) suffer.
impassive: not feeling pain; insensible. [1] L in + passivus < passus (pp patior) suffer.
impenitent: not repentant for one's behavior. [2] L in- (not) + paenitere to repent.
incompatible: inconsistent; irreconcilably disagreeing. [1] Fr compatible < L com (with) + patior suffer.
passive: receiving rather than initiating action. [1] L in + passivus < passus (pp patior) suffer.
penitent: having remorse for sins; (n) person with remorse for misdeeds. [2] L paenitere to repent.
penurious: extremely frugal; stingy. [3] L penuria want.
RELATED: dispassion impassible impassiveness impassivity incompatibility penury
COMMON: fiend [4] impatience [1] impatient [1] passion [1] passive [1] patient [1]

118. Greek: PHIL love

[1] Gk philia love, friendship

bibliophile: lover of books. [1] Gk biblos book + philia love.
philanderer: man who engages in many casual extramarital affairs. [1] Gk phileo to love + aner, andr- man.
philanthropist: giver of large sums of money to help mankind. [1] Gk philia love + anthropos man.
philosophy: investigation of principles and truths that underlie reality. [1] Gk philia love + sophia wisdom.
RELATED: philanthropy philosophical philosopher philosophize
COMMON: philatelist [1] philology [1]

119. sa- to satisfy
Latin: SAT enough

[1] L satis enough, sufficient   [2] L satur full of food
[3] OE saed sated, weary   [4] OE sadian to sate

insatiable: not possible to satisfy. [1] L satiates (pp satio) < satis enough.
satiate: to fill with more than enough; be surfeited. [1] L satiates (pp satio) < satis enough.
satirical: caricaturing human follies or institutions to ridicule them. [2] L satur < Gk satur satyr.
saturate: cause to be soaked, treated, or filled to the maximum extent. [2] L saturatus < satur full.
RELATED: satiable satiated saturated saturation unsated unsaturated
COMMON: asset [1] sad [3] sate [1] satire [2] satisfy [1]

120. wen-[1] desire, strive for
Latin: VEN

[1] L venus to love; venerer (veneratus) to revere;
    venerabilis honorable; veneratio respect

[2] L venenum love potion, poison

[3] L venia favor, forgiveness

[4] L venari to hunt

[5] OE wenian accustom, train, wean < Ger

[6] OE wunian become accustomed to, dwell < Ger

[7] OE winnan to win

[8] OE wynn pleasure, joy

[9] OE wenan to expect, imagine, think

[10] OE wyscan to desire, wish

envenom: embitter; make poisonous. [2] OF en- (cover with) + venim venom.
venerate: to revere. [1] L venerabilis < venerer revere.
venerable: meriting much respect due to age. [1] OF < L venerabilis < venerer revere.
venial: not serious; readily excused. [3] LL venialis < venia forgiveness.
venom: malice; poison esp. that secreted by an animal. [2] OF en-(cover with) + venim venom.
winsome: engaging, attractive. [8] OE wynn pleasure, joy + -sum.
RELATED: veneration wonted
COMMON: venereal [1] venison [4] Venus [1] wean [5] ween [9] win [7] wish [10] wont [6]

121. am- (nursery word)
Latin: AMO love AM/IM

[1] L amare (amatus) to love; amator lover

[2] L amicus friend

[3] L amor love

[4] L amita aunt

amatory: loving. [1] L amator < amo love.
amiable: pleasing in disposition; kind-hearted. [1] L amicabilis < amo love.
amicable: friendly; peaceable. [2] L amicabilis < amo love.
amity: peaceful relations; mutual good-will; friendship. [2] L amicus friend < amo love.
enmity: deeply held hatred. [2] L in (not) + amicus friend.
inimical: harmful; hostile. [2] L inimicus < in (not) + amicus friendly.
RELATED: enamor
COMMON: amateur [1] amigo [2] amorous [1] amour [3] archenemy [2] aunt [4] enamored [3] enemy [2] inamorata [1] paramour [3]

CHAPTER 18

Roots Referring to Simple Action or Motion

The ninth category of roots, covered in this chapter, involves simple human action or motion. Twenty roots fall within this category. Two roots have a more general meaning of doing or performing:

'deu-[2]' meaning "to do, perform, show favor, revere"
'werg-' meaning "to do"

The root 'deu-[2]' with the meanings "to do, perform, show favor, revere" is the source of the Latin 'bonus' meaning "good," 'beatus' meaning "blessed," and Greek 'dunamis' meaning "power." The second root 'werg-' meaning "to do" is the source of the Greek word 'ergon' meaning "to work" and the English words 'work,' 'bulwark,' 'wrought,' and 'wright.' Nine roots have a basic meaning of "going" with various other associated ideas:

'ei-[1]' meaning "to go"
'ers-' meaning "be in motion"
'ghredh-' meaning "to walk, go"
'gʷa-/gʷem-' meaning "go, come"
'ked-' meaning "go, yield"
'mei-[1]' meaning "change, go, move"
'sent-' meaning "to head for, go"
'wadh-[2]' meaning "to go"
'wegh-' meaning "go, move by vehicle"

The root 'ei-[1]' meaning "to go" is the source of the Latin verb 'ire' meaning "to go," 'iter' meaning "journey" and the Greek 'ienai' meaning "to go." Next 'ers-' meaning "be in motion" produced the Latin verb 'errare' meaning "make a mistake" or "to wander" and the English word 'race.' The root 'ghredh-' meaning "to walk, go" is the source of the Latin verb 'gradi' meaning "to step" or "walk" and 'gressus' meaning "step." Further 'gʷa-/ gʷem-' meaning "go, come" is the source of the Latin verb 'venire' meaning "to come," the Greek 'basis' meaning "a stepping" or "base," and the English words 'come,' 'become,' and 'welcome.'

The root 'ked-' meaning "go, yield" is the source of the Latin verb 'cedere' meaning "to go" or "to yield." Next 'mei-[1]' meaning "change, go, move" is the source of the Latin verb 'meare' meaning "to go" or "to pass," 'mutare' meaning "to change," the Greek 'ameibein' meaning "to change," and the English words 'miss,' 'mistake,' 'amiss,' 'mean,' and 'mad.' The root 'sent-' meaning "to head for, go" produced the Latin verb 'sentire' meaning "to feel" or "to perceive" and the English word 'send.' Another root 'wadh-[2]' meaning "to go" is the source of the Latin verb 'vado' meaning "to go" or "to walk." Finally 'wegh-' meaning "go, move by vehicle" produced the Latin verb 'vehere' meaning "to bear" or "carry" as well as 'via' meaning "way" or "road" and the

English words 'wee,' 'way,' 'weigh,' 'weight,' 'wag,' 'away,' and 'always.' Two roots involve absence of motion as in sitting or resting:

'kʷeie-²' meaning "rest, be quiet" and
'sed-¹' meaning "to sit."

The root 'kʷeie-²' meaning "rest, be quiet" is the source of the Latin word 'quies' meaning "rest" and the Old English 'hwil' meaning "while" and the English word 'while.' Also 'sed-¹' meaning "to sit" produced the Latin verb 'sedere' meaning "to sit" and 'sidere' meaning "to sit down" or "to settle." It is also the source for Greek 'hedra' meaning "seat" and the English words 'sit,' 'set,' 'settle,' 'seat,' 'nest,' and 'saddle.' Three roots involve accelerated motion as in running or jumping:

'kers-²' meaning "run"
'sel-⁴' meaning " to jump"
'skand-' meaning "leap, climb"

The root 'kers-²' meaning "run" is the source of the Latin verb 'currere' meaning "to run." Next 'sel-⁴' meaning " to jump" is the source of the Latin verb 'salire' meaning "to leap" or "to jump." And 'skand-' meaning "leap, climb" is the source of the Latin verb 'scandere' meaning "to climb" and Greek 'skandalon' meaning "snare" or "stumbling block." Four roots have various other ideas related to simple action:

'ag-¹' meaning "drive, draw, move"
'eue-' meaning "leave, abandon, give out"
'kad-' meaning "to fall," and
'tere-²' meaning "to cross over, pass through, overcome."

The root 'ag-¹' meaning "drive, draw, move" is the basis for the Latin verb 'agere' meaning "to act" or "to drive" and the Greek verb 'agein' meaning "to drive" or "to lead." Next 'eue-' meaning "leave, abandon, give out" is the source of the Latin verb 'vacare' meaning "to be empty," 'vastus' meaning "waste" or "empty," and the English words 'wane,' 'want,' and 'wanton.' The root 'kad-' meaning "to fall" is the source of the Latin verb 'cado' meaning "to fall" and 'casus' meaning "accident." Finally, 'tere-²' meaning "to cross over, pass through, overcome" is the source of the Latin word 'trans' meaning "across" or "over."

SOUND SHIFTS

If Indo-European, Latin, and Greek have a smooth palatal mute 'k,' then West Germanic and Old English generally has a rough palatal 'h.' Thus, 'kʷeie-²' meaning "rest, be quiet" is the source of the Latin word 'quies' meaning "rest" and the Old English 'hwil' meaning "while" and the English word 'while.'

Although Indo-European rough palatal 'gh' sound generally becomes a 'kh' sound in Latin and Greek, it can become voiced palatal 'g,' as in Germanic and Old English. The latter happens for 'ghredh-' meaning "to walk, go," which is the source of the Latin verb 'gradi' meaning "to step" or "walk" and 'gressus' meaning "step."

The Indo-European, Latin, and Greek voiced palatal mute 'g' shows up as smooth palatal 'k' in West Germanic and Old English. Thus 'werg-' meaning "to do" is the source of the Greek word 'ergon' meaning "to work" and the English words 'work,' 'bulwark,' 'wrought,' and 'wright.'

When Indo-European, Latin, and Greek have the voiced dental mute 'd,' the West Germanic and Old English form generally shows a smooth dental 't.' Thus 'sed-¹' meaning "to sit" is the source of the Latin verb 'sedere' meaning "to sit" and 'sidere' meaning "to sit down" or "to settle," the Greek 'hedra' meaning "seat," and the English words 'sit,' 'set,' 'settle,' 'seat,' 'nest,' and 'saddle.' Sometimes 'd' becomes 'b' in Latin. For example, 'deu-^{2}' meaning "to do, perform, show favor, revere" is the source of the Latin 'bonus' meaning "good" and 'beatus' meaning "blessed" and the Greek 'dunamis' meaning "power."

The w sound of Indo-European is retained in the Old English forms, but in the case of Latin it is occasionally dropped and otherwise represented by the letter 'v,' which, however, was pronounced as a w sound. Words coming directly from the Latin into English are consequently pronounced as a v sound. The original Greek w sound disappeared, becoming a rough breathing or h sound and often was dropped altogether. We see this phenomenon with the root 'wadh-^{2}' meaning "to go," which is the source of the Latin verb 'vado' meaning "to go" or "to walk." Also 'wegh-' meaning "go, move by vehicle" is the source of the Latin verb 'vehere' meaning "to bear" or "carry," 'via' meaning "way" or "road," and the English words 'wee,' 'way,' 'weigh,' 'weight,' 'wag,' 'away,' and 'always.' The root 'werg-' meaning "to do" produced the Greek word 'ergon' meaning "to work" and the English words 'work,' 'bulwark,' 'wrought,' and 'wright.'

Indo-European labiovelar 'g^w' or 'k^w' may take several forms, including a labial 'b' or 'f' in Latin or Greek, or may drop the 'g,' 'k,' or 'w.' Thus 'g^{w}a-/ g^{w}em-' meaning "go, come" is the source of the Latin verb 'venire' meaning "to come," where it retains the 'w' and drops the 'g.' In the Greek 'basis' meaning "a stepping" or "base," it takes the labial 'b.' However, the English words 'come,' 'become,' and 'welcome' show the typical sound shift from 'g' in the Indo-European forms to a 'k' in West Germanic. The root 'k^{w}eie-^{2}' meaning "rest, be quiet" is the source of the Latin word 'quies' meaning "rest," where it shows no change. It is also the source of the Old English 'hwil' meaning "while" and the English word 'while,' where the 'w' sound is retained and the 'g' sound is dropped. Twelve roots do not exhibit any of the sound shift changes covered in chapter 7:

'ag-^{1}' meaning "drive, draw, move" is the source of the Latin verb 'agere' meaning "to act" or "to drive" and the Greek verb 'agein' meaning "to drive" or "to lead."

'ei-^{1}' meaning "to go" is the source of the Latin verb 'ire' meaning "to go" and 'iter' meaning "journey" and the Greek 'ienai' meaning "to go."

'ers-' meaning "be in motion" is the source of the Latin verb 'errare' meaning "make a mistake" or "to wander" and the English word 'race.'

'eue-' meaning "leave, abandon, give out" is the source of the Latin verb 'vacare' meaning "to be empty" and 'vastus' meaning "waste" or "empty" and the English words 'wane,' 'want,' and 'wanton.'

'kad-' meaning "to fall" is the source of the Latin verb 'cado' meaning "to fall" and 'casus' meaning "accident." The root 'ked-' meaning "go, yield" is the source of the Latin verb 'cedere' meaning "to go" or "to yield."

'kers-^{2}' meaning "run" is the source of the Latin verb 'currere' meaning "to run."

'mei-^{1}' meaning "change, go, move" is the source of the Latin verb 'meare' meaning "to go" or "to pass" and 'mutare' meaning "to change," the Greek 'ameibein' meaning "to change," and the English words 'miss,' 'mistake,' 'amiss,' 'mean,'' and 'mad.'

'sel-^{4}' meaning " to jump" is the source of the Latin verb 'salire' meaning "to leap" or "to jump." The root 'sent-' meaning "to head for, go" is the source of the Latin verb 'sentire' meaning "to feel" or "to perceive" and the English word 'send.'

'skand-' meaning "leap, climb" is the source of the Latin verb 'scandere' meaning "to climb" and the Greek 'skandalon' meaning "snare" or "stumbling block."

'tere-^{2}' meaning "to cross over, pass through, overcome" is the source of the Latin word 'trans' meaning "across" or "over."

LIST OF ROOTS IN ORDER OF OCCURRENCE

The following list gives the roots in order of their occurrence in this chapter. The syllables in capital letters give sequences of letters in English words that generally indicate the root to be the origin of the word. In nearly all cases, if one sees the letters in caps in an English word, one can infer that it comes from the Indo-European root in the first column. However, there may also be some English words from the root that do not accord with the general pattern and some English words that fit the pattern but come from a different root.

122. ag-[1] drive, draw, move	AG, IG, ACT do; act; drive AG, AGOG lead AGON struggle
123. deu-[2] to do, perform, show favor, revere	BEN-, BON- good, well DYN, DYNAM power; force
124. ei-[1] to go	EO go
125. ers- be in motion	ERR stray; wander
126. eue- leave, abandon, give out	VAC empty
127. ghredh- to walk, go	GRAD, GRED, GRESS step
128. gʷa- / gʷem- go, come	VEN, VENT come BAS, BAT step; go
129. kad- to fall	CAD, CAS, CID fall, happen —> CASU chance, fate
130. ked- go, yield	CED, CESS yield, go
131. kers-[2] run	CURR, CURS, CORR, [COURS] run
132. kʷeie-[2] rest, be quiet	QUIE, QUIT rest
133. mei-[1] change, go, move	MEA go; pass MUT change
134. sed-[1] to sit	SED, SID, SESS, SIT set; settle
135. sel-[4] jump	SAL, SIL, SULT leap
136. sent- to head for, go	SENT, SENS feel; be aware
137. skand- leap, climb	SCAND, SCEND, SCENT, SCENS climb
138. tere-[2] to cross over, pass through, overcome	TRANS-, TRA- across; beyond; through
139. wadh-[2] to go	VAD, VAS go; rush
140. wegh- go, move by vehicle	VEH, VECT, VEX, VEIGH carry; convey VIA, VI, [VOY] way, road
141. werg- to do	ERG, URG work

122. ag- drive, draw, move
Latin: AG, IG, ACT do; act; drive
Greek: AG, AGOG lead AGON struggle

[1] L agere (actus) to do, act, drive, conduct, lead, weigh;
   actio, -onis action; actor driver; agitare (agitatus) to drive
[2] L ambactus servant < amb(i) around + ag- to go
[3] Gk agein drive, lead, weigh   [4] Gk axios worth, weighty, of like value
[5] Gk agonizomai contend, strive

actionable: affording ground for prosecution as a trespass or libel. [1] L ago.
actuary: official insurance statistician who calculates risk and rates. [1] L actuarius clerk < ago do.
actuate: to move or incite to action; influence. [1] L actus (pp ago) do.
agitate: stir up people to action; disturb; cause vigorous movement. [1] L agitare (freq. of agree) to drive.
ambiguous: can be understood in multiple senses; equivocal. [1] L ambi (around) + ago drive.
assay: to evaluate. [1] L exigo prove < ex (out) + ago drive.
cachet: a seal or mark indicating distinction or authenticity. [1] OF cacher (to press) < L cogere force.
castigate: to criticize; punish. [1] L castus pure + ago make.
coagulate: change into a clot from heat or fermenting; curdle; congeal. [1] L coagulatus < cogo compel.
cogency: ability to rationally convince. [1] L cogo compel < co (together) + ago drive.

cogitate: to think. [1] L co (with) + agito (freq ago) drive.

embassage: mission to a foreign government. [2] L ambactiata < ambactia mission < ambactus servant.

essay: to try; to attempt; (n) a short literary piece. [1] L ex- + agere to drive.

exacting: making rigorous demands; requiring great care. [1] L exigo determine < ex (out) + ago drive.

exigency: the state of being urgent or exigent. [1] L ex (out) + ago drive.

intransigent: not willing to compromise. [1] L in (not) + transigo come to a settlement.

litigation: legal proceedings. [1] L litigates (pp litigo) strive < lis lawsuit + agere to drive.

mitigate: to lessen in severity or relieve; alleviate. [1] L mitis mild + ago make.

navigable: having sufficient depth and width for ships to pass. [1] L navis ship + agere to drive, lead.

objurgate: berate; rebuke; scold. [1] L ob- + iurgare scold, sue at law < agere do, proceed.

prodigal: addicted to wasteful expenditure; spendthrift. [1] L pro (forth) + ago drive.

prodigy: a person with unusual or exceptional abilities; an omen. [1] L prodigium.

reactionary: ultraconservative wanting to reinstate earlier practices. [1] L re (back) + ago drive.

retroactive: a law or policy taking effect for a period prior to ratification. [1] L retro (back) + ago do.

unambiguous: clear; not vague; definite. [1] un- + L ambiguus uncertain < ambi around + agere to go.

unmitigated: not weakened or lessened in any respect. [1] un- + L mitis mild + ago make.

variegate: diversify with different colors or tints; dapple; spot; streak. [1] L varius various + ago make.

antagonism: feeling of hostility or opposition against. [5] Gk anti (against) + agonizomai strive.

axiom: postulate held as true for purposes of argument; self-evident principle. [4] Gk axios worthy.

demagogue: leader who incites. [3] Gk demos people + ago lead.

hegemony: leadership or supreme command. [3] Gk hegemonia < ago lead.

pedagogue: teacher, tutor. [3] Gk paidagogos < pais child + ago lead.

protagonist: leading character. [5] Gk protagonistes < protos first + agonistes a contestant.

stratagem: a scheme or maneuver designed to obtain an objective. [3] Gk stratos army + agein lead.

synagogue: a congregation of Jews for worship and religious study. [3] Gk syn (together) + ago bring.

RELATED: agendum antagonist antagonize castigation cogent exigent intransigent litigate mitigation pedagogy prodigality redact redactor

COMMON: act [1] activate [1] active [1] actor [1] actual [1] agenda [1] agent [1] agile [1] agony [5] allege [1] ambassador [2] cache [1] counteract [1] embassy [2] enact [1] exact [1] exacta [1] examine [1] fumigate [1] levigate [1] navigate [1] reactant [1] reaction [1] squat [1] transact [1]

123. deu-² to do, perform, show favor, revere

Latin: BEN-, BON- good, well
Greek: DYN, DYNAM power; force

[1] L bonus good   [2] L bene well
[3] L bellus handsome, fair
[4] L beare (beatus) make blessed; beatus happy, blessed;
    benignus kind, friendly, generous
[5] Gk dunamai be able; dunamis power

beatify: give great joy or happiness; exalt. [4] L beatus happy + facio do.

beneficial: advantageous; producing favorable outcomes. [2] L bene well + facio do.

beneficent: bringing about or doing good; showing charity and kindness. [2] L bene well + facio do.

benign: influencing in a favorable or harmless way; of kindly disposition. [4] L benignus kind, generous.

bonhomie: pleasant and friendly disposition. [1] Fr bon good + homme man < L bonus good + homo man

debonair: suave; carefree. [1] OF de bon aire of good disposition < L bonus good.

dynamic: pert. to energy or power in motion; energetic; forceful. [5] Gk dynamikos < dynamis power.
embellish: decorate with ornaments; add fanciful details. [3] OF embellir < L bellus.
RELATED: benefic
COMMON: beatitude [4] beau [3] beauty [3] belladonna [3] belle [3] benediction [2] benefaction [2] benefactor [2] benefit [2] benevolent [2] benignant [2] bonbon [1] bonny [1] boon [1] bonus [1] bountiful [1] bounty [1] bonanza [1] dynamics [5] dynamism [5] dynamite [5] dynamo [5] dynasty [5] embellishment [3] hydrodynamic [5]

124. ei-¹ to go
Latin: EO go

[1] L ire (pfp iens; it 3rd pers. pres. sng.) to go
[2] L initium entrance, beginning, commence   [3] L comes companion
[4] L iter journey   [5] L ianus archway
[6] L uter use
[7] Gk ienai to go   [8] Gk isthmos narrow passage

ambience: the mood or atmosphere produced by the immediate environment. [1] L ambi around + eo go.
ambit: that which bounds; a boundary; circumference. [1] L ambitus < ambio < ambi around + eo go.
circuitous: roundabout. [1] L circum around + eo go.
concomitant: accompanying in occurrence or existence. [3] L comitari accompany < comes companion.
disabuse: set someone straight about a misconception. [6] L dis + ab (from) + uter use.
entrance: to hypnotize; to fill with wonder. [1] L en- (in) + transire to go across.
imperishable: indestructible. [1] L in (not) + pereo perish < per (through) + eo go.
issue: a flowing out, giving out, or distributing; something published; a point of policy or debate. [1] L ire to go.
itinerary: proposed route and places visited on a journey. [4] L itiner < iter journey.
itinerant: constantly on the move from place to place. [4] L itiner < iter journey.
perishable: destructible. [1] L pereo perish < per (through) + eo go.
transient: of short duration; brief; not permanent; temporary. [1] L transiens (pfp transeo).
transition: to pass from one state, form, or subject to another. [1] L trans + ire to go.
transitive: verb requiring an object. [1] L transire to go over < trans (over) + ire to go.
transitory: of short duration; not permanent; temporary. [1] L trans + ire to go.
COMMON: ambient [1] ambition [1] circuit [1] coitus [1] constable [3] count [3] county [3] errant [4] exit [1] initial [2] iniate [2] ion [7] ionosphere [7] isthmus [8] janitor [5] January [5] perish [1] obituary [1] sedition [1] sudden [1] trance [1] transit [1] viscount [3]

125. ers- be in motion
Latin: ERR stray; wander

[1] L errare (erratus; pfp errans) to make a mistake, wander; error mistake
[2] ON ras rushing

aberrant: wandering; straying; abnormal. [1] L ab (from) + erro wander.
aberration: deviation from the expected, normal, or typical. [1] L ab (from) + erro wander.
erratic: lacking a regular path or course; inconsistent; deviating from the norm. [1] L errare to wander.
erroneous: marked by error; mistaken. [1] L erro wander.
unerring: not making any mistakes; invariably accurate. [1] un- + L errare to wander.
RELATED: errant unerringly
COMMON: err [1] error [1] race [2]

126. eue- leave, abandon, give out
Latin: VAC empty

[1] L vanus empty; evanesco (pfp evanescens) to vanish
[2] L vacare (vacatus; pfp vacans) to be empty
[3] L vastus empty, waste; vastare (vastatus) to ravage, lay waste
[4] OE wanian to lessen   [5] ON vanta to lack

devoid: wholly lacking. [2] L de- + vacare to be empty.
evacuate: to empty. [2] L e (out) + vacuus empty.
evanescent: passing away gradually; quickly fading; short-lived. [1] L evanesco vanish.
vacuous: empty. [2] L vacuus empty.
vaunt: to speak of boastfully; boast; exult; glory. [1] OF venter < L vanus empty.
wane: to decrease in size or strength; to decline. [4] OE wanian (to lessen).
wanton: undisciplined or unrestrained. [4] OE wanian (to lessen) + teon to pull, draw, lead.
RELATED: evanesce vacuity waste
COMMON: avoid [2] devastate [3] vacant [2] vacate [2] vacation [2] vacuum [2] vain [1] vanish [1] vanity [1] void [2] wan [4] want [5] wastrel [3]

127. ghredh- to walk, go
Latin: GRAD, GRED, GRESS step

[1] L gradi (gressus; pfp gradiens) to step, walk, go; gressus step
[2] L gradus step, stage, rank

aggressor: one who attacks or initiates hostility. [1] L ad (to) + gradior walk.
congress: a conference or assembly esp. a formal assembly. [1] L con (together) + gradior walk.
degradation: act or state of being reduced in rank or dignity; debasement. [2] L de (down) + gradior go.
digress: to wander. [1] L di (apart) + gradior step.
egress: exit. [1] L e (out) + gradior go.
gradation: orderly or continuous progression; a step in a series; grade. [2] Fr < L gradatio < gradior walk.
gradient: degree of rising or failing. [2] Fr < L gradus step < gradior walk.
graduated: ordered by steps or degrees. [2] Fr < L gradatio < gradior walk.
ingredient: that which enters into the constitution of a mixture. [1] L ingrediens (pfp ingredior) enter.
progression: advancing toward completion or a better state; improvement. [1] L pro (forward) + gradior go.
regressive: passing back; returning; retroactive. [1] L re (back) + gradior go.
retrogression: going back. [1] L retro (backward) + gradior step.
transgression: a violation of the law; a sin. [1]L trans (over) + gradior step.
RELATED: aggress aggression aggressive degrade digression progress progressive regress regression retrogress retrogressive transgress
COMMON: centigrade [2] degree [2] grade [2] gradual [2] graduate [2] retrograde [4]

128. gᵂa-/ gᵂem- go, come
Latin: VEN, VENT come
Greek: BAS, BAT step; go

[1] L venire (pfp veniens; sup. ventum) to come; adventus arrival
[2] Gk bainen go, walk, step; basis a stepping, base; -batos a going
[3] OE cuman to come   [4] OE becuman to become

advent: a coming or arrival of any important event or person. [1] L ad to + venio come.
adventitious: not inherent; extrinsic; accidental; casual; not inherited. [1]L ad (to) + venio come.
circumvent: to go around. [1] L circum (around) + venio come.
contravene: to oppose; act against. [1] L contra (against) + venio come.
convene: call together; convoke; assemble. [1] L convenio < con (together) + venio come.
conventional: conforming to general practice or standards. [1] L convenio < con (together) + venio come.
covenant: agreement. [1] L conveniens < con (together) + venio come.
eventuate: to ultimately result in. [1] L e (out) + venio come.
intervene: to come or lie between; to interpose; to interfere. [1] L inter- (inter) + venire to come.
prevenient: preceding or preventing; anticipatory; expectant. [1] L praevenio < prae (before) + venio come.
revenant: one who returns as a ghost; an apparition. [1] Fr < L re- + venire to come.
supervene: follow closely upon, but as extraneous or additional; to happen. [1] L super (over) + venio come.
venturesome: willing and inclined to take risks. [1] L adventurus (fp advenire) to arrive + OE -sum -like.
RELATED: basal contravention convenience convenient convent convention event eventual eventuality eventually eventful intervention interventionist prevene prevenience prevent preventible prevention preventive supervention
COMMON: acrobat [2] adventure [1] adventurer [1] adventurous [1] base [2] basin [2] basis [2] become [4] come [3] diabetes [2] invent [1] invention [1] inventive [1] inventor [1] preventive [1] revenue [1] venue [1] venture [1] welcome [3]

129. kad- to fall
Latin: CAD, CAS, CID fall, happen —> CASU chance, fate

[1] L cado (casus; pfp. cadens) to fall   [2] L casus accident, case; occasio, -onis opportunity

cadence: the beat or measure of movement in poetry, speech, or marching. [1] L cadens (pfp cado) fall.
cascade: a waterfall or sequence of small waterfalls. [1] Ital cascata < L cadere.
casualty: accident causing death or injury; soldiers lost for battle. [2] L casualitas accident < casus event.
casuistry: sophistical reasoning. [2] L casus case.
coincidence: agreement; correspondence usually implying accident. [1] L co + incido fall on.
decadence: deterioration esp. in morals. [1] Fr decadence < L de (down) + cado fall.
deciduous: Bot. falling off or shed at maturity; short lived. [1] L deciduus falling off < de (down) + cado fall.
incidence: frequency of occurrence; manner or extent of influence on something. [1] L in (on) + cado fall.
incidental: being a concomitant of an event but of secondary importance. [1] L in (on) + cado fall.
mischance: bad luck; misfortunate. [2] L casus accident, case.
occidental: Western. [1] Fr < L occidens (pfp occido) fall, set < ob (before) + cado fall.
recidivism: tendency to return to criminal behavior. [1] L recidivus falling back < re- + cadere to fall.
RELATED: cadent casuist decadent incident incidentally occident recidivist
COMMON: accident [1] cadaver [1] cadenza [1] case [2] casual [2] chance [2] chute [1] coincide [1] coincidental [1] decay [1] occasion [2] occasional [2]

130. ked- go, yield
Latin: CED, CESS yield, go

[1] L cedere (cessus; pfp cedens) to go, withdraw, yield
[2] L necesse inevitable, unavoidable

accede: agree to proposed terms. [1] L ad (to) + cedo yield.
accessible: easily approached, entered, or obtained. [1] L accessorius < ad (to) + cedo yield.

accessory: aiding as a cause but playing a subordinate role. [1] L accessorius < ad (to) + cedo yield.
antecedent: preceding; person or thing going before. [1] L antecedens going before < ante (before) + cedo go.
cessation: discontinuing of action; a ceasing. [1] L cessatio < cessare cease, yield.
concede: to yield or assent to. [1] L concedo concede, grant < con with + cedo yield.
decedent: a person deceased. [1] L decessus < de + cedo go.
incessant: uninterrupted; continual; without ceasing. [1] L incessans < in (priv.) + cessare to cease.
intercede: to intervene, mediate; plead for another. [1] L inter (between) + cedo go.
precedent: event or act used for following in future cases. [1] L praecedens < prae- (before) + cedere to go.
predecessor: temporally earlier occupant of a position or place. [1] L de- (away) + cedere to go.
recession: process of going back; withdrawal; falling off of business activity. [1] L re (back) + cedo go.
secession: withdrawal from an organization or association. [1] L se- (apart) + cedere to go.
unprecedented: lacking previous occurrence or example. [1] un- + L prae- (before) + cedere go.
RELATED: access antecede antecedence cede concession decease intercession recede recess recessive
COMMON: abscess [1] ancestor [1] cease [1] cession [1] exceed [1] excess [1] excessive [1] necessary [2] precede [1] proceed [1] proceedings [1] process [1] procession [1] retrocede [1] secede [1] succeed [1] succession [1] unnecessary [2]

131. kers-² run
Latin: CURR, CURS, CORR, [COURS] run

[1] L currere (cursus; pfp currens) to run; cursus course
[2] L carrus two-wheeled wagon   [3] L carpentum two-wheeled cariage

caricature: a depiction that exaggerates or distorts features for comic effect. [2] L carrus a wagon.
concur: agree on a course of action. [1] L con (together) + curro run.
concurrent: occurring at the same time. [1] L concurro < con (together) + curro run.
cursive: running, flowing; said of writing with joined letters. [1] L cursus < curro run.
cursory: superficial. [1] LL cursorius relating to running.
discourse: conversation; treatise on a subject. [1] L discursus < dis + curro run.
discursive: passing from one subject to another; rambling. [1] L discursus (pp discurro) < dis + curro run.
incur: to experience something undesirable esp. by bringing it upon oneself. [1] L in (toward) + curro run.
incursion: an unwanted entry; invasion. [1] L in (toward) + curro run.
occurrence: event presenting itself simply to notice; the happening of an event. [1] L ob (upon) + curro run.
precursor: predecessor. [1] L prae (before) + curro run.
recourse: an act of turning to a secondary less preferred approach. [1] L re- (back) + currere to run.
recurrent: occurring again or repeatedly, esp. at regular intervals. [1] L re (back) + curro run.
RELATED: incursive recur recurred recurrence
COMMON: car [2] career [2] cargo [2] carpenter [3] carry [2] charge [2] chariot [2] concourse [1] corral [1] corridor [1] corsair [1] countercurrents [1] courier [1] course [1] current [1] currency [1] curriculum [1] cursor [1] discharge [2] excursion [1] hussar [1] intercourse [1] occur [1] succor [1]

132. kʷeie-² rest, be quiet
Latin: QUIE, QUIT rest

[1] L tranquillus tranquil   [2] L quies rest, quiet
[3] L quiescere (quietus; pfp. quiescens) to rest, stop, be
    or make quiet
[4] OE hwil while

acquiesce: to drop opposition to a policy or course of action; yield; agree. [3] L ad (to) + quietus rest.
acquittal: the act of being declared innocent; exoneration. [3] L ad (to) + quietus rest.
disquiet: uneasiness or sense of disturbance. [3] L dis (not) + quietus rest.
quiescent: being in a state of repose or inaction; resting free from anxiety or agitation. [2] L quies rest.
quietude: the state of being quiet, still, or at rest. [2] L quies rest.
quittance: discharge or release as from a debt or obligation; acquittance. [2] Fr quitter < L quies rest.
requiem: hymn or service for the dead; mass for the dead. [2] L acc. of requies < re (again) + quies rest.
requital: the act of requiting or that which requites. [3] L re (again) + quietus.
tranquility: the state of being calm, undisturbed, or serene. [1] L tranquillus tranquil.
unrequited: not returned or reciprocated. [3] ME un- + re- + quiten to pay.
RELATED: acquit disquieting disquietude quiesce quiescence requite tranquil
COMMON: coy [3] quiet [3] quietus [2] quit [3] quitclaim [3] quite [3] while [4]

133. mei-¹ change, go, move
Latin: MEA go; pass MUT change

[1] L meare (meatus) to go, pass
[2] L mutare (mutatus; pfp. mutans) to change;
    mutabilitas changeableness; mutatio, -onis change
[3] L mutuus borrowed, mutual   [4] L semita sidetrack, sidepath
[5] L communis common, public   [6] L munus community service, duty
[7] L immunis exempt from public service
[8] L migrare (migratus; pfp. migrans) to change
    place of abode; move
[9] Gk ameibein to change   [10] Gk mimos mime, imitator
[11] OE gemaene common, public   [12] OE gemaedan to make insane or foolish
[13] OE missan to miss

communal: rel. to a small group of society; having shared property. [5] L communis common.
commutation: a substitution; reversal of direction; reduction in penalty. [2] L com (with) + muto change.
commutative: relating to or capable of being interchanged or exchanged. [2] L com (with) + muto change.
demean: to humble or be humbled. [11] OE de- + gemaene common < Ger.
demeanor: manner of behaving; bearing; comportment. [10] OE de- + gemaene common < Ger.
emigrate: move residence from one country or region to another. [8] L emigrare < ex- + migrare move.
immune: exempt; unresponsive; not subject to infection by a disease. [7] L immunis exempt, not contributing.
immutable: unchangeable. [2] L in (not) + mutabilis variable < muto change.
impermeable: not allowing passage; impervious. [1] L in (not) + per (through) + meo pass.
incommunicado: without opportunity to communicate with others. [5] L in- + comunicar communicate.
migratory: roving; frequently changing abode from place to place. [8] L migrare to migrate.
mimicry: the act of copying or imitating the actions of others. [10] Gk mimos mime, imitator.
munificent: very generous. [6] L munus gift + facere do.
mutable: capable of changing; fickle; unstable. [2] L mutabilis variable < muto change.
mutation: alteration; change esp. genetic. [2] L muto change.
pantomime: to communicate with bodily gestures and movements only. [10] Gk panto- all + mimos mime.
permeable: allowing passage, esp. of fluids. [1] L per (through) + meo pass.
permeate: pass through the pores or interstices of; saturate; pervade. [1] L per (through) + meo pass.
permutation: a transformation; a rearrangement of a group of objects. [2] L per (through) + muto change.

remunerative: giving back a sufficient return; profitable. [6] L re- (back) + munerari to give.

transmute: to change in nature, substance, or form; alter in essence. [2] L trans (over) + muto change.

zenith: highest point; peak. [4] L semita path.

RELATED: commutable commutator commute immunize incommutable munificently mutability mutant mutate permute remunerate transmutable

COMMON: amiss [13] amoeba [9] common [5] commonplace [5] commune [5] communicate [5] communism [5] excommunicate [5] mad [12] mean [11] migrant [8] migrate [8] mishap [13] miss [13] mistake [13] molt [2] municipal [6] mutiny [2] mutual [3] mutualism [3] mutually [3]

134. sed-[1] to sit
Latin: SED, SID, SESS, SIT set; settle
Greek: HEDR seat

[1] L sedere (sessus; pfp. sedens) to sit; subsidium
     help; sedentarius sitting
[2] L solium throne, seat
[3] L sidere to sit down, settle   [4] L nidus nest
[5] L sedes seat, residence
[6] L sedare (sedatus; pfp. sadans) to settle, calm;
     sedatio, -onis a soothing; sedamen, -minis sedative
[7] Gk hedra seat, chair, face of a geometric solid
[8] OHG sezzan to set   [9] OE sittan to sit
[10] OE setl seat   [11] OE sadol saddle
[12] OE settan to place   [13] OE nest nest
[14] OE -saeta inhabitant   [15] OE sot soot
[16] ON saeti seat

assessor: an officer who determines the amount of taxes due. [1] L assideo < ad (to) + sedeo sit.

assiduous: devoted or constant; unremitting; diligent. [1] L ad + sedeo sit,settle.

dispossess: to deprive someone of ownership, occupation, or control. [1] L possessus (pp possideo) possess.

dissident: one who strongly opposes; (adj) strongly opposing. [1] L dis- + sedens (pfp. sedere) to sit.

ersatz: inferior imitation or substitute; artificial. [8] Ger. ersetzen replace < ir- (out) + sezzan to set.

insidious: proceeding hiddenly with potential lethal effects. [1] L insidiae ambush < in- + sedeo sit.

obsessive: excessive activity as if driven by some compulsive idea. [1] L ob- + sedere (sessus) to sit.

sedate: calm; serious; dignified. [6] L sedatus composed, calm < sedeo sit.

sedentary: sluggish. [1] L sedentarius < sedens (pfp sedeo) sit.

sedimentation: material accumulating at the bottom of a liquid. [1] L sedimentum settling < sedeo sit.

sedulous: painstaking in application or attention; persevering in effort. [1] L sedulus diligent < sedeo sit.

subside: to settle; to become calm and tranquil. [3] L subsideo settle down < sub (down) + sedeo sit.

subsidiary: assisting in an inferior capacity; auxiliary. [3] L subsidarius < sub (under) + sedeo sit.

subsidy: financial aid. [1] L subsidium < sub (under) + sedeo sit.

supersede: to take the place of. [1] L super (over) + sedeo sit.

unprepossessing: not noticeably remarkable or impressive; modest. [1] un- + L possideo to possess.

RELATED: assent assess assessment assiduity assiduously polyhedron possess possession possessor sedation sedative sediment sedimentary subsidize

COMMON: beset [12] besiege [1] cathedral [7] chair [7] cosset [14] inkling [4] nest [13] niche [4] nick [4] nidulant [4] nidulate [4] nidus [4] obsess [1] onset [12] possessive [1] preside [1] reside [1] residence [1] residue [1]

saddle [11] seance [1] seat [16] see [5] session [1] set [12] settle [10] sewer [1] siege [1] sit [9] soil [2] soot [15] tetrahedron [7]

135. sel-⁴ jump
Latin: SAL, SIL, SULT leap

[1] L salire (saltus; pfp saliens) to leap, jump; saltare (saltatus; pfp saltans) to dance
[2] L salmo salmon

assail: to assault; to attack. [1] L saliens (pfp salire) to leap, jump.
desultory: passing abruptly from one thing to another; aimless; fitful. [1] L de (down) + salio leap.
exult: rejoice greatly; be jubilant. [1] L salire (saltus) to leap, jump.
resilient: springing back to a former shape or position; elastic. [1] L resilio < re (back) + salio leap.
salacious: lustful; lascivious. [1] L salax < salio leap.
salient: standing out prominently; striking; conspicuous. [1] Fr saillant < L salio leap.
saltation: a leap as in a dance; a palpitation. [1] Fr < L saltatio < salto dance < salio leap.
unassailable: not disputable; impregnable. [1] L un + ad- (onto) + salire to jump.
RELATED: desultorily resile resiliency saltant
COMMON: assault [1] insult [1] result [1] sally [1] salmon [2] saute [1] somersault [1]

136. sent- to head for, go
Latin: SENT, SENS feel; be aware

[1] L sentire (sensus; pfp. sentiens) to feel, perceive;
    sensus sense; sententia opinion
[2] OE sendan to send   [3] OE sand message, messenger

assent: to agree; to concur; (n) agreement; consent. [1] L ad + sentio feel.
consensus: a collective opinion; general agreement. [1] L con (together) + sentio feel.
dissent: disagree esp. with the majority. [1] L dis- + sentire to feel.
insensate: manifesting or marked by a lack of reason; brutish; mad. [1] L in (not) + sensus (pp sentio) feel.
insensible: imperceptible; deprived of or naturally deficient in sensation. [1] L in (not) + sensus < sentio feel.
presentiment: foreboding. [1] L prae (before) + sentio feel.
resentment: ill will held because of a real or imagined wrong done. [1] L re- + sentire to feel.
sensibility: the capability of sensation; power to perceive or feel. [1] Fr sens < L sensus (pp sentio) feel.
sensory: conveying or producing sense impulses; pert to sensation. [1] LL < sensus (pp sentio) feel.
sententious: abounding in or giving terse expression to thought. [1] Fr < L sententia opinion < sentio feel.
sentient: possessing powers of sense perception. [1] L sentiens (pfp sentio) feel.
sentiment: noble, tender, or artistic feeling. [1] Fr < L sentio feel.
RELATED: consent sensorial sentience sentimental sentimentality
COMMON: consensual [1] desensitize [1] dissension [1] dissenters [1] Godsend [3] insensitive [1] nonsense [1] nonsensical [1] resent [1] resentment [1] scent [1] send [2] sense [1] sensate [1] sensation [1] sensationalism [1] senseless [1] senselessness [1] sensible [1] sensitive [1] sensitiveness [1] sensitivity [1] sensitize [1] senseless [1] sensor [1] sensorial [1] sensual [1] sensuality [1] sensuous [1] sentence [1] sentinel [1] sentry [1] supersensory [1]

137. skand- leap, climb
Latin: SCAND,SCEND,SCENT,SCENS climb

[1] L scandere (pfp scandens) to climb; ascendo (ascensus; pfp ascendens) to mount, rise
[2] L scalae steps, ladder
[3] Gk skandalon snare, trap, stumbling block

ascendancy: paramount influence; domination; sway. [1] L ad (to) + scando climb.
condescending: looking down on; patronizing. [1] Fr condescendre < L con- + de + scando climb.
echelon: a rank; level of responsibility; a formation or division of military troops. [2] L scalae steps.
scalar: a pure number or simple quantity characterized by one number. [2] L scalaris of a ladder.
scale: to climb; to proportion; (n) an instrument or measure with marked, fixed intervals. [2] L scalae steps.
slander: false statements damaging a person's reputation. [3] Gk skandalon snare, trap.
transcendent: surpassing others. [1] L trans (beyond) + scando climb.
RELATED: ascend ascendent ascension ascent condescend transcend transcending
COMMON: descend [1] descending [1] scale [2] scan [1] scandal [3]

138. tere-² to cross over, pass through, overcome
Latin: TRANS-, TRA- across; beyond; through

[1] L trans across, over, beyond   [2] L trux savage, fierce, grim
[3] L truncus trunk

retrench: to reduce; to economize. [3] L re- + truncare < truncus trunk.
transient: of short duration; brief; not permanent; temporary. [1] L transiens (pfp transeo) go over.
trenchant: incisive; sharp; clear, vigorous, and effective. [3] OF trenchier cut < L truncus trunk.
trenchantly: in an incisive, sharp, clear, and vigorous manner. [3] OF trenchier cut < L truncus trunk.
truculent: disposed to fight, be violent, or bitterly critical. [2] L trux savage, fierce, grim.
truncate: cut off; shorten. [3] L truncus trunk.
RELATED: truculence truculently truncated
COMMON: trans- [1] transom [1] trench [3] trenchancy [3] truncheon [3] trunk [3]

139. wadh-² to go
Latin: VAD, VAS go; rush

[1] L vado to go, walk

evasive: tending or seeking to avoid, elude, or escape from. [1] L evado < e (from) + vado go.
invade: to enter with an armed force with hostile intent; encroach upon. [1] L in (into) + vado go.
invasive: tending to break into by force. [1] L evado < in (into) + vado go.
pervasive: thoroughly penetrating or permeating. [1] L per (through) + vado go.
RELATED: evasion evasiveness invasion pervade pervasiveness
COMMON: evade [1] vamoose [1]

140. wegh- go, transport by vehicle
Latin: VEH, VECT, VEX, VEIGH carry; convey VIA, VI, [VOY] way, road

[1] L vehere (vectus; pfp vehens) to bear, draw, carry
[2] L via way, road
[3] L vexare to agitate, distress   [4] L convexus convey

[5] OE wae(g)n wagon

[6] OE wegan to carry; wiht weight; waege unit of weight

[7] OE weg way

[8] OE wicga insect

[9] ME waggen to wag

[10] OF voguer to row, sail to row, sail

[11] MD wiggelen to move back and forth, wag

[12] MD wagen wagon

convection: transmission of heat by circulating currents. [1] L convectus < com- + vehere to carry.

convex: curving outward; bulging out. [4] L convexus < con (together) + veho carry.

conveyance: a means for transporting, transmitting messages, or transferring ownership. [4] L com- + via way.

deviate: to turn aside, stray. [2] L devius < de (from) + via way.

devious: deceptive; leading away from a straight course; rambling. [2] L devius < de (from) + via way.

envoy: diplomatic representative entrusted with a mission. [2] Fr envoye < envoyer send < L via way.

impervious: not to be penetrated. [2] L in (not) + per (through) + via way.

invective: railing accusation; vituperation. [1] L invectivus scolding.

inveigh: to utter vehement censure or invective. [1] OF enveir < L inveho < invectus scolding.

obviate: make irrelevant anticipated difficulties and objections. [2] LL obvio meet < ob + via way.

pervious: capable of being penetrated; permeable. [2] L per (through) + via way.

vehement: forceful and intense. [1] L vehemens < vehere to carry.

vexatious: annoying; troublesome. [3] L vexare to agitate, distress.

vogue: the current fashion or style; popular. [10] OF voguer to sail, row.

waggery: mischievous jocularity; drollery. [5] ME waggen.

RELATED: convexity deviousness deviation vehemence waggish

COMMON: always [7] away [7] convector [4] convey [4] convoy [2] earwig [8] invoice [2] obvious [2] previous [2] trivia [2] trivial [2] vector [1] vehicle [1] vex [3] vexation [3] via [2] viaduct [2] vogue [10] voyage [2] wag [9] wagon [12] wain [5] wainscot [6] way [7] waylay [7] wcc [6] weigh [6] weight [6] wiggle [11]

141. werg- to do
Greek: ERG, URG work

[1] Gk ergon work, action

[2] Gk organon tool

[3] Gk orgia secret rites

[4] OE weorc work

[5] OHG werc work

[6] OE wyrcan to work

[7] OE wryta maker, wright

[8] ON yrkja to work

energize: to invigorate; to motivate to act. [1] Gk ergon work, action.

ergonomics: design of equipment for greatest efficiency and health in use. [1] Gk ergon work + nomos law.

irksome: causing annoyance or vexation. [8] ON yrkja to work + OE -sum –like.

lethargic: being sluggish. [1] Gk lethe forgetfulness + a (without) + ergon work.

overwrought: excessively agitated or excited; overdone. [6] OE ofer- (over) + wyrcan to work.

synergy: combined and correlated force; united action. [1] Gk syn (together) + ergon work.

RELATED: lethargy synergistic thaumaturge

COMMON: allergy [1] argon [1] boulevard [5] bulwark [5] energy [1] erg [1] handiwork [4] irk [8] liturgy [1] metallurgy [1] organ [2] orgy [3] surgery [1] -urgy [1] work [4] wright [7] wrought [6]

CHAPTER 19

Roots for Actions Affecting Possession

The tenth category, covered in this chapter, refers to human actions affecting possession. Fifteen roots fall into this category. Two roots emphasize the concept of giving:

'do-' meaning "to give"
'ghabh- / ghebh-' meaning "to give or receive"

The root 'do-' meaning "to give" is the source of the Latin verb 'dare' meaning "to give," 'donare' meaning "to give," and the Greek 'didonai' meaning "to give." Next 'ghabh- / ghebh-' means "to give or receive" and is the source of the Latin verb 'habere' meaning "to hold" or "to have" and 'debere' meaning "to owe," the Old English 'giefan' meaning "to give," and the English words 'give,' 'forgive,' 'gift,' and 'gavel.' Three roots emphasize dividing or allotting:

'da-/dail-' meaning "divide"
'nem-' meaning "assign, allot"
'pere-2' meaning "grant, allot"

The root 'da-/dail-' meaning "divide" is the source of the Greek word 'demos' meaning "people" and 'daiesthai' meaning "to divide" and the English words 'tide,' 'tiding,' 'time,' 'deal,' and 'ordeal.' Next 'nem-' meaning "assign, allot" is the source of the Latin 'numerus' meaning "number," the Greek 'nemein' meaning "to allot," and the English words 'numb,' 'benumb,' and 'nimble.' Also 'pere-2' meaning "grant, allot" is the source of the Latin 'pars' meaning "to share" and 'par' meaning "equal." Six roots mean to take, seize, or snatch:

'dek-1' meaning "to take, accept"
'em-' meaning "take, distribute"
'ghend-' meaning "seize, take"
'kap-' meaning "take" ('kaput-' meaning "head" and 'kap-ro-' meaning "he-goat")
'rep-' meaning "snatch"
'reu-' meaning "tear up" ('reup-' meaning "snatch" and 'reud-' meaning "raw, wild")

The root 'dek-1' meaning "to take, accept" is the source of the Latin verb 'docere' meaning "to teach," 'dignus' meaning "worthy," and the Greek 'dokein' meaning "to appear" or "to seem." Next 'em-' meaning "take, distribute" produced the Latin verb 'emere' meaning "to buy" and 'sumere' meaning "to take" or "to buy." Another root, 'ghend-' meaning "seize, take," is the source of the Latin verb 'prehendere' meaning "to seize" and 'praeda' meaning "booty" and the English words 'get,' 'beget,' 'forget,' and 'guess.' The root 'kap-' meaning "take" ('kaput-' means "head" or 'kap-ro-' means "he-goat") is the source of the Latin verb 'capio' meaning "to take" and 'caput' meaning "head" and the English words 'behave,' 'have,' 'heavy,' 'haven,' 'haft,' 'hawk,' and 'behoove.' The root 'rep-' meaning "snatch" is the source of the Latin verb 'rapere' meaning "to seize" and 'rapina' meaning "plunder." Finally, 'reu-' "tear up" ('reup-' means "snatch" and 'reud-' meaning "raw, wild") is the source of the Latin verb 'rumpere' meaning "to break" and 'rudis' meaning "rough." It is the source of the Old English 'reafian' meaning "to plunder" and the English words 'bereave' and 'reave.' Four roots involve other concepts generally related to possession:

'ger-¹' meaning "to gather"
'peku-' meaning "wealth, property"
'wes-¹' meaning "buy, sell"
'wer-⁵' meaning "to cover"

The root 'ger-¹' meaning "to gather" is the source of the Latin word 'grex (greg-)' meaning "herd," the Greek 'ageirein' meaning "to assemble" and 'katagoria' meaning "accusation," and the English word 'cram.' Next 'peku-' meaning "wealth, property" is the source of the Latin 'pecunia' meaning "property" or "wealth" and the English words 'fee' and 'fellow.' The root 'wes-¹' meaning "buy, sell" is the source of the Latin 'venum' meaning "sale" and 'vilis' meaning "cheap." Finally, 'wer-⁵' meaning "to cover" is the source of the Latin verb 'operire' meaning "to cover" and 'aperire' meaning "to open" and the English words 'warn' and 'warranty.'

SOUND SHIFTS

The Indo-European rough palatal 'gh' sound becomes a 'kh' sound in the Latin and Greek, with the 'k' sound usually dropped in Latin. The corresponding West Germanic and Old English form is generally a voiced palatal 'g.' Thus 'ghabh- / ghebh-' meaning "to give or receive" is the source of the Latin verb 'habere' meaning "to hold" or "to have" and 'debere' meaning "to owe," the Old English 'giefan' meaning "to give," and the English words 'give,' 'forgive,' 'gift,' and 'gavel.' The root 'ghend-' meaning "seize, take" is the source of the Latin verb 'prehendere' meaning "to seize," 'praeda' meaning "booty," and the English words 'get,' 'beget,' 'forget,' and 'guess.'

If Indo-European, Latin, and Greek show a smooth palatal mute 'k,' the West Germanic and Old English usually shows a rough palatal 'h.' Hence, 'kap-' meaning "take" ('kaput-' meaning "head" and 'kap-ro-' meaning "he-goat") is the source of the Latin verb 'capio' meaning "to take" and 'caput' meaning "head" and the English words 'behave,' 'have,' 'heavy,' 'haven,' 'haft,' 'hawk,' and 'behoove.'

When Indo-European, Latin, and Greek have a voiced palatal mute 'g,' the corresponding West Germanic and Old English form is generally the smooth palatal 'k.' Thus 'ger-¹' meaning "to gather" is the source of the Latin word 'grex (greg-)' meaning "herd," Greek 'ageirein' meaning "to assemble," 'katagoria' meaning "accusation," and the English word 'cram.'

The Indo-European, Latin, and Greek smooth labial mute 'p' shows up in West Germanic and Old English as a rough labial 'f.' This sound change is clearly evident in the root 'kap-' meaning "take" ('kaput-' meaning "head" and 'kap-ro-' meaning "he-goat"), the source of the Latin verb 'capio' meaning "to take," 'caput' meaning "head," and the English words 'behave,' 'have,' 'heavy,' 'haven,' 'haft,' 'hawk,' and 'behoove.' It is also evident in 'peku-' meaning "wealth, property," the source of the Latin 'pecunia' meaning "property" or "wealth" and the English words 'fee' and 'fellow.' Again 'reu-' meaning "tear up" ('reup-' meaning "snatch" and 'reud-' meaning "raw, wild") generated the Latin verb 'rumpere' meaning "to break," 'rudis' meaning "rough," the Old English 'reafian' meaning "to plunder," and the English words 'bereave,' and 'reave.'

Where Indo-European and Latin and Greek show a voiced dental mute 'd,' the West Germanic and Old English show a smooth dental 't.' Hence, 'da-/dail-' meaning "divide" is the source of the Greek word 'demos' meaning "people" and 'daiesthai' meaning "to divide" and the English words 'tide,' 'tiding,' 'time,' 'deal,' and 'ordeal.'

The w sound of Indo-European is retained in the Old English forms. In the case of Latin it is occasionally dropped and otherwise represented by the letter 'v,' which, however, was pronounced as a w sound. The original Greek w sound disappeared becoming a rough breathing or h sound and often was dropped altogether. We see this phenomenon with the root 'wes-[1]' meaning "buy, sell," which is the source of the Latin 'venum' meaning "sale" and 'vilis' meaning "cheap." Also 'wer-[5]' meaning "to cover" is the source of the Latin verb 'operire' meaning "to cover," 'aperire' meaning "to open," and the English words 'warn' and 'warranty.'

Six roots covered here do not show any sound shift changes covered in chapter 7. The root 'dek-[1]' meaning "to take, accept" is the source of the Latin verb 'docere' meaning "to teach" and 'dignus' meaning "worthy" and the Greek 'dokein' meaning "to appear" or "to seem." Also 'do-' meaning "to give" is the source of the Latin verb 'dare' meaning "to give" and 'donare' meaning "to give" and the Greek 'didonai' meaning "to give." The root 'em-' meaning "take, distribute" is the source of the Latin verb 'emere' meaning "to buy" and 'sumere' meaning "to take" or "to buy." Further, 'nem-' meaning "assign, allot" is the source of the Latin 'numerus' meaning "number," the Greek 'nemein' meaning "to allot," and the English words 'numb,' 'benumb,' and 'nimble.' The root 'pere-[2]' meaning "grant, allot" is the source of the Latin 'pars' meaning "to share" and 'par' meaning "equal." Finally, 'rep-' meaning "snatch" is the source of the Latin verb 'rapere' meaning "to seize" and 'rapina' meaning "plunder."

LIST OF ROOTS IN ORDER OF OCCURRENCE

The following list gives the roots as they occur in the chapter. The syllables in capital letters give sequences of letters in English words generally indicating the root of origin. In nearly all cases, if one sees the letters in caps in an English word, one can infer that it comes from the Indo-European root in the first column. However, there may also be some English words from the root that do not accord with the general pattern and some English words that fit the pattern but come from a different root.

142. da-/dail- divide	DEM people
143. dek-[1] to take, accept	DIGN worth DOC, DOCT teach DOX belief; opinion
144. do- give	DA, DAT, DON give DOR, DOS, DOT give
145. em- take, distribute	EM, EMPT
146. ger-[1] to gather	GREG herd AGOR assemble; declare
147. ghabh- / ghebh- to give or receive	HAB, HIB have; hold —> HABIT dwell HABIT/HIBIT
148. ghend- seize, take	PREHEND, PREHENS, [PRAIS], [PRIS] seize
149a. kap-take/ kaput- head	CAP, CIP, CAPT, CEPT, [CEIVE,CEIPT] take CAP/CEP/CIP
149b. kap-ro- he-goat	
150. nem- assign, allot	NOM, NEM arrangement, law
151. peku- wealth, property	PECU one's own; money
152. pere-[2] grant, allot	PAR, PAIR, PEER equal PART
153. rep- snatch	RAPT seize
154a. reu- tear up	
154b. reup- snatch	RUPT break
154c. reud- raw, wild	RUD rough, crude
155. wes-[1] buy, sell	VIL base, mean
156. wer-[5] to cover	

142. da-/dail- divide
Greek: DEM people

[1] Gk demos people, land

[2] Gk daiesthai to divide

[3] Gk daimon divinity

[4] OE tid time, season; tidan to happen

[5] OE tima time, period

[6] ON tidhr occurring

[7] OE daelan to share; dal portion, lot

[8] OE ordal trial by ordeal

demagogue: leader who incites. [1] Gk demos people + ago lead.

demography: study of vital and social statistics of human populations. [1] Gk demos people + graph write.

demonic: extremely evil; devilish; fiendish. [3] Gk daimon divinity.

demotic: of or pert. to the people. [1] Gk demotikos < demos people.

endemic: prevailing among some group of people. [1] Gk endemios native < en + demos people.

pandemic: widely epidemic. [1] Gk pandemos < pas all + demos people.

pandemonium: a very great din and uproar. [3] Gk pan- all + daimon demon.

RELATED: demographic

COMMON: deal [7] democracy [1] democrat [1] demon [3] dole [7] epidemic [1] eventide [4] geodesic [2] geodesy [2] ordeal [8] tide [4] tiding [6] time [5]

143. dek-[1] to take, accept

Latin: DIGN worth DOC, DOCT teach

Greek: DOX belief; opinion

[1] L decere be fitting; decens proper

[2] L docere (doctus; pfp docens) to teach, explain; docilis teachable; doctrina instruction

[3] L decus grace, ornament, beauty

[4] L decor beauty; decorus adorned; decorare to adorn

[5] L dignus worthy, deserving, fitting

[6] L discere to learn; disciplina instruction; discipulus student

[7] Gk dokein (f doxo; pfm dedegmai) to appear, seem, think

[8] Gk dekhesthai to accept

condign: well deserved; merited; deserving. [5] L condignus < con (intens.) + dignus deserving.

decorum: proper behavior and conduct. [4] L decor seemliness, beauty.

deign: to condescend. [5] OF deigner < L dignor < dignus worthy.

disdain: to regard with proud indifference; reject. [5] L dis (apart) + dignor deem worthy.

docile: easily led. [2] L docilis teachable < doceo teach.

doctrine: belief held to be true by a group or sect. [2] Fr < L doctrina < doctor teacher < doceo teach.

document: (v) provide with written evidence. [2] Fr < L documentum lesson < doceo teach.

indignation: anger caused by actions perceived to be unjust or wrong. [5] L in- (not) + dignus worthy, fitting.

indignity: humiliating treatment; an affront to a person's status. [5] L in- (not) + dignus worthy, deserving.

indoctrinate: to instruct in doctrines or principles. [2] L in + doctrina < doceo teach.

dogmatic: stating beliefs confidently and authoritatively. [7] Gk dogma opinion < dokeo think.

doxology: hymn of praise to God. [7] Gk doxa praise + lego speak.

heterodox: varying from commonly accepted doctrines or opinions. [7] Gk heteros other + doxa opinion.

orthodox: correct in doctrine; having the commonly accepted faith. [7] Gk orthos right + dokeo think.

paradox: seemingly contradictory but true claim. [7] Gk paradoxos incredible < doxa opinion.

RELATED: decorous docility doctrinate dogma dogmatist indignant

COMMON: dainty [5] decent [1] decor [3] decorate [3] dignify [5] dignity [5] disciple [6] discipline [6] dowel [8] doctor [2] documentary [2]

144. do- give
Latin: DA, DAT, DON give
Greek: DOR, DOS, DOT give

[1] L dare (datus) to give   [2] L donum gift; donare (donatus) to give
[3] L dos dowry
[4] Gk doron a gift   [5] Gk didonai (f doso) to give; dosis a gift

antidote: a neutralizing or counteracting agent. [5] Gk antidoton < anti- + didonai to give.
condone: to pardon [2] L con (together) + dono give.
endow: give property or wealth for a source of income. [3] OF en- + douer give a dowery < L dos dowry.
extradite: to transfer a prisoner. [1] Fr < L ex (out) + traditio < trans (over) + do give.
mandate: a specific order. [1] L manus hand + do give.
perdition: eternal consignment to hell. [1] L perditus (pfp perdere) to lose < per- + dare to give.
render: to give, give back, or give what is due; to represent. [1] L re- + dare to give.
rendition: a performance of a dramatic or musical work. [1] L re- + dare to give.
RELATED: extradition
COMMON: add [1] anecdote [5] betray [1] data [1] date [1] dative [1] datum [1] die [1] donor [2] donation [2] dose [5] dot [3] dowager [3] dower [3] dowry [3] edition [1] lobster [4] Pandora [4] pardon [2] rent [1] surrender [1] thermidor [4] tradition [1] traitor [1] treason [1] vend [1] vendor [1]

145. em- take, distribute
Latin: EM, EMPT

[1] L emere (emptus; pfp emens) to obtain, buy; promptus ready; redemptio, -onis ransoming
[2] L sumere (sumptus; pfp sumens) take, obtain, buy; sumptus expense

assumption: something taken for granted; taking on a task or obligation. [2] L ad- + sumere to take.
exemplary: deserving imitation. [1] L exemplar < exemplum <ex (out) + emptus (pp emo) buy.
exemplify: to offer or be a pattern, model, or representative. [1] L ex (out) + emo buy + facio make.
exemption: dispensation giving freedom from duty or penalty. [1] L ex (out) + emo buy, take.
impromptu: done without prior planning. [1] L in promptu at hand < in (in) + promptu < promere bring forth.
peremptory: not admitting of debate or appeal; intolerant of opposition. [1] L peremptus annihilated.
preempt: to acquire or appropriate beforehand. [1] L prae (before) + emptio a buying.
presumptive: assumed to be true; apparently. [2] L prae (before) + sumo take.
presumptuous: overstepping the bounds of proper behavior. [2] L prae (before) + sumo take.
prompt: done on time without delay; (v) to cause to act; to assist. [1] L pro- (forth) + emere to take, obtain.
resumption: continuation or taking up again after interruption. [2] L re (again) + sumo take.
subsume: include under a general principle or category of wider scope. [2] L sub- (under) + sumere take.
sumptuous: lavish; splendid; very expensive. [2] L sumptuarius < sumere take.
unassuming: modest; not pretentious. [2] L un- + ad- + sumere to take.
RELATED: assume exempt preemption presume resume
COMMON: consume [2] example [1] premium [1] pronto [1] ransom [1] redeem [1] redemption [1] sample [1] vintage [1]

146. ger-¹ to gather
Latin: GREG
Greek: AGOR assemble; declare

[1] L grex (greg-) herd, flock
[2] Gk ageirein to assemble; aguris, agora marketplace
[3] Gk katagoria accusation, assertion
[4] OE crammian to stuff, cram

aggregate: bring together into a mass or sum; collected into a sum or mass. [1] L ad (to) + grex flock.
allegory: a story conveying abstract ideas or principles. [2] Gk allos other + agoreuein to speak publicly.
categorical: pert. to a category; without qualification, unequivocal; absolute. [3] Gk kategoria assertion.
congregation: an assemblage or crowd of people. [1] L con (together) + grego collect.
desegregate: abandon the separation of people by race. [1] L de (from) + se (aside) + grex flock.
egregious: excessive; usually in a bad sense; prominent; protuberant. [1] L e (out) + grex (greg-) flock.
gregarious: sociable. [1] L gregarius < grex flock.
panegyric: elaborate praise or eulogy. [2] Gk panegyrikos of an assembly.
segregate: separate into isolated groups. [1] L segregatus (pp segrego) separate < se (aside) + grex flock.
RELATED: categorize category congregate desegregation segregation
COMMON: agoraphobia [2] cram [4] paregoric [2]

147. ghabh- / ghebh- to give or receive
Latin: HAB, HIB have; hold —> HABIT dwell HABIT/HIBIT

[1] L habere (habitus) to hold, have; habilis handy; habitare (habitatus)
    to dwell; habitabilis habitable
[2] L debere (debitus; pfp debens) to owe, ought; debitio, -onis debt
[3] OE giefan to give; forgifan to give, remit, forgive
[4] ON gipt a gift   [5] OE gafol tax, debt

exhibitionistic: behaving in a manner designed to attract attention to oneself [1] L habere (habitus) to have
habitable: livable. [1] L habitabilis < habito dwell.
habitation: occupancy; dwelling place. [1] L habitatio < habito dwell.
habitual: customary; normal practice. [1] L habitualis pert. to dress < habeo have, hold.
habituate: to make accustomed as normal practice. [1] L habitualis pert. to dress < habeo have, hold.
inhibit: restrain; suppress; hold back. [1] L inhibitus < in (on) + habeo have, hold.
inhibition: mental process restraining a person from acting. [1] L in (on) + habeo have, hold.
prohibition: act of forbidding; order that forbids something. [1] L pro (before) + habeo hold.
prohibitive: preventive; discouraging action through cost or difficulty. [1] L pro (before) + habeo hold.
provender: food. [1] L praebenda state allowance < prae- pre- + habere to hold.
rehabilitate: to restore to health, normal life, or former privileges. [1] L re- + habilitare to enable.
uninhibited: not restrained, suppressed, or held back. [1] L inhibitus < in (on) + habeo have, hold.
RELATED: habitually inhabit inhabitable inhabitation inhibitor inhibitory
COMMON: able [1] cohabit [1] debit [2] debt [2] due [2] dutiful [2] duty [2] endeavor [2] exhibit [1] exhibition [1] exhibitionist [1] forgive [3] gavel [5] gift [4] give [3] habit [1] habitat [1] inhabitant [1] malady [1] misgivings [1] prohibit [1]

148. ghend- seize, take
Latin: PREHEND, PREHENS, [PRAIS], [PRIS] seize

[1] L prehendere (prehensus; pfp prehendens),
    prendere get hold of, seize, grasp

[2] L praeda booty
[3] ON geta to get   [4] OE begetan to get, beget; forgetan to forget
[5] ME gessen to guess

apprehend: grasp mentally; perceive; grasp a truth or statement. [1] L apprehendo < ad + prehendo seize.
apprehension: fear of future evil; understanding; arrest. [1] L apprehendo < ad + prehendo seize.
apprise: to give notice. [1] Fr appris < L apprehendo < ad + prehendo seize.
beget: to father; to cause the existence or occurrence of. [4] OE begetan.
comprehensible: can be understood; intelligible. [1] L comprehendo < com (together) + prehendo seize.
comprehensive: inclusive; broad in scope. [1] L comprehendo < com (together) + prehendo seize.
comprise: to include and consist of. [1] L comprehendo < com (together) + prehendo seize.
depredation: a plundering; robbery. [2] L de (thoroughly) + praeda prey.
enterprising: having the initiative to take on new projects. [1] L prehendere < prendere get hold of.
entrepreneur: one who undertakes ventures. [1] OF entreprendre undertake < L inter + prehendo take.
impregnable: not allowing penetration or capture. [1] L in- (not) + prehendere seize.
misapprehension: perceiving incorrectly; misunderstanding. [1] L apprehendo < ad + prehendo seize.
predatory: characterized by or undertaken for plundering. [2] L praedatorius < praedor < praeda booty.
pregnable: vulnerable to assault, penetration, and capture. [1] L prehendere seize.
prehensile: adapted for grasping or holding. [1] L prehensus (pp prehendo) < prendo grasp, seize.
reprehend: to chide sharply; object to forcibly; find fault with; blame. [1] L re (again) + prehendo seize.
reprehensible: deserving of blame or rebuke. [1] L re (again) + prehendo seize.
reprieve: to cancel punishment; (n) a cancellation of punishment. [1] L re- + prehendere to seize.
reprisal: injury in return. [1] Fr represaille < L re (again) + prehendo seize.
RELATED: apprehensive comprehend comprehension depreciate enterprise predator prehensible reprehension
COMMON: apprentice [1] apprenticeship [1] forget [4] get [3] guess [5] impresario [1] misdemeanor [1] osprey
[2] pregnant [1] prey [2] prison [1] prize [1] pry [1] reprise [1] spree [2] surprise [1]

149. kap- take/kaput- head/ kap-ro- he-goat
Latin: CAP, CIP, CAPT, CEPT, [CEIVE,CEIPT] take CAP/CEP/CIP CAPIT, CIPIT head

[1] L capio (captus) to seize, take; captivus prisoner
[2] L -ceps taker   [3] L caput head
[4] L caper he-goat
[5] OE haeft handle   [6] OE habban to have, hold
[7] OE hefig heavy   [8] OE haefan a haven
[9] OE hafoc hawk   [10] OE behofian to have need of

anticipatory: expecting; foreseeing and fulfilling beforehand. [1] L ante (before) + capio take.
capability: the state or quality of being able to do a certain thing, competence. [1] L capio take, hold.
capacious: spacious. [1] L capax capable, broad, roomy < capio hold.
capitulate: to surrender. [3] L capitulum chapter < caput head.
capricious: subject to impulses and whims. [3] L caput head.
captious: apt to find fault; hypercritical. [1] L captiosus deceptive.
captivate: to charm and hold someone's interest. [1] L captivus prisoner.
captivating: seizing and holding a person's attention; fascinating. [1] L captivus prisoner < capere to seize.
chattel: items of personal property. [3] OF chatel < L capitalis < caput head.
conceit: a high opinion of oneself; a fanciful or ingenious thought. [1] L capio (captus) to seize, take.

conceive: to form an idea of; think, imagine. [1] L concipio < con (together) + capio take.

concept: an abstract general notion or idea. [1] L conceptus < concipio < con (together) + capio take.

conception: egg fertilization; formation of abstract ideas and thoughts. [1] L conceptio < com- + capere take.

decapitate: kill by severing the head. [3] L de (from) + caput head.

deceptive: having power or tendency to mislead or delude. [1] L deceptus (pp decipio) deceive.

emancipation: release from bondage, slavery or any oppressive authority. [1] L e (out) + mancipo give up.

exceptionable: open to exception or objection. [1] L ex (out) + capio take.

imperceptible: not easily seen. [1] L in (not) + perceptio < perceptus (pp percipio) perceive.

incapacitate: to deprive of capacity. [1] L in + capacitas < capax < capio hold.

inception: the beginning of a process or undertaking. [1] L in- + capio (captus) to seize, take.

incipient: belonging to the first stages. [1] L incipiens (pfp incipio) begin.

misconception: a mistaken notion or misunderstanding. [1] L mis- + conceptus < con (together) + capio take.

perceptible: capable of being sensed. [1] Fr < L perceptio < perceptus (pp percipio) perceive.

perception: awareness of objects or ideas. [1] Fr < L perceptio < perceptus (pp percipio) perceive.

perceptive: discerning; showing keen awareness. [1] Fr < L perceptio < perceptus (pp percipio) perceive.

precept: a rule of conduct or action; a maxim. [1] OF < L praeceptum < praecipio admonish.

precipice: a cliff. [2] L praeceps headlong < prae (before) + capio take.

precipitate: to cause. [2] L praeceps headlong < prae (before) + capio take.

precipitous: extremely steep. [2] L praeceps headlong < prae (before) + capio take.

principal: chief; primary. [2] L principalis < princeps chief < primus first + capio take.

recapitulate: to summarize. [3] L re (again) + caput head.

receptive: ready to accept; ready to receive. [1] L receptus (pp recipere) to receive.

recipient: one who receives. [1] L re- + capio (captus) to seize, take.

recuperate: to recover from illness or loss. [1] L re- + capere to take.

susceptible: yielding readily to influence. [1] Fr < L sub (under) + capio take.

unprincipled: unscrupulous. [2] < un (not) + L principium beginning < primus first + capio take.

RELATED: ancipitous anticipate capacitance capacitor caprice deception emancipate perceive preconception principle principled susceptibility

COMMON: accept [1] acceptance [1] achieve [3] behave [6] behoove [10] biceps [3] cable [1] cacciatore [1] caddie [3] cadet [3] caitiff [1] capable[1] capacity [1] cape [3] caper [4] capital [3] capitalism [3] capitalization [3] capitate [3] capitation [3] Capricorn [4] capstan [1] captain [3] caption [1] captive [1] captivity [1] captor [1] capture [1] catch [1] cater [1] cattle [3] chapter [3] chase [1] chef [3] chief [3] chieftain [3] cop [1] copper [1] corporal [3] deceit [1] deceive [1] except [1] exception [1] exceptional [1] haft [5] have [6] haven [8] hawk [9] heavy [7] incapable [1] inconceivable [1] intercept [1] kerchief [3] mischief [3] municipal [1] municipality [1] occupant [1] occupy [1] participate [1] participating [1] participle [1] prince [1] princess [1] receipt [1] receive [1] reception [1] receptionist [1] receptacle [1] recipe [1] recover [1] triceps [3] unacceptable [1]

150. nem- assign, allot
Greek: NOM, NEM arrangement, law

[1] L numerus number, division
[2] Gk nemein to allot
[3] Gk nomos portion, custom, law
[4] Gk nomas wandering in search of pasture
[5] OE niman to take, seize
[6] OE naemel quick to seize

astronomical: enormous or immense; rel. to study of stars and the universe. [3] Gk astro- star + nomos law.

autonomous: independent in government. [3] Gk autonomia < autos self + nemo distribute, assign.

enumerate: count or name one by one. [1] L enumerare count out < ex- (out) + numerus number.
ergonomics: equipment design for greatest efficiency and health in use. [3] Gk ergon work + nomos law.
innumerable: too great in number to be counted. [1] L in- (not) + numerus number.
nemesis: retribution cause; unbeatable opponent. [2] Gk Nemesis goddess of retribution < nemein allot.
nomadic: moving about from place to place with no fixed home. [4] Gk nomas wandering for pasture.
numismatist: a collector of coins. [3] Gk nomizein to have in use < nomos custom.
RELATED: autonomic autonomist autonomy nomad numismatic
COMMON: astronomer [3] astronomy [3] benumb [5] binomial [3] Deuteronomy [2] economics [2] economy [2]
metronome [3] monomial [3] nimble [6] -nomy [3] numb [5] number [1] numeral [1] polynomial [3]

151. peku- wealth, movable property
Latin: PECU one's own; money

[1] L pecunia property, wealth; pecus cattle   [2] L peculium riches
[3] OF fie fief   [4] ON fe property, cattle

impecunious: having no money; habitually poor. [1] L im (not) + pecunia money.
peculate: appropriate public property to oneself; embezzle. [2] L peculatus < peculor defraud the public.
pecuniary: financial; relating to money. [1] L pecuniarius < pecunia wealth.
RELATED: peculator
COMMON: fee [3] fellow [4] fief [3] peculiar [2]

152. pere-² grant, allot
Latin: PAR, PAIR, PEER equal PART

[1] L pars share, part   [2] L portio part
[3] L par equal

bipartite: having two parts or participants. [1] L bi- two + partire to part < pars part.
compeer: one of equal rank; comrade; associate. [3] L com (together) + par equal.
disparage: to belittle. [3] OF des + parage rank < L dis (not) + par equal.
disparate: distinct; dissimilar; unequal. [3] L dis (not) + paro make equal.
disparity: inequality; difference. [3] L dis (not) + par equal.
impart: to give to; to bestow; to disclose; to transmit. [1] L in- (in) + partire to share < pars part.
impartial: not biased or prejudiced. [1] L im- (not) + pars part.
jeopardy: danger or risk of serious loss or injury. [1] L iocus joke + partire < pars part.
nonpareil: without equal. [3] Fr non (not) < L non + parell equal < L par equal.
parity: equality. [3] L par equal.
parse: to describe and analyze a word. [1] L pars part.
partiality: showing bias or prejudice. [1] L im- (not) + pars part.
participle: form of verb usable as an adjective. [1] L participium < pars part + capere to take.
partisan: a strong supporter of a cause, group, or idea. [1] L pars part.
partition: to split into parts. [1] L pars part.
peerless: greatly superior to anything of the same type or kind. [3] L par equal + OE –less.
proportion: quantitative relation of part to whole or other part. [2] L proportio < pro- + portione < portio part.
repartee: interchange of witty replies. [1] OF re- + partir to depart < L partire to divide < pars part.
tripartite: divided into three parts. [1] L tri- three + pars share, part.

RELATED: disparagement disparager disparaging jeopardize partial
COMMON: comparable [3] compare [3] comparison [3] pair [3] par [3] parcel [1] pari-mutual [3] part [1] participate [1] particle [1] party [1] peer [3] portion [2]

153. rep- snatch
Latin: RAPT seize

[1] L rapere (raptus) to seize; rapax, -acis grasping; rapidus swift
[2] L rapina plunder, pillage

enrapture: to fill with delight. [1] en- + L raptus (pp rapere) to seize.
rapacious: given to plundering or raping; extortionate. [1] L rapia seize.
rapt: absorbed; captured attention. [1] L raptus (pp rapere) to seize.
raptorial: seizing and devouring living prey; adapted for seizing and holding prey. [1] L rapio seize.
ravenous: extremely hungry or greedy. [2] L rapina plunder.
surreptitious: accomplished by secret or improper means; stealthy. [1] L sub (under) + rapio snatch.
RELATED: rapacity rapine
COMMON: rape [1] rapid [1] raptor [1] ravage [1] raven [1] ravish [1]

154. reu- tear up / reup- snatch / reud- raw, wild
Latin: RUPT break RUD rough, crude

[1] L usurpare (usurpatus) to usurp   [2] L rumpere (ruptus) to break
[3] L rudis rough
[4] OE reafian to plunder; bereafian to take away
[5] OF rober to rob   [6] OF robe robe

bereft: left without a loved one or one's possessions. [4] OE reafian to plunder; bereafian to take away.
disruption: cause disorder; break up. [2] L dis (apart) + rumpo break.
erudite: widely read; learned; scholarly. [3] L eruditus (pp erudio) instruct < e (from) + rudio rude.
interruption: intermission in action usually due to an hindering event. [2] L inter (off) + rumpo break.
irruption: a breaking or rushing in; a violent incursion. [2] L in (in) + rumpo break.
rudimentary: elementary; not fully developed features. [3] Fr < L rudimentum beginning < rudis rough.
rupture: breaking off or apart. [2] Fr < L ruptus broken < rumpo break.
usurp: to seize and take over without having legal authority. [1] L usurpare usurp.
RELATED: disrupt interrupt irrupt rude rudely rudeness rudiment usurpation
COMMON: abrupt [2] bankrupt [2] bereave [4] corrupt [2] corruption [2] erupt [2] eruption [2] eruptive [2] garderobe [6] reave [4] rob [5] robe [6] rout [2]

155. wes-[1] buy, sell
Latin: VIL base, mean

[1] L venum sale   [2] L vilis cheap, base

revile: to scold. [2] < re + Fr avilir cheapen < L vilis worthless.
venal: can be bought for a price; corrupt. [1] L venalis < venum sale.
vile: mean; degrading; evil. [2] Fr < vil < L vilis cheap, base.

vilify: to represent as base, mean or evil; defame; slander. [2] Fr vil < L vilis worthless + facio make.
RELATED: vilification
COMMON: vend [1]

156. wer-[5] to cover

[1] L operire (opertus; pfp. operiens) to cover
[2] L aperire (apertus; pfp. aperiens) open, uncover
[3] OF warantir to guarantee
[4] OF wer dam, fish trap
[5] OE warnian to take heed, warn
[6] OF garer to guard; garir to defend, protect
[7] OF garnir to equip

aperture: an opening. [2] L aperire to open, uncover.
covert: done hiddenly or secretly. [1] OF < L coopertus (pp cooperio) < co- (intens) + operio hide.
garnish: to decorate or embellish; to legally seize property; (n) an embellishment. [7] OF garnir to equip.
overt: open to view; not hidden. [2] OF pp ovrir < L operio open.
unwarranted: not justifiable. [3] un + OF warantir to guarantee.
warrant: to certify; affirm; (n) justification; rationale. [3] OF warantir to guarantee.
RELATED: warrant warranted warrantee warranty
COMMON: cover [1] garage [6] garment [7] garnish [7] garret [6] garrison [6] guaranty [3] kerchief [1] operculum [1] pert [2] warn [5] weir [4]

CHAPTER 20

Roots Referring to Cutting and Object Deformation

The eleventh category, covered in this chapter, refers directly to human actions that cut objects or deform them. Fifteen roots fall into this category. Five roots have a primary meaning of cutting or splitting:

'leu-[1]' meaning "loosen, divide, cut up"
'pau-[2]' meaning "cut, strike, stamp"
'skei-' meaning "cut, split"
'sker-[1]' meaning "to cut," 'skreu-' meaning "to cut, cutting tool," and 'skribh-' meaning "cut, separate, sift"
'tem-' meaning "to cut"

The root 'leu-[1]' meaning "loosen, divide, cut up" is the source of the Latin verb 'solvere' meaning "to loosen," Greek 'luein' meaning "to loosen," and the English words 'lose,' 'loss,' 'loose,' '-less,' 'leasing,' and 'forlorn.' Next 'pau-[2]' meaning "cut, strike, stamp" is the source of the Latin verb 'putare' meaning "to prune" or "to think over" and 'puteus' meaning "well." The root 'skei-' meaning "cut, split" is the source of the Latin verb 'scire' meaning "to know" and 'scindere' meaning "to split," the Greek 'schizein' meaning "to split," and the English words 'shed,' sheath,' 'sheave,' 'shin,' 'shiver,' and 'ski.' In Old English the 'sh' sounds were 'sk' sounds. Another root 'sker-[1]' meaning "to cut" ('skreu-' meaning "cut, cutting tool" and 'skribh-' meaning "cut, separate, sift") is the source of the Latin verb 'scribere' meaning "to write," 'caro, carnis' meaning "flesh," the Greek 'epikarsios' meaning "at an angle," and the English words 'share,' 'sharp,' 'shear,' 'shirt,' 'shore,' 'short,' 'shrub,' 'shard,' and 'skirt.' Finally, 'tem-' meaning "to cut" is the source of the Latin 'templum' meaning "temple" and the Greek 'temnein' meaning "to cut." One root has the idea of puncturing or pricking:

'peuk-' meaning "to prick"

The root 'peuk-' meaning "to prick" is the source of the Latin verb 'pugnare' meaning "to fight (with fists)," 'pungere' meaning "to prick," and the Greek 'pugme' meaning "fist." Three roots emphasize rubbing or pressing:

'mer-[2]' meaning "rub away, harm"
'streig-' meaning "stroke, rub, press"
'tere-[1]' meaning "rub, turn"

The root 'mer-[2]' meaning "rub away, harm" is the source of the Latin verb 'mordere' meaning "to bite," 'mors (mort-)' meaning "death," the Greek 'ambrotos' meaning "immortal," the Old English 'morthor' meaning "murder," and the English words 'murder' and 'nightmare.' Next 'streig-' meaning "stroke, rub, press" is the source of the Latin verb 'stringere' meaning "to press together" or "to bind" and the English words 'strike,' 'streak,' and 'stroke.' Also 'tere-¹' meaning "rub, turn" is the source of the Latin verb 'terere' meaning "to rub away," the Greek 'tribein' meaning "to rub," 'trogein' meaning "to gnaw," and the English words 'thread,' 'thrash,' 'thresh,' 'threshold,' and 'throw.' Three roots involve stretching or squeezing:

'(s)pen-' meaning "draw, stretch, spin"
'ten-/tenk-¹' meaning "stretch"
'treud-' meaning "squeeze"

The root '(s)pen-' meaning "draw, stretch, spin" produced the Latin verb 'pendere' meaning "to hang" or "to weigh," 'pondus (ponder-)' meaning "weight," Greek 'ponein' meaning "to toil," and the English words 'span,' 'spider,' 'spin,' and 'spindel.' Also 'ten-/tenk-¹' meaning "stretch" is the source of the Latin verb 'tendere' meaning "to stretch" or "to strive," 'tenere' meaning "to hold" or "to maintain," the Greek 'teinein' meaning "to stretch," and the English word 'thin.' Finally, 'treud-' meaning "squeeze" is the source of the Latin verb 'trudere' meaning "to thrust" and the English words 'threat' and 'thrust.' Three roots have a meaning of bending, twisting, or folding:

'pel-³' meaning "to fold ('plek-' meaning "to plait")
'terkʷ-' meaning "twist"
'wer-³' meaning "turn, bend"

The root 'pel-³' meaning "to fold (plek-' meaning "to plait") is the basis for the Latin verb 'plicare' meaning "to fold" and 'plectere' meaning "to weave," the Greek '-plos' meaning "-fold," and the English words 'fold' and 'flax.' Further 'terkʷ-' meaning "twist" is the source of the Latin verb 'torquere' meaning "to twist" and the English word 'thwart.' Finally 'wer-³' means "turn, bend" and is the source of the Latin verb 'vertere' meaning "to turn" and 'vergere' meaning "to tend toward," Greek 'rhaptein' meaning "to sew," and the English words '-ward,' 'warp,' 'weird,' 'worm,' 'worry,' 'worth,' 'wrangle,' 'wrap,' 'wrath,' 'wreath,' 'wrench,' 'wrest,' 'wrestle,' 'wring,' 'wrinkle,' 'wrist,' 'writhe,' 'wrong,' and 'wry.'

SOUND SHIFTS

The Indo-European, Latin, and Greek smooth palatal mute 'k' shows up in West Germanic and Old English as a rough palatal 'h.' For example, 'skei-' meaning "cut, split" is the source of the Latin verb 'scire' meaning "to know" and 'scindere' meaning "to split," the Greek 'schizein' meaning "to split," and the English words 'shed,' sheath,' 'sheave,' 'shin,' 'shiver,' and 'ski.' In Old English the 'sh' sounds were 'sk' sounds. Second, 'sker-¹' meaning "to cut" ('skreu-' meaning "cut, cutting tool" and 'skribh-' meaning "cut, separate, sift") is the source of the Latin verb 'scribere' meaning "to write," 'caro, carnis' meaning "flesh," Greek 'epikarsios' meaning "at an angle," and the English words 'share,' 'sharp,' 'shear,' 'shirt,' 'shore,' 'short,' 'shrub,' 'shard,' and 'skirt.'

If Indo-European, Latin, and Greek have a voiced palatal mute 'g,' the West Germanic and Old English form is a smooth palatal 'k.' Thus, 'streig-' meaning "stroke, rub, press" is the source of the Latin verb 'stringere' meaning "to press together" or "to bind" and the English words 'strike,' 'streak,' and 'stroke.'

When Indo-European and Latin and Greek show a smooth labial mute 'p,' the West Germanic and Old English show a rough labial 'f.' This sound change is clearly evident with the root 'pel-³' meaning "to fold ('plek-' meaning "to plait"), which is the source of the Latin verb 'plicare' meaning "to fold" and 'plectere' meaning "to weave," the Greek '-plos' meaning "-fold," and the English words 'fold' and 'flax.'

The third general rule cited in chapter 7 applies to one root: Initial s sounds conjoined with following consonants usually show no change in Greek, Latin, and Old English. However, they do often disappear. An initial Indo-European 's' followed by a vowel tended to become a rough breathing or 'h' in classical Greek or disappeared. The root '(s)pen-' meaning "draw, stretch, spin" is the source of the Latin verb 'pendere' meaning "to hang" or "to weigh" and 'pondus (ponder-)' meaning "weight," the Greek 'ponein' meaning "to toil," and the English words 'span,' 'spider,' 'spin,' and 'spindel.' Here the initial 's' has disappeared for both Latin and Greek.

When Indo-European, Latin, and Greek show a voiced dental mute 'd,' West Germanic and Old English show a smooth dental 't.' Thus, 'treud-' meaning "squeeze" is the source of the Latin verb 'trudere' meaning "to thrust" and the English words 'threat' and 'thrust' showing a change to 't' for the final consonant of the root.

The Indo-European, Latin, and Greek smooth dental mute 't' surfaces in West Germanic and Old English as a rough dental 'th.' Hence, 'ten-/tenk-[1]' meaning "stretch" is the source of the Latin verb 'tendere' meaning "to stretch" or "to strive" and 'tenere' meaning "to hold" or "to maintain," the Greek 'teinein' meaning "to stretch," and the English word 'thin.' Also 'tere-[1]' meaning "rub, turn" is the source of the Latin verb 'terere' meaning "to rub away" and the Greek 'tribein' meaning "to rub," 'trogein' meaning "to gnaw," and the English words 'thread,' 'thrash,' 'thresh,' 'threshold,' and 'throw.' Further, 'terkʷ-' meaning "twist" is the source of the Latin verb 'torquere' meaning "to twist" and the English word 'thwart.' Additionally, 'treud-' meaning "squeeze" is the source of the Latin verb 'trudere' meaning "to thrust" and the English words 'threat' and 'thrust.' Finally, the root 'mer-[2]' meaning "rub away, harm" is the source of the Latin verb 'mordere' meaning "to bite" and 'mors (mort-)' meaning "death." It does not have a final 't' in the root, but an appended 't' does show up in some forms. It is the source of Greek 'ambrotos' meaning "immortal," the Old English 'morthor' meaning "murder," the English words 'murder' and 'nightmare.'

The fourth rule in chapter 7 states that the w sound of Indo-European is retained in the Old English forms. In the case of Latin it is occasionally dropped and otherwise represented by the letter 'v,' which, however, was pronounced as a w sound. The original Greek w sound disappeared becoming a rough breathing or h sound and often was dropped altogether. We see this phenomena with the root 'wer-[3]' meaning "turn, bend," which is the source of the Latin verb 'vertere' meaning "to turn" and 'vergere' meaning "to tend toward." The Greek word 'rhaptein' meaning "to sew" changes to a rough breathing 'h' but is left unchanged in the English words '-ward,' 'warp,' 'weird,' 'worm,' 'worry,' 'worth,' 'wrangle,' 'wrap,' 'wrath,' 'wreath,' 'wrench,' 'wrest,' 'wrestle,' 'wring,' 'wrinkle,' 'wrist,' 'writhe,' 'wrong,' and 'wry.'

Four of the roots discussed in this chapter do not show any of the sound shift changes covered in chapter 7. The root 'leu-[1]' meaning "loosen, divide, cut up" is the source of the Latin verb 'solvere' meaning "to loosen," Greek 'luein' meaning "to loosen," and the English words 'lose,' 'loss,' 'loose,' '-less,' 'leasing,' and 'forlorn.' Another root, 'pau-[2]' meaning "cut, strike, stamp," is the source of the Latin verb 'putare' meaning "to prune" or "to think over" and 'puteus' meaning "well." Third, 'peuk-' meaning "to prick" is the source of the Latin verb 'pugnare' meaning "to fight (with fists)" and 'pungere' meaning "to prick" and the Greek 'pugme' meaning "fist." Finally, 'tem-' meaning "to cut" is the source of the Latin 'templum' meaning "temple" and the Greek 'temnein' meaning "to cut."

LIST OF ROOTS IN ORDER OF OCCURRENCE

The following list gives the roots as they are presented in this chapter. Syllables in capital letters indicate a sequence of letters in English words that shows the root to be the origin of a word. In nearly all cases, if one sees the letters in caps in an English word, one can infer that it comes from the Indo-European root in the first column. However, there may also be some English words from the root that do not accord with the general pattern and some English words that fit the pattern but come from a different root.

157. leu-[1] loosen, divide, cut	SOLV, SOLUT loosen; set free -LYSIS, -LYST, -LYTIC, LYTICAL a loosening, solution
158. mer-[2] rub away, harm	MORD, MORS bite MOR/MORT MORT death
159. pau-[2] cut, strike, stamp	PUT cut; prune away; clear up; think; suppose
160. pel-[3] to fold; plek- to plait	PLIC, PLECT, PLEX, PLI, -PLE, -PLY fold; twist; weave

161.	peuk- to prick	PUGN, PUG fight; fist PUNG, PUNCT, POINT point; prick
162.	skei- cut, split	SCI know SCIND, SCISS cut, split SCHIZ, SCHIS split; cleave
163a.	sker-[1] to cut	CARN flesh
163b.	skreu- cut, cutting tool	
163c.	skribh- cut, separate, sift	SCRIB, SCRIPT write
164.	(s)pen- draw, stretch, spin	PEND, PENS hang —> PEND, PENS, POND weigh; pay SPONT, SPONS free will, of oneself
165.	streig- stroke, rub, press	STRING, STRICT, STRAIN, STRAINT bind
166.	tem- to cut	TEMN, TOM cut
167.	ten-/tenk-[1] stretch	TEND, TENS, TENT stretch TEN, TIN, TENT, TAIN hold TENU thin TON, TEN stretch; tone
168.	tere-[1] rub, turn	TER, TRIT rub
169.	terk^w- twist	TORT twist
170.	treud- squeeze	TRUD, TRUS thrust
171.	wer-[3] turn, bend	VERT, VERS, VERT, VORS turn VERG tend toward, bend

157. leu-[1] loosen, divide, cut apart

Latin: SOLV, SOLUT loosen; set free
Greek: -LYSIS, -LYST, -LYTIC, -LYTICAL a loosening, solution

[1] L solvere (solutus) to loosen, untie, pay,
    set sail; solutus free; solutio, -onis payment
[2] Gk luein to loosen, release, untie
[3] OE -leosan to lose; forleosan to forfeit, lose   [4] OE leas free from, lacking
[5] OE los loss   [6] ON lauss loose

absolute: without restriction or relation; unconditional. [1] L absolutus < ab (from) + solvo loose.
absolve: free from obligation or liability; free from sin or its penalties. [1] L ab (from) + solvo loose.
dissolute: abandoned; profligate. [1] L dissolutus (pp dissolvo) loosen.
dissolution: changing into a fluid; breakup of an assembly or organization. [1] L dissolvo loosen.
indissoluble: cannot be dissolved; cannot be broken up. [1] L dissolutus loosen (pp dissolvo).
insolvent: bankrupt. [1] L in (not) + solvo loosen, solve.
irresolute: wavering; hesitating. [1] L in (not) + re (again) + solvo loosen.
resolution: being of fixed purpose, determined, constant. [1] L re (again) + solvo loosen.
resolve: fixed purpose; determination to do something. [1] L re (again) + solvo loosen.
soluble: capable of dissolving; susceptible of being solved or explained. [1] Fr < L solubilis < solvo solve.
solvent: assets exceed liabilities; (n) substance that dissolves other substances. [1] L dissolvo loosen.
analysis: separating a whole into its parts to determine function or relationship. [2] Gk ana (up) + lyo loose.
catalyst: unchanged agent that accelerates or retards chemical processes. [2] Gk kata (entirely) + lyo loose.
dialysis: kidney disease treatment removing waste from the blood. [2] Gk dia (apart) + lyo loose.
electrolysis: separating ions by electricity; hair removal by electric needle. [2] Gk elektron + lyo loose.
psychoanalysis: exposing repression to treat mental disorders. [2] Gk psyche mind + ana (up) + lyo loose.
RELATED: absolution analyst analytic analyze catalytic irresoluteness resolute
COMMON: dissoluble [1] dissolve [1] forlorn [4] irresolution [1] irresolvable [1] leasing [4] -less [4] loose [6] lorn [3] lose [5] loss [5] lyo- [1] lyso- [1] -lyte [1] -lytic [1] palsy [1] paralysis [1] resoluteness [1] resolvable [1] resolve [1] solute [1] solution [1] solvable [1] solve [1]

158. mer-² rub away, harm
Latin: MORD, MORS bite MOR/MORT MORT death

[1] L mors (mort-) death

[2] L mori (mortuus) to die; mors, mortis death

[3] L immortalis immortal

[4] L mortarium mortar

[5] L mordere (morsus; pfp mordens) to bite;
   mordax, -acis biting; morsus bite

[6] L morbus disease

[7] Gk ambrotos immortal, divine
   (a + -mbrotos, brotos mortal)

[8] OE mare goblin, incubus

[9] OE morthor murder

amortize: extinguish a debt using a sinking fund. [1] Fr amortir < amortissant < L ad (to) + mors death.
morbid: diseased; unwholesome; gruesome. [6] L morbidus diseased < morbus disease.
mordacious: biting or given to biting; sarcastic. [5] L mordax < mordeo bite.
mordant: biting; pungent; fixing. [5] Fr < L mordens (pfp mordeo) bite.
moribund: dying; at the point of death; coming to an end. [2] L moribundus < morior die.
mortality: having a limited span of life; death rate. [1] L mortalitas < mors, mortis death.
mortification: feeling of humiliation or great shame; self-denial. [1] LL mortifico kill.
remorse: regret; sorrow over past misdeeds. [5] L re- + mordere to bite.
RELATED: mordacity moribundity mortify
COMMON: ambrosia [7] immortal [3] immortality [3] morsel [5] mortal [1] mortally [1] mortar [4] mortgage [2] mortician [2] mortuary [2] murder [9] nightmare [8]

159. pau-² cut, strike, stamp
Latin: PUT cut; prune away; clear up; think; suppose

[1] L putare (putatus) to prune, clean, think over, reflect
[2] L puteus well

discount: (v) reduce in price; dismiss as unimportant. [1] OF dis + conter count < L com- + putare think.
discountenance: to disapprove. [1] L dis (apart) + computo < com (together) + puto reckon.
disputable: open to question or challenge; doubtful. [1] Fr disputer < L disputo < dis (apart) + puto reckon.
disputatious: given to engaging in arguments. [1] Fr disputer < L dis (apart) + puto reckon.
dispute: a controversy; an argument. [1] Fr disputer < L disputo < dis (apart) + puto reckon.
disrepute: lack or loss of reputation; ill repute. [1] L dis (not) + re (again) + puto think.
impute: to set to the account of someone; charge. [1] L in (in) + puto reckon.
indisputable: cannot be questioned or doubted. [1] Fr disputer < L disputo < dis (apart) + puto reckon.
pitfall: a hidden danger or trouble; trap formed by ground cavity. [2] OE pytt (< L puteus well) + feallan.
putatively: supposedly. [1] Fr putatif < L puto think.
raconteur: a clever and skillful story teller. [1] OF re- + aconter to count up.
recount: to describe a sequence of events. [1] L re + com- + putare to think.
reputable: being worthy of honor and esteem. [1] L putare (putatus) to prune, think over.
unaccountable: cannot be explained; lacking responsibility for. [1] L un- + ad- + computare to sum up.
RELATED: disputation imputation imputative putative
COMMON: account [1] accountable [1] amputate [1] compute [1] reputation [1] reputed [1]

160. pel-³ to fold; plek- to plait

Latin: PLIC, PLECT, PLEX, PLI, -PLE, -PLY fold; twist; weave

[1] L -plus -fold   [2] L -plex -fold
[3] L plicare (plicatus; pfp plicans) to fold;
    simplicitas, -tatis simplicity
[4] L plectere (plexus) weave, plait, entwine
[5] Gk -plos, -ploos -fold
[6] OE -feald -fold; fealdan to fold   [7] OE fleax flax

complicity: the act or state of being an accomplice. [4] L complexus < com (together) + plecto braid.
deploy: to arrange, position, or distribute; to put into use. [3] L plicatus (pfp plicare) to fold.
duplicity: tricky deceitfulness; double-dealing. [3] Fr duplicite < duplex < L duo two + plico fold.
explicable: capable of explanation. [3] L explicatus < ex (out) + plico fold.
explicate: to clear from obscurity; to explain. [3] L explicatus < ex (out) + plico fold.
explicit: plainly expressed or that plainly expresses; definite; not implied. [3] L ex (out) + plico fold.
exploit: a deed esp. an heroic action. [3] L explicare to unfold < ex (out) + plico fold.
implicate: to connect with; to incriminate; to imply. [3] L in- (in) + plicare to fold.
implicative: tending to imply or implicate. [3] L in (in) + plico fold.
implicit: absolute; implied. [3] L implicitus (pp implico) < in (in) + plico fold.
imply: to logically necessitate as a consequence; indicate implicitly. [3] L implicare < in- (in) + plicare to fold.
manifold: of many kinds or forms. [6] L multus many + OE -feald –fold.
multiplicity: having many forms; a great many. [2] L multus many + -plex –fold.
perplexity: bewilderment; confusion. [4] OF perplexite < LL perplexitas < per + plexus < plectere twist.
plait: to braid or pleat. [3] OF pleit < L plicatus (pp plico) fold.
pliable: easily bent or twisted; flexible; easily persuaded or controlled. [3] Fr < L plicans (pfp plico) fold.
plight: an unfortunate situation. [3] L plicare to fold.
replica: the duplicate as of a picture; a copy; reproduction. [3] L re (again) + plico fold.
replication: a reply; a repetition or copy; reverberation; echo. [3] L re (again) + plico fold.
supplication: a humble entreaty or request as a prayer to God. [3] L supplicatus < sub (under) + plico.
RELATED: duplicitous implication perplex perplexed pliability pliableness pliant replicant replicate replicative supplicate
COMMON: accomplice [4] application [3] apply [3] complex [4] complexion [4] complexity [4] complicate [3] complication [3] display [3] duplicate [3] duplication [3] employ [3] flax [7] fold [6] -fold [6] multifold [6] multiplex [2] multiple [1] multiplicand [3] multiplier [3] multiplication [3] octuple [1] pleat [3] -ploid [5] ply [3] reply [3] quadruple [1] quintuple [1] septuple [1] sextuple [1] triple [1]

161. peuk- to prick

Latin: PUGN, PUG fight; fist PUNG, PUNCT, POINT point; prick

[1] L pugil pugilist; pugnus fist; pugnare (pfp pugnans) to fight with the fist
[2] L pungere (punctus; pfp pungens) to prick; punctus point
[3] Gk pugme fist

compunction: self-reproach for wrong-doing; slight regret. [2] L com (intens.) + pungo sting.
expunge: to erase or delete. [2] L ex (out) + pungo prick.
impugn: to call in question; gainsay. [1] L in (against) + pugno fight.

oppugn: militate against; conflict with; oppose; to assail with argument. [1] L ob (against) + pugno fight.

poignant: piercing; bitter; severe; sharp; pungent; biting. [2] Fr < L pungo prick.

pugnacious: quarrelsome; disposed or inclined to fight. [1] L pugnax < pugno fight.

punctilious: very nice or exact in the observance of forms of etiquette. [2] L punctus point.

pungent: painful to the nerves or mind as by sharp points; sharp; caustic. [2] L pungens < pungo prick.

repine: to be discontented or fretful; complain; murmur. [2] L re (again) + pungo prick.

repugnant: offensive to taste or feeling; exciting aversion or repulsion. [1] OF < re (back) + pugnus fist.

RELATED: impugnable poignancy pugnaciousness pugnacity punctilio

COMMON: bung [2] pink [2] point [2] pointillism [2] pounce [2] pugilism [1] pugilist [1] pugil stick [1] punctual [2] punctuate [2] punctuation [2] puncture [2] pygmaean [3] Pygmy [3]

162. skei- cut, split

Latin: SCI know SCIND, SCISS cut, split

Greek: SCHIZ,SCHIS split; cleave

[1] L scire (pfp sciens) to know; scientia knowledge; conscientia joint knowledge; conscius aware

[2] L scindere (scissus) to split   [3] L scutum shield

[4] Gk schizein (eskismai) to split

[5] OE scinu shin   [6] OE scitan to defecate

[7] OE sceadan to separate   [8] OE sceath sheath

[9] OE skidh log, snowshoe   [10] ME sheve pulley

[11] ME shivere splinter

abscissa: horizontal line on a graph showing distance from the zero co-ordinate. [2] L ab (off) + scindo cut.

conscience: faculty telling a person what is wrong. [1] Fr < L conscientia < con (together) + scio know.

conscientious: governed or dictated by conscience. [1] L conscientia < con (together) + scio know.

exscind: to cut off; sever from a body or organization. [2] L exscindo < ex (out) + scindo cut.

nescience: the state of not knowing; ignorance. [1] L nescio be ignorant.

omniscience: infinite knowledge. [1] L omnis all + sciens knowing.

prescience: foresight. [1] Fr < L prae (before) + scio know.

rescind: to make void as an act; repeal. [2] L re (again) + scindo cut.

schismatic: tending to cause division. [4] Gk schisma split.

schizophrenic: disorder exhibiting withdrawal and delusions of grandeur. [4] Gk schizo divide + phren mind.

unconscionable: beyond reasonable bounds; unscrupulous. [1] L conscientia < con (together) + scio know.

RELATED: conscientiousness conscionable nescient omniscient prescient schism unconscionably unconscious unconsciousness

COMMON: abscission [2] conscious [1] consciousness [1] esquire [3] nice [1] nicety [1] plebiscite [1] recission [2] schizo- [4] science [1] sciolism [1] sciolist [1] scission [2] scissors [2] scissure [2] sheath [8] sheave [10] shed [7] shin [5] shit [6] shiver [11] ski [9] squire [3]

163. sker-¹ to cut —> skreu- to cut, cutting tool / skribh- cut, separate, sift

Latin: SCRIB, SCRIPT write CARN flesh

[1] L scribere (scriptus; pfp scribens) to scratch, incise, write; scriba clerk; scriptura writing

[2] L caro, carnis flesh   [3] L curtus short

[4] L corium leather   [5] L scruta trash

[6] L cortex bark

[7] Gk epikarsios at an angle (cf epi)

[8] Ital scarpa embankment

[9] OE sceard cut, notch

[10] OE scieran to cut

[11] OE scear plowshare; scearu portion

[12] OE scear scissors

[13] OE scort short

[14] OE skyrte skirt

[15] OE scora shore

[16] OE scearp sharp

[17] OE scrybb shrub

[18] ON skor notch, tally

[19] ON skrap remains

[20] ON skrapa scrapa to scratch

[21] LG scheren to move to and fro

[22] MD scherm shield

[23] MD schrabben to scrape; schrobben to scrape

[24] OF escauberc scabbard

[25] OF eskirmir to fight with swords

ascribe: attribute or assign a cause or source; assign as a quality or attribute. [1] L ad (to) + scribo write.

bias: partiality or prejudice against; systematic sampling error. [7] Gk epikarsios slanted, at an angle.

carnage: great human slaughter. [2] Fr carnage < L caro, carnis flesh.

carnal: of the body. [2] L carnalis < caro flesh.

carnivorous: flesh-eating. [2] L caro flesh + voro devour.

carrion: decaying flesh. [2] L caro flesh.

circumscribe: to draw a line or figure around; confine within bounds. [1] L circum (around) + scribo write.

conscript: to force into government service. [1] L con (together) + scribo write.

crone: ugly, old woman. [2] L caro flesh.

curt: short, terse, or abrupt in manner or speech. [3] L curtus short.

curtail: reduce; shorten. [3] L curtus short.

excoriate: wear or strip off the skin; abrade; denounce. [4] L ex (off) + corium skin.

incarnadine: flesh colored; pink; red. [2] Fr incarnadin < L incarnatus < in (in) + caro, carnis flesh.

incarnation: the act of becoming embodied in human form. [2] L incarnatus < in (in) + caro, carnis flesh.

indescribable: beyond the power of description. [1] L in (not) + de (down, from) + scribo write.

inscrutable: mysterious; difficult or impossible to understand. [5] L in- (in) + scrutabilis discoverable.

nondescript: person or thing difficult to describe. [1] L non + descriptus < de (fully) + scribo write.

prescript: prescribed as a rule or model; laid down. [1] L prae (before) + scribo write.

proscribe: to outlaw or prohibit; condemn as a doctrine or practice. [1] L pro (before) + scribo write.

scrip: document entitling to receive something else of value. [1] OF escript < L scriptus (pp scribo) write.

scrutinize: (v) to observe carefully in detail. [5] L scrutinium < scrutor examine.

shard: a broken piece of an earthen vessel; potsherd. [9] OE sceard (cut, notch).

superscription: an upper or outer inscription. [1] L super (over) + scribo write.

transcription: act of copying or recopying. [1] L trans (over) + scribo write.

underscore: to stress; to emphasize. [18] ME under- + scoru twenty.

RELATED: ascription biased carnally conscribe circumscription conscription incarnate prescribe prescription prescriptive proscription proscriptively scrutiny superscribe superscript transcribe transcript

COMMON: carnate [2] carnation [2] carnival [2] carnivorous [2] charnal [2] cortex [6] describe [1] descriptive [1] escarpment [8] inscribe [1] inscription [1] manuscript [1] outskirts [14] postscript [1] scabbard [24] score [18] scrabble [23] scrap [19] scrape [20] screen [22] scribal [1] scribe [1] scribble [1] scrimmage [25] script [1] scriptural [1] scripture [1] scrub [23] serif [1] share [11] sharp [16] shear [10,12] sheer [21] shirt [14] shore [15] short [13] shrub [17] skirmish [25] skirt [14] subscript [1] subscribe [1] subscription [1]

164. (s)pen- draw, stretch, spin

Latin: PEND, PENS hang —> PEND, PENS, POND weigh; pay SPONT, SPONS free will, of oneself

[1] L pendere (pfp pendens) hang, be
   uncertain; pendere (pensus) weigh, value;
   pensare weigh, consider
[2] L pondo by weight
[3] L pondus (ponder-) weight; ponderare
   (ponderatus; pfp ponderans) to weigh, ponder
[4] L sponte of one's own accord, spontaneously
[5] Gk penia lack, poverty
[6] Gk ponos toil; ponein to toil deriv. penesthai to toil
[7] OE spinnan to spin
[8] OE spinel spindel
[9] OE spann distance
[10] MD spange clasp

append: to attach [1] L ad to + pendo hang
compendium: an abridgment; a brief, comprehensive summary. [1] L com (together) + pendo weigh.
compensatory: made in return for; remuneration for. [1] L com (together) + penso weigh.
counterpoise: induce equilibrium by counterbalancing weights. [1] L contra (against) + pensum weight.
despondent: dejected in spirit; disheartened. [4] L de (from) + spondeo promise.
dispensation: a distribution; divine arrangement of world affairs. [1] L dispenso < dis (apart) + pendo weigh.
equipoise: equilibrium; balanced in weight and power. [1] OF pois < L aequus equal + pensum weight.
expenditure: outlay; disbursement; expense. [1] L ex (out) + pendo weigh.
geoponic: rel. to agriculture. [6] Gk ge earth + ponos toil; ponein to toil.
impend: hang over; be imminent; threaten. [1] L impendeo < in (on) + pendeo hang.
imponderable: something that cannot be evaluated precisely. [3] L in- + pondero < pendo weigh.
indispensable: cannot be left out; necessary for a purpose. [1] L dispenso < dis (apart) + pendo weigh.
penchant: a strong inclination in favor of something. [1] Fr pencher incline < L pendeo hang.
pendant: something that hangs for ornament or for use. [1] L pendeo hang.
pendulous: hanging esp. so as to swing. [1] L pendulus pendulous.
pensile: pendant and swaying; pendulous; suspended; hanging loosely. [1] L pensilis < pendeo hang.
pensive: in quiet reflection; with a touch of sadness. [1] Fr pensif < L pensare weigh < pendo weigh.
ponderous: having weight, bulk; very impressive. [3] L pondero < pondus weight < pendo weigh.
preponderance: a force overbalancing the weight of other factors. [3] L prae (before) + pondero weigh.
propensity: disposition; tendency. [1] L propensus < propendeo < pro (forward) + pendeo hang.
recompense: to return or give an equivalent to; repay. [1] L re (again) + com (together) + pendo weigh.
responsive: inclined to reply or answer; being in accord or sympathy. [4] L re (again) + spondeo promise.
spontaneous: not compelled, caused, or planned. [4] LL spontaneus < sponte free will.
stipend: a regular payment of a fixed amount. [1] L stips a small payment + pendere to weigh, pay.
suspension: hung from a support; float in a fluid; cessation from operation. [1] L sub (under) + pendo hang.
RELATED: appendage appendix compensate compensation despond despondence dispense dispensable dispensatory dispenser equiponderant equiponderate expend expendable expense expensive impending pendency pending pensively pensiveness preponderant preponderate preponderous propend respond response responsibility responsible spontaneity suspend suspense suspender
COMMON: appendicitis [1] avoirdupois [1] depend [1] dependency [1] dependent [1] independence [1] independent [1] interdependence [1] interdependent [1] painter [1] pansy [1] pend [1] pendulum [1] -penia [5] pension [1] penthouse [1] perpendicular [1] peso [1] poise [1] ponder [3] ponderable [3] pound [2] span [9] spangle [10] spend [1] spider [7] spin [7] spindel [8]

165. streig- stroke, rub, press
Latin: STRING, STRICT, STRAIN, STRAINT bind

[1] L stringere (strictus; pfp stringens)
  draw tight, press together, bind, touch, prune
[2] L stria furrow, channel
[3] OE strican to stroke   [4] OE strica stroke, line
[5] OE strac stroke

astringent: tending to contract or draw together organic tissues; constipative. [1] L ad + stringo bind fast.
constrain: compel by physical or moral means. [1] OF constraindre < L constringo < con (with) + stringo bind.
constraint: something inhibiting movement or action. [1] OF constraindre < L con (with) + stringo bind.
constrict: contracting or compressing to make smaller and more narrow. [1] L con (together) + stringo bind.
prestige: distinction, standing, honor, or esteem. [1] L praestigiae tricks < prae- (pre-) + stringere draw tight.
restraint: means hindering movement or action; holding back. [1] L re (back) + stringo bind.
restrictive: tending or operating to keep within limits or bounds; confine. [1] L re (back) + stringo bind.
striated: having narrow channels; thin parallel lines. [2] L stria furrow.
stricture: severe criticism. [1] L strictura < strictus (pp stringo) bind.
stringent: keeping closely to strict requirements; rigid; severe. [1] L stringo bind < stringens compress.
RELATED: astriction astringe constriction constrictive nonrestrictive restrain restrained restrict restriction stria striation stringency
COMMON: distress [1] district [1] strain [1] strait [1] streak [4] stress [1] strict [1] strike [3] stroke [5]

166. tem- to cut
Greek: TEMN, TOM cut

[1] L templum temple, shrine   [2] L contemnare to despise
[3] Gk temnein to cut; tomos a cut, section; tome a cutting

anatomy: science of the structure of animals and plants. [3] Gk ana (up) + temno cut.
atomistic: composed of many small separate, disparate elements. [3] Gk temnein to cut.
contemn: to despise; scorn. [2] L contemno < com- (intens.) + temnere despise.
contemplate: to attend to and consider. [1] L com- (with) + templum temple.
contempt: a feeling of scorn or disrespect; showing disrespect for. [2] L contemptus (pp contemnare) despise.
dichotomy: division. [3] Gk dicha in two + temno cut.
epitome: a representative example. [3] Gk epi (upon) + temno cut.
tome: volume. [3] Gk tomos.
RELATED: anatomic diatomic diatomaceous
COMMON: atom [3] atomic [3] entomo- [3] entomology [3] temple [1] -tome [3] -tomy [3]

167. ten- stretch /tenk-¹ stretch
Latin: TEND,TENS,TENT stretch TEN, TIN, TENT, TAIN hold TENU thin
Greek: TON, TEN stretch; tone

[1] L tendere (tentus; pfp tendens) to stretch, extend,
  strive, aim
[2] L portendere to predict, stretch out before;
  portentum omen
[3] L tenere (pfp tenens) to hold, keep, maintain;
  tenax, -acis tenacious; pertinax, -acis stubborn
[4] L tenuis thin, rare, fine   [5] L tener tender, delicate

[6] Gk teinein to stretch; tasis a stretching　　　　[7] Gk tetanos stiff, rigid
[8] Gk tenon tendon　　　　　　　　　　　　　　　[9] Gk tonos string, sound, pitch
[10] OE thynne thin

abstinence: voluntary refraining from esp. intoxicating drinks; self-denial. [3] L ab (from) + teneo hold.
attentive: giving close consideration to matters esp. to the desires of others. [1] L ad- + tendere to stretch .
attenuate: to make thin small or fine; draw out; emaciate. [4] L ad + tenuis thin.
con´tent: all that a thing contains; the constituent elements of a concept. [3] L con (together) + teneo hold.
contention: competition; controversy; an assertion in an argument. [3] Fr < L con (together) + teneo hold.
contentious: quarrelsome. [3] Fr < L contentio < contentus < contineo < con (together) + teneo hold.
continence: moderation; self-control esp. in engaging in sexual activity. [3] L con (together) + teneo hold.
continuity: the state of being unbroken without cessation or interruption. [3] L con (together) + teneo hold.
countenance: facial expression; the face; approve. [3] L continentia demeanor < con (together) + teneo hold.
discountenance: put to shame; discourage; frown on. [3] L dis (not) + con (together) + teneo hold.
distend: to stretch. [1] L dis (apart) + tendo stretch.
extensive: spatially very large, prolonged in time, or broad in scope. [1] L ex (out) + tendo stretch.
extent: range or scope of presence or occurrence. [1] L ex- + tendere.
extenuating: mitigating, excusing, lessening degree of guilt. [4] L ex (out) + tenuis thin.
impertinent: insolent; rude; intrusive; irrelevant; pointless. [3] L in (not) + per (through) + teneo hold.
incontinent: not controlling appetites; unchaste. [3] L in (not) + continens < con (together) + teneo hold.
intensive: maximizing production from a resource. [1] L intensus (pp intendo) < in (toward) + tendo stretch.
intention: a settling of the mind on doing a certain act; purpose. [1] L intentus < in (toward) + tendo stretch.
intone: to speak with a singing tone. [9] L in- (in) + tonos tone.
malcontent: a rebel; a troublemaker; one always dissatisfied. [3] L mal + contentus (pp continere) to restrain.
ostensible: apparent. [1] L ostendo exhibit.
ostentatious: pretentious public display; showy; displaying wealth. [1] L ostento (freq ostendo) exhibit.
pertain: to be connected, associated, relevant, appropriate, or suitable. [3] L per (intens.) + teneo hold.
pertinacious: tenacious of purpose; stubbornly maintaining. [3] L per (through) + tenax < teneo hold.
pertinent: relevant; just to the purpose; to the point. [3] L per (intens.) + teneo hold.
portend: give warning of a future fortunate or unfortunate occurrence. [2] L portendere fortell.
pretentious: giving an outward show of importance or intelligence. [1] L prae (before) + tendo stretch.
retentive: having the power and tendency to keep and maintain possession. [3] L re (back) + teneo hold.
retinue: the retainers attending a person of rank; an escort. [3] Fr retenue < L re (back) + teneo hold.
sustain: uphold as a weight; support; endure; keep up, maintain. [3] L sub (under) + teneo hold.
sustenance: food for supporting and maintaining life. [3] L sub (under) + teneo hold.
tenable: capable of being held, maintained, or defended. [3] L teneo hold.
tenacious: unyielding; holding opinions or rights strongly; determined. [3] L tenax < teneo hold.
tenant: occupy; lessee of lands or property. [3] Fr tenant (pfp tenir) < L teneo hold.
tendentious: having a purposed aim. [1] Ger. tendenz < L tendo stretch.
tender: to formally offer (usually for payment). [1] L tendere to stretch, extend, hold forth.
tenet: an opinion, principle, or doctrine believed or maintained as true. [3] L tenet he holds < teneo hold.
tensile: pert. to tension; capable of extension. [1] L tensus (pp tendo) stretch.
tension: being stretched tight; mental strain. [1] L tensio a stretching < tensus (pp tendo) stretch.
tenuous: thin; slim; delicate; weak; flimsy. [4] L tenuis thin.
tenure: holding in possession; permanent possession; the period of holding. [3] L tenere to hold.
untenable: not capable of being held, maintained, or defended. [3] un + L teneo hold.
baritone: male voice with a range between bass and tenor. [9] Gk barys deep + tonos tone < teino stretch.
hypertension: high blood pressure. [6] Gk hyper (over) + L tensio a stretching < tensus (pp tendo) stretch.

isotonic: having equal tones or tension. [9] Gk isos equal + tonos accent, tone.

monotony: boredom; tediousness and repetitiousness of living. [9] Gk mono- + tonos string, sound, pitch.

tonic: something that invigorates or refreshes. [9] Gk tonos a stretching, tone.

RELATED: abstain abstention abstinent attenuated contentiousness extend extensibility extension extenuate incontinence intend intense intension intensity intensiveness intent intently intentness intentiveness pertinacity portent portentous pretence pretend pretender retain retainer retent retention retentiveness sustainable tenaciously tenacity tenancy tendentiously tense (adj) tenuity tenuousness unostentatious

COMMON: attend [1] contain [3] container [3] containment [3] contend [3] contentment [3] continent [3] continue [3] continual [3] continued [3] continuous [3] detain [3] detention [3] discontent [3] entertain [3] entertainment [3] hypotenuse [6] lieutenant [3] maintain [3] maintenance [3] monotone [9] monotonous [9] obtain [3] proton [9] tenace [3] tend [1] tender [5] tendency [1] tendon [8] tendril [5] tenement [3] teno- [8] tenor [3] tent [1] tentacle [1] tetanus [7] thin [10] tone [9]

168. tere-[1] rub, turn
Latin: TER, TRIT rub

[1] L terere (tritus) rub away, thresh, wear out

[2] L tribulum threshing sledge

[3] L tersus ppr tergere to cleanse

[4] Gk tornos tool for drawing a circle, a circle

[5] Gk trauma hurt, wound

[6] Gk tribein rub, thresh, pound, wear out

[7] Gk trogein to gnaw

[8] Gk tragema sweetmeat

[9] OE thraed thread

[10] OE therscan thresh

[11] OE threscold doorsill

[12] OE thrawan to turn, twist

[13] MD drillen to drill

[14] OF truant beggar

attrition: wearing down through rubbing or friction. [1] L attritus (pp attero) < ad + tero rub.

contour: the shape of a surface; lines representing shape. [4] com- + Gk tornos tool for drawing a circle.

contrition: penitence; repentance; sorrow over past misdeeds. [1] L contritus < contero bruise.

detrimental: causing injury, harm, or damage. [1] L detrimentum < de- + terere to rub.

diatribe: a bitter and abusive criticism or denunciation. [6] Gk diatribe lecture < dia + tribein to rub.

terse: concise; to the point. [3] L tarsus (pp tergere) to cleanse.

threadbare: worn out; worn or frayed (cloth). [9] OE thraed thread + baer bare.

trauma: serious physical or emotional injury or shock. [5] Gk trauma hurt, wound.

tribulation: trouble. [2] Fr < L tribulatus (pp tribulo) press.

trite: used so often as to be made commonplace; worn out. [1] L tero (pp tritus) rub.

RELATED: attrite contrite detrital detritic traumatic triteness trituration

COMMON: attorney [4] detour [4] detriment [1] dredge [8] drill [13] return [4] thrash [10] thread [9] thresh [10] threshold [11] throw [12] trout [7] truant [14] turn [4] turncoat [4]

169. terkʷ- twist
Latin: TORT twist

[1] L torquere (tortus) to twist; tortuosus full of twists; tortus twisted

[2] MLG dwer oblique

[3] ON thverr transverse

athwart: crosswise; obstructing; against. [3] ME a- + thwert across.

contortionist: person who twists into unusual and difficult positions. [1] L con (with) + torqueo twist.

distortion: twisting out of shape; a misrepresentation. [1] L dis (apart) + torqueo twist.
extort: to obtain by threat of violence. [1] L ex (out) + torqueo twist.
extortionate: exorbitant; involving use of threats to obtain something. [1] L ex (out) + torqueo twist.
retort: a reply esp. a retaliatory curt, witty, or snappish reply. [1] L re- (back) + torquere (tortus) to twist.
tortuous: winding; full of curves, twists, and turns; devious. [1] L tortuosus < tortus twisted.
RELATED: contort contortion distort tortuosity tortuousness
COMMON: queer [2] retrousse [1] torque [1] torture [1] torturous [1]

170. treud- squeeze
Latin: TRUD, TRUS thrust

[1] L trudere (trusus) to thrust, push
[2] OE threat oppression, use of force   [3] ON thrystra to squeeze, compress

abstruse: difficult to understand; hidden; concealed. [1] L abs (from, away) + trudo thrust, push.
extrude: to force thrust or push out; drive out or away; expel. [1] L ex (out) + trudo thrust.
intrusive: tending to enter in where not wanted or permitted. [1] L in (in) + trudo thrust.
obtrusive: tending to obtrude; obtruding; pushing. [1] L ob (before) + trudo thrust.
protrude: to project out or forth. [1] L protrusus < pro (forth) + trudo thrust.
unobtrusive: not very noticeable or bothersome; not conspicuous. [1] L ob (before) + trudo thrust.
RELATED: intrude intruder intrusion obtrude protrusion
COMMON: threat [2] thrust [3]

171. wer-³ turn, bend
Latin: VERT, VERS, VERT, VORS turn VERG tend toward, bend

[1] L vertere (versus) to turn; versus turned; versare
    (versatus) to turn, twist; versari to stay, behave
[2] L vergere (pfp vergens) to turn, tend toward   [3] LL brucus heather
[4] OF riber to be wanton   [5] L verber whip, rod
[6] L vermis worm
[7] Gk rhombus rhombus, magic wheel   [8] Gk rhaptein to sew
[9] OE -weard toward; inweard inward   [10] OE wrigian to turn, bend, go
[11] OE weorth worth, valuable   [12] OE weorthan to befall
[13] OE wyrd fate, destiny   [14] OE writha band
[15] OE writhan to twist, torture   [16] OE wrath angry
[17] OE wyrgan to strangle   [18] OE wringan to twist
[19] ME wrong wrong   [20] ME wranglen to wrangle
[21] OE wrencan to twist   [22] OE gewrinclian to wind
[23] MLG wriggeln to wriggle   [24] OE wrist wrist
[25] OE wraestan to twist   [26] OE weorpan to throw away
[27] ME wrappen to wrap   [28] OE wyrm worm
[29] OF guietre gaiter

adversary: an opponent or enemy. [1] L ad + verto turn.
adverse: antagonistic; harmful; unfavorable. [1] L ad + verto turn.
adversity: a condition of hardship or affliction; misfortune or calamity. [1] L ad + verto turn.
advert: refer incidentally. [1] L ad + verto turn.

animadversion: criticism or censure; taking notice of an offense. [1] L animus mind + ad (to) + verto turn.

aversion: dislike of; reluctance toward. [1] L averto < a (from) + verto turn.

avert: avoid; ward off; prevent; turn from. [1] L averto < a (from) + verto turn.

awry: askew; off-course. [10] OE a + wrigian.

brusque: abrupt and blunt in speech or manner. [3] Fr < LL brucus heather.

controvert: to dispute, disagree. [1] L contra (against) + verto turn.

convergence: to cause or tend toward one point. [2] L con (with) + vergo incline.

conversant: having knowledge of. [1] L conversor live with < converto < con (with) + verto turn.

con´verse: an opposite or contrary with positions reversed. [1] L conversus < con (with) + verto turn.

divergent: moving apart from a common point; departing from the usual. [2] L di (apart) + vergo incline.

divers: more than one; several; of different kinds; various. [1] Fr < L diversus (pp diverto) < verto turn.

diverse: having differing and distinct elements and characteristics. [1] L dis- (aside) + vertere turn.

diversion: act of turning aside or deflecting; an amusement or entertainment. [1] L diversus < verto turn.

extrovert: person primarily interested in others and things outside. [1] L extra (outside) + verto turn.

inadvertent: unintentional; not properly attentive. [1] L in (not) + ad (to) + verto turn.

incontrovertible: not disputable. [1] L in (not) + contra (against) + verto turn.

introvert: to direct inward. [1] L intro (within) + verto turn.

inverse: opposite in order or effect; reciprocal. [1] L in (in) + verto turn.

invert: reverse in position or order. [1] L in (not) + verto turn.

malversation: evil or corrupt conduct; misconduct as in public office. [1] L male bad + versatio turning.

obverse: the facing side, opp. to reverse; the side meant to be seen. [1] L ob (toward) + verto turn.

perverse: willfully wrong or erring; unreasonable; refractory. [1] L perversus < per (through) + verto turn.

prosaic: belonging to prose; dull. [1] L prosa prose < pro- (forward) + vertere to turn.

retroversion: a tipping or bending backward. [1] L retro (backward) + verto turn.

reverberate: echo and reecho repeatedly; with prolonged effect. [5] L re- + verberere to beat < verber whip.

revert: to go back to an earlier condition or belief. [1] L re- (again) + vertere turn.

rhapsody: expression of great feeling; bliss. [8] Gk rhapsoidein recite poems < rhaptein sew + oide song.

ribald: showing lewd or vulgar humor. [4] OF riber to be wanton < Ger.

subversive: tending to undermine and destroy a government or organization. [1] L sub (under) + verto turn.

transverse: running or lying across; intersecting a system of lines. [1] L trans + verto turn.

traverse: pass across or through; cross; cross and recross. [1] OF traverser < L trans (across) + verto turn.

universal: applying to all things without exception; cosmic in scope. [1] L vertere (versus) to turn.

untoward: vexatious; not yielding readily; refractory; perverse; uncouth. [9] OE un +(to) + weard ward.

versatile: competent at many endeavors; usable for many functions. [1] L versare (versatus) to turn, twist.

vertex: highest point; apex; top. [1] L verto turn.

vortex: a whirling, spiraling mass of water or air. [1] L verto turn.

wry: dry or ironic (of humor); twisted or bent. [10] OE wrigian (to turn, bend, go).

RELATED: advertisement averse controversial controversy controvertible converge convergent converging conversation conversationalist conversely conversion controversy convertible diverge divergence diverging diversification diversity divert extroversion inadvertence inadvertently inversion obvert perversion perversity pervert retroversion retrovert ribaldry subversion subvert transversal versatility versification versify

COMMON: advertency [1] advertise [1] anniversary [1] avert [1] briar [3] converse [1] convert [1] diversify [1] divorce [1] gaiter [29] invertebrate [1] inward [11] peevish [1] perversity [1] prose [1] reverse [1] reversibility [1] rhombus [7] stalwart [11] universe [1] university [1] verge [2] vermicelli [6] vermin [6] verse [1] version [1] versus [1] vertebra [1] vertical [1] vertigo [1] -ward [9] warp [26] weird [13] worm [28] worry [17] worth [11,12] wrangle [20] wrap [27] wrath [16] wreath [14] wrench [21] wrest [25] wrestle [25] wriggle [23] wring [18] wrinkle [22] wrist [24] writhe [15] wrong [19] wroth [16]

CHAPTER 21

Roots Indicating Setting, Placing, Circular Motion, Throwing, and Thrusting

The twelfth category of roots, covered in this chapter, refers directly to human actions involving setting, placing, circular motion, throwing, and thrusting. Twelve roots fall within this category. Four roots emphasize striking or thrusting:

'bhau-' meaning "to strike"
'kae-id-' meaning "to strike"
'pel-[6]' meaning "thrust, strike, drive"
'per-[4]' meaning "to strike"

The root 'bhau-' meaning "to strike" is the source of the Latin verb 'refutare' meaning "to drive back" and the English words 'beat,' 'beetle,' and 'buttock.' Next 'kae-id-' meaning "to strike" is the source of the Latin verb 'caedere' meaning "to cut" or 'to strike." The root 'pel-[6]' meaning "thrust, strike, drive" is the source of the Latin verb 'pellere' meaning "to push" or "to drive" and 'polire' meaning "to polish," the Greek 'plesios' meaning "near," and the English words 'felt,' 'anvil,' and 'filter.' Finally, 'per-[4]' meaning "to strike" is the source of the Latin verb 'premere' meaning "to press." Three roots have a primary meaning of throwing:

'g^wele-[1]' meaning "throw, reach, pierce"
'mittere-' meaning "send off, throw"
'ye-' meaning "throw, impel"

The root 'g^wele-[1]' meaning "throw, reach, pierce" is the source of the Greek 'ballein' meaning "to throw" and the English words 'kill,' 'quell,' and 'quail.' The root 'mittere-' meaning "send off, throw" is the source of the Latin verb 'mitto' meaning "to send." Also 'ye-' meaning "throw, impel" is the source of the Latin verb 'iacere' meaning "to throw" and the Greek 'hienai' meaning "to send" or "to throw." Three roots designate placing or standing:

'dhe-' meaning "to set out"
'stel-' meaning "to put, stand"
'sta-' meaning "stand"

The root 'dhe-' meaning "to set out" is the source of the Latin verb 'facere' meaning "to do" or "to make" and 'factum' meaning "deed," the Greek 'thesis' meaning "a placing," and the English words 'do,' 'deed,' 'deem,' and 'doom.' Next 'stel-' meaning "to put, stand" is the source of the Latin 'locus' meaning "place" and 'stultus' meaning "foolish," the Greek 'stellein' meaning "to send," and the English words 'stilt,' 'stilted,' and 'stall.' Also 'sta-' meaning "stand" is the source of the Latin verb 'stare' meaning "to stand" and 'sistere' meaning "to set," the Greek 'statos' meaning "standing," and the English words 'stall,' 'stalwart,' 'stand,' 'standard,' 'starboard,' 'starling,' 'stead,' 'steed,' 'steer,' 'stem,' 'stool,' 'stow,' 'stud,' and 'understand.' Two roots involve rolling or revolving:

'kʷel-¹' meaning "revolve, move around, sojourn, dwell"
'wel-³' meaning "turn, roll"

The root 'kʷel-¹' meaning "revolve, move around, sojourn, dwell" is the source of the Latin verb 'colere' meaning "to cultivate" or "to inhabit," the Greek 'kuklos' meaning "wheel" and 'telos' meaning "end" or "result." It is also the source of the Old English 'hweol' meaning 'wheel' and thus the English word 'wheel.' Second, 'wel-³' meaning "turn, roll" is the source of the Latin verb 'volvere' meaning "to roll," the Greek 'helix' meaning "spiral object," and the English words 'walk,' 'well,' 'wallow,' and 'willow.'

SOUND SHIFTS

When Indo-European exhibits a rough labial 'bh' sound, Latin and Greek have an 'f' sound (represented by 'ph' in English words coming from Greek). The corresponding West Germanic and Old English form is generally the voiced labial 'b.' Thus 'bhau-' meaning "to strike" is the source of the 'fu' in the Latin verb 'refutare' meaning "to drive back" and the English words 'beat,' 'beetle,' and 'buttock.'

The Indo-European, Latin, and Greek smooth labial mute 'p' in West Germanic and Old English becomes a rough labial 'f.' This sound change is clearly evident with the root 'pel-⁶' meaning "thrust, strike, drive," which is the source of the Latin verb 'pellere' meaning "to push" or "to drive" and 'polire' meaning "to polish." It is also the source of Greek 'plesios' meaning "near" and the English words 'felt,' 'anvil,' and 'filter.'

If Indo-European, Latin, and Greek have the smooth palatal mute 'k,' the corresponding West Germanic and Old English form is generally the rough palatal 'h.' Thus 'kʷel-¹' meaning "revolve, move around, sojourn, dwell" produces the Old English 'hweol' meaning 'wheel' and thus the English word 'wheel.' The 'k' becomes 'h,' and the 'w' sound is retained.

When Indo-European, Latin, and Greek have a voiced palatal mute 'g,' West Germanic and Old English normally have a smooth palatal 'k.' Hence 'gʷele-¹' meaning "throw, reach, pierce" generated the English words 'kill,' 'quell,' and 'quail' showing change of 'g' to 'k' with the 'w' sound sometimes retained and sometimes not.

The Indo-European labiovelars 'gʷ' or 'kʷ' exhibit different changes in Latin or Greek. They may change to a labial 'b' or other mute form, or the 'g,' 'k,' or 'w' may get dropped. The root 'gʷele-¹' meaning "throw, reach, pierce" shows a change to labial 'b' for Greek 'ballein' meaning "to throw." For 'kʷel-¹' meaning "revolve, move around, sojourn, dwell," which is the source of the Latin verb 'colere' meaning "to cultivate" or "to inhabit," the 'w' sound is dropped. In the Greek, 'kuklos' meaning "wheel" and 'telos' meaning "end" or "result" come from this root.

If Indo-European had a rough dental 'dh' sound, the Greek shows a 'th' sound. But Latin does not have the 'th' sound, and we find that the 'dh' becomes an 'f' as if it were a 'bh.' The corresponding West Germanic and Old English form is generally the voiced dental 'd.' This is demonstrated by the root 'dhe-' meaning "to set out," which is the source of the Latin verb 'facere' meaning "to do" or "to make" and 'factum' meaning "deed." It is also the source of the Greek 'thesis' meaning "a placing" and the English words 'do,' 'deed,' 'deem,' and 'doom.'

The third general rule in chapter 7 for sibilants is that the initial s sounds conjoined with following consonants usually show no change in Greek, Latin, and Old English. However, they do frequently disappear. An initial Indo-European 's' followed by a vowel tended to become a rough breathing or 'h' in classical Greek. This applies to 'stel-' meaning "to put, stand," which is the source of the Latin 'locus' meaning "place" and 'stultus' meaning "foolish," the Greek 'stellein' meaning "to send," and the English words 'stilt,' 'stilted,' and 'stall.'

The w sound of Indo-European is retained in the Old English forms. In the case of Latin, it is occasionally dropped and otherwise represented by the letter 'v,' which, however, was pronounced as a w sound. The original Greek w sound disappeared becoming a rough breathing or h sound and often was dropped altogether. We see this phenomenon with the root 'wel-³' meaning "turn, roll," which is the source of the Latin verb 'volvere' meaning "to roll," of the Greek 'helix' meaning "spiral object," and of the English words 'walk,' 'well,' 'wallow,' and 'willow.'

Five of the roots covered here do not show any sound shift changes discussed in chapter 7: 'kae-id-' meaning "to strike" as the source of the Latin verb 'caedere' meaning "to cut" or 'to strike," 'mittere-' meaning "send off, throw" as the source of the Latin verb 'mitto' meaning "to send," 'per-⁴' meaning "to strike" as the source of the Latin verb 'premere' meaning "to press," 'sta-' meaning "stand" as the source of the Latin verb 'stare' meaning "to stand" and 'sistere' meaning "to set," the Greek 'statos' meaning "standing," and the English words 'stall,' 'stalwart,' 'stand,' 'standard,' 'starboard,' 'starling,' 'stead,' 'steed,' 'steer,' 'stem,' 'stool,' 'stow,' 'stud,' and 'understand.' Finally, the root 'ye-' meaning "throw, impel" is the source of the Latin verb 'iacere' meaning "to throw" and the Greek 'hienai' meaning "to send" or "to throw."

LIST OF ROOTS IN ORDER OF OCCURRENCE

The following list gives the roots as they are discussed in this chapter. Syllables in capital letters show a sequence of letters found in English words that generally indicates the root is the origin. In nearly all cases, if one sees the letters in caps in an English word, one can infer that it comes from the Indo-European root in the first column. However, there may also be some English words from the root that do not accord with the general pattern and some English words that fit the pattern but come from a different root.

172. bhau- to strike
173. dhe- to set out — FAC, FACT, FECT, -FIC, -FY do; make; cause FAC/FEC/FIC
THEM, THE, THET, THEC, THEK put; place
174. gʷele-¹ throw, reach, pierce — BAL, BALL, BOL, BL throw
175. kae-id- to strike — CID, CIS cut; kill
176. kʷel-¹ revolve, sojourn, move around, dwell — CYCL circle TELEO, TEL end; complete
177. mittere- send off, throw — MITT, MISS, MISE send; let go
178. pel-⁶ thrust, strike, drive — PELL, PULS drive, push PEL/PULS
179. per-⁴ strike — PREM, PRIM, PRIN, PRESS press
180. stel- to put, stand — STELL, -STLE, STOL send; place LOC, LOCAT place
181. sta- stand — STO, STAT, STIT, SIST put in place; cause to stand; stand STAT, STAS stand
182. wel-³ turn, roll — VOLV, VOLU roll
183. ye- throw, impel — JACI, JECT, JACU throw JAC/JEC

172. bhau- to strike

[1] L confutare restrain, suppress   [2] L refutare (refutatus) to drive back, rebut
[3] L battuere to beat, knock
[4] OE beatan to beat   [5] OE bytl hammer, mallet
[6] OE buttuc end, strip of land   [7] OF bouter to strike, push
[8] ON beysta to beat

abate: lessen in intensity or degree. [3] L ad- + battere to beat.
browbeat: to intimidate; to bully; to domineer. [4] OE bru + beatan to beat.
buttress: anything that serves to support or reinforce esp. a wall. [4] OF bouter (strike against).
confute: to overwhelm by argument. [1] L confuto < con (together) + futo pour.
irrefutable: cannot be proven false. [2] L in- (not) + refuto repel.
lambaste: give a beating; thrash; to berate. [8] lam + ON beysta beat.

rebuttal: showing falsity of; presenting arguments against. [7] OF rebouter < re + bouter strike.
refute: prove false. [2] L refuto repel.
RELATED: confutation rebut
COMMON: abut [7] battledore [5] beat [4] beetle [5] butt [7] buttock [6] button [7]

173. dhe- to set out, set, put
Latin: FAC, FACT, FECT, -FIC, -FY do; make; cause FAC/FEC/FIC
Greek: THEM, THE, THET, THEC, THEK put; place

[1] L abdomen belly
[2] L condere (conditus) to put together, establish,
    presume
[3] L condire season, flavor
[4] L facere (factus; pfp faciens) to do, make;
    factum deed
[5] L facies shape, face   [6] L officium service
[7] L facilis feasible, easy   [8] L fas divine law, right
[9] L farium making
[10] Gk theke receptacle   [11] Gk thema proposition
[12] Gk tithemi (f theso; pfm tetheimai) to put;
    thesis a placing; thetis placed
[13] OE dom judgment   [14] OE daed doing, deed
[15] OE don to do   [16] OE -dom state, condition
[17] OE deman to judge

abscond: leave suddenly for an unknown location. [2] L com (together) + do put.
affectation: artificial, unnatural behavior. [4] L ad + facio do.
artifacts: products of human craft, agency, or conception. [4] L ars art + facio make.
artifice: a clever or artful method; deception; ingenuity. [4] L ars art + facio make.
defection: act of leaving and disowning one's country or associations. [4] L defectus < de (from) + facio do.
deficit: a shortfall or insufficiency; amount of shortfall. [4] L deficere to desert, be wanting < facere make.
disaffection: discontent; estrangement. [4] Fr < dis + affecter < L affecto aspire to < ad to + facio do.
discomfit: defeat the purposes of; frustrate; to rout; vanquish. [4] L dis (apart) + con (intens.) + facio do.
edifice: a building (especially large). [4] L aedes building + facio make.
edify: to instruct. [4] L aedifico < aedes building + facio make.
efface: erase or wipe out; act to be unnoticeable. [5] OF esfacer < L ex- + face face < facies.
effectual: able to produce the desired result. [4] L ex- + facere to make.
effectuate: to produce or bring about. [4] L effectus (pp efficere) < cx- + facere to make.
efficacy: power to produce an effect; effective energy. [4] L efficax < efficio < ex (out) + facio do.
efficiency: using resources effectively and with little waste. [4] L efficiens (pfp efficio) < ex (out) + facio do.
façade: front of a building. [5] Fr < L facies face.
facet: one of several aspects of a subject; a flat surface of a gemstone. [5] L facies shape, face.
facile: easy of performance; easily acquired; readily mastered. [7] Fr < L facilis easy < facio do.
facilitate: make easier. [7] L facilitas < facilis facile.
faction: a number of persons combined for a common purpose. [4] Fr < L factio < factus (pp facio) do.
faculty: a natural or acquired ability. [7] L facultas < facul < facio do.
feasible: practicable; that may be done. [4] Fr faisable < faire < L facio do.
feckless: purposeless; weak; careless. [4] Scots feck effect + less < L ex- + facere to make.

indefeasible: incapable of defeat or being set aside. [4] OF defeisance < defaire defeat < L facio do.

ineffectual: not producing the desired result. [4] L efficax < efficio < ex (out) + facio do.

inefficacious: not able to produce the desired result. [4] L in- (not) + efficax < efficio < ex (out) + facio do.

malefactor: one who commits a crime. [4] L male ill + facio do.

malfeasance: unlawful or wrongful action; wrongdoing in general. [4] Fr < L facio do.

mortify: to affect with humiliation or vexation; to subdue the passions. [4] LL mortifico kill.

multifaceted: having many aspects or implications. [5] L multus many + facies shape, face.

nefarious: infamous due to wickedness. [8] L nefas crime < ne- (not) + fas divine law.

officious: intermeddling with what is not one's concern. [4] Fr < L officium < opus work + facio do.

pontificate: to speak pompously. [4] L pons bridge + facio make.

putrefy: to decay. [4] L putreo be putrid + facio make.

qualified: competent; meets the criteria needed to engage in an activity. [4] L qualis such + facio make.

rarified: made rare or less dense. [4] L rarus rare + facio make.

recondite: abstruse; not readily understood; concealed. [2] L re- + condere put together, preserve.

soporific: causing or tending to produce sleep. [4] L sapor sleep + facio make.

superficial: (adj) near the surface; shallow; cursory; hasty. [5] L superficies < super (over) + facies face.

surfeit: to feed to fulness or satiety; overfeed. [4] L super (over) + facio do.

vilify: to represent as base, mean or evil; defame; slander. [4] Fr vil < L vilis worthless + facio make.

anathema: a curse or ban. [12] Gk anathema curse < ana (up) + tithemi place.

antithesis: direct opposite or contradictory. [12] Gk anti + tithemi place.

epithet: descriptive adjective. [12] Gk epi (on) + tithemi put.

hypothesis: an assumption as a basis of reasoning. [12] Gk hypo (under) + tithemi place.

synthesis: a combining of separate elements or ideas into one. [12] Gk syn (together) + tithemi place.

synthetic: made artificially; not natural. [12] Gk syn (together) + tithemi place.

thematic: relating to the main idea or motif. [11] Gk thematikos < thema theme.

thesis: proposition defended in argument; postulate; essay required for a degree. [12] Gk tithemi place.

RELATED: affected affection affectionate affective antithetic beneficence defect efficacious factious hypothetical metathetic metathetical rarefy refection

COMMON: abdomen [1] affair [4] affect [4] amplify [4] apothecary [10] beatify [4] benefaction [4] beneficent [4] beneficiary [4] boutique [10] chafe [4] coefficient [4] comfit [4] condiment [3] confect [4] confection [4] confetti [4] counterfeit [4] deed [14] deem [17] deface [5] defeat [4] defeatist [4] deficient [4] difficulty [7] disaffected [4] discomfit [4] disinfectant [4] do [15] doff [15] -dom [16] don [15] doom [13] doomsday [13] effect [4] effective [4] efficient [4] face [5] facial [5] -facient [4] facility [7] facsimile [4] fact [4] -faction [4] factitious [4] factitive [4] factor [4] factory [4] fashion [4] feat [4] feature [4] fetish [4] -fic [4] -fy [4] fordo [15] forfeit [4] hacienda [4] indeed [14] infect [4] infectious [4] justify [4] magnify [4] manufacture [4] modify [4] multifarious [9] nullify [4] office [6] olfactory [4] omnifarious [9] parenthesis [12] perfect [4] petrified [4] petrify [4] photosynthesis [12] pluperfect [4] proficient [4] profit [4] prosthesis [12] rectify [4] sacrifice [4] satisfy [4] stultify [4] suffice [4] sufficient [4] surface [5] theme [11] tick [10] unify [4] vivify [4]

174. gᵂele-¹ /gᵂel- throw, reach, pierce
Greek: BAL, BALL, BOL, BL throw

[1] Gk ballein (pfm beblemai) to throw

[2] Gk ballizein to dance

[3] OE cwellan to kill; cwealm death

[4] ME killen to kill

[5] MD quelen to be ill, suffer

diabolic: devilish. [1] Gk diabolikos < diabolos devil.

hyperbola: two-branched plane curve generated by conic section. [1] Gk hyper (beyond) + ballein throw.

hyperbole: poetic or rhetorical overstatement; exaggeration. [1] Gk hyper (over, above) + ballo throw.
metabolism: processes in living cells that sustain life. [1] Gk metabole change < meta- + ballein throw.
palaver: to make empty or idle talk; flatter. [1] Gk paraballein to compare < para (beside) + ballein throw.
parable: a short, simple story with a moral or spiritual lesson. [1] Gk ballein (pfm beblemai) to throw.
problematic: involving a difficulty or an uncertainty needing a solution. [1] Gk pro (before) + ballo throw.
quail: to cower; to tremble in fear. [5] MD quelen to be ill, suffer.
qualm: feeling of sickness; twinge of conscience; sensation of misgiving. [3] OE cwealm death.
quell: suppress; pacify. [3] OE cwellan to kill < Ger.
RELATED: diabolical parabolically problem
COMMON: ball [2] ballad [2] ballet [2] ballistics [1] devil [1] emblem [1] embolism [1] kill [4] killjoy [4] parable [1] parabola [1] parley [1] parliament [1] parlor [1] symbol [1]

175. kae-id- to strike
Latin: CID, CIS cut; kill

[1] L caedere (caesus; pfp caedens) to cut, strike; recido (recisus; pfp recidens) to cut back

concise: expressed with few words; succinct. [1] L com- + caedere to cut.
excise: remove esp. by cutting; (n) indirect tax. [1] L ex- + caedere to cut.
incisive: sharp, penetrating thought or action. [1] L in- + caedere to cut.
précis: concise summary. [1] Fr < L prae- + caedere to cut.
precise: accurate; exact. [1] L prae- + caedere to cut.
recision: act of annulling or canceling. [1] L resisio (pfp recidere) cut back < re- (back) + caedere to cut.
RELATED: conciseness concision incise incision incisor precise preciseness precision
COMMON: cement [1] chisel [1] circumcise [1] decide [1] decisive [1] indecisive [1] scissor [1]

176. kʷel-¹ revolve, move around, sojourn, dwell
Latin: COL, CULT inhabit, cultivate
Greek: CYCL circle TELEO, TEL end; complete

[1] L colere (cultus) to till, cultivate, inhabit	[2] L collum neck
[3] Gk kuklos circle, wheel	[4] Gk polos axis of a sphere
[5] Gk boukolos cowherd	[6] Gk telos consummation, perfection, end, result
[7] Gk palin again	
[8] OE hweol wheel	[9] ON hals neck, ship's bow

accolade: an expression of praise or high honor. [2] L ad- + collum neck.
bucolic: of the countryside; rustic; pastoral. [5] Gk boukolikos < bous cow + kolos herdsman.
décolleté: low-cut neckline. [2] L de-+ collum neck.
encyclical: a letter sent by the Pope to the clergy regarding church matters. [3] Gk en (in) + kyklos a circle.
encyclopedic: showing vast, comprehensive knowledge. [3] Gk enkyklios in a circle + paideia education.
epicycle: circle with its center following the path of a greater circle. [3] Gk epi (upon) + kyklos a circle.
palindrome: a word or words that read the same forward or backward. [7] Gk palin (again) + dromos run.
polarize: to induce to separate to opposite poles or positions. [4] Gk polos axis, sky.
talisman: object believed to have or confer magic powers. [6] Gk telesma consecration < telein consecrate.
teleology: study of goals or final causes; being directed toward a goal. [6] Gk teleos an end + lego speak.
RELATED: polarization talismanic

COMMON: bicycle [3] collar [2] colony [1] cult [1] cultivate [1] culture [1] cycle [3] cyclo- [3] cyclone [3] ency-clopedia [3] hawse [9] pole [4] pulley [4] tricycle [3] wheel [8]

177. mittere- send off, throw
Latin: MITT, MISS, MISE send; let go MIT/MIS

[1] L mitto (missus; pfp mittens) to send

compromise: agreement made by mutual concessions. [1] L con (together) + pro (forth) + mitto send.
demise: death; loss of authority. [1] Fr demettre (pp demis) resign < L demitto < de (down) + mitto send.
dismiss: discharge; reject. [1] L dis- + mittere to send.
emissary: messenger. [1] L emissarius < emissus (pp emitto) < e (out) + mitto send.
intermit: interrupt, suspend. [1] L inter (between) + mitto send.
intermittent: starting and stopping at intervals. [1] L inter (between) + mitto send.
missive: a letter sent or designed to be sent. [1] L missus (pp mitto) send.
noncommittal: not expressing a decided opinion. [1] < non not + L committo < com (together) + mitto send.
premise: an assumed proposition serving as a foundation for an argument. [1] L missus (pp mitto) send.
promissory: of the nature of a promise; an engagement to pay. [1] L promissum < pro (forth) + mitto send.
remiss: negligent or careless in preforming obligations. [1] L re- + mittere to send.
remission: abatement; release from a debt or penalty; pardon. [1] L re- + mittere to send.
submissive: yielding; obedient; docile. [1] OF < L submissio < submissus < sub (under) + mitto send.
surmise: form opinions or conjectures on slight evidence. [1] OF pp surmettre accuse < L sub + mitto sent.
RELATED: remit remittance transmit transmitter
COMMON: admit [1] admittance [1] admission [1] commissary [1] commission [1] commit [1] commitment [1] committal [1] committee [1] compromise [1] dismissal [1] emission [1] emit [1] intermission [1] message [1] mes-senger [1] missal [1] missile [1] mission [1] missionary [1] omission [1] omit [1] permissible [1] permission [1] permit [1] permitting [1] promise [1] remitted [1] submit [1] transmission [1] unremitting [1]

178. pel-⁶ thrust, strike, drive
Latin: PELL, PULS drive, push PEL/PULS

[1] L pellere (pulsus; pfp pellens) push, drive, strike
[2] L polire make smooth, polish   [3] L interpolis refurbished
[4] L appellare (appellatus; pfp appellans) to address, call
[5] L compellare (compulsus; pfp compellans) to accost, address
[6] Gk plesios near
[7] OE anfilte anvil   [8] OE felt felt
[9] ML filtrum filter < Ger

appellation: name or designation. [4] L appellare to entreat.
compelling: forceful; needing urgent action. [5] L compellatio < com (together) + pello drive.
compulsive: unable to resist urges. [5] L compulsus (pp compello) < com (together) + pello drive.
dispel: to rid of; to scatter. [5] L dis- (apart) + pellere to drive.
expulsion: driving out. [1] L expulsio < expello < ex (out) + pello thrust.
extrapolation: an estimate projected from known values. [3] (by analogy with 'interpolate'< L interpolare alter).
impel: drive or urge to action; propel. [1] L in- + pellere to drive.
infiltrate: to slip behind enemy lines. [9] ML in- + filtrum filter < Ger.

interpolate: insert between or into. [3] L interpolis < interpolare alter < inter between + polire to polish.

propellant: fuel that provides thrust for a rocket. [1] L pro- (forward) + pellere to push, drive, strike.

propulsive: driving or thrusting forward. [1] L pro- (forward) + pellere (pulsus) to push, drive, strike.

repeal: revoke a law or official act; (n) process of revoking an act. [4] L re- (back) + appellare to address, call.

repel: drive back or away; cause feeling of repugnance. [1] L re- + pellere to drive.

repulsive: exciting a feeling of aversion or disgust. [1] L repulses (pp repello) repel < re (back) + pello drive.

RELATED: compel compellable compulsion compulsiveness compulsory expel extrapolate repellant repulse repulsion

COMMON: anvil [7] appeal [4] dispel [1] felt [8] filter [9] filtrate [9] impulse [1] peal [4] pelt [1] plesiosaur [6] polish [2] propel [1] propellant [1] pulsate [1] pulse [1] push [1] rappel [4]

179. per-[4] strike
Latin: PREM, PRIM, PRIN, PRESS press

[1] L premere (pressus) to press, oppress; pressus pressure

compress: firmly press together; reduce data stored or transmitted. [1] L com- + premere (pressus) to press.

impressment: the act of seizing and forcing into public service. [1] L in (in) + premo press.

imprimatur: official approval or sanction. [1] L imprimere to imprint < in- + premere press.

irrepressible: that cannot be restrained. [1] L in (not) + re (back) + premo press.

oppressive: burdensome; tyrannical; producing depression. [1] L oppressus < ob (against) + premo press.

repress: to keep forcibly under restraint; suppress; crush; overpower. [1] L re (back) + premo press.

reprimand: strong rebuke. [1] L reprimere to restrain < re- + premere press.

suppress: put down or to an end by force; withhold from publication. [1] L sub (under) + premo press.

RELATED: impress impression impressionable impressionism impressionistic impressive oppress oppression oppressor repression repressive suppression suppressor

COMMON: compressible [1] compression [1] compressor [1] depress [1] depression [1] depressant [1] espresso [1] express [1] expression [1] imprint [1] pregnant [1] press [1] pressure [1] print [1] reprimand [1] reprisal [1] suppress [1]

180. stel- put, place, stand
Latin: LOC, LOCAT place
Greek: STELL,-STLE,STOL send; place

[1] L locus place; loco (locatus) to place, lend   [2] L stolidus stupid

[3] L stultus foolish

[4] Gk stellein put in order, prepare, send

[5] ME stilte crutch, stilt < Ger   [6] OE steall standing place, stable

allocate: to apportion. [1] L ad + locus place.

apostle: person sent out on a special mission esp. one of Jesus' twelve disciples. [4] Gk apo (off) + stello send.

collocation: putting side by side, together, or in order. [1] L col (together) + locatus (pp loco) < locus place.

couchant: lying down. [1] OF couchier lie down < L collocare < col- (together) + locare to place.

epistle: a letter. [4] Gk epistole < epi (to) + stello send.

forestall: hold off, hinder, prevent. [6] OE steall (standing place, stable).

milieu: an environment; the setting. [1] OF milieu < L medius middle + locus place.

peristaltic: pert. to alternate waves. [4] Gk peri (around) + stalsis constriction < stello place.

stalemate: a deadlock; neither of two opposing sides can make further progress. [6] OE steall (standing place).
stilted: artificially formal. [5] ME stilte < Ger.
stolid: showing little emotion; impassive. [2] L stolidus stupid.
stultify: make ineffectual or to appear foolish. [3] L stultus foolish + facere make.
RELATED: apostolate epistolary peristalsis stultification stultifying
COMMON: dislocation [1] dislocative [1] locate [1] location [1] locus [1] stall [6] translocate [1] translocation [1]

181. sta- stand
Latin: STO, STAT, STIT, SIST put in place; cause to stand; stand
Greek: STAT, STAS stand

[1] L stare (pfp stans) to stand

[2] L stamen thread of the warp

[3] L statim at once

[4] L statio a standing still; station

[5] L -stitium a stoppage

[6] L destinare (destinatus) to make firm, establish

[7] L obstinare (obstinatus) to set one's mind on, persist

[8] L stabulum stable

[9] L status manner, posture; statura stature; statuere (statutus) set up, decide; superstes witness

[10] L sistere (status; pfp sistens) to set, place, stand still, stop

[11] L postis post

[12] L stabilis standing firm, steady

[13] L instaurare (instauratus) to restore, set upright again

[14] L restaurare (restauratus) to restore, repair, rebuild

[15] Gk statos placed, standing

[16] Gk histani (aor. stani) to set, place; stasis

[17] Gk histos web, tissue

[18] Gk stoa porch

[19] Gk stulos pillar

[20] Gk stalassein to drip

[21] OE stede place < Ger

[22] OE steda stallion, studhorse

[23] OE stod horse breeding

[24] OE stol stool

[25] OE standan to stand, understandan to know

[26] OE stathol foundation

[27] OE stefn stem, tree trunk

[28] OE stow place

[29] OE stuthu post, prop

[30] OE steor- a steering; stieran to steer

[31] ME sterne boat stern

arrest: to stop motion or growth; to detain under legal custody. [1] L ad- + re- + stare to stand.
consist: be constituted of; to have as its foundation, substance or nature. [10] L con (together) + sisto stand.
consistent: agreeing with itself; compatible with other acts or statements. [10] L con (together) + sisto stand.
constituency: body of voters. [9] L constituens (pfp constituo) < con (together) + statuo place.
constituent: a component or part of something. [9] L constituens (pfp constituo) < con (together) + statuo place.
constitute: to make up; be equivalent to. [9] L constituere to set up < com- + statuere to set up.
destitute: very poor; completely lacking in resources. [9] L de- + statuere to set.
establishmentarian: supporting the existing social order. [9] L stabilis standing firm, steady + ment.
existentialism: philosophy of a purposeless world. [10] L ex (out) + sisto set < sto stand.
extant: still existing. [1] L ex (out) + sto stand.
inconsistency: internal disagreement; incompatibility with other statements. [10] L con (together) + sisto stand.

institution: an established organization or usage belonging to society. [9] L in (in) + statuo set up.

interstice: an opening in anything or between things; cranny. [10] Fr < L inter (between) + sisto stand.

obstetrician: doctor who cares for women during and after pregnancy. [1] L ob- (opposite) + stare stand.

obstinate: unreasonably resolved in a purpose or opinion; stubborn. [7] L ob (before) + sto stand.

persistent: refusing to quit; constantly repeated. [10] L per (through) + sisto cause to stand.

reinstatement: putting back in a former state or condition. [9] L re (again) + in + status standing < sto stand.

restitution: restoration or compensation for loss. [9] Fr < L re (again) + statuo set up.

restive: impatient of control; unruly; restless; fidgety. [1] Fr restif < rester remain < L re (behind) + sto stand.

solstice: the time of year when the sun is at its greatest declination. [3] Fr < L sol sun + sto stand.

staid: sober; sedate; steady. [1] OF ester < L sto stand.

stanch: to stop flow esp. of blood; to allay. [1] L stare (prp stans) to stand.

stanchion: an upright bar forming a principle support. [1] LL stantia chamber < stans (pfp sto) stand.

statistics: mathematical analysis of numerical data esp. population characteristics. [9] L statuere set up.

subsistence: continuance in existence; real being; sustenance. [10] L subsisto < sub (under) + sisto stand.

substance: the material of which anything is constituted. [1] Fr < L substantia < sub (under) + sto stand.

substantial: being real, solid and material; having significant value or quantity. [1] L sub- + stare to stand.

substantiate: to establish as a position or a truth; verify. [1] L substantia < sub (under) + sto stand.

substantive: denoting substance and what is essential. [1] LL substantivus < sub (under) + sto stand.

substitution: replacing something with another thing. [9] L substituo < sub (under) + statuo < sto stand.

apostasy: desertion of one's faith, religion, party, or principles. [16] Gk apo (off) + histemi stand.

ecstasy: rapture or enthusiasm. [16] Gk ekstasis ecstasy < ek (out) + stasis standing < histemi stand.

peristyle: columns encircling a building or a court. [19] Gk peristulon < peri- (around) + stulos pillar.

stalactite: icicle-like deposit on roof of a cavern. [20] Gk stalaktos dripping < stalassein to drip.

stalagmite: icicle-like deposit on floor of a cavern. [20] Gk stalagmos dropping < stalassein to drip.

stasis: a state of rest produced by a balance among acting forces. [16] Gk stasis stationariness.

static: lack of motion; at rest or in equilibrium. [15] Gk statikos causing to stand < histemi stand.

stoic: person unaffected by good or bad fortune; impassive. [18] Gk Stoa Poikile 'Painted Porch.'

stalwart: strong; firm of resolve; (n) steadfast supporter. [26] OE stathol foundation + weorth valuable.

steadfast: remaining firm, not swerving. [21] OE stede + faest fixed, fast < Ger.

RELATED: apostate consistence consistency ecstatic histology inconsistence inconsistent institutional institute interstitial persist restitute statics stoical subsist subsistent substantiate substitute substituent transubstantiate transubstantiation

COMMON: armistice [5] assist [10] bestow [28] circumstance [1] circumstantial [1] constable [8] constancy [1] constant [1] constitution [9] contrast [1] cost [1] desist [10] destine [6] distance [1] distant [1] establish [12] estate [9] exist [10] existence [10] histo- [17] insist [10] insistent [10] instant [1] obstacle [1] obstetrics [1] obstinate [7] oust [1] post [11] prostate [16] prostitute [9] resist [10] resistance [10] rest [1] restore [14] stable [8] stage [1, 9] stall [26] stamina [2] stance [1] stand [1, 25] standard [1, 25] standardization [1] stanza [1] starboard [30] starling [26] stat [3] -stat [15] state [9] stateless [9] stately [9] statement [9] statesman [9] station [4] stationary [4] stato- [15] statue [9] statuesque [9] stature [9] status [9] statute [9] statutory [9] stay [1] stead [21] steed [22] steer [30] stern [31] stool [24] store [13] stow [28] stud [23, 29] superstition [9] superstitious [9] system [16] transistor [10] understand [25] withstand [25]

182. wel-³ turn, roll
Latin: VOLV, VOLU roll
Greek: HELIC, HELIX spiral

[1] L volvere (volutus) to roll; volumen, -minis roll;
    volubilis revolving, changeable; volutare tumble about

[2] L valva door leaf

[3] L valles, vallis valley

[4] Gk Helene Helen

[5] Gk helix spiral object

[6] MLG welteren to roll < Ger

[7] OHG walzan to roll, waltz

[8] OE welig willow

[9] OE wealcan to roll, toss

[10] OE wiella a well

[11] OHG wallon to roam

[12] OF walet roll, knapsack

[13] OE wealwian to roll in mud

convoluted: very complex and difficult to follow. [1] L con (together) + volvo roll.

devolution: the act of delivering to another; a passing to a successor. [1] L de (down) + volvo roll.

evolve: to develop gradually. [1] L evolvo unroll < e (out) + volvo roll.

helix: three dimensional curve on the surface of a cylinder or cone. [5] Gk helix.

involuted: having a complex or intricate nature. [1] L in- + volvo roll.

involvement: being a part of or connected with an act, enterprise, or movement. [1] L in (in) + volvo roll.

revolution: make a circuit; major change in government, procedures, or ideas. [1] L re (back) + volvo turn.

voluble: having a flow of words or fluency in speaking. [1] Fr < L volubilis, volutes (pp volvo) turn, roll.

voluminous: taking up much space. [1] Fr < L volumen < volutus < volvo turn, roll.

welter: a disordered jumble; to roll and toss about. [6] ME welteren (toss about) < Ger.

RELATED: convolve convolution devolve evolution evolutionism evolutionist involve revolutionary volubly

COMMON: gaberdine [11] Helen [4] helicopter [5] revolt [1] revolve [1] revolver [1] vail [3] vale [3] valley [3] valve [2] vault [1] volt [1] volume [1] walk [9] wallet [12] wallow [13] waltz [7] well [10] willow [8]

183. ye- throw, impel

Latin: JACI, JECT, JACU throw JAC/JEC

[1] L iacere (iactus) to throw, lay; iaculum javelin; iacere (iacens) to lie down; iactare (iactatus) buffet

[2] Gk hienai, send, throw

abject: miserable [1] L jacio throw

adjacent: lying next to or near. [1] L adiacere to lie near < ad- (toward) + iacere to lie.

conjecture: surmise; guess; offer an idea or explanation. [1] L con (with) + jacio throw.

gist: the main idea; the essential point. [1] L iacere.

interjection: an interposition; part of speech showing sudden emotion. [1] L inter (between) + jacio throw.

jactation: the act of throwing. [1] L jactatio < jacto (freq. jacio) hurl.

jettison: cast overboard. [1] OF getaison < L jactatio < jacio hurl.

objective: existing independently apart from experience or thought;(n) goal. [1] L ob (before) + jacio throw.

projectile: an object shot or thrown at high speed or long distance. [1] L pro (forth) + jacio throw.

projection: a jutting out or forth; prediction made from a series of data. [1] L pro (forth) + jacio throw.

subjective: proceeding or taking place within the thinking subject. [1] L sub (under) + jacio throw.

trajectory: path described by a moving projectile. [1] L trajectus (pp trajicio) < trans (over) + jacio throw.

RELATED: ejaculation injection injector interject

COMMON: adjective [1] catheter [2] deject [1] dejected [1] ejaculate [1] eject [1] enema [2] inject [1] jet [1] jetsam [1] jetty [1] joist [1] jut [1] object [1] project [1] reject [1] subject [1] subjectivism [1]

CHAPTER 22

Roots Referring to Doing, Working, Leading, Joining, and Washing

The thirteenth category of roots, covered in this chapter, refers directly to human actions not included in other categories, including doing, working, leading, joining, and washing. Seventeen roots fall into this category. Three roots involve leading or pulling:

'deuk-' meaning "to lead"
'per-[2]' meaning "lead, pass over"
'tragh-' meaning "pull, drag"

The root 'deuk-' meaning "to lead" is the source of the Latin verb 'ducere' meaning "to lead" and the English words 'tug,' 'tie,' 'tow,' 'wanton,' 'taut,' 'team,' and 'teem.' Next 'per-[2]' meaning "lead, pass over" is the source of the Latin verb 'portare' meaning "to carry" and 'porta' meaning "gate," the Greek 'petra' meaning "rock" and 'poros' meaning "passage," and the English words 'ford,' 'ferry,' 'fare,' 'warfare,' 'welfare,' 'fern,' and 'wayfaring.' Third, 'tragh-/dhragh-' meaning "pull, drag" is the source of the Latin verb 'trahere' meaning "to pull, draw, or drag" and the English words 'drag,' 'draw,' dray,' and 'draft.' Four roots involve joining or closing:

'ar-' meaning "to fit together"
'klau-, kleu-' meaning "hook, peg"
'pag-/pak-' meaning "fasten"
'yeug-' meaning "to join"

The root 'ar-' meaning "to fit together" is the source of the Latin 'ars' meaning "craft" and 'ratio' meaning "reason," the Greek 'arthron' meaning "joint," and the English words 'arm,' 'read,' 'dread,' 'hatred,' 'kindred,' and 'riddle.' Also 'klau-, kleu-' meaning "hook, peg" is the source of the Latin verb 'claudere' meaning "to close" and 'clavis' meaning "key" and the Greek 'kleiein' meaning "to close." The root 'pag-/pak-' meaning "fasten" is the source of the Latin verb 'pangere' meaning "to fasten" and 'pax (pacis)' meaning "peace," the Greek 'pegnuni' meaning "to fasten," and the English word 'fang.' Finally, 'yeug-' meaning "to join" is the source of the Latin verb 'iungere' meaning "to join," 'iugum' meaning "yoke," and the English word 'yoke.' Three roots involve pouring or filling:

'gheu-' meaning "pour"
'leu(e)-' meaning "to wash"
'pele-[1]' meaning "to fill, be abundant"

The root 'gheu-' meaning "pour" is the source of the Latin verb 'fundere' meaning "to pour out" and the English words 'gush' and 'gut.' Next 'leu(e)-' meaning "to wash" is the source of the Latin verb 'lavere' meaning "to wash" and the English words 'lye' and 'lather.' Third, 'pele-[1]' meaning "to fill, be abundant" is the source of the Latin verb 'plere' meaning "fill" and 'plenus' meaning "full," the Greek 'plethein' meaning "to be full," and the English words 'fill,' 'full,' and 'folk.' Two roots have a meaning of spreading or strewing:

'pete-' meaning "to spread"
'(s)preg-²' meaning "jerk; strew, sprinkle, squirt" and the related 'sper-⁴' meaning "to strew"

The root 'pete-' meaning "to spread" is the source of the Latin verb 'pandere' meaning "to spread out," the Greek 'petalon' meaning "leaf," and the English words 'fathom.' Second, '(s)preg-²' meaning "jerk; strew, sprinkle, squirt" (and the related 'sper-⁴' meaning "to strew") is the source of the Latin verb 'spargere' meaning "to scatter" or "to sprinkle," the Greek 'sperma' meaning "seed," and the English words 'spread,' 'sprawl,' 'spray,' 'sprit,' and 'sprout.' Five roots refer to various miscellaneous actions:

'leid-' meaning "play, jest"
'med-' meaning "take appropriate measures"
'op-¹' meaning "work, produce"
'pet-' meaning "rush, fly"
'tele-' meaning "lift, support, weigh"

The root 'leid-' meaning "play, jest" is the source of the Latin verb 'ludere' meaning "to play." Also, 'med-' meaning "take appropriate measures" is the source of the Latin verb 'moderari' meaning "moderate" and 'modus' meaning "measure" and the English words 'empty,' 'meet,' 'must,' and 'mote.' Next 'op-¹' meaning "work, produce" is the source of the Latin 'opus' meaning "work." The root 'pet-' meaning "rush, fly" is the source of the Latin verb 'petere' meaning "to seek," the Greek 'piptein' meaning "to fall," and the English word 'feather.' Finally, 'tele-' meaning "lift, support, weigh" is the source of the Latin 'latus' meaning "carried" and 'tollere' meaning "to lift" and Greek 'talanton' meaning "weight."

SOUND SHIFTS

The Indo-European, Latin, and Greek smooth labial mute 'p' shows up in West Germanic and Old English forms generally as a rough labial 'f.' This sound change is clearly evident for five of the roots: 'pag-/pak-' meaning "fasten" is the source of the Latin verb 'pangere' meaning "to fasten" and 'pax (pacis)' meaning "peace," the Greek 'pegnuni' meaning "to fasten," and the English word 'fang.' Next 'pele-¹' meaning "to fill, be abundant" is the source of the Latin verb 'plere' meaning "fill" and 'plenus' meaning "full," the Greek 'plethein' meaning "to be full," and the English words 'fill,' 'full,' and 'folk.' Third, 'per-²' meaning "lead, pass over" is the source of the Latin verb 'portare' meaning "to carry" and 'porta' meaning "gate," the Greek 'petra' meaning "rock," 'poros' meaning "passage," and the English words 'ford,' 'ferry,' 'fare,' 'warfare,' 'welfare,' 'fern,' and 'wayfaring.' Fourth, 'pet-' meaning "rush, fly" is the source of the Latin verb 'petere' meaning "to seek," the Greek 'piptein' meaning "to fall," and the English word 'feather.' Finally, 'pete-' meaning "to spread" is the source of the Latin verb 'pandere' meaning "to spread out," the Greek 'petalon' meaning "leaf," and the English word 'fathom.'

The Indo-European rough palatal 'gh' sound becomes a 'kh' sound in Greek but may take several forms in Latin including 'f.' The corresponding West Germanic and Old English form is generally a voiced palatal 'g.' Thus 'gheu-' meaning "pour" is the source of the Latin verb 'fundere' meaning "to pour out" and the English words 'gush' and 'gut.'

When Indo-European, Latin, and Greek have a smooth palatal mute 'k,' the West Germanic and Old English generally has a rough palatal 'h.' Hence, 'deuk-' meaning "to lead" is the source of the Latin verb 'ducere' meaning "to lead." The English words 'tug,' 'tie,' 'tow,' 'wanton,' 'taut,' 'team,' and 'teem' derived from this root exhibit various ways of assimilating the 'h' to vowels and suffixes.

If Indo-European, Latin, and Greek have the voiced palatal mute 'g,' the corresponding West Germanic and Old English form is generally the smooth palatal 'k.' Thus 'yeug-' meaning "to join" is the source of the Latin verb 'iungere' meaning "to join" and 'iugum' meaning "yoke" and the English word 'yoke.'

If Indo-European, Latin, and Greek show a voiced dental mute 'd,' the West Germanic and Old English show a smooth dental 't.' Hence, 'deuk-' meaning "to lead" is the source of the Latin verb 'ducere' meaning "to lead" and the English words 'tug,' 'tie,' 'tow,' 'wanton,' 'taut,' 'team,' and 'teem.' Also 'med-' meaning "take appropriate measures" is the source of the Latin verb 'moderari' meaning "moderate" and 'modus' meaning "measure" and the English words 'empty,' 'meet,' 'must,' and 'mote.' The final 'd' of the root becomes a 't' in English.

When Indo-European, Latin, and Greek exhibit a smooth dental mute 't,' West Germanic and Old English exhibit a rough dental 'th.' Thus 'pet-' meaning "rush, fly" is the source of the Latin verb 'petere' meaning "to seek," the Greek 'piptein' meaning "to fall," and the English word 'feather' showing change to a 'th' for the final 't' of the root. Second, 'pete-' meaning "to spread" is the source of the Latin verb 'pandere' meaning "to spread out," the Greek 'petalon' meaning "leaf," and the English word 'fathom.'

If Indo-European has a rough dental 'dh' sound, the Greek has a 'th' sound. Latin, however, does not have the 'th' sound, and we find that the 'dh' then takes other forms. The corresponding West Germanic and Old English form is generally a voiced dental 'd.' Hence, 'tragh-/dhragh-' meaning "pull, drag" is the source of the Latin verb 'trahere' meaning "to pull, draw, or drag" and the English words 'drag,' 'draw,' dray,' and 'draft.'

Seven of the roots covered here do not show any sound shift changes requiring notice: 'ar-' meaning "to fit together" is the source of the Latin 'ars' meaning "craft" and 'ratio' meaning "reason," the Greek 'arthron' meaning "joint," and the English words 'arm,' 'read,' 'dread,' 'hatred,' 'kindred,' and 'riddle'; 'klau-, kleu-' meaning "hook, peg" is the source of the Latin verb 'claudere' meaning "to close" and 'clavis' meaning "key" and the Greek 'kleiein' meaning "to close"; 'leid-' meaning "play, jest" is the source of the Latin verb 'ludere' meaning "to play"; 'leu(e)-' meaning "to wash" is source of the Latin verb 'lavere' meaning "to wash" and the English words 'lye' and 'lather'; 'op-[1]' meaning "work, produce" is the source of the Latin 'opus' meaning "work"; '(s)preg-[2]' meaning "jerk; strew, sprinkle, squirt" (and the related 'sper-[4]' meaning "to strew") is the source of the Latin verb 'spargere' meaning "to scatter" or "to sprinkle," the Greek 'sperma' meaning "seed," and the English words 'spread,' 'sprawl,' 'spray,' 'sprit,' and 'sprout'; and 'tele-' meaning "lift, support, weigh" is the source of the Latin 'latus' meaning "carried" and 'tollere' meaning "to lift" and the Greek 'talanton' meaning "weight."

LIST OF ROOTS IN ORDER OF OCCURRENCE

The following list gives the roots as they are ordered in this chapter. Syllables in capital letters give sequences of letters found in English words that generally indicate the root to be the origin of the word. In nearly all cases, if one sees the letters in caps in an English word, one can infer that it comes from the Indo-European root in the first column. However, there may also be some English words from the root that do not accord with the general pattern and some English words that fit the pattern but come from a different root.

184. ar- to fit together	ART art, skill; ARTIC joint ORD, ORDIN order; rank; series; ORN adorn RAT reason; RIT
185. deuk- to lead	DUC, DUCT lead
186. tragh- pull, drag	TRAH, TRACT, [TRAI] draw; drag
187. gheu- pour	FUND, FUS, [FOUND] pour —> FUND [FOUND] bottom
188. klau-, kleu- hook, peg	CLAV, CLAUD, CLAUS, CLUD, CLUS, CLOS lock, shut, close
189. leid- play, jest	LUD, LUS play, deceive
190. leu(e)- to wash	LU, LAV, LUV, LUT, LOT wash
191. med- take appropriate measures	MOD measure; fit; suitable

192. op-¹ work, produce   OPER work
193. pag-/pak- fasten   PAC, PEAS, PEAC peace
194. pele-¹ to fill, be abundant   PLEN, PLET, PLE, PLI, -PLY fill
195. per-² lead, pass over   PORT carry —> PORT entrance; gate; harbor
196. pet- rush, fly   PET seek, attack
197. pete- to spread   PAND, PANS, PASS spread; extend
198a. (s)preg-² jerk; strew, sprinkle, squirt   SPAR, SPERS sprinkle
198b. sper-⁴ to strew   SPERM, SPERMAT, SPOR seed, sowing
199. tele- lift, support, weigh   LAT bear, carry
200. yeug- to join   JUNCT, JOIN join

184. ar- fit together/ ord- to arrange/ re(i)- to reason, count
Latin: ART art, skill; ARTIC joint ORD, ORDIN order; rank; series; ORN adorn RAT reason; RIT
Greek: ARTHR joint ARITHM number

[1] L arma tools, arms   [2] L ars art, skill, craft
[3] L artus joint
[4] L ordo order; ordinare (ordinatus; pfp ordinans) to arrange;
    ordinatus arranged, orderly
[5] L ordiri (pfp ordiens) to begin, begin speaking; orsa, -orum
    speech, beginnings
[6] L ornare (ornatus) to adorn; ornatus equipped, decorated
[7] L reri (ratus) to believe, judge, consider, confirm; ratio
    reason, calculation; rationalis reasonable
[8] L ritus rite, custom, usage
[9] Gk harmos joint, shoulder   [10] Gk aristos best
[11] Gk arithmos number   [12] Gk arthron joint
[13] OE earm arm   [14] OE raedan to advise
[15] OE raeden condition   [16] OE raedels opinion, riddle
[17] OHG rim number, series

aristocracy: government by an elite or privileged ruling class. [10] Gk aristos best + kratia < krateo rule.
arraign: to bring before a court. [7] L ad (to) + ratio reason.
articulate: clear in expression; very able in speech; to enunciate clearly. [3] L articulus (dim. artus) joint.
artifacts: nonessential objects or features produced by human agency. [2] L ars art + facere make.
artifice: a clever or crafty, often deceptive, action or strategy to achieve an end. [2] L ars art + fex maker.
artisan: person skilled in a craft. [2] L artitus skilled in the arts < ars art.
artless: lacking in cleverness, skill, or deception; natural; ignorant. [2] L ars art + less < OE leas (without).
inarticulate: not distinct. [3] L in (not) + articulus (dim. artus) joint.
inert: destitute of inherent power to move; chemically neutral. [2] L iners < in (not) + ars art.
inertia: tendency to remain in the same state of motion; preference for the status quo. [2] L in (not) + ars art.
inordinate: immoderate; without restraint. [4] L in (not) + ordinatus < ordo order.
insubordination: unwillingness to submit to authority. [4] L in- (not) + sub- + ordinare to set in order.
irrational: not showing use of reason; at odds with reason. [7] L in- (not) + rationalis < ratio, rayion- (reason).
ordain: to decree, enact, install. [4] OF ordener < L ordino set in order.
ordinal: indicating the order. [4] Fr ordinal < L ordinalis < ordior begin.
ordinate: distance from the horizontal axis of a geometric graph. [4] L ordino set in order.

ordnance: military weapons. [4] OF < L ordinans (pp ordino) set in order.
ornate: very elaborate, flowery, and showy architectural decoration. [6] L ornare to embellish.
ornery: uncooperative; perverse; contrary. [4] alt. of ordinary < L ordo order.
primordial: first in time; existing from the beginning. [5] L primordialis < primus first + ordior begin.
prorate: divide proportionately; proportion on the basis of a given rate. [7] L pro (for) + rata rate.
ratify: formally approve, confirm. [7] L reri to reckon + ficare to do.
ratiocination: deduction of conclusions from premises; reasoning. [7] L ratiocinatus < ratio reason.
rationale: reason for believing or doing something. [7] L rationalis < ratio reason.
rationalize: to give reasons justifying questionable behavior; to make rational. [7] L rationalis < ratio reason.
subordinate: of lower rank or class; to subdue; to place in a lower class. [4] L ordinare set in order.
suborn: persuade a person to do an unlawful act esp. commit perjury. [6] L sub- secretly + ornare equip.
RELATED: insubordinate
COMMON: adorn [6] alarm [1] arithmetic [11] arm [13] armada [1] armadillo [1] armature [1] army [1] arraign [7] art [2] arthro- [12] article [3] artist [2] co-ordinate [4] co-ordination [4] disarm [1] dread [14] extraordinary [4] harmony [9] hatred [15] kindred [15] logarithm [11] order [4] orderly [4] ordinariness [4] ordinary [4] ordnance [4] ornament [6] rate [7] ratio [7] read [14] reason [7] rhyme [17] riddle [16] riet [8]

185. deuk- to lead
Latin: DUC, DUCT lead

[1] L ducere (ductus) to lead
[2] L educare (eductus) to lead out, bring up
[3] OE teon to pull, draw, lead.
[4] OE togian to draw, drag
[5] OE tigan to bind
[6] OE team descendent. family, team
[7] OE teman to beget

abduction: a carrying away unlawfully; kidnapping. [1] L ab (from) + duco lead.
adduce: to bring forward for consideration; cite; allege. [1] L ad + duco lead.
conducive: contributing to a result. [1] L con (together) + duco lead.
conduction: having the power of guiding; be a medium of transmission. [1] L con (together) + duco lead.
conduit: pipe or channel; means of transmission. [1] Fr < L com- + ducere lead.
deduce: to derive by reasoning. [1] L deduco < de (down) + duco lead.
educe: call forth; draw out; deduce; evoke. [1] L e (out) + duco lead.
endue: furnish with a quality or attribute. [1] OF enduir to lead in, induct < L inducere < in- + ducere lead.
induce: to persuade or cause someone to follow a course of action; to cause. [1] L in (in) + duco lead.
induct: to bring in, initiate, or install a person into an office or group. [1] L in (in) + duco lead.
induction: bringing forth evidence to warrant a general statement. [1] Fr < L inductio < in (in) + duco lead.
irreducible: not having a more elementary and fundamental state. [1] L in (not) + re (back) + duco lead.
productivity: capability for generating output by some activity. [1] L productus < pro + duco lead.
redoubt: an enclosed usually temporary fortification. [1] Fr redoute < L reducere withdraw.
reproduction: act of bringing forward or exhibiting afresh; producing again. [1] L re (again) + pro + duco lead.
seduction: inducing to violate proper conduct esp. in sexual activity. [1] L sub- + ducere lead.
subdued: defeated; overcome; toned down. [1] L sub- + ducere (ductus) to lead.
traduce: willfully misrepresent character; defame; slander. [1] L traduco < trans (over) + duco lead.
RELATED: adducent adductive conduce conducent conduct conductance deducible ductility inductive traducer traducible traducingly traduction
COMMON: abduct [1] aqueduct [1] con [1] deduct [1] doge [1] douche [1] ducal [1] duchess [1] duchy [1] duct [1] ductile [1] duke [1] educate [2] introduce [1] introduction [1] produce [1] product [1] production [1] reduce [1]

reduction [1] seduce [1] semiconductor [1] subdue [1] taut [4] team [6] teem [7] tie [5] tow [4] transducer [1] tug [3] viaduct [1] wanton [3]

186. tragh- draw, drag, move
Latin: TRAH, TRACT, [TRAI] draw; drag

[1] L trahere (tractus; pfp trahens) to pull, draw, drag; tractabilis manageable
[2] OE draege thing drawn

abstract: (v) separate out elements; (adj)general; (n) summary. [1] L abs (from) + traho draw.
contract: reduce size by pulling together; legal agreement. [1] L contractus < con (with) + traho draw.
detract: to take away from; belittle; reduce the value of. [1] L detrahere to remove < de- (from) + traho draw.
distraught: bewildered. [1] L distraho < dis (apart) + traho draw.
entrain: to drag after oneself; draw along. [1] Fr entrainer < en + trainer < LL trahino < traho draw.
entreat: to beg; earnestly entreat. [1] L en- + tractare to draw.
intractable: stubborn; unruly; difficult to treat. [1] L in (not) + tractabilis < tracto handle < traho draw.
protracted: drawn out; prolonged. [1] L pro- + trahere to drag.
retract: withdraw, revoke, or disavow; draw back or draw in. [1] L re (back) + traho draw.
tractable: easily led or controlled; manageable; readily handled. [1] L tractabilis < traho draw.
treatise: a long systematic written document covering a subject. [1] L trahere to draw.
RELATED: abstraction abstractive attraction attractive contractual detraction entreaty protract retractable tractability
COMMON: attract [1] contractor [1] detraction [1] detractor [1] distract [1] distraction [1] dray [2] extract [1] extraction [1] maltreatment [1] mistreated [1] portrait [1] portraiture [1] portray [1] portrayal [1] retrace [1] retreat [1] subtract [1] subtraction [1] tracer [1] tracery [1] tract [1] traction [1] tractor [1] trail [1] trailer [1] train [1] trait [1] treat [1] treatable [1] treatment [1] treaty [1] trawl [1] trawler [1] withdrawn [2]

187. gheu- pour
Latin: FUND, FUS, [FOUND] pour —> FUND [FOUND] bottom

[1] L fundere (fusus) to melt, pour out, spread, scatter;
   profundus deep
[2] L futilis untrustworthy, useless
[3] Gk khaos unformed mass, space
[4] OE guttas intestines < Ger   [5] ME gushen to gush
[6] ON gustr cold wind blast   [7] ON geysa to gush

chaotic: highly disordered and confused. [3] Gk khaos unformed mass, space.
confound: confuse or amaze; perplex. [1] L confundo < con (together) + fundo pour.
diffuse: to spread out. [1] L dis (apart) + fundo pour.
dumbfound: to confound; to perplex. [1] OE dumb + L fundere to pour.
effusive: gushing; unrestrainedly expressing. [1] L ex (out) + fundo pour.
fundamental: constituting a foundation; indispensable; essential. [1] L fundamentum < fundus bottom.
fusillade: a rapid discharge or barrage esp. of bullets. [1] L fusilis < fusus (pfp fundere) to melt.
fusion: uniting or merging together; merging together by application of heat. [1] L fundere (fusus) to melt.
futile: failed, useless. [2] L futilis that easily pours out.
infusion: the process of introducing or instilling into; pouring into. [1] L infusus < in (into) + fundo pour.
profound: intellectually deep. [1] L profundus deep.

profusion: condition of plenty; supplied in great abundance. [1] L pro (forth) + fundo pour.
suffuse: to overspread. [1] L sub (under) + fundo pour.
RELATED: affusion effuse effusion futility infuse profundity profuse transfusion
COMMON: confuse [1] fondue [1] font [1] found [1] fundamentalist [1] funnel [1] fuse [1] geyser [7] gush [5] gust [6] gusty [6] gut [4] refund [1] refuse [1] transfuse [1]

188. klau-/ kleu- hook, peg
Latin: CLAV, CLAUD, CLAUS, CLUD, CLUS, CLOS lock, shut, close

[1] L claudere (clausus) to shut, close; includere (inclusus)
    to enclose, hinder
[2] L clavis key   [3] L clavus nail
[4] L clava club
[5] Gk kleis key   [6] Gk kleiein to close
[7] Gk kleistos closed
[8] OE hleor cheek

claustrophobia: fear of being in a small space. [1] L claustrum enclosure (< claudo) + Gk phobos fear.
cloister: to seclude; (n) a quiet secluded place. [1] L claustrum enclosure < claudere to close.
closure: a closing or shutting up; an end to. [1] L clausus (pp claudo) close.
cloy: to satiate as with sweetness; surfeit. [3] Fr clouer to nail < L clavus nail.
conclave: a secret council or society. [2] F < L conclave < con (with) + clavis key.
conclusive: decisive; putting an end to doubt. [1] Fr < L con (with) + claudo shut.
disclose: make known; uncover. [1] L dis- + claudere close.
enclave: area within foreign territory. [2] Fr enclaver < L inclavo < in (in) + clavis key.
inclusive: broad in scope; comprehensive. [1] L includere to enclose < in- + claudo close.
occlude: absorb a gas by a solid; obstruct; shut out or off. [1] L occludo < ob (before) + claudo close.
preclude: prevent; render impossible by antecedent action. [1] L prae (before) + claudo shut.
reclusive: seeking to retire from the world, be solitary. [1] Fr < L re (back) + claudo shut.
seclusion: kept apart from company or society; withdrawn from others. [1] L se (aside) + claudo shut.
RELATED: cloying conclude conclusion include occluded occlusion recluse seclude
COMMON: clause [1] claustrophobia [1] clavicle [2] clavier [2] clef [2] close [1] closet [1] exclude [1] exclusive [1] leery [8]

189. leid- play, jest
Latin: LUD, LUS play, deceive

[1] L ludus game, play; ludere (lusus) to play; eludere (elusus) to outmaneuver

allude: to hint at or refer to indirectly. [1] L ad (to) + ludo play.
collusion: a secret agreement for a fraudulent purpose; conspiracy. [1] L col (together) + ludo play.
delude: to mislead or deceive. [1] L de (from) + ludo play.
elusive: difficult to pin down, describe, or comprehend. [1] L e-, ex- + ludere to play.
illusion: a deceiving, false appearance. [1] L illusio < in (on) + ludo play.
illusory: deceiving, false appearance. [1] L illusio < in (on) + ludo play.
interlude: anything filling time between events. [1] OF entrelude < L inter (between) + ludus play.
ludicrous: calculated to excite laughter; droll; ridiculous. [1] L ludicrus < ludo play.

prelude: introductory part to a musical composition or play. [1] L pre- (before) + ludus game, play.
RELATED: allusion allusive collusory delusion elude
COMMON: postlude [1]

190. leu(e)- to wash
Latin: LU, LAV, LUV, LUT, LOT wash

[1] L lavere to wash (-luere)   [2] L lavare (lautus; pfp lavans) to wash
[3] L lavatrina, latrina bath, latrine
[4] OE leag lye [5] OE lethran lather

ablution: a washing or cleansing. [1] L abluens (pfp abluo) < ab + luo wash.
alluvial: left by departing water. [1] L ad (to) + luo wash.
antediluvian: from before the flood; antiquated; primitive. [1] L ante (before) + di (apart) + luo wash.
deluge: a great flood or massive downpour; (v) to overwhelm; to inundate. [1] L dis- (apart) + lavere to wash.
dilute: to reduce in concentration or value. [1] L dis- + lavere to wash (-luere).
diluvial: pertaining to the flood. [1] L di (apart) + luo wash.
lavish: extravagant; give in great abundance. [2] L lavare to wash.
COMMON: lather [5] latrine [3] launder [2] laundry [2] lavatory [2] lave [2] lotion [1] lye [4]

191. med- take appropriate measures
Latin: MOD measure; fit; suitable

[1] L mederi (meditus; pfp medens) to look after, heal, cure
[2] L meditari (meditatus; pfp meditans) to think about,
    consider, intend, practice
[3] L modestus moderate
[4] L moderari (moderatus) to restrain, moderate, control
[5] L modus measure, size, limit; modulari (modulatus) to
    play music, measure; modicus limited
[6] OE metan to measure < Ger   [7] OE gemaete commensurate, fit
[8] OE motan to have occasion, permission, or obligation
[9] OE aemetta rest, leisure   [10] OE mod disposition

commodious: well adapted to need; convenient. [5] L commodus < com (together) + modus measure.
immoderate: not restrained; excessive. [4] L immoderatus unrestrained < in (not) + moderari moderate.
irremediable: cannot be corrected or repaired. [1] L in- (not) + re- + mederi to heal.
meditation: thoughtful reflection; contemplation. [2] L meditari (meditatus) to think about, consider.
mete: measure out; allot. [6] OE metan < Ger.
mode: the manner or way of doing something; the current style. [5] L modus manner, tune.
modicum: a moderate amount; a little. [5] L modus measure.
modulation: act or process of shifting in key or frequency. [5] L modulatus (pp modulor) measure.
moodiness: having frequent periods of gloom or depression. [10] OE mod disposition + ness.
outmoded: not in fashion; obsolete. [5] OE ut (out) + L modus manner, tune.
premeditate: to plan beforehand. [2] L pre- (before) + meditari (meditatus) to think about, consider.
remediable: can be corrected or repaired. [1] L re- + mederi to heal.
remedial: providing relief or correction. [1] L re- + mederi to heal.

RELATED: accommodation immoderation immoderately modal modality moderate modulate premeditated
COMMON: accommodate [5] commode [5] commodity [5] demodulate [5] demodulator [5] empty [9] immodest [3] immodesty [3] medical [1] medicate [1] medicine [1] medico [1] meditate [2] meet [7] mod [5] model [5] modem [5] moderator [4] modern [5] modernism [5] modernity [5] modest [3] modesty [3] modification [5] modifier [5] modify [5] modular [5] module [5] mold [5] mood [10] mote [8] must [8] remedy [1]

192. op-¹ work, produce abundantly
Latin: OPER work

[1] L opus work; operari (operatus; pfp operans) to work;
   opera work

[2] L officium service

[3] L opulentus rich, wealthy

[4] L omnis all

[5] L optimus best

[6] L copia plenty

copious: plentiful. [6] L copiosus < copia abundance.
inoperative: not working or not having any effect. [1] L in (not) + opera work.
inured: accustomed or used to undesirable states of affairs. [1] in + OF eure < L opus work.
officious: intermeddling with what is not one's concern. [2] Fr < L officium < opus work + facio do.
omnibus: comprehending many classes or things; a bus. [4] L omnibus (dat. pl. of omnis) all.
optimist: one who always expects affairs to turn out well. [5] L optimus best.
optimum: most favorable condition or amount. [5] L optimus best.
opulent: (adj) having large wealth; profuse; wealthy. [3] Fr < L opulens < opes riches.
opus: creative composition ordered by number. [1] L opus work.
RELATED: inure opulence
COMMON: co-operate [1] copy [6] cornucopia [6] maneuver [1] manure [1] office [2] officinal [1] omni- [4] opera [1] operate [1] operation [1] operational [1] operative [1] operator [1] opus [1]

193. pag-/pak- fasten
Latin: PAC, PEAS, PEAC peace

[1] L pangere (panctus; pfp pangens) to fasten, drive
   in, fix, agree upon

[2] L pax, pacis peace

[3] L pacisci (pacitus) to agree

[4] L palus stake

[5] L palu spade

[6] L pagus district

[7] L pagina trellis, page

[8] L propagare (propagatus) to propagate

[9] Gk pegnuni to fasten, coagulate; pagos mass, hill

[10] OE fang plunder, booty; Ger fanhan to seize

appease: to calm matters esp. by yielding to demands. [2] Fr apaiser < L ad (to) + pax peace.
compact: dense; smaller than typical; concise; (v) press together. [1] L com- + pangere to fasten.
dispatch: to send on a mission; to finish off. [1] Sp despachar < L impingere to dash against.
impact: collision of bodies; effect on something. [1] L impingere push against < in- + pangere fasten.
impale: to penetrate with a sharp pointed object. [4] L in- + palus stake.
impinge: encroach upon. [1] L impingere < in- (against) + pangere to fasten.
pacific: pert. to the making of peace; inclined to peace; peaceable; calm. [2] L pax peace + facio make.

pacifist: person opposed to war or use of force. [2] L pax peace + facio make.
propagate: produce offspring; pass on to future generations; spread ideas or beliefs. [8] L propagare propagate.
travail: arduous work; trials and difficulties. [4] L tri- three + palus stake.
RELATED: pacifism pacify
COMMON: fang [10] newfangled [10] pacifier [2] pact [3] pagan [6] page [7] pageant [7] pale [4] palette [5] palisade [4] patio [3] pay [3] peace [3] peasant [6] pectin [9] peel [5] pole [4] travel [4]

194. pele-¹ to fill, be abundant
Latin: PLEN, PLET, PLE, PLI, -PLY fill
Greek: POLY- many

[1] L plenus full

[2] L plus more

[3] L plere to fill; implere (impletus) to fill; complere (completus)
    fill up; complementum a complement
[4] L plebs, plebes the people, multitude
[5] Gk polus many

[6] Gk plethein be full

[7] Gk pleon, pleion more
[8] OE full full

[9] OE fyllan to fill

[10] OE folc people

complementary: fitting in harmoniously and filling a lack. [3] L complementum < com (intens.) + pleo fill.
compliant: being in accordance with a law, request, or demand. [3] L com- + plere to fill.
compliment: an expression of admiration. [3] L complementum < compleo < com (intens.) + pleo fill.
expletive: an interjection, often profane. [3] L ex (out) + pleo fill.
fitful: characterized by intermittent or irregular activity or occurrence. [8] OE fitt struggle + full full.
fulsome: offensive from excess of praise; indelicate; lustful; wanton. [8] ME ful full + sum some.
hoi polloi: the common people. [5] Gk hoi polloi.
implement: carry into effect; fulfill; tool used in work. [3] L impleo fill up < in (in) + pleo fill.
impletion: the act of filling; state of being full; that which fills. [3] L impleo fill up < in (in) + pleo fill.
manipulation: skillful execution; psychological control. [3] L manipulus handful < manus hand + pleo fill.
nonplus: to bring to a stand by disconcerting; puzzle; perplex. [2] L non (not) + plus more.
plebeian: common; inferior; pert. to the common people. [4] L plebeius < plebs the common people.
plebiscite: popular vote to decide a proposal. [4] L plebiscitum < plebs the people + scitum decree.
plenipotentiary: person with full powers esp. a diplomatic representative. [1] L plenus full + potens powerful.
plenitude: the state of being full, complete, or abounding. [1] L plenitudo < plenus full.
plethora: a great abundance or excess. [6] Gk plethein to be full.
replenish: to fill again; resupply or restock. [1] L re (again) + plenus full.
replete: full to the uttermost; lavishly stocked; abounding; complete; perfect. [3] L re (again) + pleo fill.
RELATED: complement compliance fulsomeness manipulate manipulative manipulator nonplussed replenishment repletion repletive
COMMON: accomplish [3] complete [3] completeness [3] completion [3] comply [3] deplete [3] fill [9] folk [10] full [8] plebe [4] plenty [1] pleonasm [7] pluperfect [2] plural [2] plus [2] poly- [5] polygamist [5] polymer [5] supplementary [3] supplement [3] supplier [3] supply [3] surplus [2]

195. per-² lead, pass over
Latin: PORT carry —> PORT entrance; gate; harbor
Greek: PETR, PETER rock

[1] L portus harbor   [2] L porta gate
[3] L portare (portatus) to carry
[4] Gk petra cliff, rock   [5] Gk poros journey, passage
[6] ON fjordhr inlet < Ger   [7] OE faran to go on a journey, get along
[8] OE ferian to transport   [9] OE fearn fern
[10] OE ford river crossing point

comport: to conduct (oneself); to be compatible; agree. [3] L com (together) + porto carry.
deportation: act of sending away forcibly, banishing. [3] L de (from) + porto carry.
deportment: conduct or behavior; demeanor; bearing. [3] L de (from) + porto carry.
ford: shallow place in a river permitting crossing by vehicle or on foot. [10] OE ford.
importune: press urgently or frequently. [1] L importunus troublesome < in (not) + portus harbor.
inopportune: not advantageous or occurring at an advantageous time. [1] L ob- (to) + portus harbor.
insupportable: that is not endurable; insufferable; intolerable. [3] L in (not) + sub (beneath) + porto carry.
opportunist: person who uses every available circumstance for gain. [1] L ob (to) + portus harbor.
petrify: to change organic matter into stone. [4] Gk petra rock + L facere to make.
porous: easily penetrated; allowing easy penetration by gas or liquid. [5] Gr poros passage < poron pierce.
purport: signify; mean; (n) what is conveyed. [3] OF purporter intend < L pre (before) + porto carry.
rapport: harmony of relation; sympathetic relation. [3] Fr < L reporto < re (again) + porto carry.
sportive: related to or fond of sport or play; frolicsome; wanton. [3] L de (away) + porto carry.
supporting: holding up; providing for; aiding; corroborating. [3] L sub- (from below) + portare to carry.
transport: (n) strong emotion; (v) to enrapture; to move from one place to another. [3] L trans + porto carry.
RELATED: comportment deport disporting importunate importunity opportune purported purportedly sport sportsman support
COMMON: emporium [6] export [3] exporter [3] fare [7] fern [9] ferry [8] fieldfare [7] firth [6] fjord [6] gaberdine [7] import´ [3] im´port [3] importance [3] important [3] importation [3] opportunity [1] parsley [4] passport [1] petro- [4] petroleum [4] pier [4] porch [2] pore [5] port [1, 2, 3] portable [3] portage [3] portal [2] porter [2,3] portfolio [3] porthole [1] portico [2] portly [3] portmanteau [1] Portugal [1] report [3] reportable [3] reporter [3] saltpeter [4] supporter [3] transportation [3] unreportable [3] warfare [7] wayfarer [7] wayfaring [7] welfare [7]

196. pet- rush, fly
Latin: PET seek, attack
Greek: PTER wing

[1] L petere (petitus; pfp petens) to go toward, ask for, seek; impetus attack; petitio, -onis claim
[2] L penna, pinna feather, wing
[3] L propitius favorable, gracious; propitiare (propitiatus) to soothe, appease
[4] Gk piptein to fall; ptotos falling, fallen; ptosis a fall; ptoma a fall, fallen body, corpse
[5] Gk potamos (-amo-) rushing water, river
[6] OE fether feather

appetence: strong craving or propensity; instinct or tendency. [1] L ad (to) + peto seek.
asymptote: a line toward which a curve converges. [4] Gk a (not) + syn (together) + piptein to fall.
competence: having sufficient ability or skill. [1] L competere strive together < com (together) + peto seek.
impetuous: impulsive, quick, unthinking action. [1] L impetuosus < impeto rush upon < in + peto.
impetus: force causing bodies to continue on course; main force motivating action. [1] L impetus < in + peto.
panache: spirited self-confidence. [2] Fr panache plum, verve < L pinna wing.

pinnate: having feathers or wings. [2] L penna feather.

perpetual: lasting for eternity or an unlimited duration. [1] L per- (through) + petere to go toward.

perpetuate: to prolong or continue for an unlimited period. [1] L per- (through) + petere to go toward.

petulant: displaying capricious fretfulness; insolently wanton. [1] L petulans < peto attack.

pinnacle: the highest point; a spire or high pointed rock formation. [2] L pinnaculum < pinna feather.

propitiate: to appease. [3] L propitiatus (pp propitio) render favorable, appease.

propitious: facing favorable circumstances; auspicious. [3] L propitiatus (pp propitio) render favorable.

repetition: act of doing or saying over; reiterating; that which is repeated. [1] L re (again) + peto seek.

symptom: an attribute or event which acts as a sign of a causing event. [4] Gk syn (with) + piptein fall.

unpropitious: not auspicious; facing unfavorable circumstances. [3] L un + propitiatus render favorable.

RELATED: appetency appetent competent competency petulance repeat repeating repetitious

COMMON: appetite [1] compete [1] competition [1] feather [6] hippopotamus [5] pen [2] -petal [1] petition [1] pin [2]

197. pete- to spread
Latin: PAND, PANS, PASS spread; extend

[1] L pandere (passus) to spread out, open, explain; passus dishevelled
[2] L pater (pfp patens) to lie open, extend; patens, -entis open; patulus open
[3] Gk petalon leaf   [4] Gk patane platter
[5] OE foethm fathom

compass: go around; comprehend; (n) device indicating direction; scope. [1] L com- + pandere spread out.

encompass: to surround or enclose; to include. [1] L com- + pandere spread out.

expansive: talkative; tending to increase in scope; broad in scope. [1] L ex- + pandere (passus) spread out.

fathom: (v) understand; comprehend; (n) 6 feet of water depth. [5] OE foethm (outstretched arms).

impasse: a situation that reaches a deadlock with further progress impossible. [1] L in- (not) + passer to pass.

pan: harshly criticize. [4] L patina platter < Gk patane.

passé: out of date or fashion. [1] Fr < L passus (pfp pandere) to spread out, scatter.

patent: evident, obvious; (n) grant of sole rights to profit from an invention. [2] L pater (pfp patens) lie open.

patina: surface coloration produced by use and age. [4] Gk patane platter.

spawn: to cause; produce; produce offspring; (n) eggs. [1] L ex- + pandere to spread out.

surpass: go beyond in capacity or power; exceed. [1] Fr surpasser < passer pass < L passus step.

trespass: to sin or transgress; to infringe on another's rights or time. [1] L trans- (over) + passus step.

unfathomable: cannot be understood or comprehended. [5] OE un- (not) + foethm (outstretched arms).

RELATED: compassable patently patinate

COMMON: expand [1] expansion [1] pace [1] pass [1] passage [1] passport [1] petal [3]

198. (s)preg-[2] jerk; scatter
Latin: SPAR, SPERS sprinkle
sper-[4] to strew
Greek: SPERM, SPERMAT, SPOR seed, sowing

[1] L spargere (sparsus; pfp spargens) to scatter, sprinkle,
    divide; sparsio, -onis a scattering
[2] ME sprenklen to sprinkle
[3] Gk sperma sperm, seed   [4] Gk spora a sowing, seed

[5] Gk sporas scattered, dispersed; speirein to scatter

[6] OE spreawlian to sprawl

[7] OE -spraedan spread

[8] OE -sprutan to sprout

[9] OE spreot pole

[10] Swed sprygg brisk

aspersion: a disparaging or derogatory remark. [1] L ad (to) + spargo sprinkle.

disperse: scatter; widely distribute; break up light. [1] L dispergere scatter < spargo sprinkle.

intersperse: insert or interleave at regular intervals between items. [1] L inter- (between) + spargo sprinkle.

sparse: distributed thinly; scattered. [1] L sparsus < spargo scatter.

sporadic: irregular; scattered; occasional. [5] Gk sporadikos < sporas < speiro scatter.

spry: active and vigorous. [10] Swed sprygg brisk.

RELATED: asperse aspersive diaspore dispersion sparsely sporiferous

COMMON: bowsprit [9] sperm [3] sporo- [4] sprawl [6] spray [7] spread [7] sprinkle [2] sprit [9] sprout [8]

199. tele- lift, support, weigh
Latin: LAT bear, carry

[1] L latus borne, carried

[2] L tolerare (toleratus) to bear, endure;
   tolerabilis bearable; toleratio, -onis an enduring

[3] L talio reciprocal punishment

[4] L tollere (sublatus; pfp tollens) to lift, raise

[5] Gk telos tax, charge

[6] Gk talanton balance, weight

[7] Gk Tantalos "the suffering king"

[8] Gk Atlas (Atlant-)

ablation: removal; amputation; wasting as of rocks or glaciers. [1] L ablatio < ablatus < ab + latus carried.

collate: to put in order; to compare critically. [1] L col (together) + latus borne.

correlation: close correspondence or relation; degree of relation. [1] L cor + relatus < re- + latus borne.

dilate: to expand. [1] L di (apart) + latus carried.

dilatory: causing delay or postponement; tardy; slow. [1] LL dilatorius < dilatus < latus delay.

elated: elevated in spirit. [1] L ex (out) + latus borne.

extol: give high praise. [4] L ex- + tollere to lift.

irrelation: lack of relation. [1] Fr < L relatio < in + relatus related < re (back) + latus borne.

oblation: act of offering something esp. to a deity. [1] L ob (out) + latus borne.

philately: stamp collecting. [5] Gk philos love + a (without) + telos tax.

prelate: high-ranking member of the clergy, usually bishops. [1] L praelatus < prae- + latus brought.

relation: condition of being connected; connected by blood. [1] Fr < L relatio < re (back) + latus borne.

retaliation: paying back in kind; returning evil for evil. [3] L talio reciprocal punishment.

superlative: elevated to the highest degree; of supreme excellence. [1] L super (over) + latus borne.

tantalize: excite with a reward but keep it always out of reach. [7] Gk Tantalos.

RELATED: collation correlate correlative dilation legislator retaliate

COMMON: Atlantic [8] atlas [8] elate [1] elation [1] legislation [1] relate [1] relative [1] talent [6] tolerable [2] tolerate [2] toll [5] translate [1]

200. yeug- to join
Latin: JUNCT, JOIN join JUNCT
Greek: ZYGO join

[1] L iugum yoke   [2] L iuxta close by
[3] L jungere (iunctus) to join, yoke
[4] OE geoc yoke

adjoin: be next to or contiguous with. [3] L adiungere to join to < ad- (to) + iungere to join.

adjunct: auxiliary; assistant; in a subordinate position. [3] L ad (to) + jungo join.

conjoin: to unite. [3] L con (together) + jungo join.

conjugal: pertaining to marriage. [3] L conjugalis < con (together) + jungo join.

conjugation: union; inflection of a verb. [1] L conjugo yoke together < con (together) + jugum yoke.

conjunct: joined; (n) an entity joined or associated. [3] L con- (with) + iungere to join.

disjoin: to separate. [3] OF < L dis (apart) + jungo join.

disjunction: separation; proposition asserting one of two joined statements is true. [3] L dis + jungo join.

enjoin: to prescribe, impose, or prohibit with emphasis. [3] L jungere (iunctus) to join, yoke.

injunction: an order or command esp. a legal court order. [3] L in (into) + jungo join.

juncture: act of joining; junction. [3] L junctio < jungo join.

junta: a small ruling body esp. in Central and South America. [3] L jungere (iunctus) to join, yoke.

juxtapose: place close together; make contiguous. [2] L juxta (near) + positio < positus (pp pono) place.

rejoinder: a sharp reply esp. to rebut. [3] L jungere (iunctus) to join, yoke.

subjoin: add at the end; attach. [3] L sub (under) + jungo join.

subjugate: to subdue; conquer; enslave. [1] L sub (under) + jugum yoke.

RELATED: conjugate disjointed juxtaposition subjunctive

COMMON: adjust [2] conjunction [3] join [3] joinder [3] joint [3] jointure [3] jostle [2] joust [2] jugular [1] junction [3] rejoin [3] yoke [4]

PART 3

ADDITIONAL VOCABULARY FROM DIFFERENT LANGUAGES

CHAPTER 23

Words with Latin Roots (A–J)

There are many important words that do not have one of the two hundred Indo-European roots featured in the previous thirteen chapters as their source. This chapter and the following four chapters list many additional words from other roots. The most important words to learn are in italics. Many other words worth learning are in the lists as well. Students should concentrate on the words in italics. If students have time, they can spend additional effort on the words that have not been highlighted, perhaps on a second pass through these chapters. The words in these final five chapters have been separated according to linguistic or other sources. This chapter covers words coming from Latin roots with initial letter from A to J. Each word is given a short definition and has an indication of its origin.

abase: to degrade; to reduce in rank or prestige. L ad- + bassus low.

abash: to embarrass or disconcert someone. OF esbahir < baer to gape < L badare bay.

abate: lessen in intensity or amount. OF abattre < L ad- + battuere beat.

abeyance: suspended temporarily. Fr a- + bayer gape, stare at < L badare bay.

abhor: to view with horror or loathing. L ab- (from) + horrere to shudder, be terrified.

abortive: futile; failing to achieve the objective. L abortari to disappear < ab- + oriri to appear.

abrasive: causing wear; having a manner that grates on others. L ab- + radere to scrape.

abstemious: consuming sparingly or in moderation. L ab- (away) + temum liquor.

adulation: extravagant praise; servile and extravagant flattery. L adulor fawn.

affinity: condition of close relationship; mutual attraction. L ad (to) + finis end.

affirmation: assert to be true. L affirmare < ad + firmare < firmus strong.

affix: to attach to. L ad- + figere to fasten.

affliction: suffering or pain; a cause of suffering and pain. L ad- + fligare to strike.

affront: to offend openly and intentionally. OF afronter < L ad- + frons (front-) face.

aftermath: period subsequent to an event; consequences of an event. OE after + maeth mowing.

agrarian: pert. to agriculture and rural matters. L agrarius < ager field.

ambidextrous: equally adept with either hand. L ambi- (on both sides) + dexter right-handed.

amend: to alter or correct; to change a proposed law or policy measure. L ex- + mendum defect.

amenities: things contributing to comfort. L amoenus pleasant.

amoral: not following moral principles; not subject to moral reasoning. L a + mos manner, custom.

anterior: before; in front; earlier in time. L ante (before).

antiquated: out of date; no longer useful. L antiquus former, antique.

apex: highest point; peak; vertex. L apex top.

aplomb: upright posture; assurance, self-confidence; poise. OF a plomb < L plumbum lead.

appall: to horrify or cause great dismay. L ad (to) + pallere to grow pale.

apparition: a ghostly appearance. L apparitus (pp apparere) to appear.

aptitude: innate ability; quickness to learn. LL aptitudo aptitude < aptus apt.

arable: cultivatable (land). L arare to plow.

arbitrary: not based on necessity or principle. L arbiter.

arbiter: person chosen to settle a dispute. L arbiter.

array: arrange in an orderly fashion; (n) an orderly arrangement; (math) a matrix. OF arraier < VL arredare.

arrears: to be behind in paying debts or fulfilling obligations. L ad- + retro (behind).

asseverate: to affirm or aver emphatically or solemnly. L ad + severus serious.

astute: shrewd and discerning. L astus craft.

atavism: intermittent heredity; reversion to an ancestral type or trait. L atavus < avus grandfather.

audit: to check financial accounts for correctness and legality. L audire to hear.

aural: pertaining to hearing. L aura ear.

auroral: pertaining to the dawn. L aurora.

auspicious: favorable; propitious. L auspex a diviner < avis bird + specio view.

avarice: great desire for wealth. L avarus greedy < avare to desire.

aviary: enclosure for keeping birds. L avis bird.

avidity: strong and eager appetite or relish; greediness. L avidus eager.

avuncular: of or pertaining to an uncle. L avunculus < dim. avus grandfather.

bailiwick: a local area of interest or authority. ME bailiff + wik town < L vicus neighborhood.

bellicose: warlike. L bellum war.

belligerent: disposed to engage in warfare. Fr belligerant (waging war) < L belligerare wage war.

bestial: subhuman; brutal; beastly. L bestia beast.

bibulous: given to drinking alcoholic beverages. L bibulus < bibere to drink.

bilateral: involving two sides; reciprocal. L bi two + latus a side.

bourgeois: of the middle class or conforming to its standards. Fr bourg < L burgus fortified place.

bovine: of cows or related ruminants; sluggish. L bovinus < bos ox.

bravado: a pretended or false show of bravery. Sp bravada swagger < L barbarus.

calumny: slander; malicious statements made to damage someone's reputation. L calvor deceive.

candor: frankness; openness. L candere to shine.

canine: of or related to dogs. L canis dog.

cant: tedious, empty talk with commonplaces, jargon, or false piety. L cantare to sing.

carnivorous: flesh-eating. L caro flesh + voro devour.

catenate: to connect like the links of a chain; form into a chain of series. L catena chain.

caucus: a meeting of political party meetings to choose leaders or policies. L caucus drinking vessel.

cavalcade: a series; a procession of riders or carriages. L caballus horse.

cavalier: (adj) acting arrogantly and disregarding others; (n) knight or chivalrous gentleman. L caballus horse.

cavil: to find fault over trivial and petty matters. L cavillor < cavilla jeering.

celerity: speed; quickness of motion. L celeritas < celer swift.

celestial: related to the sky or heavens; divine; sublime. L caelestis < caelum sky.

celibate: (adj) not engaging in sexual intercourse. L caelibatus < caelebs unmarried.

centrifugal: force pushing away from the center or axis. L centrum center + fugere to flee.

cerebral: pertaining to the brain. L cerebrum brain.

challenging: requiring dedication of all abilities and resources to achieve; intriguing. L calumnia trickery.

citadel: fortress on a hill. Ital cittadella little city < L civitas < civis citizen.

cite: to quote. L cito (freq cieo) call.

clandestine: done secretly; concealed. L clandestinus < clam in secret.

clangor: loud sounds as of many large bells ringing; a din. L clangere to clang.

claustrophobia: abnormal fear of being in a small place. L claustrum enclosure + Gk phobos fear.

coddle: to boil gently. L caldum hot drink < calidus warm, hot.

coercion: act of compelling by force, threats, or intimidation. L coercere < co- + arcere enclose, confine.

cohere: to hold together resisting separation; form a consistent whole. L co (together) + haereo stick.

cohesion: process of sticking or holding together. L co (together) + haereo stick.

cohort: a company or band. L cohors company of soldiers.

collaborate: to work together esp. scientific and intellectual work. L com- + laborare to work.

collateral: coincidental, attendant, or secondary; forfeitable security. L col (with) + lateralis < latus side.

colligate: to tie, group or fasten together. L colligatus < col + ligo bind.

colorless: dull; lacking variety; devoid of interest. L color.

combustible: capable of burning. L com- + ambi- + urere to burn.

comfortless: disconsolate; forsaken; left with nothing to alleviate distress. L com- + fortis strong + OE –less.

commemorate: do something to provide a memorial for. L commemorare remind < memor mindful.

comminute: to reduce to minute particles; crush; pulverize. L com (intens.) + minuo diminish.

commiserate: to sympathize with; feel sorry for. L com- + miserari to pity.

compile: combine text or information materials together. L com- + pila heap, pillar.

concatenate: to connect. L con (with) + catena chain.

concave: curved like the inside of a ball. L com- + cavus hollow.

concentric: having the same center. L com- + centrum center.

concoct: devise a plan; contrive; produce with mixed ingredients. L coquere to cook.

concupiscence: undue or illicit sexual desire; lust; any inordinate appetite. Fr < L con (intens.) + cupio desire.

condemn: express strong disapproval of; to declare unfit for use. L com- + damnare to sentence.

condolence: expression of sympathy. L condolere < com (with) + doleo grieve.

configuration: the arrangement of or set up. L com- + figura form, shape.

confiscate: to seize by government authority. L com- + fiscus treasury.

conflate: combine into one. L conflare < com- + flare to blow.

congeal: to change from a fluid to a solid. L con (together) + gelo freeze < gelu cold.

congruent: fitting together; identical; compatible; harmonious; consistent. L congruere to agree.

connive: to cooperatively scheme together esp. in wrongdoing. L conivere close the eyelids, be indulgent.

connubial: pertaining to matrimony. L con (together) + nubo marry.

consanguinity: blood relationship. L con (together) + sanguis blood.

conservatism: belief in maintaining the traditional order esp. in politics. L con- + servare preserve.

conserve: using resources carefully avoiding waste. L com- + servare to keep, preserve.

considerate: showing care for the feelings of others; done with deliberation. L considerare < sidus star.

console: to sympathize with; to comfort; to encourage. L com- + solari comfort, console.

consort: wife or husband. L con (together) + sors lot.

consternate: to cause alarm, dismay, or confusion. L sternere (pp stratus) to throw down.

construe: to take to be the meaning; to interpret. L construere to build.

contemporary: of the same time; current; of the present time. L com- + tempus time + -arius –ary.

context: the setting or surroundings that give words or events their meaning. L texere weave.

contusion: a bruise. L contundere to beat < com- + tundere to beat.

conundrum: a seemingly insoluble problem or dilemma. L quonandrum (16th Cent).

conviction: judgment of guilt; strong belief. L com- + vincere to conquer.

convulse: shake violently involuntarily or from strong emotion. L convellere (convuls-) < com- + vellere pull.

corrode: slow erosion of a metal. L com- + rodere to gnaw.

corrugated: having parallel grooves and ridges. L com- + rugare to wrinkle.

counterpart: something corresponding to another in function or action. L contra + pars part.

couplet: two lines that rhyme. Fr < L copula bond, pair.

courteous: polite; showing consideration for others. L cohors courtyard, retinue.

covetous: desirous of something belonging to someone else. L cupiditas < cupere to desire.

crevice: a narrow crack or fissure. L crepo creak, crack.

crisp: firm but brittle; fresh; concise. L crispus.

cuisine: food especially elegantly prepared food. L coquere to cook.

culinary: related to cooking and kitchens. L culinarius < culina kitchen.

culminate: to reach the highest point or goal; to end. L culminatus < culmen top.

cumulative: increasing by summing successive additions. L cumulus heap, mass.

cupidity: an inordinate wish for possession; avarice. L cupiditas < cupio desire.

daub: to touch up or smear with paint or other liquid material. L de- + albus white.

daunt: discourage. L domare to tame.

debacle: sudden failure, collapse, or defeat. OF desbacler to bar < L de- + baculum rod.

debilitate: to weaken in strength or health. L debilis weak.

debris: rubble or wreckage from accidents and natural disasters; litter. VL de- + brisare to break.

decoy: an artificial or live animal used to lure game for hunting; (v) to lure as if by a decoy. L de- + cavea.

decrepit: enfeebled through infirmity or old age. L de + crepo crack.

definite: clearly defined or precise; certain. L de- + finis boundary, limit.

definitive: determinate; explicit; positive; bringing to an end; conclusive. L definio < de (off) + finis end.

defunct: no longer living, existing, or in use; dead. L de (off) + fungor discharge, perform.

delighted: filled with pleasure or happiness. L de + lactare < lacere to entice.

delineate: to draw in outline; to trace out. L delineatus < de (off) + linea line.

delirium: a state of disorientation or delusion usually from sickness. L delirium < de- + lira furrow.

demarcation: act of setting boundaries or limits; a distinction. L de- + marcar to mark.

demur: to offer objections; take exception; delay; hesitate. L de (from) + mora delay.

denouement: the unravelling of the plot of a play or novel. Fr < de (from) + nouer tie < L nodus knot.

denounce: condemn; accuse. L de- + nuntiare announce < nuntius messenger.

depict: to represent by picture or art; to describe. L de- + pingere to picture.

deplore: strongly disapprove of. L de- + plorare to wail.

depravity: moral degradation and perversion. L de (thoroughly) + pravus crooked, depraved.

deprecate: indicate disapproval of; disparage. L de- + precari to pray.

depreciate: decrease in value. L de (down) + pretium price.

derivative: obtained or adapted from some prior source. L derivo < de (from) + rivus stream.

desiccate: to thoroughly dry out. L desiccare < de- + siccare to dry up < siccus dry.

despoil: to plunder; deprive of. L de (intens.) + spolium spoil.

despondent: being discouraged or dejected. L spondere pledge.

deterrent: something which discourages or prevents action. L de- + terrere to frighten.

devotee: a dedicated practitioner of a specific form of activity. L de- + vovere to pledge, vow.

devout: diligent to fulfill religious obligations; reverent; pious. L de- + vovere to pledge, vow.

dilapidated: in a state of neglect or broken-down condition. L dis- + lapidare to throw stones.

diminution: reduction or decrease. L minutia smallness < minuere.

dire: causing terrible consequences. L dirus fearsome, terrible.

disarray: a state of confusion or disorder. OF arraier < VL arredare.

disburse: to pay from a fund. L bursa purse.

discrepancy: a disagreement or difference; state or point of variance. L dis (apart) + crepo break.

disinter: to dig up from a grave or tomb. L dis- + terra land.

dismember: to break off or pull off the limbs or parts of. L dis- + membrum limb.

dissection: the act of cutting apart or of analyzing in detail. L dis- + secare to cut up.

disparate: different in kind; having dissimilar elements. L dis- (apart) + parare to prepare.

disseminate: to scatter or spread widely or abroad. L dis- + seminare to sow < semen seed.

dissertation: formal essay. L dissero discuss.

divest: to deprive; strip off; sell assets. L devestio < de (from) + vestis clothing.

divulge: to make something private known. L dis- + vulgare to spread < vulgus commoners.

doleful: sorrowful, sad. OF dol < L doleo feel pain.

domicile: a main residence; a home. L domus house.

dubious; arousing questions, doubt, and uncertainty. L dubius doubtful.

dubitable: questionable; doubtful; uncertain. L dubitabilis < dubitare to doubt.

dulcet: sweet to the taste or to the ear; mentally pleasing. L dulcis sweet.

duplicity: double-dealing; intentional deception. L duplex double.

eccentric: not following the conventions and norms; odd. Gk ek- (out of) + kentron center < kentein prick.

effigy: a dummy or likeness representing a person or member of a group. L ex- + fingere to shape.

effrontery: brazenness; presumptuousness. L ex (out) + frons forehead.

ego: the self; conceit. L ego I.

egocentric: self-centered. L ego I + center < Gr kentron.

egotism: excessive focus on self; self-conceit. L ego I.

elicit: bring out; draw out. L elicitus < e (out) + lacere allure.

emaciated: very thin; starved; scrawny. L ex- + maciare make thin.

emanate: to flow forth or proceed as from a source; originate. L e (from) + mano flow.

embark: get on a ship or in a vehicle; begin a venture. L in- + barca boat.

emend: improve by editing text. L e + mendum defect, fault.

emulate: to strive to equal or surpass; vie with. L aemulatus (pp aemulor) < aemulus striving to equal.

endorse: sign on the back; acknowledge by signing; give support to; stand behind. L en + dorsum back.

enervating: depriving of nerve, vigor; weaken. L e (out) + nervus nerve.

entice: to lure by playing on desires. L in- + titio firebrand.

ennui: boredom, weariness. Fr < L odium hatred.

enunciate: pronounce clearly; set out precisely. L ex- + nuntiare announce < nuntius messenger.

equilibrium: a balance of opposing forces. L aequalis equal.

equestrian: pertaining to horses. L equester < equus horse.

equine: pertaining to horses. L equus horse.

eradicate: pull out by the roots; wipe out; thoroughly destroy. L eradicatus < ex (out) + radix root.

erode: wear down by rubbing or scraping. L erodere < ex- + rodere to gnaw.

escapade: a prank; an adventurous act. L ex- + cappa cloak.

espouse: give one's support to; to marry. Fr < L sponsus (pp spondeo) promise.

estranged: alienated; made hostile. L extraneare disown < extraneus foreign < exter outward.

evince: show; manifest; exhibit; make evident. L ex- + vincere to conquer.

exaggerated: overstated; represented to be much greater than is actually the case. L ad- + gerere to bring.

excise: indirect tax. OF acceis < L ad- + census tax.

excerpt: segment selected from a document, film, or music. L exerptus < ex- + carpere pluck.

exhaustive: thorough; complete. L ex- + haurire to draw.

exhort: to incite. L ex (out) + hortor urge.

exhume: to dig out of the earth; disinter. L ex (from) + humus ground.

exonerate: to release from blame. L ex- + onus burden.

exorbitant: unreasonable; excessive (esp. of price). L e (out) + orbita track.

expatriate: banish or exile; move to and take up allegiance in a foreign country. L ex- (out) + pater father.

expurgate: to clear as a book, of whatever is objectionable. L ex (out) + purgo cleanse.

extraneous: not essential; irrelevant. L extraneous < extra (outside).

extravagant: spending lavishly, excessively, and wastefully; unreasonable. L extra- + vagari to wander.

exude: to slowly discharge; to have abundantly. L ex- + sudare to sweat.

farina: meal or flour obtained from cereals. L far (coarse meal).

fascinate: to compel interest or attraction; to charm. L fascinare cast a spell < fascinum evil spell, amulet.

fatigued: tired; weary from exertion. L fatigare.

fauna: animals of a specified region or period. LL Faunus god of fertility.

favor: to regard with friendship or approval; to prefer; be partial to. L favere to be favorable.

feigned: pretended; imitated; not real. L feindre < fingo shape.

feint: a pretended attack or action to distract attention away from the intended target. L figura form.

felon: one who has committed a felony, that is, a major crime. L fel bile.

fictitious: imaginary; not genuine. L fingere to shape.

figment: made up; not real. L figura form, shape.

figurative: symbolic; metaphorical. L figura form, shape.

finale: the conclusion of a musical performance. L finalis < finis end.

finesse: ability to handle delicate and difficult situations skillfully and adroitly. Fr fin (fine) < L finio finish.

finite: bounded or limited in number, time, or space. L finis end.

fissile: capable of being split or separated into layers; tending to split. L fissilis < fissus (pp findo) cleave.

fissure: a long crack; process of separating into groups or factions. L fissura < findo split.

flair: a knack; elegance of action. LL flagrare < fragrare to emit an odor.

flatulent: having excessive gas in the bowels; windiness; vanity. L flatus a blowing < flo blow.

flexible: easily bent without breaking or being damaged; pliable; adaptable. L flexus (pp flecto) bend.

foment: incite; instigate. L fomentum poultice < fomentum warm lotion.

forensic: pert. to debate, courts of law, or establishing evidence for courts. L forensis < forum market-place.

fornication: sexual intercourse between unmarried partners. L fornicari < fornix arch, vault, brothel.

forte: a strong point of one's abilities; something a person excels in. L fortis strong.

fortitude: strength enabling one to endure adversity. L fortitudo < fortis strong.

fraternal: pertaining to brothers or comrades. L frater brother.

fraudulent: involving swindling or deceit; gained through swindling. L fraudulentus < fraus, fraud- deceit.

frugality: quality of exercising economy or being sparing and thrifty. Fr < L frugalis < frux fruit.

fruition: the accomplishment realized by an endeavor; the result. L fruitus (pp frui) enjoy.

frustrate: to prevent from achieving a goal; to provoke discouragement. L frustrari < frustra in vain.

furor: a public commotion or uproar. L furere to rage.

garner: to obtain; accumulate; gather and store. L granarium < granum grain.

gaudy: showy but tasteless. L gaudere to rejoice.

gerund: a verbal noun. L gerundium < gerundus (gerundive) gero carry.

gestation: pregnancy, carrying young; inception of a plan. L gestatio < gero bear, carry.

gesticulate: make motions of limbs or body while speaking for emphasis. L gesticulus < gerere to behave.

glacial: extremely slow movement; freezing cold. L glacies ice.

glutton: person who consumes excessive food and drink. L glutto glutton.

gorge: (n) a deep ravine; (v) to glut with food. L gurges throat; gulf, whirlpool.

grandeur: greatness, splendor, magnificence, or eminence. Fr < L grandis great.

grandiose: great in scale; magnificent; pompous and affected greatness. L grandis great.

gustatory: related to taste (the sense). L gustus taste.

gusto: the enthusiasm or relish for action. L gustus taste.

herbivorous: feeding on herbs. L herba herb + voro devour.

hermetic: sealed airtight; totally protected from outside interest. NL hermetical alchemical.

hiatus: break; interruption; pause. L hiatus (pp hio) gape.

hibernate: to go into an inactive or dormant state esp. during winter. L hibernalis < hiems winter.

homage: acknowledgement of allegiance; public showing of respect. L hominaticum service of a vassel.

homicide: act of killing a person. L homo human being, man + caedo kill.

hortatory: encouraging. L hortativus < hortor urge.

humanist: one concerned mainly with human welfare and interests. L humanus belonging to a man.

hybrid: something of mixed or dissimilar origins. L hibrida mongrel.

illicit: not lawful. L in- (not) + licitus lawful.

imbibe: to drink; to saturate with liquid. L im (in) + bibo drink.

immaculate: spotlessly clean; pure; without fault. L in- (not) + macula spot.

immanent: remaining within; indwelling; inherent. L in (in) + maneo remain.

impalpable: imperceptible to touch; intangible; unreal; incorporeal. LL in (in) + palpabilis < palpo touch.

imperative: expressing a command; necessary and unavoidable. L imperare to command < parare prepare.

impious: acting in violation of religious duties and not showing reverence for the divine. L in- (not) + pius dutiful.

implausible: not believable. L in- + plaudere.

impotent: lacking power to perform esp. sexual relations. Fr < L impotens < in (not) + potens powerful.

imprecation: a curse. L in- (towards) + precari to entreat, pray.

impunity: not subject to punishment or penalty. L impunitas < in (not) + poena punishment < Gk poine fine.

inane: lacking in sense. L inanis (empty, lacking sense).

incandescence: emitting light from being heated; very intense or brilliant. L in- + candere to shine.

incarcerate: to imprison. L in (in) + carcer jail.

incendiary: tending to cause a fire or to inflame passions. L incendere to set fire to, kindle.

incentive: reward or threatened punishment used to motivate action. L in- + cantare to sing.

incite: provoke to action. L incitare urge forward < in- + citare stipulate < ciere put in motion.

incoherent: not comprehensible, inconsistent, confusing. L in- (not) + co (together) + haereo stick.

incongruous: not compatible or harmonious; inconsistent. L in- (not) + congruere to agree.

incumbent: (adj) dependent on; obligatory; (n) an office holder. L in- + cumbere to recline.

indefatigable; tireless. L in- (not) + de- + fatigare to weary.

indefinite: vague; indistinct; not specifiable in number or kind. L in (not) + de (from) + finio to limit, bound.

indelible: permanent; not erasable or capable of being washed away. L in- + delebilis < delere to wipe out.

indenture: binding contract for service for a specified period. OF endenter < L in (in) + dens tooth.

indomitable: unconquerable. L in- (not) + domare to tame.

indubitable: undeniably true. L in (not) + dubius < duo two.

inebriated: drunken. L inebriatus (pp inebrio) make drunk.

inept: clumsy; incompetent. L ineptus < in- (not) + aptus suitable.

ineptitude: clumsiness; inability to act competently or appropriately. L ineptus < in- (not) + aptus suitable.

inevitable: cannot be avoided or prevented. L in- + evitabilis < evitare to shun.

infernal: related to hell; diabolical; awful. L infernus hell.

infinitesimal: too small to be measured. L in (priv.) + finites (pp finio) to limit, bound.

infirmity: a physical weakness or frailty. L in- + firmus firm, strong.

inflated: expanded by filling with gas or air; excessively enlarged; swollen; pretentious. L in- + flare blow.

ingest: to take into the body. L ingestus < in (into) + gero carry, bear.

inherent: innate; essential characteristic. L in- + haerare to stick, adhere.

inimitable: cannot be imitated; not matchable. L imitare to imitate.

innuendo: suggestion or hint about some person or thing; indirect aspersion; insinuation. L innuo nod.

inseminate: to insert semen into. L in- + seminare to sow < semen seed.

insinuate: to suggest subtly. L insinuo wind in < in (in) + sinus winding.

instigate: provoke or urge to do. L instigare to goad, incite.

inter: to bury. L in- (in) + terra land.

intimidate: make afraid; deter by threats. L in (in) + timidus afraid, fearful.

intriguing: causing curiosity or interest. L intricare to entangle, perplex.

intuitive: perceived without involving thinking; instinctive, untaught. L intueor < in (on) + tueor look.

inveterate: firmly established; deep-rooted; confirmed in a particular character or habit. L in (in) + vetus old.

invigorate: to give strength, vitality, or energy. L in- + vigere be lively.

invincible: cannot be defeated. L in- (not) + vincere to conquer.

invulnerable: too strong to be attacked successfully, or damaged, or wounded. L in- (not) + vulnus wound + -able.

iridescent: brilliant or lustrous in color. L iris, irid- rainbow.

irradicable: cannot be uprooted or eliminated. L in- (not) + radix root.

irreparable: not capable of being restored to sound condition. L in- (not) + re (again) + parare to prepare.

iterate: to utter or do again; repeat. L iterum again < is he.

jeopardy: danger or risk of serious loss or injury. L iocus joke + partire < pars part.

jocose: of the nature of a joke; humorous. L jocosus < jocus joke.

jolly: very cheerful; merry; joyful. ME joli.

joyful: filled with pleasure and delight. L gaudere to rejoice.

joyless: cheerless; gloomy; unhappy; dismal. L gaudere to rejoice.

joyous: feeling great pleasure and delight. L gaudere to rejoice.

jubilation: having or expressing great joy; rejoicing. L jubilo shout for joy.

CHAPTER 24

Words with Latin Roots (L–V)

There are many important words that do not have one of the two hundred Indo-European roots featured in chapters 10 to 22 as their source. This chapter offers additional words from Latin roots with initial letter from L to V. The most important words to learn are in italics. Many other words worth learning are in the lists as well. Students should concentrate on the words in italics. If students have time, they can spend additional effort on the words that have not been highlighted, perhaps on a second pass through these chapters. Each word is given a short definition and has an indication of its origin.

lachrymose: sorrowful; tearful. L lacrima tear.

lament: grieve, mourn. L lamentum lament.

languish: to become weak; to exist in dispiriting or miserable conditions. L languere to be weak.

largess: (or largesse) great generosity; gifts given with great generosity. L largus plentiful..

lassitude: feeling of weariness or lack of energy. L lassus weary.

latent: potential but undeveloped and not active or evident; hidden. L latens (ppr lateo) lie hidden.

lateral: pert to or being on the side of. L lateralis, latus a side.

latitude: degrees from the equator in degrees; not subject to restraints. L latitudo < latus broad.

lenient: permissive; indulgent. L leniens pacifying < lenis soft.

lethal: able to cause death; devastating. L letum death.

liaison: person serving as a communication link; an affair. L ligare to bind.

liberal: advocating minimal restrictions; generous; not strict; broad-minded. L liberalis < liber free.

libertarian: one who rejects any form of determinism; advocate of maximum civil liberties. L liber free.

lineage: descendants from the same ancestor. L linealis < linea linen thread.

linear: pertaining to, or composed of lines. L linealis < linea linen thread.

linguistic: related to languages. L lingua language.

longevity: long-lived or tendency to live long. L longus long + aevum age.

lucrative: very profitable. L lucrativus < lucrum profit.

lurid: giving a ghastly or dull-red light; dismal; fig. ghastly and sensational; pale; wan. L luridus pale.

luxuriant: showing abundant growth; producing abundantly. L luxuria excess, luxury.

malodorous: having a foul or bad smell. L malus bad + odor smell.

marine: pertaining to the sea or navigation. Fr marin < L marinus < mare sea.

marital: related to marriage. L maritus married.

maritime: by the sea or related to the sea or navigation. L maritimus < mare sea.

martial: related to war and fighting. L Martialis < Mars Mars.

materialism: belief physical things only are real; striving mostly for material things. L materia matter.

maternal: pertaining to the mother and motherhood. L mater mother.

matrix: breeding ground or nurturing environment; a mathematical array. L matrix < mater mother.

maul: to batter or beat; to handle roughly. L malleus hammer, mallet.

meddlesome: interfering or intruding where unwelcome. L miscere (pp mictus) to mix + OE -sum –like.

mediate: to settle differences between parties; (adj) being in the middle. L medius middle.

mélange: a mixture of diverse elements. Fr < L miscere to mix.

memorable: notable and worth remembering. L memor mindful.

memorandum: written note or record for communication. L memor mindful.

ménage: the persons of a household collectively. Fr < L manere to remain.

menagerie: a diverse group; an enclosure with live wild animals. Fr < L manere to remain.

mendicant: one who begs; (adj) relying on begging for sustenance. L mendicare to beg < mendum a defect.

menial: of monotonous work done by servants or others of low estate. L mansio house.

mercenary: (adj) seeking monetary gain. L merces wages, prices.

mercurial: changeable in temperament. L Mercurius Mercury.

minuscule: very small. L minisculus rather small < minor smaller.

minute: extremely small, insignificant. L minutia smallness < minuere to lessen.

minutiae: small, usually petty, details. L minutia smallness < minuere to lessen.

mirage: an illusory sight of apparent water; an illusion. L mirari to wonder at < mirus wonderful.

mobile: able to move or be moved; not fixed in place. L movere to move.

momentous: of very great significance and consequence. L momentum movement.

morale: a group attitude of confidence and willingness to perform its tasks. L moralis < mos manner.

moratorium: suspension of an activity; temporary suspension of an obligation. L mora delay.

mores: a group's customs, moral beliefs, and ways. L mos (manner, custom).

motif: a repeated or central theme or design in a work of art or literature. L movere to move.

mulish: stubborn and obstinate. L mulus.

mutinous: unruly; disposed to rebellion, especially of sailors against ship officers. L movere to move.

nebulous: having its parts confused or mixed; hazy; indistinct. L nebula cloud.

nepotism: business or political favoritism given to relatives. L nepos, nepot- grandson, nephew.

nexus: a connected group; the core or links between group elements. L nectere (pp nexus) to tie, bind.

nocturnal: occurring or active at night rather than in daylight. L nocturnus nightly < nox night.

node: knob, knot, or connecting point. Fr < L nodus knot.

noisome: disgusting; foul; dangerous. OF anoier to annoy < L odium hatred.

nonchalant: unconcerned; casual. Fr non- (non) + chaloir cause concern to < L calere heat up.

nuance: subtle shade of difference in meaning. L nubes cloud, shade.

nuptial: related to marriage and weddings. L nuptialis < nubere to marry, take a husband.

nurture: bringing up with care. L nutrire to suckle.

nutrient: healthful food ingredient useful to the body. L nutrire suckle, nourish.

obeisance: bending the knee in courtesy or reverence. OF obeissance < L ob-(to) + audire hear.

obese: excessively fat. L obesus fat.

obfuscate: to obscure to cause confusion and difficulty in perceiving. L ob (to) + fuscus dark.

obligatory: morally or legally binding; compulsory. L ob- + ligare to bind.

obliging: accommodating; willing and ready to comply. L ob- (to) + ligare to bind.

obscurity: darkness; difficulty of perception or understanding. L obscurus dark.

observant: alert and quick to notice; watchful; diligent to obey laws and principles. L ob- + servare.

obstreperous: making a great disturbance; clamorous; boisterous; unruly. L ob (before) + strepo roar.

odious: causing great displeasure, dislike, or hatred. L odium hatred.

ominous: threatening; giving warning of imminent danger or evil. L omen omen.

omnipotent: able to do anything logically possible. L omnis all + potens powerful.

omnivorous: eating everything. L omnis all + voro eat.

onerous: burdensome; oppressive. L onerosus < onus burden.

orientation: a general tendency; alignment relative to points of the compass or another object. L oriens rising sun.

ossify: to become rigid or bonelike. L os bone + fy.

palatable: acceptable as a policy or outcome; acceptable in taste for eating. L palatum palate.

pallid: unusually pale in complexion; dull. L pallere to be pale.

palpable: that may be touched or felt; readily perceived; obvious. LL palpabilis < palpo touch.

palpitate: to tremble or shake rapidly. L palpitare (freq palpo) feel.

parry: to deflect, ward off, or evade a thrust or attack. L parare to try to get, prepare, equip.

pastoral: rural; related to herding; related to activity of a pastor. L pastor shepherd.

patrician: an aristocrat; person with noble manners and tastes. L patres enrolled fathers < pater father.

patronize: act condescendingly; be a regular customer of; sponsor. L pater father.

pavilion: an open-air tent or roofed structure used for shelter or for exhibitions. L papilio butterfly, tent.

penal: serving to punish for an offense. L poena penalty < Gk poine fine.

peregrination: travel; wandering. L per (through) + ager land.

peruse: to examine carefully. L per- + ME usen to use.

picaresque: pertaining to pirates or rogues esp. clever rogues. Fr < Sp pocarosco < L piccare picaro.

picayune: small Spanish coin; person or thing of trifling value. Fr picaillon farthing < L piccare to pierce.

pied: patchy or splotched of color. L pica magpie.

piety: devoutness; strict observance of religious requirements. L pietas < pius pious.

pigment: substance used for painting and coloring. L pigmentum < pingere to paint.

piquant: having an agreeably pungent or tart taste; provocative; racy. Fr piquancy < L piccare to pierce.

pique: a feeling of slight irritation or resentment. Fr piquer prick, sting < L piccare to pierce.

pillage: to plunder and take as spoil. L pileus felt cap.

pillory: to ridicule; (n) wooden structure on a post used to punish offenders. L pila heap, pillar.

pious: dutifully performing religious duties and showing reverence for the divine. L pius dutiful.

pittance: a very small amount especially of money. L pietas piety < pius dutiful.

plaintive: sad; lamenting; mournful. L planctus (pp plangere) to lament, strike one's breast.

plaudits: praise or applause. L plaudere to applaud.

plausible: credible; likely to be true. L plaudere to applaud.

plenipotentiary: possessing full power or authority to act. L plenus full + potens powerful.

plumb: weighted line used to test water depth or verticality; (v) determine depth or verticality. L plumbum lead.

plummet: plunge or decline steeply. OF plommet (dim plom, plum) < L plumbum lead.

possibility: a thing, event, or statement that may become true. OF < L possibilis < posse be able.

posthumous: occurring after a person's death. L post (after) + humus earth.

postulate: to assume for the sake of argument; (n) an unproved assumption. L postulare to request.

potable: drinkable; (n) a beverage. L potus a drink.

potent: physically powerful; efficacious; strong. L potens (pp possum) be able.

potentate: one having great power or sway; a sovereign. Fr potentat < L potens powerful.

potential: not actual; latent; possible; (n) capacity for coming into existence. L potentia power < posse be able.

potion: a liquid mixture used for medicinal, magical, or poisonous purposes. L potio a drink.

praise: expressions of admiration or commendation; acclaim; to applaud. L pretium price.

precarious: very unstable or insecure. L precarius obtained by entreaty < precari to entreat.

precocious: early development and maturity. L prae- pre- + coquere cook, ripen.

predominate: to exhibit a presence, power, or influence exceeding all others. L prae + dominari to rule.

prefigure: to produce beforehand something that foreshadows later developments. L figura form.

preserve: maintain intact and unharmed; area of special protection. L prae- pre- + servare preserve.

pretext: pretended reason concealing the true purpose. L praetexere disguise < prae- + texere weave.

primeval: belonging to the first ages; primitive in time. L primaevus < primus first + aevum age.

procrastinate: to put off what ought to be done for a later time. L pro (for) + crastinus of tomorrow.

profligate: (adj) very wasteful; dissolute. L pro (forward) + fligare < fligere to strike down.

promiscuous: not discriminating or selective esp. in sexual partners. L pro- + miscere (pp mictus) to mix.

protégé: a person whose career is advanced by someone of higher status. L pro- + tegere to cover.

proxy: one authorized to act for another; the authorization to act for another. L pro + curare to care for.

prune: cut off branches to improve growth or shape; to remove what is unneeded. L pro- (in front) + rota wheel.

prurient: excessively interested in sex. L pruriens (pp prurire) to yearn for.

pulverize: to crush or grind into powder. L pulvis, pulver- dust.

pummel: to batter as with the fists. L pomum fruit.

purge: to purify; to rid of guilt; to rid of people considered undesirable. L purgo cleanse.

putrefy: to cause decay. L im (not) + putreo be putrid.

putrid: rotten and foul smelling. L im (not) + putreo be putrid.

quadrilateral: four-sided closed figure. L quadri four + lateris side.

quibble: raising trivial distinctions to avoid an issue; an irrelevant objection. L quibus (who, which).

quip: a witty remark. L quippe indeed < quid (what).

rabid: mad; unreasonably zealous; fanatical; violent; furious; raging. L rabidus < rabio rave.

radical: proceeding from the root or foundation; favoring extreme change. L radix root.

raiment: clothing. OF arreement array < VL arredere.

ramification: consequence of an event or state of affairs. L ramus branch + facio make.

rancid: disagreeable; rank; nasty. L rancere to stink, be rotten.

rancorous: exhibiting spite and malice; hateful. OF < L ranceo be rancid.

raze: demolish; shave. L radere to scrape.

recant: formal disavowal or retraction of a statement or belief. L re- + cantare to sing.

recrudescence: a breaking out afresh; a reappearance; return. L re (again) + crudesco grow raw.

redolent: fragrant; reminiscent. L re- + olere to smell.

redoubtable: formidable; deserving honor. OF redouter to dread < L re- + dubius doubtful.

redress: to make amends; remedy; (n) reparation. OF re- + drecier to arrange.

reimburse: to pay back; to refund. L re- + in + bursa bag.

reinforcing: strengthening; bolstering; shoring up. OF re- + en- + force < L fortis strong.

reiterate: to repeat. L re- + iterum (again).

rejuvenate: to restore to youthful or new condition. L re- + iuvenis young.

relentless: persistent and unremitting. L re- + lentus sticky + -less.

reliable: dependable, trustworthy, responsible. L re- + ligare to bind.

relinquish: to give up or surrender; to set aside; to release. L re- + linquere to leave.

relish: to take great pleasure in; (n) a strong liking for or appetite for; zest. L re- + laxare to loosen.

renounce: formally give up; disown. L re- + nuntiare announce < nuntius messenger.

reparable: capable of being restored to sound condition. L re- + parare to prepare, put in order.

repast: a meal; to eat. L re- + pascere to feed.

repertoire: the set of songs or plays that a player or company can perform. L repertus < re- + parire to beget.

repudiate: disavow previous statements or commitments; reject emphatically. L repudium divorce.

requisite: necessary; required. L re- + quaerere to seek.

reserve: (n) something kept for future use; (v) keep back, retain. L reservare < re- + servare keep.

reservation: something held back or committed for a future use; a qualification. L re- + servare keep.

resplendent: brilliant, dazzling. L re- + splendere to shine.

resuscitate: to revive. L re (again) + sub (under) + cito summon.

revulsion: feeling of loathing or disgust. L revellere to tear back < re- + vellere to tear.

ridiculous: worthy of contempt and laughter; foolish; absurd. L ridiculus < rideo laugh.

rigidity: stiffness; inflexibility; fixedness. L rigere to be stiff.

rigor: strictness; exactness. L rigere to be stiff.

risibility: laughability; ludicrousness; being amusing. Fr risible < L risibilis < rideo laugh.

rivalrous: seeking to compete with and surpass. L rivalis < rivus stream.

rivulet: tiny stream. L rivulus < rivus stream.

ruse: a deceptive scheme. OF ruser to drive back < L re- + causari to give as a reason.

rustic: related to country life; coarse; unsophisticated; roughly finished. L rus country.

sanguine: of buoyant disposition; hopeful; confident; having the color of blood. L sanguis blood.

sartorial: related to tailors and tailored clothing. L sarcire to mend.

scourge: a whip; something that causes widespread affliction or devastation. L ex- + corriga thong.

secular: not spiritual or religious. L saeculum generation, age.

serpentine: long and winding as a snake. L serpere to creep.

sever: to cut off, divide, or separate. L separare < se- (apart) + parare to prepare.

shambles: a mess; condition of devastation and disorder. L scamnum bench.

sinecure: an office having emoluments with few or no duties. L sine (without) + cura care.

sinister: suggestive of impending trouble or evil. L sinister on the left, unlucky.

sinuous: with many curves. L sinuosus < sinus bend.

solace: comfort in the face of misfortune or sorrow; source of comfort. L solor comfort.

solstice: time when the sun is furthest from the celestial equator. L solstitium < sol sun.

somnolent: sleepy. L somnus sleep.

stagnant: not flowing or moving. L stagnare < stagnum swamp.

stellar: outstanding; related to stars. L stella star.

stipulate: lay down or specify as a condition. L stipulor (pp stipulatus) bargain for.

straying: deviating from the proper or normal course; to wander. L strata paved road.

strident: shrill; harsh. L stridere make harsh sounds.

stupefy: daze; astonish. L stupefacere < stupere to be stunned + facere to make stupid.

sublime: majestic; noble; inspiring; excellent. L sublimis uplifted.

subliminal: not consciously (but perhaps subconsciously) perceived. L sub- + limen threshold.

subterfuge: an action used for escape or concealment; a false excuse. L subter (below) + fugio flee.

subtle: hard to detect or describe; perceptive. L subtilis < sub (beneath) + tela web.

succulent: juicy and sweet. L succulentus < succus juice.

succumb: to be overcome by force or desire; give in; to die. L sub- + cumbere to lie down.

sudatory: efficacious in exciting perspiration; perspiring. L sudatorius < sudatus (pp sudo) sweat.

supplant: to replace; usurp by intrigue. L sub- + planta sole of foot.

surveillance: observation of; watching. OF sur + veillier < L vigil watchful.

tacit: existing, inferred, or implied without being directly stated; implicit. L tacitus < taceo be silent.

tandem: having identical parts arranged with one directly behind the other. L tandem at last.

temperate: moderate; showing self-restraint. L temperatus (pp temperare) to temper.

temporal: related to time or to the material world; not eternal; secular. L tempus time.

temporize: finding excuses and means to delay or gain time. L tempus time.

tentative: provisional; hesitant. L tentatus (ppr tentare) to try.

tepid: lukewarm; unenthusiastic; half-hearted. L tepidus < tepere to be lukewarm.

terrestrial: related to the earth or land. L terra earth.

torpor: stupor; dullness; loss of sensation or motion. L torpeo be numb.

torrent: a heavy downpour or outpouring; a heavy turbulent flow. L torrere to burn.

torrid: extremely hot; scorching; passionate; rapid. L torrere to dry, parch, burn.

transplant: relocate something esp. a plant; (n) relocated entity. L trans + plantare plant.

travesty: grotesque or exaggerated likeness or imitation. L trans- + vestire to dress.

tremulous: quivering or shaking; timid. L tremulus trembling < tremere to tremble.

tutelage: providing guardianship or instruction; under a guardian or tutor. L tutela < tueri (tutus) to guard.

ubiquitous: found everywhere. L ubique (everywhere).

unctuous: greasy; flattering; unduly suave. Fr onction < L unctio < ungo anoint.

unfeigned: genuine; not pretended. OE un + L feindre < fingo shape.

unilateral: one-sided; action on the part of but one of the parties. L uni one + latus, lateris side.

unique: the only one of its kind; without any equivalent. L unicus.

useful: beneficial to the purpose at hand; productive. L uti (use) + OE full.

vacillate: to waver indecisively between different courses of action. L vacillare to waver.

vagabond: a nomad; a wanderer. L vagari to wander.

vaporize: convert to a gaseous form. L vapor (steam, vapor).

velocity: speed or rate of motion. L velox fast.

vent: (n) opening for release of fumes; (v) forcefully express; discharge via an opening. L ex- + ventus wind.

verdant: abundant with green vegetation. L viridis green.

vestige: a remaining trace or evidence of something that once existed. L vestigium.

vicarious: experienced empathetically or from description or imagination. L vicarius vicarious < vix change.

vicissitude: a change of fortune; alternate occurrence or succession. L vicissitudo < vicis (gen. vix) change.

vie: to contend for superiority. L invitare to invite.

vigor: strength or energy. L vigere be lively.

virile: manly; exhibiting masculine strength and powers. L vir man.

virtuoso: outstanding skilled musician or artist. L virtus excellence.

virulent: extremely infectious or toxic; hateful; antagonistic. L virus poison.

visceral: felt instinctively; felt "from the gut." L viscera intestines.

viscous: thick, sticky, and resisting flow. L viscosus < viscum birdlime.

vitriolic: scathing and abusive. L vitreus < vitrum glass.

volant: able to fly; agile. L volo to fly.

volatility: tendency to be explosive, changeable, or easily influenced. L volatilis < volo fly.

voracious: gluttonous; insatiable. L vorax < voro devour.

vulnerable: susceptible to injury or attack. L vulnerare to wound < vulnus wound.

CHAPTER 25

Words with Greek Roots

There are many important words that do not have one of the two hundred Indo-European roots featured in chapters 10 to 22 as their source. This chapter offers additional words from Greek roots. The most important words to learn are in italics. Many other words worth learning are in the lists as well. Students should concentrate on the words in italics. If students have time, they can spend additional effort on the words that have not been highlighted, perhaps on a second pass through these chapters. Each word is given a short definition and has an indication of its origin.

acrophobia: an abnormal fear of high places. Gk akros topmost + phobos fear.

aesthetic: pert to beauty, taste, or the fine arts; artistic. Gk aisthetikos perceptive, underlying beauty.

amalgamate: to mix together, unite, or alloy. Gk malagma soft mass.

amass: to accumulate a large amount of. L ad- + massa lump < Gk maza a lump, barley cake.

aperiodic: not occurring at fixed intervals. Gk a- (without) + periodos < peri (around) + hodos way.

apocalypse: a revelation esp. of the end of the world; a total destruction. Gk apo (from) + kalypto cover.

apoplexy: fit of great anger or rage; a stroke. OF apoplexie < Gk apo- + plessein to strike.

archetype: a primitive or standard pattern or model; a prototype. Gk archos chief + typos < typto strike.

aria: a vocal solo with accompaniment. Gk aer air.

aromatic: having a pleasant smell or fragrance. Gk aroma aromatic herb.

asceticism: practicing self-denial. Gk asketikos < askein to work, exercise.

aseptic: free of bacteria or contamination. Gk a- (without) + sepsis rotten.

asteroid: a miniplanet orbiting the sun. Gk aster, astron star.

astral: related to stars. Gk astron < aster star.

atrophy: wasting away; deterioration. Gk a + trepho nourish < trophe food.

atypical: not characteristic; abnormal. Gk a (priv.) + typos type.

austere: stern, somber; plain and unadorned; ascetic. Gk austeros harsh.

authenticate: to prove the genuineness of. Gk authentes author.

canvass: to poll; to solicit orders or votes. LL canna reed < Gk kannabis.

cataclysm: violent upheaval or deluge causing major changes. Gk kata + klao break.

cataract: a large waterfall; opaqueness in the eye reducing vision. Gk kata (down) + arassein to strike.

catastrophic: quality of being calamitous or disastrous. Gk katastrophe < kata (down) + strepho turn.

catechism: elementary religious book. Gk kata (down) + echo sound.

caustic: burning; corrosive. Gk kaustikos < kaio burn.

cauterize: to cut with a hot iron. Gk kauterion (dim kauter) a searing iron < kaio burn.

cenotaph: monument for the dead. Gk kenos empty + taphos tomb.

chameleon: lizard that changes color. Gk chamai on the ground + leon lion.

charisma: an unusual personal magnetism or charm. Gk kharisma divine grace, favor.

chasm: a gorge or narrow but deep opening in the earth. Gk khasma yawning gulf, chasm.

chimera: an absurd and groundless fancy. Gr chimaira < chimairos he goat.

chiropractic: healing by manipulating. Gk cheir hand + praktikos practical < prasso do.

choleric: quick to be angered or show anger. Gk kholera < khole bile.

chromatic: pert. to color. Gk chroma color.

chromosome: microscopic rod-shaped bodies carrying genes. Gk chroma color + soma body.

collage: a collection of materials or text pasted or assembled together. Gk kola.

colossal: so enormous as to produce awe and amazement; immense. Gk kolossos.

comatose: related to or affected by coma; abnormally sleepy. Gk koma slumber.

conic: cone shaped. Gr konikos < konos peak.

contrivance: clever or ingeneous scheme or device. L com- + tropus manner < Gk tropos manner.

coup: a brilliant success; a coup d'etat. Fr < Gk kolaphos a blow.

cubical: volume with approximately equal length, width, and height. Gk kubos.

cygnet: young swan. L cycnus < Gk kyknos swan.

cynic: negative person who attributes base motives to human actions. Gk kunikos < kuon dog.

despot: a tyrant; one with absolute power. Gk despotes master, lord.

diapason: full range of notes. Gk.

didactic: pert. to teaching; expository. Gk didaktikos apt to teach.

dilemma: a choice between two or more undesirable options. Gk di- two + lemma proposition.

diocese: district of bishop. Gk dioikesis < dia through + oikeo dwell.

draconian: extremely harsh or severe. Gk Drako.

dromedary: one-humped domestic camel. Gk dromas running.

eclipse: sunlight cut off by a planet or moon; a decline; (v) to surpass; to obscure. Gk leipein leave.

ecology: science of environment. Gk oikos home + logy.

economics: science of the production and distribution of wealth. Gk oikos house + nomos law.

ecumenical: general; universal. Gk oikumene whole world < oikeo inhabitant.

elegy: lament for a dead person. Gk elegeia < elegos mournful song.

ellipsis: omission of words needed for complete and correct grammatical constructions. Gk leipein leave.

emetic: inducing vomiting. Gk emetikos < emeo vomit.

empyreal: from the highest region of heaven; celestial. Gk empyros in the fire < en (in) + pyr fire.

enigma: something puzzling and inexplicable. Gk ainigma < ainos tale.

entropy: measure of closed system randomness; transmission information loss. Gk en- + trope change.

eolithic: stone age. Gk eos dawn + lithos stone.

eon: very long period of time. Gk aion age.

ephemeral: living only one day; transitory; momentary; fleeting. Gk ephemera day.

epoch: a specific historical period usually distinguished by some characteristic. Gk epokhe a point in time.

epochal: momentous; unparalleled. Gk epokhe a point in time.

ethereal: airy; celestial; otherworldly. Gk aither < aitho burn.

euthanasia: painless death. Gk eu well + thanatos death.

exhilarating: causing a feeling of energy, giddiness, or refreshment. Gk ex- + hilaros gay.

exodus: a going forth or out. Gk ex (out) + hodos way.

exotic: strange or unusual; foreign. Gk ex, ek (out of).

galaxy: large system of stars. Gk galaxis < gala milk.

gambit: a chess opening sacrificing a pawn or piece for positional advantage. Gk kampe a bending, winding.

geriatrics: care for the aged. Gk gero old.

glucose: sugar. Gk glykys sweet.

gynecology: science of women's diseases. Gk gynaikos (gen. of gyne) woman + logy.

gyrate: to spin; oscillate around a fixed point. Gk gyros circle.

gyroscope: rotating wheel that maintains its orientation. Gk gyros round, a circle + scope.

hector: (n) domineering fellow; bully. Gk Hektor.

hemophilia: disease characterized by inability of the blood to clot. Gk haima blood + philia love.

hemorrhage: discharge of blood from a ruptured blood vessel. Gk haima blood + rhegnymi break.

heresy: a doctrine that contradicts established religious doctrines. Gk hairesis school < haireo take.

hermitage: monastery. Gk eremites < eremos solitary.

hexagon: six-sided polygon. Gk hex six + gonia corner.

hieroglyphic: picture or symbol representing words; hard to read. Gk hieros sacred + glypho carve.

hilarity: great merriment, fun, and good spirits. Gk hilaros gay.

hormone: internal secretion. Gr hormao excite L oriri.

hypochondria: fancies of bad health. Gk hypo + khondros granule, cartilege (L frendere grind refrain).

hypothermia: dangerously low body temperature. Gk hyps- + therme heat.

icon: an image; an object of devotion. Gk eikon < eikenai to seem.

iconoclastic: attacking established beliefs, institutions, and ideas. Gk eikon image + klao break.

idiosyncrasy: peculiar characteristic of a person or group. Gk idio- personal + krasis a mixing.

kinetics: science of pure motion. Gk kineo move.

labyrinth: a maze. Gk laburinthos.

larceny: stealing; theft. Gk latron pay, hire.

machinations: underhanded schemes; plots. Gk mekhane.

masticate: to chew. Gk mastizo chew.

methodical: proceeding in a deliberate and orderly manner. Gk meta + odos way, journey.

metropolis: a major city. Gk meter mother + polis city.

miasma: polluting exhalations; malarial poison. Gk miasma pollution.

misogynist: hater of women. Gk miseo hate + gyne woman.

monastic: rel. to the life of a monastery; contemplative; austere. Gk monazein to live alone.

monochrome: painting with shades of a single color. Gk monos single, one + chroma color.

monolith: a single fashioned piece or block of stone. Gk monos single, one + lithos stone.

myriad: a great many. Gk myrios numberless < myrioi ten thousand.

nautical: rel. to ships and sailing. Gk nautikos < naus ship.

neolithic: pert. to a later Stone Age. Gk neos new, recent + lithos stone.

nostalgia: longing for the past. Gk nostos a return home.

octamerous: having eight parts. Gr oktas < okto eight.

orthogonal: right-angled. Gk orthogonius < ortho straight + gonia angle.

ostracize: to exclude or banish from a group. Gk ostrakon potsherd.

pachyderm: elephant. Gk pachys thick + derma skin.

palindrome: a word or words that read the same forward or backward. Gk palin again + dromos run.

panacea: remedy for all ills. Gk pas all + akos cure.

paranoia: extreme distrust of others and fear of persecution. Gk para- beyond + nous mind.

parochial: church operated; provincial. OF < L parochia for paroecia < Gk para beside + oikos house.

pentagon: five-sided polygon. Gk penta five + gonia corner.

periodic: recurring at fixed intervals. Gk periodos < peri (around) + hodos way.

phalanx: any massed body. Gk phalanx battle-line, bone, or finger, or toe.

phobia: an irrational fear of a specific situation or thing; a strong fear. Gk phobos panic, flight, fear.

phoenix: mythical bird that rose from its ashes; something of very great excellence. Gk phoenix.

politic: judicious, tactful, shrewd. Gk polis city.

polyglot: person who speaks or writes several languages. Gk poly many + glotta tongue.

polygon: an enclosed plane figure with several angles and sides. Gk poly many + gon angle.

practicable: feasible; usable. Gk prassein do, make.

pragmatic: practical. Gk pragmatikos versed in affairs < prasso do.

pragmatism: practicality; belief truth only known by results. Gk pragmatikos versed in affairs < prasso do.

proselyte: convert. Gk proselytos < pros to + elthein come.

prototype: initial working model used as a basis for future production. Gk protos first + typos type.

punitive: inflicting penalties; punishing. L punire (punitus) to punish < Gk poine fine, penalty.

pyre: a heap of wood or other solid fuel for burning a corpse in a funeral rite. Gk pyr fire.

pyromaniac: person with a compulsion to start destructive fires. Gk pyr fire + mania madness.

retrieve: to get back; to find and bring back. L re- + Gk tropos a turn, way, manner.

scheme: a plan, often devious, conceived in some detail. Gk schema shape.

seismic: caused by an earthquake. Gk seismos earthquake < seio shake.

simian: rel. to monkeys or other apes. L simia ape < Gk simos blunt nosed.

spatula: flat, broad instrument. Gk spathe broadsword.

stigma: a mark of infamy or token of disgrace; a blot on one's good name. L < Gr stigma < stizo prick.

strategem: a scheme or maneuver designed to achieve an objective. Gk strategema < strategos general.

subpoena: a summons to give testimony. L sub (under) + poena penalty < Gk poine fine.

syncopation: dropping middle sounds; music stressing normally weak beats. Gk syn (together) + kopto cut.

synod: a council or assembly esp. of church officials. Gk sunodos assembly < syn (with) + hodos way.

tactics: skillful use of assets (esp. military forces) to effect desired results. Gk taktikos < tasso arrange.

technical: involving specialized practical knowledge or skills. Gk tekhnikos of art < tekne art, skill.

therapeutic: having or showing powers of healing. Gk therapeutikos to serve, treat.

thermal: rel. to heat; retaining heat. Gk thermos warm, hot; therme heat.

thespian: rel. to drama. Gk Thespis.

titanic: colossal; of enormous size, scope, or power. Gk Titan.

torso: the human body without head and limbs. L thyrsus < Gk thursos.

toxic: poisonous. Gk toxon bow.

tropism: tendency for living creatures to be attracted or repulsed by certain stimuli. Gk tropos a turning.

utopia: an ideal, perfect society. Gk ou (not) + topos place.

xenophobia: fear or hatred of foreigners or strangers. Gk xenos strange, foreign + phobos fear.

zealot: person fervently or fanatically committed to a cause. Gk zelos zeal.

zephyr: a light breeze. Gk Zephuros.

CHAPTER 26

Words with Germanic Roots

There are many important words that do not have one of the two hundred Indo-European roots featured in chapters 10 to 22 as their source. This chapter offers additional words from Germanic roots. The most important words to learn are in italics. Many other words worth learning are in the lists as well. Students should concentrate on the words in italics. If students have time, they can spend additional effort on the words that have not been highlighted, perhaps on a second pass through these chapters. Each word is given a short definition and has an indication of its origin.

aghast: feeling great dismay or shock. OE gast (ghost).
akimbo: with hands on hips. ON kengboginn < keng bent + bogi bow.
aloof: distant, reserved. OE a + luff (windward part of a ship).
asunder: separated completely. OE on (on) + sunder (apart).
atone: to pay for a sin or wrong; to expiate. OE aet (at, near, by) + an one.
bask: to revel in warmth or pleasure. ME basken.
bawdy: lewd or risqué. OLG bald (bold, merry).
begrudge: to envy; to give reluctantly. OE be- + grudge.
beguile: take advantage of by deceit; charm. OE be + OF guile (cunning, deceit).
belated: done too late. OE be- + laet (late).
belie: give a false appearance; misrepresent. OE beleogan (to deceive with lie).
belittle: disparage; assert to lack importance. OE lyt (little).
bequeath: pass something on to another. OE be- + cwethan (to say).
besmirch: to soil or stain. ME be- + smorchen.
bevy: a group of. ME bevee.
bicker: to squabble; quarrel. ME bickeren (to attack).
bivouac: a temporary camp. MHG bei- beside + Wacht watch.
blasé: unconcerned; uninterested. MD blasen to blow up, swell.
bode: to portend. OE bodian (to announce).
bolt: (v) break away suddenly; to secure with a bar; (n) a bar used to lock. OE bolt (heavy arrow).
braggart: a boaster. ME brag (ostentatious).
brisk: moving with vigor and energy; invigorating. Scand.
bristling: taking offense; responding angrily. OE byrst (bristle).
brook: to put up with; endure; tolerate. OE brucan (use, enjoy).
brunt: the greatest burden or impact. ME brunt.
burnish: to polish by rubbing. OF burnir (polish).
carping: complaining; whining. ON karpa to boast
chaff: worthless material esp. that removed from grain during threshing. OE caef (chaff).

chastisement: punishment. ME.

clamber: to scramble up a slope. OE climban (to climb).

cleave: to adhere to; to split. OE cleofan (to split; cling to).

cleft: divided; (n) a crack or crevice. OE cleofan (to split; cling to).

clout: amount of influence or power. OE clut (cloth patch).

couturier: dressmaker. Fr.

cretinism: dwarfism caused by a thyroid deficiency. Fr cretin < L Christianus Christian.

cringe: shrink back in fear. OE cringan (to give way).

dale: valley. OE dael.

dank: damp and humid. Scand.

deadlock: inability to proceed; a tie. OE dead + loc (bolt, bar).

debase: to reduce in value or dignity < de + base.

decant: to pour off gently. Fr decanter < de (from) + OF cant (edge).

delve: to search carefully; to dig. OE delfan (to dig).

detached: disconnected; standing apart. OF de + attachier (to attach) < Ger.

dint: effort; a dent. OE dynt (dent).

dogged: tenaciously persevering. OE docga.

doughty: brave; valiant; redoubtable; boastful. OE dyhtig.

douse: to throw water on; to drench; to immerse. ME douse (to strike).

dowdy: shabby; lacking style. ME doude (ugly or shabby woman).

dregs: sediments; worst parts; leftovers. ON dregg.

drifting: carried along by currents; moving aimlessly without purpose. ME drove (herd).

drivel: foolish talk. OE dreflian.

drone: continuing monotonous hum, sound, or speech. OE dran.

dross: refuse or impurity in melted metal; slag; cinders; waste matter; refuse. OE dros < dreosan.

drudgery: tedious, unenjoyable work. OE dreogan (to work, suffer).

dwindle: to gradually decrease by small amounts until little is left. OE dwinan (to shrink).

earthy: of the earth; worldly; indecent. OE eorthe (earth).

encroach: slowly move beyond previous limits. OF encrocher < en in + croc hook < Ger.

enfranchise: to give the right to vote; set free OF franc frank, free

endearment: action producing affection; expression of affection. OE en + deore (dear) + ment.

fallow: plowed, unseeded land. OE fealh (fallow land).

fawn: show excessive favor and attention to please. OE faegan (glad).

faze: to disconcert. OE fesian.

fell: (v) cut or knock down. OE fellan.

fettle: state of fitness. E.

fickle: changeable; capricious; unstable. OE ficol (deceitful).

firebrand: one who stirs up trouble. OE fyr (fire) + brand (torch).

flatter: to give excessive or insincere compliments. ON flatr.

fledgling: bird learning to fly; inexperienced person; (adj) untried or inexperienced. OE fleogan (fly).

flotsam: floating ship wreckage; discarded objects OF floter (float).

fluster: to make agitated or confused. ME flostring (agitation).

fop: a vain man concerned primarily with his appearance and manners. ME fob (trickster).

foreboding: an intuition of coming misfortune; a portent. OE fore (in front) + bodian (to announce).

forgo: to relinquish or waive; to abandon. OE forgan (go away, forgo) < for- + gan (to go).

foster: to promote development; nurture; (adj) unrelated persons giving parental care. OE fostor (food).

fraught: filled with some characteristic. MD vracht (freight).

fray: fight. OF affrayer < L ex (from) + fridus peace < OHG fridu peace.

frizzle: to make crisp or curly. OF friser.

gait: the manner or rhythm of foot movement when walking or running. ON gata (path).

gall: to injure or render sore by friction; abrade; excoriate; irritate; harass. OE gealla (gall).

gambol: to skip sportively about; a skipping about in sport. Ital gamba (leg).

gammon: to hoodwink; to gamble; a hoax. OE gamen (sport).

gape: to open wide the mouth; to gaze with mouth open. ON gapa.

gay: happy; cheerful; merry. ME gai.

ghastly: revolting or terrifying; very serious; very unpleasant. ME gasten (to terrify).

giddy: lightheaded; dizzy; frivolous. OE gidig.

glib: speaking fluently without sincerity. D glibberen (freq glippen) slide.

gloat: to express or feel great self-satisfaction; to take pleasure in a rival's misfortune. Scand.

gloomy: dreary; dismal; pessimistic. ME gloumen (to become dark).

glower: to look angrily or sullenly; to frown. ME gloren.

gnarled: having knots and misshapened; roughened. ME knarre (knot in wood).

goad: to urge on. OE gad.

gouache: a method of water color painting with opaque colors using honey and gum. Fr.

grimace: to distort the features. Fr.

grist: a thing used to one's advantage. OE.

grovel: to act in a servile or subservient manner. ON grufa (to grovel).

grub: to toil unceasingly. ME grubben, grobben.

grueling: prolonged and exhausting. ME grue (horrible).

guileless: free of deceit and treachery. OF guile (cunning, deceit) + less.

haggard: worn and gaunt in appearance. OF hagard.

haggle: to dicker or bargain over price; to argue over; (n) an argument. ME haggen < ON hoggva.

hail: to acclaim; to greet. OE haeil (be healthy).

hamper: (v) prevent free action or progress. ME hamperen.

harbor: provide a home or shelter for; nourish; (n) sheltered inlet for ships anchorage. OE herebeorg (lodging).

harrowing: causing great distress and fear. ME harwe.

heedful: attentive to circumstances; mindful. OE hedan.

heedless: thoughtless; careless. OE hedan heed + -less.

heinous: hateful; atrocious. Fr haineux < OF hair (hate).

heyday: period of great vigor. OE heah (high) + daeg (day).

higgle: dispute about trifling matters. Corr. haggle.

hoary: white with age; ancient. OE har (hoary).

hodgepodge: a jumble of diverse elements. ME hochepot < OF (stew).

hoodwink: to deceive; fool. OE hod + wincian (wink).

hone: to sharpen. OE han (stone).

hopeless: despairing; foreseeing no possible good outcome. OE hopian + -less.

hovel: a small mean hut or house. ME hovel (hut).

hover: to float or flutter in place in the air. ME hoveren.

hoyden: tomboy. MD heyden (heathen).

hue: color; shade or tint. OE hiw (color, appearance, form).

insightful: showing the essential or truth of a matter. OE in- + sihth (something seen).

interloper: person unauthorized to enter another's place or trade. Fr entre (between) + D looper (runner).

jaded: worn out; sated. ME iade (nag) <? Swed jalda (mare).

knave: a dishonest mischievous person; medieval servant. OE cnafa (male servant).

knoll: a small round hill. OE cnoll (knoll).

laggard: straggler; (adj) falling behind. ME lag-(last).

lampoon: to ridicule or satirize a person or organization. Fr lamper (to gulp down) < Ger.

lewd: focused on sex and sexual desire. OE laewede (lay, ignorant).

liege: feudal lord. OF < MHG ledic (free).

lithe: supple. OE lithe (flexible, mild).

loath: reluctant; not inclined. OE lath (hateful, loathsome).

loathe: to strongly dislike. OE lathian (to hate or loathe).

lobbyist: one who tries to influence legislation. LL lobia < OHG louba (arbor).

lofty: of great height; exalted; grand. ME loft (sky, upstairs room).

loiter: to linger in a place; to dawdle. ME loitren (to idle time away).

loll: to leisurely pass time. MD lollan (to doze).

lope: to run at an easy steady pace. MD lopen (to run).

lout: a stupid and clumsy person. OE lutan.

lull: (v) cause to sleep; to induce to let down the guard; (n) interval of calm or lessened activity. ME lullen.

lurk: to lie in ambush; be around just out of sight. ME lurken.

maelstrom: violent conditions; enormous whirlpool. MD malen (whirl) + stroom (stream).

marred: damaged; disfigured; spoiled. OE mierran (to impede).

maw: mouth of a voracious animal. OE maga (stomach).

morass: something that greatly slows down or impedes progress; low, soggy ground. OF mareis.

mottled: spotted; blotched. ME mot (speck).

mournful: sorrowful; feeling grief. OE murnan.

mummery: pretentious show; performance by costumed merrymakers. OF mommerie < momer (mum).

murky: very dark and gloomy; indistinct; obscure. OE mirce.

needy: very poor; indigent; impoverished. OE neod (distress, necessity).

oaf: a clumsy or dumb person. ON alfr (elf).

ordure: filth; excrement; feces. OF < ord (foul, nasty)

pall: to grow wearisome; (n) a gloomy or dark atmosphere. ME pallen (to grow feeble).

parched: extremely dry. ME parchen.

penniless: without money; destitute. OE penig + -less.

poseur: given to posing or attitudinizing. Fr.

prattle: chatter meaninglessly. MD praten.

*quagmire: difficult to cross, marshy, soggy land; a predicament. OE *cwabba.*

queasy: feeling nausea or uneasiness. ME coisy.

rankle: to irritate. OE ranc (strong).

rant: express angrily; to rave; (n) angry expression; raving. D ranten.

rash: done without adequately taking the risks into account; reckless; foolhardy. MLG rasch (fast).

raspy: a grating sound. ME raspen.

reek: to be permeated with smoke or other unpleasantness. OE reocan (to expose to smoke).

rend: to tear apart. OE rendan.

rife: widespread in occurrence; numerous. OE ryfe.

roster: a list of names. D roosten (to roast).

rue: to regret; to feel remorse for. OE hwreowian (to repent).

ruthless: lacking any mercy or pity. ME ruthe + -less.

saga: Scandinavian narrative about legends and history. ON saga (a saying, narrative).

saunter: to walk with a leisurely pace. ME santren (to muse).

scanty: lacking or barely sufficient. ON skammr (short).

scoff: to deride; to show scorn. ME scof (mockery).

scold: to angrily rebuke, berate; or reprove. ME scolde (an abusive person).

scuttle: to sink a ship; to annul; to scurry. ME skottell.

sear: to wither or cause to wither; dry up; to render callous or insensible; harden. OE searian (wither).

seedy: shabby; unkempt; dilapidated. OE soed (seed).

shackle: a metal fetter used to restrain prisoners; a restraint on progress. OE sceacel (fetter).

sinewy: lean; tough; muscular; strong. OE sinewe.

skinflint: a miserly person. ON skinn + OE flint.

slacken: to slow down, lessen, or ease. OE slaec (loose, careless).

slake: to render inoperative by satisfying a desire; quench; appease. OE sleacian < slaec slack.

slither: glide or slide like a snake. OE slidan (to slide).

slovenly: careless, negligent, or untidy in appearance. D sloof (untidy woman).

sluggish: slow, inactive. ME slugge (lazy person).

skulk: to steal about; to lurk in concealment; to shirk obligations. ME skulken.

smirk: a self-satisfied smile. OE smercian (to smile).

smolder: to continue to burn with only wisps of smoke; to continue in a suppressed state. OE smorian (to smoke).

snivel: to complain; to sniffle. ME snivelen.

sodden: soaked; soggy; dull in mind. ME soden (boiled).

sparing: exhibiting restraint in spending or use of resources; economical. OE sparian.

spurn: reject with disdain; scorn. OE spurnan.

stiffening: becoming more rigid and inflexible. OE stif.

stiff-necked: obstinate; stubborn; arrogant. OE stif + hnecca.

stint: to restrain within fixed limits; provide scantily; a fixed amount; a bound. OE styntan (blunt).

strew: to spread around; to scatter. OE streowian (strew).

sully: to injure the brightness or purity of; soil; defile; tarnish; also fig. OE sylian < sol (mire).

sultry: very hot and humid. ME sulter (to swelter).

swagger: walk arrogantly or insolently; strut. OF souage.

swarthy: having a dark hue; of dark or sunburned complexion; tawny. OE sweart.

table d'hote: a common table for guests; course meal served at a fixed price. Fr (table of host) < L tabula board.

tarry: to delay before acting; to wait. ME tarien.

tawdry: showy without elegance; excessively ornamented; gaudy. Cor St Audrey < OE Aethylthryth.

thrive: prosper; flourish. ON thrifa (to seize).

throng: a very large crowd; (v) to crowd into. OE gethrang.

touchstone: a fine-grained dark stone as jasper used to test the fineness of gold.

ungainly: clumsy. OE un + Ice gegnligr (straight).

unkempt: not combed; not tidy. OE un + cemban (comb).

unscathed: unharmed; without a scratch. ME un- + skathen < ON.

unyielding: not conceding due to persuasion or pressure; resolutely staying the course. OE un- + geldan (pay).

uproarious: accompanied by or making violent disturbance and noise. D op (up) + roeren (stir).

vagrant: a nomad; a wanderer. OF wacrer (to wander) < Ger.

vanguard: front-most troops in battle; leaders in a movement. Fr avaunt (before) < L ante + garde guard.

varlet: a low menial or subordinate; formerly a page. OF varlet (valet) < VL.

waft: to carry gently and lightly with a waving motion in air or water. OE wafian (wave).

waif: a homeless or abandoned person or animal. ME waif (ownerless property).

waive: to relinquish a claim or right; to put off. ME waif (ownerless property).

watchfulness: quality of being vigilant and on the lookout. OE waeccan (to watch) + full + -ness.

wearisome: tedious; tiresome. OE wearig + -some.

wheedle: to persuade by flattery; coax; obtain by cajoling or coaxing. Ger. wedeln (wag the tail).
whet: to sharpen; to stimulate. OE (hwettan).
wholesome: good for health or well being. ME holsom.
wince: to involuntarily flinch from pain or distress. OF guencir < Ger.
wily: full of cunning. ON vel trick.
windfall: an unexpected gain of something of great value. OE wind (wind) + feallan (to fall).
wizen: to become or cause to become withered; shrunken; withered. OE wisnian (with).
woe: calamity; distress. OE wa (woe!).
woeful: distressful, miserable; wretched. OE wa (woe) + full.

CHAPTER 27

Words with Miscellaneous Origins

There are many important words that do not have one of the two hundred Indo-European roots featured in chapters 10 to 22 as their source. This chapter offers additional words from various sources: French, Italian, Spanish, various other languages, imitative words, and words of unknown origin. The most important words to learn are in italics. Many other words worth learning are in the lists as well. Students should concentrate on the words in italics. If students have time, they can spend additional effort on the words that have not been highlighted, perhaps on a second pass through these chapters. Each word is given a short definition and has an indication of its origin.

French

abet: to encourage; to urge on; to help. OF a- + beter (to bait).

askew: sitting sideways. OF eskiuer.

baffle: to confuse or perplex. Fr bafouer (to ridicule).

bizarre: odd; very peculiar or unusual. .Sp bizarro (brave).

brandish: to wave menacingly. OF brand sword.

buccaneer: a pirate; a reckless adventurer. Fr boucan (barbecue frame) < Tupian.

camaraderie: rapport among friends. OF camarade (roommate).

chicanery: trickery; use of subterfuges. OF chicaner (to quibble).

cliché: overused expression. Fr clicher (to stereotype).

clique: a small tightly knit group of friends. OF clique (latch).

crotchety: contrary and eccentric. OF croche (a hook).

cumbersome: awkward to handle because of size or weight. OF combre (hindrance).

deranged: insane; having normal arrangements disturbed. OF de- + renc (line, row).

dismantle: to disassemble; tear down. OF des- + mantel (cloak).

fleece: to defraud or swindle; to shear sheep; (n) sheep coat. OF fleos.

flinch: to recoil or shrink involuntarily. OF flenchir.

fracas: a brawl; a serious fight. Ital fracassare (to make an uproar).

franchise: grant of rights (often limited to an area of operation) to a person or group. OF franc (frank, free).

gauche: socially awkward. OF gauchir (to turn aside, walk clumsily).

gaunt: very lean and bony; starved; desolate. OF gant < Scand?

gibe: to heckle; to deride. OF giber (to play).

grapple: to come to grips with; to wrestle; to struggle for dominance. OF grape (hook).

grate: to shred with a shredder; to irritate; to make a grinding sound. OF grater (to scrape).

grudging: not willing; reluctant. OF grouchier.

gullible: easily duped or tricked. OF goule (throat).

harbinger: a precursor that foreshadows something to come. OF herberge (lodging).

hurtle: to move with great speed and force; to hurl. ME hurten < OF hurter (to bang into).

maim: to injure permanently. OF mahaignier (to maim).

marquee: large tent or canopy; theater sign promoting actors. Fr marquise (canopy) < marche (border area).

pivotal: being of crucial importance; being the point on which events or issues turn. OF pivot (pivot).

refurbish: to clean up, brighten up, and replace worn items; to renovate. ME re- + OF fourbir.

reverie: a daydream. OF rever (to dream).

ruffian: a thug or rowdy person. Old Ital ruffiano.

staccato: abrupt, crisp unconnected sounds. Ital staccare (to detach) < OF de- + attachier.

taint: to partially spoil or infect; show a moral deficiency. OF ataindre (to attain, touch upon).

trifling: something of little importance; small amount. OF trufle (mockery) < truffe (deception).

vignette: a short literary sketch or scene. OF vigne (vine).

wince: to involuntarily flinch from pain or distress. OF guencir < Ger.

Other Sources

mammoth: monstrous; huge; (n) an extinct elephant with large tusks. Russ mamut.

pariah: an outcast. Tamil parai.

scapegoat: one that is given the blame for the sins of others. < trans of Heb 'ez ozel (goat that escapes).

tycoon: a very wealthy, influential, and powerful businessman. Jap taikun (a shogun title).

yen: a strong inclination or craving. Chin uen (hope, wish).

Semitic

alcove: a recess or secluded part of a room or garden. Arab al- the + qubba (vault).

Armageddon: Biblical final battle just prior to Christ's Second Coming. Heb har (mountain) + Megiddo.

arsenal: a store or supply esp. of weapons. Arab dar (house) + as sinaa (manufacture).

azure: light blue with purplish hue. Arab al- the + lazaward (azure).

balmy: having a pleasant fragrance or soothing agent. Gk balsamon.< Arab.

behemoth: a very great and powerful animal or entity. Heb behemot (beast).

cabal: plot; persons secretly united for some private purpose; intrigue, conspiracy. Heb qabbalah (secret doctrine).

cabala: any occult or mystic system. Heb qabbalah (reception) < qabal receive.

carafe: coffee bottle. Fr carafe.

cherubic: characteristic of winged angels. Heb kerub.

cipher: a zero or nonentity; code for encrypting secret messages. Arab safira (to be empty).

decipher: to decode coded text or interpret obscure text. L de- + cifra < Arab safira (to be empty).

encipher: to encode text. L de- + cifra < Arab safira (to be empty).

haphazard: random; lacking an observable pattern. ON happ + hazard < Arab al the + zahr (gaming die).

hazardous: dangerous; risky. Arab al the + zahr (gaming die).

hegira: a flight from danger. Arab hijra (departure) < hajara to depart.

horde: a large crowd or swarm. Old Turkic ordu.

iota: a miniscule amount. Gk iota (iota) < Phoenician.

leviathan: a very large or monstrous creature or object. Heb liwyatan.

lionize: to treat someone as a celebrity. Gk leon < Sem.

messianic: rel. to a savior or liberator. Heb masiah (anointed).

nabob: a person of high status and wealth. Arab nuwwab (deputy).

nadir: lowest point. ML < Arab nazir (opposite the zenith).

Philistinism: blind conventionalism; devotion to low aims. Heb Pelistim (Philistine).

sabotage: destruction of property esp. to hinder war operations. OF cabot < Arab or Turk.

shibboleth: a test word or pet phrase; a watchword. Heb sibbolet (torrent of water cf. Judges 12:4-6)
wadi: a valley containing the bed of a watercourse usually dry. Arab wadi.

Imititative

blurt: to impulsively utter.
dupe: person readily deceived or used as a tool. OF huppe hoopoe < L upupa
flippant: speaking with inappropriate frivolity.
gibberish: meaningless talk or writing.
humdrum: uninteresting; dull; boring.
snicker: a stifled laugh.
titter: to giggle nervously.
whimsical: capricious; acting on impulse or fancy [from whim-wham].

Unknown

askance: disapproving or suspicious.
befuddle: to confuse or perplex.
blighted: wilted from plant disease; showing impaired growth.
bludgeon: to hit or beat as with a heavy club; (n) a heavy club.
bogus: fake; false; not genuine.
flabbergasted: astonished; astounded.
hoax: a scheme used to swindle or deceive people.
limber: bending easily; flexible; supple.
prod: to incite or goad to act; to poke cattle with a pointed object; (n) pointed object used to poke.
quaff: to drink with gusto.
quandary: state of puzzlement or perplexity.
quizzical: questioning; puzzled.
scurry: to move hurriedly.
sham: a fake; (adj) fake; not genuine.
squander: to waste; miss an opportunity.
stymie: to obstruct; to puzzle.
turmoil: state of confusion, commotion.

Names

argosy: a large richly laden ship or fleet of ships; a rich source. Ital Ragusea < Ragusa.
Benthamite: adherent to utilitarian ethics which aims at the greatest happiness for society. [Jeremy Bentham].
billingsgate: vulgar and abusive language. [Billingsgate area of London].
bowdlerize: purging sensual material or skewing the contents of books or articles by omissions. [Thomas Bowdler].
boycott: to try to punish by stopping all buying from and selling to organizations or countries. [Charles Boycott].
canter: easy gallop. [Canterbury, England].
charlatan: fraud, quack. [Cerreto, Italy].
chauvinism: zealous patriotism. [Nicholas Chauvin].
debunk: demonstrate the falsity of. [Am de- + Bunscombe (county in N.C.)].
epicure: lover of good food. [Gk Epikouros the Greek philosopher].
galvanize: to stimulate to action; to coat with zinc. [Luigi Galvani].

gargantuan: a person of great size and appetites. [Rabelais' Gargantua].

hermaphrodite: an animal having both male and female reproductive organs. [Gk Hermes + Aphrodite].

jeremiad: a lament tale of woe; in sarcasm. [Jeremiah (the OT prophet)].

Lilliputian: exceedingly small in stature or size; trivial. [Lilliput in Jonathan Swift's Guliver's Travels].

limerick: a humorous verse of five lines in anapestic meter. [Limerick, Ireland].

Luddite: one opposing technological advancement and change. [Ned Ludd].

Machiavellian: following expediency and deceitful means to achieve political objectives. [Niccolo Machiavelli].

martinet: a rigid disciplinarian. [Fr < Jean Martinet].

masochist: one who derives pleasure from being abused or mistreated. [Leopold von Sacher-Masoch].

maudlin: made foolish by liquor; foolishly and tearfully affectionate. OF maudlin < Magdalen.

maverick: one who acts independently against established practices. [Samuel Maverick].

mesmerize: to hypnotize; to enthrall. [Frank Mesmer].

narcissism: love of oneself. Gk Narcissus mythical youth in love with himself.

odyssey: a long adventurous voyage; a quest. [Odysseus].

Olympian: (adj) superior or surpassing; (n) one who is superior. Gk Olympia.

pander: to cater to people's base appetites and weaknesses; to procure for sex. Gk Pandaros.

platonic: rel. to the philosophy of Plato; attraction of a spiritual and non-physical nature. Gk Plato.

Procrusteanize: to ruthlessly force to conform to an arbitrary standard. Gk Prokroustes < prokruein stretch out.

protean: readily assuming different forms or aspects; changeable. L Proteus < Gk.

Pyrrhic: victory at such great cost that it effectively is a defeat. Gk Pyrrhus King of Epirus.

rodomontade: to boast; bluster; brag; bragging; vainglorious boasting. Ital Rodomonte (by Boiardo).

sadistic: being cruel and abusive toward others; deriving pleasure from abuse of others. [Donatien de Sade].

saturnine: melancholic; gloomy. L Saturnus Saturn.

serendipity: fortuitous, but accidental occurrence or discovery. [fairy tale title].

simony: traffic in sacred things. Gk Simon (of Acts 8:18-19).

solecism: breach of grammar or etiquette; an incongruity. Gk soloikos (speaking incorrectly cf. Soloi of Cilicia).

Solomonic: showing immense wisdom to decide difficult questions. [Solomon, King of Israel].

sphinx-like: a mysterious person especially one who speaks riddles. Gk Sphinx.

References

The Official SAT Study Guide: For the New SAT. 2004 New York: College Entrance Examination Board.

The American Heritage Dictionary of the English Language. 2000. 4th ed. Boston: Houghton Mifflin.

Bodmer, F. 1972. *The Loom of Language.* New York: W. W. Norton.

Cassell's Latin English Dictionary. 1987. New York: Macmillan.

Flesch, R. 1962. *The Art of Readable Writing.* New York: Macmillan.

Funk & Wagnalls College Standard Dictionary of the English Language. 1943. New York: Funk & Wagnalls.

Kaye, S. 1989. *Writing under Pressure.* New York: Oxford University Press.

10 Real SATs. 2003 New York: College Entrance Examination Board.

Pokorny, J. 1959. *Indogermanisches etymologisches worterbuch.* Bern: Francke.

Watkins, C., ed. 2000. *The American Heritage Dictionary of Indo-European Roots.* Boston: Houghton Mifflin.

Webster's New Universal Unabridged Dictionary. 1983. 2nd ed. New York: Simon and Schuster.

DATE DUE

ınⁿ⁶

MAY 1 7 2006		
GAYLORD		PRINTED IN U.S.A.